KILLING THE HOST

How Financial Parasites and Debt Destroy the Global Economy

MICHAEL HUDSON

www.michael-hudson.com
www.islet-verlag.de

Cover: Anonymus after Pieter Bruegel (I): The Big Fish Eat the Little Fish, Satire on the Fall of Johan van Oldenbarnevelt, 1619.
Grandibus exigui sunt pisces piscibus esca. Siet sone dit hebbe ick zeer langhe gheweten / dat die groote vissen de cleyne eten. 1619.
https://commons.wikimedia.org/wiki/File:T_Recht_ondersoec_der_Staten_001.jpg

Hudson, Michael, 1939–
Killing the host. How financial parasites and debt destroy the global economy.
Michael Hudson
ISBN 13: 978-3-9814842-8-1

Acknowledgements

The initial idea to popularize my more academic *The Bubble and Beyond* came from my agent Mel Flashman, who arranged for its German publication. This book includes apolitical commentary on the U.S., Irish, Latvian and Greek economies, much of which I originally published in Counterpunch, so it is appropriate that Jeffrey St. Clair is publishing this as a Counterpunch e-book. He has made many helpful editorial suggestions that I have followed.

Constructive ideas for how to structure the book came from Dave Kelley and Susan Charette, who reviewed early drafts and helped me focus its logic. Lynn Yost and Cornelia Wunsch have handled the typesetting and publication with great patience.

I have published parts of some chapters in this book on the website Naked Capitalism, maintained by Yves Smith and Lambert Strether to cover global finance, and on CounterPunch. A good number of articles cited also have come from these two sites.

Jeffrey Sommers and Igor Pimenov provided much of the information on Latvia, and Jorge Vilches filled me in on Argentina. Fruitful ongoing discussion has come from David Graeber, Steve Keen, Michael Perelman, Bertell Ollman and Randy Wray.

Yves Smith and Lambert Strether at *Naked Capitalism* for providing the best economic coverage of global finance, including many of the articles cited and quoted in this book, along with *CounterPunch* for political reporting.

My wife, Grace Hudson, provided a loving and supportive environment without which I would not have been able to write this book. The dedication therefore belongs to her.

Table of Contents

III. Austerity as a Privatization Grab

IV. There Is an Alternative

Introduction

I did not set out to be an economist. In college at the University of Chicago I never took a course in economics or went anywhere near its business school. My interest lay in music and the history of culture. When I left for New York City in 1961, it was to work in publishing along these lines. I had served as an assistant to Jerry Kaplan at the Free Press in Chicago, and thought of setting out on my own when the Hungarian literary critic George Lukacs assigned me the English-language rights to his writings. Then, in 1962 when Leon Trotsky's widow, Natalia Sedova died, Max Shachtman, executor of her estate, assigned me the rights to Trotsky's writings and archive. But I was unable to interest any house in backing their publication. My future turned out not to lie in publishing other peoples' work.

My life already had changed abruptly in a single evening. My best friend from Chicago had urged that I look up Terence McCarthy, the father of one of his schoolmates. Terence was a former economist for General Electric and also the author of the "Forgash Plan." Named for Florida Senator Morris Forgash, it proposed a World Bank for Economic Acceleration with an alternative policy to the existing World Bank – lending in domestic currency for land reform and greater self-sufficiency in food instead of plantation export crops. My first evening's visit with him transfixed me with two ideas that have become my life's work.

First was his almost poetic description of the flow of funds through the economic system. He explained why most financial crises historically occurred in the autumn when the crops were moved. Shifts in the Midwestern water level or climatic disruptions in other countries caused periodic droughts, which led to crop failures and drains on the banking system, forcing banks to call in their loans. Finance, natural resources and industry were parts of an interconnected system much like astronomy – and to me, an aesthetic thing of beauty. But unlike astronomical cycles, the mathematics of compound interest leads economies inevitably into a debt crash, because the financial system expands faster than the underlying economy, overburdening it with debt so that crises grow increasingly severe. Economies are torn apart by breaks in the chain of payments.

That very evening I decided to become an economist. Soon I enrolled in graduate study and sought work on Wall Street, which was the only practical way to see how economies really functioned. For the next twenty years, Terence and I spoke about an hour a day on current economic events. He had translated *A History of Economic Doctrines: From the Physiocrats to Adam Smith*, the first English-language version of Marx's *Theories of Surplus Value* – which itself was the first real history of economic thought. For starters, he told me to read all the books in its bibliography—the Physiocrats, John Locke, Adam Smith, David Ricardo, Thomas Malthus, John Stuart Mill and so forth.

The topics that most interested me—and the focus of this book—were not taught at New York University where I took my graduate economics degrees. In fact, they are not taught in any university departments: the dynamics of debt, and how the pattern of bank lending inflates land prices, or national income accounting and the rising share absorbed by rent extraction in the Finance, Insurance and Real Estate (FIRE) sector. There was only one way to learn how to analyze these topics: to work for banks. Back in the 1960s there was barely a hint that these trends would become a great financial bubble. But the dynamics were there, and I was fortunate enough to be hired to chart them.

My first job was as mundane as could be imagined: an economist for the Savings Banks Trust Company. No longer existing, it had been created by New York's then-127 savings banks (now also extinct, having been grabbed, privatized and emptied out by commercial bankers). I was hired to write up how savings accrued interest and were recycled into new mortgage loans. My graphs of this savings upsweep looked like Hokusai's "Wave," but with a pulse spiking like a cardiogram every three months on the day quarterly dividends were credited.

The rise in savings was lent to homebuyers, helping fuel the post-World War II price rise for housing. This was viewed as a seemingly endless engine of prosperity endowing a middle class with rising net worth. The more banks lend, the higher prices rise for the real estate being bought on credit. And the more prices rise, the more banks are willing to lend – as long as more people keep joining what looks like a perpetual motion wealth-creating machine.

The process works only as long as incomes are rising. Few people notice that most of their rising income is being paid for housing. They feel that they are saving – and getting richer by paying for an investment that will grow. At least, that is what worked for sixty years after World War II ended in 1945.

But bubbles always burst, because they are financed with debt, which expands like a chain letter for the economy as a whole. Mortgage debt service absorbs more and more of the rental value of real estate, and of homeowners' income as new buyers take on more debt to buy homes that are rising in price.

Tracking the upsweep of savings and the debt-financed rise in housing prices turned out to be the best way to understand how most "paper wealth" has been created (or at least inflated) over the past century. Yet despite the fact that the economy's largest asset is real estate — and is both the main asset and largest debt for most families — the analysis of land rent and property valuation did not even appear in the courses that I was taught in the evenings working toward my economics PhD.

When I finished my studies in 1964, I joined Chase Manhattan's economic research department as its balance-of-payments economist. It was proved another fortunate on-the-job training experience, because the only way to learn about the topic was to work for a bank or government statistical agency. My first task was to forecast the balance of payments of Argentina, Brazil and Chile. The starting point was their export earnings and other foreign exchange receipts, which served as a measure of how much revenue might be paid as debt service on new borrowings from U.S. banks.

Just as mortgage lenders view rental income as a flow to be turned into payment of interest, international banks view the hard-currency earnings of foreign countries as potential revenue to be capitalized into loans and paid as interest. The implicit aim of bank marketing departments — and of creditors in general — is to attach the entire economic surplus for payment of debt service.

I soon found that the Latin American countries I analyzed were fully "loaned up." There were no more hard-currency inflows available to extract as interest on new loans or bond issues. In fact, there was capital flight. These countries could only pay what they already owed if their banks (or the International Monetary Fund) lent them the money to pay the rising flow of interest charges. This is how loans to sovereign governments were rolled over through the 1970s. Their foreign debts mounted up at compound interest, an exponential growth that laid the ground for the crash that occurred in 1982 when Mexico announced that it couldn't pay. In this respect, lending to Third World governments anticipated the real estate bubble that would crash in 2008. Except that Third World debts were written down in the 1980s (via Brady bonds), unlike mortgage debts.

My most important learning experience at Chase was to develop an accounting format to analyze the balance of payments of the U.S. oil industry.

Standard Oil executives walked me through the contrast between economic statistics and reality. They explained how using "flags of convenience" in Liberia and Panama enabled them to avoid paying income taxes either in the producing or consuming countries by giving the illusion that no profits were being made. The key was "transfer pricing." Shipping affiliates in these tax-avoidance centers bought crude oil at low prices from Near Eastern or Venezuelan branches where oil was produced. These shipping and banking centers – which had no tax on profits – then sold this oil at marked-up prices to refineries in Europe or elsewhere. The transfer prices were set high enough so as not to leave any profit to be declared.

In balance-of-payments terms, every dollar spent by the oil industry abroad was returned to the U.S. economy in only 18 months. My report was placed on the desks of every U.S. senator and congressman, and got the oil industry exempted from President Lyndon Johnson's balance-of-payments controls imposed during the Vietnam War.

My last task at Chase dovetailed into the dollar problem. I was asked to estimate the volume of criminal savings going to Switzerland and other hide-outs. The State Department had asked Chase and other banks to establish Caribbean branches to attract money from drug dealers, smugglers and their kin into dollar assets to support the dollar as foreign military outflows escalated. Congress helped by not imposing the 15 percent withholding tax on Treasury bond interest. My calculations showed that the most important factors in deter-mining exchange rates were neither trade nor direct investment, but "errors and omissions," a euphemism for "hot money." Nobody is more "liquid" or "hot" than drug dealers and public officials embezzling their country's export earnings. The U.S. Treasury and State Department sought to provide a safe haven for their takings, as a desperate means of offsetting the balance-of-pay-ments cost of U.S. military spending.

In 1968 I extended my payments-flow analysis to cover the U.S. economy as a whole, working on a year's project for the (now defunct) accounting firm of Arthur Andersen. My charts revealed that the U.S. payments deficit was entirely military in character throughout the 1960s. The private sector – for-eign trade and investment – was exactly in balance, year after year, and "for-eign aid" actually produced a dollar *surplus* (and was required to do so under U.S. law).

My monograph prompted an invitation to speak to the graduate economics faculty of the New School in 1969, where it turned out they needed someone to teach international trade and finance. I was offered the job immediately after my lecture. Having never taken a course in this subject at NYU, I thought teaching would be the best way to learn what academic theory had to say about it.

I quickly discovered that of all the subdisciplines of economics, international trade theory was the silliest. Gunboats and military spending make no appearance in this theorizing, nor do the all-important "errors and omissions," capital flight, smuggling, or fictitious transfer pricing for tax avoidance. These elisions are needed to steer trade theory toward the perverse and destructive conclusion that any country can pay any amount of debt, simply by lowering wages enough to pay creditors. All that seems to be needed is sufficient devaluation (what mainly is devalued is the cost of local labor), or lowering wages by labor market "reforms" and austerity programs. This theory has been proved false everywhere it has been applied, but it remains the essence of IMF orthodoxy.

Academic monetary theory is even worse. Milton Friedman's "Chicago School" relates the money supply only to commodity prices and wages, not to asset prices for real estate, stocks and bonds. It pretends that money and credit are lent to business for investment in capital goods and new hiring, not to buy real estate, stocks and bonds. There is little attempt to take into account the debt service that must be paid on this credit, diverting spending away from consumer goods and tangible capital goods. So I found academic theory to be the reverse of how the world actually works. None of my professors had enough real-world experience in banking or Wall Street to notice.

I spent three years at the New School developing an analysis of why the global economy is polarizing rather than converging. I found that "mercantilist" economic theories already in the 18th century were ahead of today's mainstream in many ways. I also saw how much more clearly early economists recognized the problems of governments (or others) relying on creditors for policy advice. As Adam Smith explained,

> a creditor of the public, considered merely as such, has no interest in the good condition of any particular portion of land, or in the good management of any particular portion of capital stock. ... He has no inspection of it. He can have no care about it. Its ruin may in some cases be unknown to him, and cannot directly affect him.[1]

The bondholders' interest is solely to extricate as much as they can as quickly as possible with little concern for the social devastation they cause. Yet they have managed to sell the idea that sovereign nations as well as individuals have

---

[1] *Wealth of Nations*, Book V.3.57.

a moral obligation to pay debts, even to act on behalf of creditors instead of their domestic populations.

My warning that Third World countries would not be able to pay their debts disturbed the department's chairman, Robert Heilbroner. Finding the idea unthinkable, he complained that my emphasis on financial overhead was distracting students from the key form of exploitation: that of wage labor by its employers. Not even the Marxist teachers he hired paid much attention to interest, debt or rent extraction.

I found a similar left-wing aversion to dealing with debt problems when I was invited to meetings at the Institute for Policy Studies in Washington. When I expressed my interest in preparing the ground for cancellation of Third World debts, IPS co-director Marcus Raskin said that he thought this was too far off the wall for them to back. (It took another decade, until 1982, for Mexico to trigger the Latin American "debt bomb" by announcing its above-noted inability to pay.)

In 1972 I published my first major book, *Super Imperialism: The Economic Strategy of American Empire*, explaining how taking the U.S. dollar off gold in 1971 left only U.S. Treasury debt as the basis for global reserves. The balance-of-payments deficit stemming from foreign military spending pumped dollars abroad. These ended up in the hands of central banks that recycled them to the United States by buying Treasury securities—which in turn financed the domestic budget deficit. This gives the U.S. economy a unique free financial ride. It is able to self-finance its deficits seemingly *ad infinitum*. The balance-of-payments deficit actually ended up financing the domestic budget deficit for many years. The post-gold international financial system obliged foreign countries to finance U.S. military spending, whether or not they supported it.

Some of my Wall Street friends helped rescue me from academia to join the think tank world with Herman Kahn at the Hudson Institute. The Defense Department gave the Institute a large contract for me to explain just how the United States was getting this free ride. I also began writing a market newsletter for a Montreal brokerage house, as Wall Street seemed more interested in my flow-of-funds analysis than the Left. In 1979 I wrote *Global Fracture: The New International Economic Order*, forecasting how U.S. unilateral dominance was leading to a geopolitical split along financial lines, much as the present book's international chapters describe the strains fracturing today's world economy.

Later in the decade I became an advisor to the United Nations Institute for Training and Development (UNITAR). My focus here too was to warn that

Third World economies could not pay their foreign debts.[2] Most of these loans were taken on to subsidize trade dependency, not restructure economies to enable them to pay. IMF "structural adjustment" austerity programs—of the type now being imposed across the Eurozone—make the debt situation worse, by raising interest rates and taxes on labor, cutting pensions and social welfare spending, and selling off the public infrastructure (especially banking, water and mineral rights, communications and transportation) to rent-seeking monopolists. This kind of "adjustment" puts the class war back in business, on an international scale.

The capstone of the UNITAR project was a 1980 meeting in Mexico hosted by its former president Luis Echeverria. A fight broke out over my insistence that Third World debtors soon would have to default. Although Wall Street bankers usually see the handwriting on the wall, their lobbyists insist that all debts can be paid, so that they can blame countries for not "tightening their belts." Banks have a self-interest in denying the obvious problems of paying "capital transfers" in hard currency.

My experience with this kind of bank-sponsored junk economics infecting public agencies inspired me to start compiling a history of how societies through the ages have handled their debt problems. It took me about a year to sketch the history of debt crises as far back as classical Greece and Rome, as well as the Biblical background of the Jubilee Year. But then I began to unearth a pre-history of debt practices going back to Sumer in the third millennium BC. The material was widely scattered through the literature, as no history of this formative Near Eastern genesis of Western economic civilization had been written.

It took me until 1984 to reconstruct how interest-bearing debt first came into being – in the temples and palaces, not among individuals bartering. Most debts were owed to these large public institutions or their collectors, which is why rulers were able to cancel debts so frequently: They were cancelling debts owed to themselves, to prevent disruption of their economies. I showed my

---

[2]   My major articles were "The Logic of Regionalism in History and Today," "The Objectives of Regionalism in the 1980s," and "A Regional Strategy to Finance the New International Economic Order," in Davidson Nicol, Luis Echeverria and Aurelio Peccei, eds., *Regionalism and the New International Economic Order* (1981); "The Structure of the World Economy: A Northern Perspective," in Erwin Laszlo and Joel Kurtzman, eds., *The Structure of the World Economy and Prospects for a New International Economic Order* (1980); and "The United States and the NIEO," in Laszlo and Kurtzman, eds., *The United States, Canada and the New International Economic Order* (1979).

findings to some of my academic colleagues, and the upshot was that I was
invited to become a research fellow in Babylonian economic history at Harvard's Peabody Museum (its anthropology and archaeology department).

Meanwhile, I continued consulting for financial clients. In 1999, Scudder,
Stevens & Clark hired me to help establish the world's first sovereign bond
fund. I was told that inasmuch as I was known as "Dr. Doom" when it came
to Third World debts, if its managing directors could convince me that these
countries would continue to pay their debts for at least five years, the firm
would set up a self-terminating fund of that length. This became the first sovereign wealth fund—an offshore fund registered in the Dutch West Indies and
traded on the London Stock Exchange.

New lending to Latin America had stopped, leaving debtor countries so
desperate for funds that Argentine and Brazilian dollar bonds were yielding
45 percent annual interest, and Mexican medium-term *tessobonos* over 22 percent. Yet attempts to sell the fund's shares to U.S. and European investors failed.
The shares were sold in Buenos Aires and San Paolo, mainly to the elites who
held the high-yielding dollar bonds of their countries in offshore accounts.
This showed us that the financial managers would indeed keep paying their
governments' foreign debts, as long as they were paying themselves as "Yankee
bondholders" offshore. The Scudder fund achieved the world's second highest-
ranking rate of return in 1990.

During these years I made proposals to mainstream publishers to write a
book warning about how the bubble was going to crash. They told me that
this was like telling people that good sex would stop at an early age. Couldn't
I put a good-news spin on the dark forecast and tell readers how they could
get rich from the coming crash? I concluded that most of the public is interested in understanding a great crash only *after* it occurs, not during the run-up
when good returns are to be made. Being Dr. Doom regarding debt was like
being a premature anti-fascist.

So I decided to focus on my historical research instead, and in March 1990
presented my first paper summarizing three findings that were as radical
anthropologically as anything I had written in economics. Mainstream economics was still in the thrall of an individualistic "Austrian" ideology specu-
lating that charging interest was a universal phenomena dating from Paleolithic
individuals advancing cattle, seeds or money to other individuals. But I found
that the first, and by far the major creditors were the temples and palaces of
Bronze Age Mesopotamia, not private individuals acting on their own.
Charging a set rate of interest seems to have diffused from Mesopotamia to
classical Greece and Rome around the 8th century BC. The rate of interest in

each region was not based on productivity, but was set purely by simplicity for calculation in the local system of fractional arithmetic: $^1/_{60}$ per month in Mesopotamia, and later $^1/_{10}$ per year for Greece and $^1/_{12}$ for Rome.[3]

Today these ideas are accepted within the assyriological and archaeological disciplines. In 2012, David Graeber's *Debt: The First Five Thousand Years* tied together the various strands of my reconstruction of the early evolution of debt and its frequent cancellation. In the early 1990s I had tried to write my own summary, but was unable to convince publishers that the Near Eastern tradition of Biblical debt cancellations was firmly grounded. Two decades ago economic historians and even many Biblical scholars thought that the Jubilee Year was merely a literary creation, a utopian escape from practical reality. I encountered a wall of cognitive dissonance at the thought that the practice was attested to in increasingly detailed Clean Slate proclamations.

Each region had its own word for such proclamations: Sumerian *amargi*, meaning a return to the "mother" (*ama*) condition, a world in balance; Babylonian *misharum*, as well as *andurarum*, from which Judea borrowed as *deror*, and Hurrian *shudutu*. Egypt's Rosetta Stone refers to this tradition of amnesty for debts and for liberating exiles and prisoners. Instead of a sanctity of debt, what was sacred was the regular *cancellation* of agrarian debts and freeing of bond-servants in order to preserve social balance. Such amnesties were not destabilizing, but were essential to preserving social and economic stability.

To gain the support of the assyriological and archaeological professions, Harvard and some donor foundations helped me establish the Institute for the Study of Long-term Economic Trends (ISLET). Our plan was to hold a series of meetings every two or three years to trace the origins of economic enterprise and its privatization, land tenure, debt and money. Our first meeting was held in New York in 1994 on privatization in the ancient Near East and classical antiquity. Today, two decades later, we have published five volumes rewriting the early economic history of Western civilization. Because of their contrast with today's pro-creditor rules—and the success of a mixed private/public economy—I make frequent references in this book to how earlier societies resolved their debt problems in contrast with how today's world is letting debt polarize and enervate economies.

------

[3] "Did the Phoenicians Introduce the Idea of Interest to Greece and Italy—And if So, When?" in Gunter Kopcke, ed., *Greece Between East and West: 10ᵗʰ – 8ᵗʰ Centuries BC* (Berlin: 1992):128–143, subsequently expanded in "How Interest Rates Were Set, 2500 BC – 1000 AD: *Máš, tokos* and *fænus* as metaphors for interest accruals," *Journal of the Economic and Social History of the Orient* 43 (Spring 2000):132–161.

By the mid-1990s a more realistic modern financial theory was being developed by Hyman Minsky and his associates, first at the Levy Institute at Bard College and later at the University of Missouri at Kansas City (UMKC). I became a research associate at Levy writing on real estate and finance, and soon joined Randy Wray, Stephanie Kelton and others who were invited to set up an economics curriculum in Modern Monetary Theory (MMT) at UMKC. For the past twenty years our aim has been to show the steps needed to avoid the unemployment and vast transfer of property from debtors to creditors that is tearing economies apart today.

I presented my basic financial model in Kansas City in 2004,[4] with a chart that I repeated in my May 2006 cover story for *Harper's*. The *Financial Times* reproduced the chart in crediting me as being one of the eight economists to forecast the 2008 crash.[5] But my aim was not merely to predict it. Everyone except economists saw it coming. My chart explained the exponential financial dynamics that make crashes inevitable. I subsequently wrote a series of op-eds for the *Financial Times* dealing with Latvia and Iceland as dress rehearsals for the rest of Europe and the United States.

The disabling force of debt was recognized more clearly in the 18th and 19th centuries (not to mention four thousand years ago in the Bronze Age). This has led pro-creditor economists to exclude the history of economic thought from the curriculum. Mainstream economics has become censorially pro-creditor, pro-austerity (that is, anti-labor) and anti-government (except for insisting on the need for taxpayer bailouts of the largest banks and savers). Yet it has captured Congressional policy, universities and the mass media to broadcast a false map of how economies work. So most people see reality as it is written—and distorted—by the One Percent. It is a travesty of reality.

Spouting ostensible free market ideology, the pro-creditor mainstream rejects what the classical economic reformers actually wrote. One is left to choose between central planning by a public bureaucracy, or even more cen-

---

[4] "Saving, Asset-Price Inflation, and Debt-Induced Deflation," in L. Randall Wray and Matthew Forstater, eds., *Money, Financial Instability and Stabilization Policy* (Edward Elgar, 2006): 104–124, and "The New Road to Serfdom: An illustrated guide to the coming real estate collapse," *Harpers*, Vol. 312 (No. 1872), May 2006: 39–46. I have republished these and related articles in *The Bubble and Beyond* (ISLET 2012), which forms the academic background of the present book.

[5] Dirk Bezemer, "Why some economists could see the crisis coming," *Financial Times*, September 7, 2009. For a roster of financial Cassandras see Alphaville, *Financial Times*, July 13, 2009: "Who saw it coming and the primacy of accounting," posted by Tracy Alloway.

tralized planning by Wall Street's financial bureaucracy. The middle ground of a mixed public/private economy has been all but forgotten—denounced as "socialism." Yet every successful economy in history has been a mixed economy.

To help provide a remedy, this book explains how the upsweep of savings and debt has been politicized to control governments. The magnitude of debt tends to grow until a financial crash, war or political write-down occurs. The problem is not merely debt, but savings on the "asset" side of the balance sheet (mostly held by the One Percent). These savings mostly are lent out to become the debts of the 99 Percent.

As for financial dynamics in the business sector, today's "activist share-holders" and corporate raiders are financializing industry in ways that undercut rather than promote tangible capital formation and employment. Credit is increasingly predatory rather than enabling personal, corporate and government debtors to earn the money to pay.

This pattern of debt is what classical economists defined as unproductive, favoring unearned income (economic rent) and speculative gains over profits earned by employing labor to produce goods and services. I therefore start by reviewing how the Enlightenment and original free market economists spent two centuries trying to prevent precisely the kind of *rentier* dominance that is stifling today's economies and rolling back democracies to create financial oligarchies.

To set the stage for this discussion, it is necessary to explain that what is at work is an Orwellian strategy of rhetorical deception to represent finance and other *rentier* sectors as being part of the economy, not external to it. This is precisely the strategy that parasites in nature use to deceive their hosts that they are not free riders but part of the host's own body, deserving careful protection.

The Parasite, the Host, and Control of the Economy's Brain

Biological usage of the word "parasite" is a metaphor adopted from ancient Greece. Officials in charge of collecting grain for communal festivals were joined in their rounds by their aides. Brought along to the meals by these functionaries at public expense, the aides were known as parasites, a non-pejorative term for "meal companion," from the roots *para* (beside) and *sitos* (meal).

By Roman times the word came to take on the meaning of a superfluous freeloader. The parasite fell in status from a person helping perform a public function to become an uninvited guest who crashed a private dinner, a stock character in comedies worming his way in by pretense and flattery.[6]

Medieval preachers and reformers characterized usurers as parasites and leeches. Ever since, many economic writers have singled out bankers as parasites, especially international bankers. Passing over into biology, the word "parasite" was applied to organisms such as tapeworms and leeches that feed off larger hosts.

To be sure, leeches have long been recognized as performing a useful medical function: George Washington (and also Josef Stalin) were treated with leeches on their deathbeds, not only because bleeding the host was thought to be a cure (much as today's monetarists view financial austerity), but also because leeches inject an anti-coagulant enzyme that helps prevent inflammation and thus steers the body to recovery.

The idea of parasitism as a positive symbiosis is epitomized by the term "host economy," one that welcomes foreign investment. Governments invite bankers and investors to buy or finance infrastructure, natural resources and industry. Local elites and public officials in these economies typically are sent to the imperial or financial core for their education and ideological indoctrination to accept this dependency system as mutually beneficial and natural. The home country's educational cum ideological apparatus is molded to reflect this creditor/debtor relationship as one of mutual gain.

---

[6] Athenaeus, *Banquet of the Scholars* VI.234–236, and Carl Zimmer, *Parasite Rex* (New York, 2000), p. 2.

Smart vs. self-destructive parasitism in nature and in economies

In nature, parasites rarely survive merely by taking. Survival of the fittest cannot mean their survival alone. Parasites require hosts, and a mutually beneficial symbiosis often results. Some parasites help their host survive by finding more food, others protect it from disease, knowing that they will end up as the beneficiaries of its growth.

A financial analogy occurred in the 19th century when high finance and government moved closer together to fund public utilities, infrastructure and capital-intensive manufacturing, especially in armaments, shipping and heavy industry. Banking was evolving from predatory usury to take the lead in organizing industry along the most efficient lines. This positive melding took root most successfully in Germany and its neighboring Central European countries under public sponsorship. Across the political spectrum, from "state socialism" under Bismarck to Marxist theorists, bankers were expected to become the economy's central planners, by providing credit for the most profitable and presumably socially beneficial uses. A three-way symbiotic relationship emerged to create a "mixed economy" of government, high finance and industry.

For thousands of years, from ancient Mesopotamia through classical Greece and Rome, temples and palaces were the major creditors, coining and providing money, creating basic infrastructure and receiving user fees as well as taxes. The Templars and Hospitallers led the revival of banking in medieval Europe, whose Renaissance and Progressive Era economies integrated public investment productively with private financing.

To make this symbiosis successful and free immune to special privilege and corruption, 19th-century economists sought to free parliaments from control by the propertied classes that dominated their upper houses. Britain's House of Lords and senates throughout the world defend the vested interests against the more democratic regulations and taxes proposed by the lower house. Parliamentary reform extending the vote to all citizens was expected to elect governments that would act in society's long-term interest. Public authorities would take the lead in major capital investments in roads, ports and other transportation, communications, power production and other basic utilities, including banking, without private rent-extractors intruding into the process.

The alternative was for infrastructure to be owned in a pattern much like absentee landlordship, enabling rent-extracting owners to set up tollbooths to charge society whatever the market would bear. Such privatization is contrary to what classical economists meant by a free market. They envisioned a market free from rent paid to a hereditary landlord class, and free from interest and monopoly rent paid to private owners. The ideal system was a morally fair market in which people would be rewarded for their labor and enterprise, but would not receive income without making a positive contribution to production and related social needs.

Adam Smith, David Ricardo, John Stuart Mill and their contemporaries warned that rent extraction threatened to siphon off income and bid up prices above the necessary cost of production. Their major aim was to prevent landlords from "reaping where they have not sown," as Smith put it. Toward this end their labor theory of value (discussed in Chapter 3) aimed at deterring landlords, natural resource owners and monopolists from charging prices above cost-value, opposing governments controlled by rentiers.

Recognizing how most great fortunes had been built up in predatory ways, through usury, war lending and political insider dealings to grab the Commons and carve out burdensome monopoly privileges led to a popular view of financial magnates, landlords and hereditary ruling elite as parasitic by the 19th century, epitomized by the French anarchist Proudhon's slogan "Property is theft."

Instead of creating a mutually beneficial symbiosis with the economy of production and consumption, today's financial parasitism siphons off income needed to invest and grow. Bankers and bondholders desiccate the host economy by extracting revenue to pay interest and dividends. Repaying a loan – amortizing or "killing" it – shrinks the host. Like the word amortization, mortgage ("dead hand" of past claims for payment) contains the root mort, "death." A financialized economy becomes a mortuary when the host economy becomes a meal for the financial free luncher that takes interest, fees and other charges without contributing to production.

The great question – in a financialized economy as well as in biological nature – is whether death of the host is a necessary consequence, or whether a more positive symbiosis can be developed. The answer depends on whether the host can remain self-steering in the face of a parasitic attack.

Taking control of the host's brain/government

Modern biology provides the basis for a more elaborate social analogy to financial strategy, by describing the sophisticated strategy that parasites use to control their hosts by disabling their normal defense mechanisms. To be accepted, the parasite must convince the host that no attack is underway. To siphon off a free lunch without triggering resistance, the parasite needs to take control of the host's brain, at first to dull its awareness that an invader has attached itself, and then to make the host believe that the free rider is helping rather than depleting it and is temperate in its demands, only asking for the necessary expenses of providing its services. In that spirit bankers depict their interest charges as a necessary and benevolent part of the economy, providing credit to facilitate production and thus deserving to share in the surplus it helps create.

Insurance companies, stockbrokers and underwriters join bankers in aiming to erase the economy's ability to distinguish financial claims on wealth from real wealth creation. Their interest charges and fees typically eat into the circular flow of payments and income between producers and consumers. To deter protective regulations to limit this incursion, high finance promotes a "value-free" view that no sector exploits any other part. Whatever creditors and their financial managers take is deemed to be fair value for the services they provide (as Chapter 6 describes).

Otherwise, bankers ask, why would people or companies pay interest, if not to pay for credit deemed necessary to help the economy grow? Bankers and also their major customers – real estate, oil and mining, and monopolies – claim that whatever they are able to extract from the rest of the economy is earned just as fairly as new direct investment in industrial capital. "You get what you pay for," is used to justify any price, no matter how ridiculous. It is circular reasoning playing with tautologies.

The most lethal policy sedative in today's mainstream orthodoxy is the mantra that "All income is earned." This soporific illusion distracts attention from how the financial sector diverts the economy's nourishment to feed monopolies and rent-extracting sectors surviving from past centuries, now sup-plemented by yet new sources of monopoly rent, above all in the financial and money management sectors. This illusion is built into the self-portrait that today's economies draw to describe their circulation of spending and produc-tion: the National Income and Product Accounts (NIPA). As presently designed, the NIPA neglect the distinction between productive activities and "zero sum" transfer payments where no overall production or real gain takes place, but income is paid to one party at another's expense. The NIPA duly report the revenue of the Finance, Insurance and Real Estate (FIRE) sector and monop-olies as "earnings." These accounts have no category for what classical econo-mists called economic rent — a free lunch in the form of income siphoned off without a corresponding cost of labor or enterprise. Yet a rising proportion of what the NIPA report as "earnings" actually derive from such rents.

The Chicago School's Milton Friedman adopted the rentier motto as a cloak of invisibility: "There Is No Such Thing As A Free Lunch" (TIN-STAAFL). That means there are no parasites taking without giving an equivalent value in return – at least, no private sector parasites.[7] Only government regulation is condemned, not rent-extraction. In fact, taxation of rentiers – the recipients of free-lunch income, "coupon clippers" living off government bonds or rental properties or monopolies – is denounced rather than endorsed, as was the case for Adam Smith, John Stuart Mill and their 19th-century free market followers.

David Ricardo aimed his rent theory at Britain's landlords while remaining silent about the financial rentiers – the class whose activities John Maynard Keynes playfully suggested should be euthanized. Landed proprietors, financiers and monopolists were singled out as the most visible free lunchers – giving them the strongest motive to deny the concept in principle.

Familiar parasites in today's economy include Wall Street's investment bankers and hedge fund managers who raid companies and empty out their pension reserves; also, landlords who rack-rent their tenants (threatening eviction if unfair and extortionate demands are not met), and monopolists who gouge consumers with prices not warranted by the actual costs of production. Commercial banks demand that government treasuries or central banks cover their losses, claiming that their credit-steering activity is necessary to allocate resources and avoid economic dissolution. So here again we find the basic rentier demand: "Your money, or your life."

A rentier economy is one in which individuals and entire sectors levy charges for the property and privileges they have obtained, or more often that their ancestors have bequeathed. As Honoré de Balzac observed, the greatest fortunes originated from thefts or insider dealings whose details are so lost in the mists of time that they have become legitimized simply by the force of social inertia.

At the root of such parasitism is the idea of rent extraction: taking without producing. Permitting an excess of market price to be charged over intrinsic cost-value lets landlords, monopolists and bankers charge more for access to

---

[7] For Friedman this means that public services that appear to be free are always paid for in some way. The idea often is abbreviated as TANSTAAFL to give a faux populist hue: "There Ain't No Such Thing As a Free Lunch." The classical idea of economic rent as a free lunch, by contrast, refers to unearned private-sector income that often exceeds the magnitude of earned income.

land, natural resources, monopolies and credit than what their services need to cost. Unreformed economies are obliged to carry what 19th-century journalists called the idle rich, 20th-century writers called robber barons and the power elite, and Occupy Wall Street call the One Percenters.

To prevent such socially destructive exploitation, most nations have regulated and taxed rentier activities or kept such potential activities (above all, basic infrastructure) in the public domain. But regulatory oversight has been systematically disabled in recent years. Throwing off the taxes and regulations put in place over the past two centuries, the wealthiest One Percent have captured nearly all the growth in income since the 2008 crash. Holding the rest of society in debt to themselves, they have used their wealth and creditor claims to gain control of the election process and governments by supporting lawmakers who un-tax them, and judges or court systems that refrain from prosecuting them. Obliterating the logic that led society to regulate and tax rentiers in the first place, think tanks and business schools favor economists who portray rentier takings as a contribution to the economy rather than as a subtrahend from it.

History shows a universal tendency for rent-extracting conquerors, colonizers or privileged insiders to take control and siphon off the fruits of labor and industry for themselves. Bankers and bondholders demand interest, landlords and resource appropriators levy rents, and monopolists engage in price gouging. The result is a rentier-controlled economy that imposes austerity on the population. It is the worst of all worlds: Even while starving economies, economic rent charges render them high-cost by widening the margin of prices over intrinsic, socially necessary costs of production and distribution.

Reversing classical reforms since World War II, and especially since 1980

The great reversal of classical Industrial Era reform ideology to regulate or tax away rentier income occurred after World War I. Bankers came to see their major market to be real estate, mineral rights, and monopolies. Lending mainly to finance the purchase and sale of rent-extracting opportunities in these sectors, banks lent against what buyers of land, mines and monopolies could squeeze out of their rent-extracting "tollbooth" opportunities. The effect was to pry away the land rent and natural resource rent that classical economists expected to serve as the natural tax base. In industry, Wall Street became the "mother of trusts," creating mergers into monopolies as vehicles to extract monopoly rent.

Precisely because a "free lunch" (rent) was free – if governments did not tax it away – speculators and other buyers sought to borrow to buy such rent-extracting privileges. Instead of a classical free market ideal in which rent was paid as taxes, the free lunch was financialized – that is, capitalized into bank loans, to be paid out as interest or dividends.

Banks gained at the expense of the tax collector. By 2012, over 60 percent of the value of today's homes in the United States is owed to creditors, so that most rental value is paid as interest to banks, not to the community. Home ownership has been democratized on credit. Yet banks have succeeded in promoting the illusion that the government is the predator, not bankers. The rising proportion of owner-occupied housing has made the real estate tax the most unpopular of all taxes, as if property tax cuts do not simply leave more rental income available to pay mortgage lenders.

The result of a tax shift off of property is a rising mortgage debt by home-buyers paying access prices bid up on bank credit. Popular morality blames victims for going into debt – not only individuals, but also national governments. The trick in this ideological war is to convince debtors to imagine that general prosperity depends on paying bankers and making bondholders rich – a veritable Stockholm Syndrome in which debtors identify with their financial captors.

Today's policy fight is largely over the illusion of who bears the burden of taxes and bank credit. The underlying issue is whether the economy's prosperity flows from the financial sector's credit and debt creation, or is being bled by increasingly predatory finance. The pro-creditor doctrine views interest as reflecting a choice by "impatient" individuals to pay a premium to "patient" savers in order to consume in the present rather than in the future. This free-choice approach remains mute about the need to take on rising levels of personal debt to obtain home ownership, an education and simply to cover basic break-even expenses. It also neglects the fact that debt service to bankers leaves less to spend on goods and services.

Less and less of today's paychecks provide what the national accounts label as "disposable income." After subtracting FICA withholding for taxes and "forced saving" for Social Security and Medicare, most of what remains is ear-marked for mortgages or residential rent, health care and other insurance, bank and credit card charges, car loans and other personal credit, sales taxes, and the financialized charges built into the goods and services that consumers buy.

Biological nature provides a helpful analogy for the banking sector's ideological ploys. A parasite's toolkit includes behavior-modifying enzymes to make the host protect and nurture it. Financial intruders into a host economy use

Junk Economics to rationalize rentier parasitism as if it makes a productive contribution, as if the tumor they create is part of the host's own body, not an overgrowth living off the economy. A harmony of interests is depicted between finance and industry, Wall Street and Main Street, and even between creditors and debtors, monopolists and their customers. Nowhere in the National Income and Product Accounts is there a category for unearned income or exploitation.

The classical concept of economic rent has been censored by calling finance, real estate and monopolies "industries." The result is that about half of what the media report as "industrial profits" are FIRE-sector rents, that is, finance, insurance and real estate rents – and most of the remaining "profits" are monopoly rents for patents (headed by pharmaceuticals and information technology) and other legal privileges. Rents are conflated with profit. This is the terminology of financial intruders and rentiers seeking to erase the language and concepts of Adam Smith, Ricardo and their contemporaries depicting rents as parasitic.

The financial sector's strategy to dominate labor, industry and government involves disabling the economy's "brain" – the government – and behind it, democratic reforms to regulate banks and bondholders. Financial lobbyists mount attacks on public planning, accusing public investment and taxes of being a deadweight burden, not as steering economies to maximize prosperity, competitiveness, rising productivity and living standards. Banks become the economy's central planners, and their plan is for industry and labor to serve finance, not the other way around.

Even without so conscious an aim, the mathematics of compound interest turns the financial sector into a wedge to push large sectors of the population into distress. The buildup of savings accruing through interest that is recycled into new lending seeks out ever-new fields for indebtedness, far beyond the ability of productive industrial investment to absorb (as Chapter 4 describes).

Creditors claim to create wealth financially, simply by asset-price inflation, stock buybacks, asset stripping and debt leveraging. Lost from sight in this exercise in deception is how the financial mode of wealth creation engorges the body of the financial intruder, at odds with the classical aim of rising output at higher living standards. The Marginalist Revolution looks nearsightedly at small changes, taking the existing environment for granted and depicting any adverse "disturbance" as being self-correcting, not a structural defect leading economies to fall further out of balance. Any given crisis is said to be a natural product of market forces, so that there is no need to regulate and tax the rentiers. Debt is not seen as intrusive, only as being helpful, not as capturing and transforming the economy's institutional policy structure.

A century ago socialists and other Progressive Era reformers advanced an evolutionary theory by which economies would achieve their maximum potential by subordinating the post-feudal rentier classes – landlords and bankers – to serve industry, labor and the common weal. Reforms along these lines have been defeated by intellectual deception and often outright violence by the vested interests Pinochet-Chile-style to prevent the kind of evolution that classical free market economists hoped to see – reforms that would check financial, property and monopoly interests.

So we are brought back to the fact that in nature, parasites survive best by keeping their host alive and thriving. Acting too selfishly starves the host, putting the free luncher in danger. That is why natural selection favors more positive forms of symbiosis, with mutual gains for host and rider alike. But as the volume of savings mounts up in the form of interest-bearing debt owed by industry and agriculture, households and governments, the financial sector tends to act in an increasingly shortsighted and destructive ways. For all its positive contributions, today's high (and low) finance rarely leaves the economy enough tangible capital to reproduce, much less to feed the insatiable exponential dynamics of compound interest and predatory asset stripping.

In nature, parasites tend kill hosts that are dying, using their substance as food for the intruder's own progeny. The economic analogy takes hold when financial managers use depreciation allowances for stock buybacks or to pay out as dividends instead of replenishing and updating their plant and equipment. Tangible capital investment, research and development and employment are cut back to provide purely financial returns. When creditors demand austerity programs to squeeze out "what is owed," enabling their loans and investments to keep growing exponentially, they starve the industrial economy and create a demographic, economic, political and social crisis.

This is what the world is witnessing today from Ireland to Greece – Ireland with bad real estate debt that has become personal and taxpayer debt, and Greece with government debt. These countries are losing population to accelerating emigration. As wages fall, suicide rates rise, life spans shorten, and marriage and birth rates plunge. Failure to reinvest enough earnings in new means of production shrinks the economy, prompting capital flight to less austerity-ravaged economies.[8]

---

[8] Michael Perelman reminds me that most biological parasites that steer their hosts along a suicidal path only do so in order to pass their progeny into new hosts. But today's financial parasites threaten to destroy the host economy without having any alternatives. Their short-termism also is destroying the global environment, education systems, and is dismantling infrastructure. The ensuring crash may leave financial parasites with no new worlds to colonize, destroying the host and its rider together.

Who will bear the losses from the financial sector's over-feeding on its industrial host?

The great political question confronting the remainder of the 21st century is which sector will receive enough income to survive without losses degrading its position: the industrial host economy, or its creditors?

For the economy at large, a real and lasting recovery requires constraining the financial sector from being so shortsighted that its selfishness causes a system-wide collapse. The logic to avoid this a century ago was to make banking a public function. The task is made harder today because banks have become almost impenetrable conglomerates attached Wall Street speculative arbitrage activities and casino-type derivative bets to the checking and saving account services and basic consumer and business lending, creating banks Too Big To Fail (TBTF).

Today's banks seek to prevent discussion of how over-lending and debt deflation cause austerity and economic shrinkage. Failure to confront the economy's limits to the ability to pay threatens to plunge labor and industry into chaos.

In 2008, we watched a dress rehearsal for this road show when Wall Street convinced Congress that the economy could not survive without bailing out bankers and bondholders, whose solvency was deemed a precondition for the "real" economy to function. The banks were saved, not the economy. The debt tumor was left in place. Homeowners, pension funds, city and state finances were sacrificed as markets shrank, and investment and employment followed suit. "Saving" since 2008 has taken the form of paying down debts to the financial sector, not to invest to help the economy grow. This kind of "zombie saving" depletes the economy's circular flow between producers and consumers. It bleeds the economy while claiming to save it, much like medieval doctors.

Extractive finance leaves economies emaciated by monopolizing their income growth and then using its takings in predatory ways to intensify the degree of exploitation, not to pull the economy out of debt deflation. The financial aim is simply to extract income in the form of interest, fees and amortization on debts and unpaid bills. If this financial income is predatory, and if capital gains are not earned by one's own labor and enterprise, then the One Percent should not be credited with having created the 95 percent of added income they have obtained since 2008. They have taken it from the 99 Percent.

If banking really provides services equal in value to the outsized wealth it has created for the One Percent, why does it need to be bailed out? When the financial sector obtains all the economic growth following bailouts, how does this help industry and employment, whose debts remain on the books? Why weren't employment and tangible capital investment bailed out by freeing them from their debt overhead?

If income reflects productivity, why have wages stagnated since the 1970s while productivity has soared and the gains extracted by banks and financiers, not labor? Why do today's National Income and Product Accounts exclude the concept of unearned income (economic rent) that was the main focus of classical value and price theory? If economics is really an exercise in free choice, why have proselytizers for the rentier interests found it necessary to exclude the history of classical economic thought from the curriculum?

The free luncher's strategy is to sedate the host to block these questions from being posed. This censorial mirage is the essence of post-classical economics, numbed by pro-rentier, anti-government, anti-labor "neoliberals." Their logic is designed to make it appear that austerity, rent extraction and debt deflation is a step forward, not killing the economy. Future generations may see the degree to which this self-destructive ideology has reversed the Enlightenment and is carving up today's global economy as one of the great oligarchic takeovers in the history of civilization. As the poet Charles Baudelaire quipped, the devil wins at the point where he is able to convince the world that he doesn't exist.

The Twelve Themes of this Book

1. A nation's destiny is shaped by two sets of economic relationships. Most textbooks and mainstream economists focus on the "real" economy of production and consumption, based on the employment of labor, tangible means of production and technological potential.

    This tangible Economy #1 is wrapped in a legal and institutional network of credit and debt, property relations and ownership privileges, while Economy #2 is centered on the Finance, Insurance and Real Estate (FIRE) sector. This "debt and ownership" economy transforms its economic gains into political control to enforce payment of debts and to preserve property and natural resource or monopoly rent privileges (typically inherited).

    Interest and rents are transfer payments from Economy #1 to Economy #2, but mainstream economics depicts all income as being earned productively, even by absentee landlords and Wall Street speculators receiving rentier overhead and interest. The operative fiction is the assumption that everyone earns in proportion to what they contribute to production. The National Income and Product Accounts (NIPA) treat whatever revenue these individuals are able to extract as a contribution to Gross Domestic Product (GDP), as if their exorbitant incomes reflect high productivity. Their "output" is defined as equal to their revenue, so GDP should really be thought of as Gross National Cost. There seems to be no such thing as economic parasitism or unnecessary costs of living and doing business. No free lunch is recognized, and hence no Economy #2 that does not contribute productively to Economy #1.

2. Today's banks don't finance tangible investment in factories, new means of production or research and development – the "productive lending" that is supposed to provide borrowers with the means to pay off their debt. Banks largely lend against collateral already in place, mainly real estate (80 percent of bank loans), stocks and bonds. The effect is to transfer ownership of these assets, not produce more.

3. Borrowers use these loans to bid up prices for the assets they buy on credit: homes and office buildings, entire companies (by debt-leveraged buyouts), and infrastructure in the public domain on which to install tollbooths and charge access rents. Lending against such assets bids up their prices – Asset-Price Inflation.

4. Paying off these loans with interest leaves less wage or profit income available to spend on consumer goods or capital goods. This Debt Deflation is

the inevitable successor to Asset-Price Inflation. Debt service and rent charges shrink markets, consumer spending, employment and wages.

5. Austerity makes it harder to pay debts, by shrinking markets and causing unemployment. That is why John Maynard Keynes urged "euthanasia of the rentier" if industrial capitalism is to thrive. He hoped to shift the focus of fortune-seeking away from banking, and implicitly from its major loan markets in absentee landlordship and privatization of rent-extracting monopolies.

6. Mainstream policy pretends that economies are able to pay their debts without reducing their living standards or losing property. But debts grow exponentially faster than the economy's ability to pay as interest accrues and is recycled (while new bank credit is created electronically). The "magic of compound interest" doubles and redoubles savings and debt balances by purely mathematical laws that are independent of the economy's ability to produce and pay. Economies become more debt-leveraged as claims for payment are concentrated in the hands of the One Percent.

7. Debts that can't be paid, won't be. The question is: how won't they be paid? There are two ways not to pay. The most drastic and disruptive way (euphemized as "business as usual") is for individuals, companies or governments to sell off or forfeit their assets. The second way to resolve matters is to write down debts to a level that can be paid. Bankers and bondholders prefer the former option, and insist that all debts can be paid, given the "will to do so," that is, the will to transfer property into their hands. This is the solution that mainstream monetarist economists, government policy and the mass media popularize as basic morality. But it destroys Economy #1 to enrich the 1 percent who dominate Economy #2.

8. A Bubble Economy may postpone the collapse if banks lend on easier terms to enable borrowers to bid up prices for real estate and other assets. This inflation becomes the only way creditors can be paid as the economy becomes increasingly more debt-ridden. It enables debtors to pay their creditors by borrowing more against collateral becoming higher priced. Indeed, new lending and debt must grow exponentially to sustain this kind of bubble, just as new subscribers are needed to sustain a chain letter or Ponzi scheme.

    After 2001, rising asset prices tempted homebuyers to borrow to buy assets, paying the interest by borrowing against their asset-price gains. But what seemed at first to be a self-inflating perpetual motion machine led to a crash when current income did not cover the interest charge. By 2007, speculators stopped buying and started to sell off property, crashing its price. The debts were left in place, causing negative equity.

9. Banks and bondholders oppose debt write-downs to bring debt in line with earnings and historical asset valuations. Creditor demands for payment run the economy in the interest of the financialized Economy #2 instead of protecting the indebted production-and-consumption Economy #1. The effect is to drive both economies bankrupt.

10. The financial sector (the One Percent) backs oligarchies. Eurozone creditors recently imposed "technocrats" to govern debt-strapped Greece and Italy, and blocked democratic referendums on whether to accept the bailouts and their associated austerity terms. This policy dates from the 1960s and '70s when the IMF and U.S. Government began backing creditor-friendly Third World oligarchies and military dictatorships.

11. Every economy is planned. The question is, who will do the planning: banks or elected governments? Will planning and structuring the economy serve short-term financial interests (making asset-price gains and extracting rent) or will it promote the long-term upgrading of industry and living standards?

    Banks denounce public investment and a tax shift off wages onto rentier wealth as "the road to serfdom." But strong public regulation is needed to prevent economies from polarizing between debtors and creditors, and to block the financial sector from imposing austerity and setting the economy on the road to debt peonage.

12. The financial sector's drive to increase its political power has a fatal fiscal dimension: Whatever economic rent that remains untaxed is "free" to be pledged to the banks as interest. Banks therefore advocate un-taxing real estate, natural resource rent and monopoly price gouging. This is the opposite from the classical policy of taxing and de-privatizing economic rent and asset-price ("capital") gains.

    Classical value and price theory demonstrates that a rent tax does not increase prices, but is paid out of rent, absorbing the excess of price over intrinsic cost-value. That was the policy aim of free market economists from the Physiocrats and Adam Smith through John Stuart Mill and the Progressive Era. By the late 19th century it was called socialism, which originally meant freeing markets from the political legacy of feudal privileges to enclose the Commons and privatized public infrastructure.

Part I
From the Enlightenment to Neo-*Rentier* Economies

1
The Financial Sector's Rise to Power

A century ago nearly everyone expected that as prosperity and wage levels increased, people would save more and have less need to go into debt. In the 1930s John Maynard Keynes worried that the increasing propensity to save would lead people to spend less on goods and services, causing unemployment to rise unless public spending increased. Yet by 2008 the U.S. domestic saving rate fell below zero. Not only individuals but also real estate, industry and even government are becoming more indebted – or in economist-speak, "dis-saving."

Trying to rise into the middle class these days is a road to debt peonage. It involves taking on mortgage debt to buy a home of one's own, student loans to get the education needed to get a good job, an automobile loan to drive to work, and credit-card debt just to maintain one's living standards as the debtor falls deeper and deeper in the hole. Many recent graduates find that they have to pay so much on their student loans that they must live at home with their parents and cannot afford to get married and start a family, much less qualify for a mortgage. That is why consumer spending has not risen since 2008. Even when income rises, many families find their paychecks eaten up by debt service.

That is what debt deflation means. Income paid to creditors is not available for spending on goods and services. In the 1930s, Keynes feared that as economies got richer they would save more of their income, causing a shortfall in market demand. The problem today is that "saving" is not a result of people having more income than they want to spend. National income statistics count as "saving" the income spent on paying down debt. So the problem that Keynes feared – inadequate market demand – comes from being debt-strapped, not from earning too much money. Debt deflation leads to defaults and foreclosures, while bondholders and banks get bailed out at government expense.

In the workplace, many employees are so deep in debt that they are afraid to complain about working conditions out of fear losing their jobs and thus missing a mortgage payment or utility bill, which would bump their credit-card interest rates up to the penalty range of circa 29 percent. This has been called the debt-traumatized worker effect, and it is a major cause of wage stagnation.

Finance and land rent: How bankers replaced the landed aristocracy

The Norman Conquest of Britain in 1066 and similar conquests of the land in other European realms led to a constant fiscal struggle over who should receive the land's rent: the king as his tax base, or the nobility to whom the land had been parceled out for them to manage, nominally on behalf of the palace. Increasingly, the hereditary landlord class privatized this rent, obliging kings to tax labor and industry.

This rent grab set the stage for the great fight of classical free market economists, from the French Physiocrats to Adam Smith, John Stuart Mill, Henry George and their contemporaries to tax land and natural resource rents as the fiscal base. Their aim was to replace the vested aristocracy of rent recipients with public taxation or ownership of what was a gift of nature – the sun that the Physiocrats cited as the source of agriculture's productive powers, inherent soil fertility according to Ricardo, or simply the rent of location as urbanization increased the value of residential and commercial sites.

Classical value and price theory was refined primarily to measure this land rent as not reflecting an expenditure of labor or enterprise (in contrast to buildings and other capital improvements), but as a gift of nature and hence national patrimony.

The main aim of political economy for the past three centuries has been to recover the flow of privatized land and natural resource rent that medieval kings had lost. The political dimension of this effort involved democratic constitutional reform to overpower the rent-levying class. By the late 19th century political pressure was rising to tax landowners in Britain, the United States and other countries. In Britain a constitutional crisis over land taxation in 1910 ended the landed aristocracy's power in the House of Lords to block House of Commons tax policy. Sun Yat-Sen's revolution in China in 1911 to overthrow the Qing dynasty was fueled by demands for land taxation as the fiscal base. And when the United States instituted the income tax in 1913, it fell mainly on *rentier* income from real estate, natural resources and financial gains. Similar democratic tax reform was spreading throughout the world.

By the turn of the 20th century land was passing out of the hands of the nobility to be democratized – on credit. That was the only way for most families to acquire a home. Mortgage credit promises to enable homebuyers to obtain security of their living space – and in the process, buy an asset rising in value. A rising share of personal saving for most of the population took the form of paying down their mortgages, building up their equity in real estate as the major element in their net worth.

Yet no economist anticipated how far-reaching the results would be, or that real estate would become by far the major market for bank lending from North America to Europe. Nor was it expected that real estate prices would be raised not so much by raw population growth (the man/land ratio) as by increasingly leveraged bank credit, and by rising public services increasing site values ("location, location and location") without recapturing this publicly created value in property taxes, which were cut.

The result of "democratizing" real estate on credit is that most of the rental income hitherto paid to a landlord class is now paid to banks as mortgage interest, not to the government as classical doctrine had urged. Today's financial sector thus has taken over the role that the landed aristocracy played in feudal Europe. But although rent no longer supports a landed aristocracy, it does not serve as the tax base either. It is paid to the banks as mortgage interest. Homebuyers, commercial investors and property speculators are obliged to pay the rental value to bankers as the price of acquiring it. The buyer who takes out the biggest mortgage to pay the bank the most gets the asset. So real estate ends up being worth whatever banks will lend against it.

Finance as the mother of monopolies

The other form of rent that Adam Smith and other classical economists sought to minimize was that of natural monopolies such as the East India Companies of Britain, France and Holland, and kindred special trade privileges. This was what free trade basically meant. Most European countries kept basic infrastructure in the public domain – roads and railroads, communications, water, education, health care and pensions so as to minimize the economy's cost of living and doing business by providing basic services at cost, at subsidized rates or even freely.

The financial sector's aim is not to minimize the cost of roads, electric power, transportation, water or education, but to maximize what can be charged as monopoly rent. Since 1980 the privatization of this infrastructure has been greatly accelerated. Having financialized oil and gas, mining, power utilities, financial centers are now seeking to de-socialize society's most important infrastructure, largely to provide public revenue to cut taxes on finance, insurance and real estate (FIRE).

The United States was early to privatize railroads, electric and gas utilities, phone systems and other infrastructure monopolies, but regulated them through public service commissions to keep prices for their services in line with the basic costs of production. Yet since the 1980s these natural infrastructure monopolies have been taken out of the public domain and privatized with little regulation. The pretense is that by financing privatization of public enterprises, bank credit and financialized management help make economies more efficient. Thatcherism has been a disaster, most notoriously in the former Soviet economies since 1991, Carlos Slim's telephone monopoly in Mexico, U.S. pharmaceutical companies and cable TV. The reality is that debt service (interest and dividends), exorbitant management fees, stock options, underwriting fees, mergers and acquisitions add to the cost of doing business.

Property speculators and buyers of price-gouging opportunities for monopoly rent on credit have a similar operating philosophy: "rent is for paying interest." The steeper the rate of monopoly rent, the more privatizers will pay bankers and bond investors for ownership rights. The financial sector ends up as the main recipient of monopoly rents and land rents, receiving what the landlord class used to obtain.

What is so remarkable is that all this has been done in the name of "free markets," which financial lobbyists have re-defined as freedom *from* public ownership or regulation. The financial sector has managed to mobilize anti-government ideology to pry away the public domain and lobby to block regulation legislation. Government planning is accused of being inherently bureaucratic, wasteful and often corrupt, as if the history of privatization deals is not one of corrupt insider dealing and schemes to obtain rights for rent extraction that makes such economies much less competitive.

Financializing industry to turn profits into interest and stock buybacks

Early in the 20th century the wave of the future promised to see banks throughout the world do what they were doing best in Germany and Central Europe: coordinating industrial links with government and acting as forward planners (Chapter 7). Academic textbooks draw appealing pictures of banks financing capital formation. Low interest rates are held to spur industrial investment by making it more profitable to borrow.

But banks rarely fund new means of production. They prefer to lend for mergers, management buyouts or raids of companies already in place. As for bondholders, they found a new market in the 1980s wave of high-interest "junk-bond" takeovers. Lower interest rates make it easier to borrow and take over companies – and then break them up, bleed them via management fees, and scale back pensions by threatening bankruptcy.

Like other sectors, industry was expected to become more debt-free. Bank lending focused on trade financing, not capital investment. Economists urged industry to rely mainly on equity so as to prevent bondholders and other creditors from taking over management and keeping it on a short leash. But industry has become financialized, "activist shareholders" treat corporate industry as a vehicle to produce financial gains. Managers are paid according to how rapidly they can increase their companies' stock price, which is done most easily by debt leveraging. This has turned the stock market into an arena for asset stripping, using corporate profits for share buybacks and higher dividend payouts instead of for long-term investment (Chapter 8). These practices are widely denounced in the financial press, but the trend is not being checked (Chapter 9).

Financializing industry thus has changed the character of class warfare from what socialists and labor leaders envisioned in the late 19th century and early 20th century. Then, the great struggle was between employers and labor over wages and benefits. Today's finance is cannibalizing industrial capital, imposing austerity and shrinking employment while its drive to privatize monopolies increases the cost of living.

The financial takeover of government

Central banks were supposed to free government from having to borrow from private bondholders. But budget deficits have increased the power of financial lobbyists who have pushed politicians to reverse progressive income taxation and cut taxes on capital gains. Instead of central banks monetizing deficit spending to help the economy recover, they create money mainly to lend to banks for the purpose of increasing the economy's debt overhead. Since 2008 the U.S. Federal Reserve has monetized $4 trillion in Quantitative Easing credit to banks. The aim is to re-inflate asset prices for the real estate, bonds and stocks held as collateral by financial institutions (and the One Percent), not to help the "real" economy recover.

The situation is worst in the Eurozone. The European Central Bank has authorized €1 trillion ("Whatever it takes," as its head Mario Draghi said) to buy bonds from banks but refuses to lend anything to governments on principle, even though budget deficits are limited to only 3 percent of GDP. This imposes fiscal deflation on top of debt deflation. Governments are forced to rely on bondholders and, increasingly, to sell off the public domain.

All this is contrary to what classical economists urged. Their objective was for governments elected by the population at large to receive and allocate the economic surplus. Presumably this would have been to lower the cost of living and doing business, provide a widening range of public services at subsidized prices or freely, and sponsor a fair society in which nobody would receive special privileges or hereditary rights.

Financial sector advocates have sought to control democracies by shifting tax policy and bank regulation out of the hands of elected representatives to nominees from world's financial centers. The aim of this planning is not for the classical progressive objectives of mobilizing savings to increase productivity and raise populations out of poverty. The objective of finance capitalism is not capital formation, but acquisition of rent-yielding privileges for real estate, natural resources and monopolies.

These are precisely the forms of revenue that centuries of classical economists sought to tax away or minimize. By allying itself with the *rentier* sectors and lobbying on their behalf – so as to extract their rent as interest – banking and high finance have become part of the economic overhead from which classical economists sought to free society. The result of moving into a symbiosis with real estate, mining, oil, other natural resources and monopolies has been to financialize these sectors. As this has occurred, bank lobbyists have urged that land be un-taxed so as to leave more rent (and other natural resource rent) "free" to be paid as interest – while forcing governments to tax labor and industry instead.

To promote this tax shift and debt leveraging, financial lobbyists have created a smokescreen of deception that depicts financialization as helping economies grow. They accuse central bank monetizing of budget deficits as being inherently inflationary – despite no evidence of this, and despite the vast inflation of real estate prices and stock prices by predatory bank credit.

Money creation is now monopolized by banks, which use this power to finance the transfer of property – with the source of the quickest and largest fortunes being infrastructure and natural resources pried out of the public domain of debtor countries by a combination of political insider dealing and debt leverage – a merger of kleptocracy with the world's financial centers.

The financial strategy is capped by creating international financial institutions (the International Monetary Fund, European Central Bank) to bring pressure on debtor economies to take fiscal policy out of the hands of elected parliaments and into those of institutions ruling on behalf of bankers and bondholders. This global power has enabled finance to override potentially debtor-friendly governments.

Financial oligarchy replaces democracy

All this contradicts what the 18th, 19th and most of the 20th century fought for in their drive to free economies from landlords, monopolists and "coupon clippers" living off bonds, stocks and real estate (largely inherited). Their income was a technologically and economically unnecessary vestige of past conquests – privileges bequeathed to subsequent generations.

When parliamentary reform dislodged the landed aristocracy's control of government, the hope was that extending the vote to the population at large would lead to policies that would manage land, natural resources and natural monopolies in the long-term public interest. Yet what Thorstein Veblen called the vested interests have rebuilt their political dominance, led by the financial sector which used its wealth to gain control of the election process to create a neo-*rentier* society imposing austerity.

A cultural counter-revolution has taken place. If few people have noticed, it is because the financial sector has rewritten history and re-defined the public's idea of what economic progress and a fair society is all about. The financial alternative to classical economics calls itself "neoliberalism," but it is the opposite of what the Enlightenment's original liberal reformers called themselves. Land rent has *not* ended up in government hands, and more and more public services have been privatized to squeeze out monopoly rent. Banks have gained control of government and their central banks to create money only to bail out creditor losses, not to finance public spending.

The next few chapters review the classical analysis of value, price and rent theory to show how "free lunch" economic rent has been taken away from the public domain by the financial sector. Instead of creating the anticipated symbiosis with industry, as was hoped a century ago, finance has backed the rent-extracting sectors. And instead of central banks creating money to finance their budget deficits, governments are now forced to rely on bondholders, leaving it up to commercial banks and other creditors to provide the credit that economies need to grow.

The result is that today's society is indeed moving toward the central planning that financial lobbyists have long denounced. But the planning has been shifted to financial centers (Wall Street, the City of London or Frankfurt). And its plan is to create a neo-*rentier* society. Instead of helping the host economy grow, banking, bond markets and even the stock market have become part of a predatory, extractive dynamic.

This destructive scenario would not have been possible if memory of the classical critique of *rentiers* had remained at the center of political discussion. Chapter 2 therefore reviews how three centuries of Enlightenment reform sought to free industrial capitalism from the *rentier* overhead bequeathed by feudalism. Only by understanding this legacy can we see how today's financial counter-Enlightenment is leading us back to a neo-feudal economy.

Marxism diagnosed the main inner contradiction of industrial capitalism to be that its drive to increase profit by paying labor as little as possible would dry up the domestic market. The inner contradiction of finance capitalism is similar: Debt deflation strips away the economy's land rent, natural resource rent, industrial profits, disposable personal income and tax revenue – leaving economies unable to carry their exponential rise in credit. Austerity leads to default, as we are seeing today in Greece.

The financial sector's response is to double down and try to lend enough to enable debtors to pay. When this financial bubble bursts, creditors foreclose on the public domain of debtor economies, much as they foreclose on the homes of defaulting mortgage debtors. Central banks flood the economy with credit in an attempt to inflate a new asset-price bubble by lowering interest rates. U.S. Treasury bonds yield less than 1 percent, and the interest rate on German government bonds is actually negative, reflecting the "flight to safety" when debt write-downs look inevitable.

In the end even zero-interest loans cannot be paid. Shylock's loan to the Merchant of Venice for a pound of flesh was a zero-interest loan. The underlying theme of this book thus can be summarized in a single sentence: Debts that can't be paid, won't be paid. But trying to pay such debts will plunge economies into prolonged depression.

2

The Long Fight to Free Economies From Feudalism's *Rentier* Legacy

If you do not own them, they will in time own you. They will destroy your politics [and]
corrupt your institutions.

Cleveland mayor Tom Johnson (1901–09) speaking of power utilities

Classical economics was part of a reform process to bring Europe out of the feudal era into the industrial age. This required overcoming the power of the landed aristocracy, bankers and monopolies to levy charges that were unfair because they did not reflect actual labor or enterprise. Such revenue was deemed "unearned."

The original fight for free markets meant freeing them *from* exploitation by rent extractors: owners of land, natural resources, monopoly rights and money fortunes that provided income without corresponding work – and usually without tax liability. Where hereditary rental and financial revenue supported the richest aristocracies, the tax burden was shifted most heavily onto labor and industry, in addition to their rent and debt burden.

The classical reform program of Adam Smith and his followers was to tax the income deriving from privileges that were the legacy of feudal Europe and its military conquests, and to make land, banking and monopolies publicly regulated functions. Today's neoliberalism turns the word's original meaning on its head. Neoliberals have re-defined "free markets" to mean an economy free *for* rent-seekers, that is, "free" of government regulation or taxation of unearned *rentier* income (rents and financial returns).

The best way to undo their counter-revolution is to revive the classical distinction between earned and unearned income, and the analysis of financial and debt relations (the "magic of compound interest") as being predatory on the economy at large. This original critique of landlords, bankers and monopolists has been stripped out of the current political debate in favor of what is best characterized as trickle-down junk economics.

The title of Adam Smith's chair at the University of Edinburgh was Moral Philosophy. This remained the name for economics courses taught in Britain and America through most of the 19th century. Another name was Political Economy, and 17th-century writers used the term Political Arithmetic. The common aim was to influence public policy: above all how to finance government, what best to tax, and what rules should govern banking and credit.

The French Physiocrats were the first to call themselves *économistes*. Their leader François Quesnay (1694-1774) developed the first national income models in the process of explaining why France should shift taxes off labor and industry onto its landed aristocracy. Adam Smith endorsed the view of the Marquis de Mirabeau (father of Honoré, Comte de Mirabeau, an early leader of the French Revolution) that Quesnay's *Tableau Économique* was one of the three great inventions of history (along with writing and money) for distinguishing between earned and unearned income. The subsequent debate between David Ricardo and Thomas Malthus over whether to protect agricultural landlords with high tariffs (the Corn Laws) added the concept of land rent to the Physiocratic analysis of how the economic surplus is created, who ends up with it and how they spend their income.

The guiding principle was that everyone deserves to receive the fruits of their own labor, but not that of others. Classical value and price theory provided the analytic tool to define and measure unearned income as overhead classical economics. It aimed to distinguish the necessary costs of production – value – from the unnecessary (and hence, parasitic) excess of price over and above these costs. This monopoly rent, along with land rent or credit over intrinsic worth came to be called *economic rent*, the source of *rentier* income. An efficient economy should minimize economic rent in order to prevent dissipation and exploitation by the *rentier* classes. For the past eight centuries the political aim of value theory has been to liberate nations from the three legacies of feudal Europe's military and financial conquests: land rent, monopoly pricing and interest.

Land rent is what landlords charge in payment for the ground that someone's forbears conquered. Monopoly rent is price gouging by businesses with special privileges or market power. These privileges were called patents: rights to charge whatever the market would bear, without regard for the actual cost of doing business. Bankers, for instance, charge more than what really is needed to provide their services.

Bringing prices and incomes into line with the actual costs of production would free economies from in these rents and financial charges. Landlords do not have to work to demand higher rents. Land prices rise as economies become more prosperous, while public agencies build roads, schools and public transportation to increase site values. Likewise, in banking, money does not "work" to pay interest; debtors do the work.

Distinguishing the return to labor from that to special privilege (headed by monopolies) became part of the Enlightenment's reform program to make economies more fair, and also lower-cost and more industrially competitive. But the rent-receiving classes – *rentiers* – argue that their charges do not add to the cost of living and doing business. Claiming that their gains are invested productively (not to acquire more assets or luxuries or extend more loans), their supporters seek to distract attention from how excessive charges polarize and impoverish economies.

The essence of today's neoliberal economics is to deny that any income or wealth is unearned, or that market prices may contain an unnecessary excessive rake-off over intrinsic value. If true, it would mean that no public regulation is necessary, or public ownership of infrastructure or basic services. Income at the top is held to trickle down, so that the One Percent serve the 99 Percent, creating rather than destroying jobs and prosperity.

The Labor Theory of Value serves to isolate and measure Economic Rent

Up to medieval times most families produced their own basic needs. Most market trade occurred mainly at the margin, especially for imported goods and luxuries. Not until the 13th century's revival of trade and urbanization did an analytic effort arise to relate market prices systematically to costs of production.

This adjustment was prompted by the need to define a fair price for bankers, tradesmen and other professionals to charge for their services. At issue was what constituted exploitation that a fair economy should prevent, and what was a necessary cost of doing business. This discussion took place in the first centers of learning: the Church, which founded the earliest universities.

The Churchmen's theory of Just Price was an incipient labor theory of value: The cost of producing any commodity ultimately consists of the cost of labor, including that needed to produce the raw materials, plant and equipment used up in its production. Thomas Aquinas (1225–74) wrote that bankers and tradesmen should earn enough to support their families in a manner appropriate for their station, including enough to give to charity and pay taxes.

The problem that he Aquinas and his fellow Scholastics addressed was much like today's: it was deemed unfair for bankers to earn so much more for the services they performed (such as transferring funds from one currency or realm to another, or lending to business ventures) than what other professionals earned. It resembles today's arguments over how much Wall Street investment bankers should make.

The logic of Church theorists was that bankers should have a living standard much like professionals of similar station. This required holding down the price of services they could charge (e.g., by the usury laws enacted by most of the world prior to the 1980s), by regulating prices for their services, and by taxing high incomes and luxuries.

It took four centuries to extend the concept of Just Price to ground rent paid to the landlord class. Two decades after the Norman Conquest in 1066, for instance, William the Conqueror ordered compilation of the Domesday Book (1086). This tributary tax came to be privatized into ground rent paid to the nobility when it revolted against the greedy King John Lackland (1199-1216). The Magna Carta (1215) and Revolt of the Barons were largely moves by the landed aristocracy to avoid taxes and keep the rent for themselves, shift the fiscal burden onto labor and the towns. The ground rent they imposed thus was a legacy of the military conquest of Europe by warlords who appropriated the land's crop surplus as tribute.

By the 18th century, attempts to free economies from the rent-extracting privileges and monopoly of political power that originated in conquest inspired criticisms of land rent and the aristocracy's burdensome role ("the idle rich"). These flowered into a full-blown moral philosophy that became the ideology driving the Industrial Revolution. Its political dimension advocated democratic reform to limit the aristocracy's power over government. The aim was not to dismantle the state as such, but to mobilize its tax policy, money creation and public regulations to limit predatory rentier levies. That was the essence of John Stuart Mill's "Ricardian socialist" theory and those of America's reform era with its anti-trust regulations and public utility regulatory boards.

Tax favoritism for rentiers and the decline of nations

What makes these early discussions relevant today is that economies are in danger of succumbing to a new rentier syndrome. Spain might have used the vast inflows of silver and gold from its New World conquests to become Europe's leading industrial power. Instead, the bullion it looted from the New World flowed right through its economy like water through a sieve. Spain's aristocracy of post-feudal landowners monopolized the inflow, dissipating it on luxury, more land acquisition, money lending, and more wars of conquest. The nobility squeezed rent out of the rural population, taxed the urban population so steeply as to impose poverty everywhere, and provided little of the education, science and technology that was flowering in northern European realms more democratic and less stifled by their landed aristocracy.

The "Spanish Syndrome" became an object lesson for what to avoid. It inspired economists to define the various ways in which rentier wealth – and the tax and war policies it supported – blocked progress and led to the decline and fall of nations. Dean Josiah Tucker, a Welsh clergyman and political economist, pointed out in 1774 that it made a great difference whether nations obtained money by employing their population productively, or by piracy or simply looting of silver and gold, as Spain and Portugal had done with such debilitating effects, in which "very few Hands were employed in getting this Mass of Wealth … and fewer still are supposed to retain what is gotten." [9]

The parallel is still being drawn in modern times. In The Great Reckoning (1991), James Dale Davidson and Lord William Rees-Mogg write with regard to the glory days of Spain's "century of gold" (1525 to 1625 AD):

> Leadership of the Spanish government was totally dominated by tax-consuming interests: the military, the bureaucracy, the church, and the nobility. … Spain's leaders resisted every effort to cut costs. …Taxes were tripled between 1556 and 1577. Spending went up even faster... By 1600, interest on the national debt took 40 percent of the budget. Spain descended into bankruptcy and never recovered.

Despite its vast stream of gold and silver, Spain became the most debt-ridden country in Europe – with its tax burden shifted entirely onto the least affluent, blocking development of a home market. Yet today's neoliberal lobbyists are urging similar tax favoritism to un-tax finance and real estate, shift the tax burden onto labor and consumers, cut public infrastructure and social spending, and put rentier managers in charge of government. The main difference from Spain and other post-feudal economies is that interest to the financial sector has replaced the rent paid to feudal landlords. And as far as economic discussion is concerned, there is no singling out of rentier income as such. Nor is there any discussion of the decline and fall of nations. Neoliberal happy talk is all about growth – automatically expanding growth of national income and GDP, seemingly ad infinitum with no checks on the super-rich elites' self-serving policies.

The main distinction between today's mode of conquest and that of 16th-century Spain (and 18th-century France) is that it is now largely financial, not

---

[9] Josiah Tucker, *Four Tracts on Political and Commercial Subjects* [1774] (2nd ed., Gloucester 1776, pp. 21–26). For a modern discussion see Erik Reinert, *How Rich Countries got Rich… and why Poor Countries Stay Poor* (London, Constable, 2007), pp. 84–90.

military. Land, natural resources, public infrastructure and industrial corporations are acquired by borrowing money. The cost of this conquest turns out to be as heavy as overt military warfare. Landlords pay out their net rent as interest to the banks that provide mortgage credit for them to acquire property. Corporate raiders likewise pay their cash flow as interest to the bondholders who finance their takeovers. Even tax revenue is increasingly earmarked to pay creditors (often foreign, as in medieval times), not to invest in infrastructure, pay pensions or spend for economic recovery and social welfare.

Today's monopolization of affluence by a rentier class avoiding taxes and public regulation by buying control of government is the same problem that confronted the classical economists. Their struggle to create a fairer economy produced the tools most appropriate to understand how today's economies are polarizing while becoming less productive. The Physiocrats, Adam Smith, David Ricardo and their successors refined the analysis of how rent-seeking siphons off income from the economy's flow of spending.

The classical critique of economic rent

Classical value theory provides the clearest conceptual tools to analyze the dynamics that are polarizing and impoverishing today's economies. The labor theory of value went hand-in-hand with a "rent theory" of prices, broadening the concept of economic rent imposed by landholders, monopolists and bankers. Rent theory became the basis for distinguishing between earned and unearned income. Nearly all public regulatory policy of the 20th century has followed the groundwork laid by this Enlightenment ideology and political reform from John Locke onward, defining value, price and rent as a guide to progressive tax philosophy, anti-monopoly price regulation, usury laws and rent controls.

Defenders of landlords fought back. Malthus argued that landlords would not simply collect rent passively, but would invest it productively to increase productivity. Subsequent apologists simply left unearned income out of their models, hoping to leave it invisible so that it would not be taxed or regulated. By the end of the 19th century, John Bates Clark in the United States, and similar trivializers abroad, defined whatever income anyone made as being earned, simply as part of a free market relationship. Debt service and rent made little appearance in such models, except to "trickle down" as market demand in general, and to finance new investment. (Chapter 6 will deal with this pedigree of today's financial lobbying.)

Instead of acknowledging the reality of predatory rentier behavior, financial lobbyists depict lending as being productive, as if it normally provides borrowers with the means to make enough gain to pay. Yet little such lending has occurred in history, apart from investing in trade ventures. Most bank loans are not to create new means of production but are made against real estate, financial securities or other assets already in place. The main source of gain for borrowers since the 1980s has not derived from earnings but seeing the real estate, stocks or bonds they have bought on credit rise as a result of asset-price inflation – that is, to get rich from the debt-leveraged Bubble Economy.

What makes classical economics more insightful than today's mainstream orthodoxy is its focus on wealth ownership and the special privileges used to extract income without producing a corresponding value of product or service. Most inequality does not reflect differing levels of productivity, but distortions resulting from property rights and other special privileges. Distinguishing between earned and unearned income, classical economists asked what tax philosophy and public policy would lead to the most efficient and fair prices, incomes and economic growth.

Government was situated to play a key role in allocating resources. But although nearly all economies in history have been mixed public/private economic systems, today's anti-government pressure seeks to create a one-sided economy whose control is centralized in Wall Street and similar financial centers abroad.

Democratic political reforms were expected to prevent this development, by replacing inherited privilege with equality of opportunity. The aim was to do away with such privileges and put everyone and every business on an equal footing. Economies were to be freed by turning natural monopolies and land into public utilities.

This is how classical free market reforms evolved toward socialism of one form or another on the eve of the 20th century. The hereditary landlord class was selling its land to buyers on credit. That is how land and home ownership were democratized. The unanticipated result has been that banks receive as mortgage interest the rental income formerly paid to landlords. The financial sector has replaced land ownership as the most important rentier sector, today's post-industrial aristocracy.

In the years leading up to World War I, it seemed that finance was becoming industrialized, that is, mobilized to support industrial prosperity in the context of democratic reforms to extend voting rights to males without regard for property ownership, and then to women. The stranglehold of hereditary aristocracies seemed on its way to being ended. In Britain, the House of Lords lost its ability to block revenue bills passed by the House of Commons in 1910.

Finance vs. industry

Today's financial sector is raiding what were expected a century ago to become the social functions of capital. The objective of most lending is to extract interest charges by attaching debt to real estate rent, corporate profits and personal income streams, turning them into a flow of interest charges. The "real" economy slows in the face of these exponentially growing financial claims (bank loans, stocks and bonds) that enrich primarily the One Percent. Instead of finance being industrialized, industry has become financialized. The stock and bond markets have been turned into arenas for debt-leveraged buyouts and asset stripping (described in Chapters 9 and 10 below).

These dynamics represent a counter-revolution against classical ideas of free markets. Today's neoliberal tax and financial philosophy is corrosive and destructive, not productive. Instead of promoting industry, capital formation and infrastructure, finance has moved into a symbiosis with the other rentier sectors: real estate, natural resource extraction, and natural monopolies. Acquisition of rent-yielding privileges on credit (or simply by insider dealing and legal maneuvering) does not require the fixed capital investment that manufacturing entails. Chapter 3 will discuss rentier privileges in general, and Chapter 4 will explain the purely financial mathematics of increasing saving and debt by the "magic of compound interest" without concern for the needs of labor and industry.

3

The Critique and Defense of
Economic Rent, from Locke to Mill

The main substantive achievement of neoliberalization … has been to redistribute, rather than to generate, wealth and income. [By] 'accumulation by dispossession' I mean … the commodification and privatization of land and the forceful expulsion of peasant populations; conversion of various forms of property rights (common, collective, state, etc.) into exclusive private property rights; suppression of rights to the commons; … colonial, neocolonial, and imperial processes of appropriation of assets (including natural resources); …and usury, the national debt and, most devastating of all, the use of the credit system as a radical means of accumulation by dispossession. … To this list of mechanisms we may now add a raft of techniques such as the extraction of rents from patents and intellectual property rights and the diminution or erasure of various forms of common property rights (such as state pensions, paid vacations, and access to education and health care) won through a generation or more of class struggle. The proposal to privatize all state pension rights (pioneered in Chile under the dictatorship) is, for example, one of the cherished objectives of the Republicans in the US.

David Harvey, *A Brief History of Neoliberalism* (Oxford, 2005), pp. 159–60.

The phenomena cited by Harvey represent opportunities for rent extraction. Neoliberals claim that such special privileges and expropriation of hitherto public assets promote economic efficiency. Classical free marketers defined the rents they yielded as neither earned nor necessary for production to occur. They were a post-feudal overhead.

The year 1690 usually is treated as the takeoff point for the classical distinction between earned and unearned wealth and its income stream. At issue then was the contrast between real wealth created by labor, and special privileges – mainly post-feudal overhead – from which society could free itself and thus lower its cost structure.

John Locke's guiding axiom was that all men have a natural right to the fruits of their labor. A corollary to this logic was that landlords have a right *only* to what they themselves produce, not to exploit and appropriate the labor of their tenants:

> Though the earth and all inferior creatures be common to all men, yet every man has a property in his own person ... The labour of his body and the work of his hands, we may say, are properly his. Whatsoever then he removes out of the state that nature hath provided and left it in, he hath mixed his labour with, and joined to it something that is his own, and thereby makes it his property. ... For this labour being the unquestionable property of the labourer, no man but he can have a right to what that is once joined to, at least where there is enough and as good left in common for others.[10]

Locke wrote here as if most rent derived from the landlords' own labor, not that of their tenants or the economy at large. He also did not distinguish between the original conquerors or appropriators and their heirs. It was as if the benefit of earlier labor (or conquest) should be inherited down through the generations. Yet Locke's labor theory of property and wealth ownership set the stage for distinguishing between the portion of land rent that resulted from its owner's expenditure of labor and capital investment, and what was received simply from ownership rights without labor effort. This contrast guided tax reform down through the Progressive Era in the early 20th century.

Despite his conflation of former and present landholder's labor, Locke's exposition initiated a centuries-long discussion. By the 19th century the rising price of land sites was seen as occurring independently of effort by landlords. The rent they charged reflected prosperity by the rest of the economy, not their own effort. Economists call this kind of gain a *windfall*. It is like winning a lottery, including in many cases the inheritance lottery of how much wealth one's parents have.

Classical economists argued that labor and capital goods require a cost necessary to bring them into production. Labor must receive wages sufficient to cover its basic subsistence, at living standards that tend to rise over time to sustain personal investment in better skills, education and health. And capital investment will not take place without the prospect of earning a profit.

More problematic are accounting for land and natural resources. Production cannot take place without land, sunlight, air and water, but no labor or capital cost is necessary to provide them. They can be privatized by force, legal right or political fiat (sale by the state). For example, Australia's richest person, Gina Rinehart, inherited from her prospector father the rights to charge for access to the iron ore deposit he discovered.[11] Much of her wealth has been spent in lobbying to block the government from taxing her windfall.

---

[10] John Locke, "Of Property," *The Second Treatise of Civil Government* (New York: 1947), p.134.

[11] Forbes calculated her 2012 wealth as $28 billion, making her the fourth richest woman in the world. See Tom Treadgold, "Australia's $17 billion Woman On the Road To Becoming A Whole Lot Richer," *Forbes*, March 21, 2014.

Classical economists focused on this kind of property claim in defining a fair distribution of income from land and other natural resources as between their initial appropriators, heirs and the tax collector. At issue was how much revenue should belong to the economy at large as its natural patrimony, and how much should be left in the hands of discoverers or appropriators and their descendants. The resulting theory of economic rent has been extended to monopoly rights and patents such as those which pharmaceutical companies obtain to charge for their price gouging.

The history of property acquisition is one of force and political intrigue, not labor by its existing owners. The wealthiest property owners have tended to be the most predatory – military conquerors, landed aristocracies, bankers, bondholders and monopolists. Their property rights to collect rent for land, mines, patents or monopolized trade are legal privileges produced by the legal system they control, not by labor. Medieval land grants typically were given to royal companions in return for their political loyalty.

This land acquisition process continued from colonial times down through America's land grants to the railroad barons and many other political giveaways to supporters in most countries, often for bribery and similar kinds of corruption. Most recently, the post-Soviet economies gave political insiders privatization rights to oil and gas, minerals, real estate and infrastructure at giveaway prices in the 1990s. Russia and other countries followed American and World Bank advice to simply give property to individuals, as if this would automatically produce an efficient (idealized) Western European-style free market.

What it actually did was to empower a class of oligarchs who obtained these assets by insider dealings.[12] Popular usage coined the word "grabitization" to describe "red company" managers getting rich by registering natural resources, public utilities or factories in their own name, obtaining high prices for their shares by selling large chunks to Western investors, and keeping most of their receipts for these shares abroad as flight capital (about $25 billion annually since 1991 for Russia). This neoliberal privatization capped the Cold War by dismantling the Soviet Union's public sector and reducing it to a neo-feudal society.

The great challenge confronting post-Soviet economies is how to undo the effects of these kleptocratic grabs. One way would be to re-nationalize them. This is difficult politically, given the influence that great wealth is able to buy.

---

[12] "Report: 110 People Own 35 Pct of Russia's Wealth," *Johnson's Russia List*, October 10, 2013, #24, summarizing an October 9 report by the Credit Suisse Research Institute.

A more "market oriented" solution is to leave these assets in their current hands but tax their land or resource rent to recapture portions of the windfall for the benefit of society.

Without such restructuring, all that Vladimir Putin can do is informal "jawboning": pressuring Russia's oligarchs to invest their revenue at home. Instead of making the post-Soviet economies more like the productive ideal of Western Europe and the United States in their reformist and even revolutionary heyday a century ago, these economies are going directly into neo-liberal *rentier* decadence.

The problem of how an economy can best recover from such grabitization is not new. Classical economists in Britain and France spent two centuries analyzing how to recapture the rents attached to such appropriations. Their solution was a rent tax. Today's vested interests fight viciously to suppress their concept of economic rent and the associated distinction between earned and unearned income. It would save today's reformers from having to reinvent the methodology of what constitutes fair value. Censoring or rewriting the history of economic thought aims at thwarting the logic for taxing rent-yielding assets.

The Physiocrats develop national income accounting

Seeking to reform the French monarchy in the decades preceding the 1789 Revolution, the Physiocrats popularized the term *laissez faire*, "let us be." Coined in the 1750s to oppose royal regulations to keep grain prices and hence land rents high, the school's founder, Francois Quesnay, extended the slogan to represent freedom from the aristocracy living off its rents in courtly luxury while taxes fell on the population at large.

Quesnay was a surgeon. The word Physiocracy reflected his analogy of the circulation of income and spending in the national economy with the flow of blood through the human body. This concept of circular flow inspired him to develop the first national income accounting format, the *Tableau Économique* in 1759 to show how France's economic surplus – what was left after defraying basic living and business expenses – ended up in the hands of landlords as groundrent.

Within this circle of mutual spending by producers, consumers and landlords, the Physiocrats attributed the economic surplus exclusively to agriculture. But *contra* Locke, they did not characterize landlords as taking rent by virtue of their labor. The crop surplus was produced by the sun's energy. This logic underlay their policy proposal: a Single Tax on land, *l'impôt unique*. Taxing land rent would collect what nature provided freely (sunlight and land) and hence what should belong to the public sector as the tax base.

The 19th century came to characterize landlords and other *rentiers* as the Idle Rich. But in an epoch when France was an autocratic state whose landed aristocracy was backed by the Church and royal organs, it would not have been politically viable to claim that they did not deserve their rents. Hoping to promote a fiscal revolution by reformers drawn from the ranks of these elites, Quesnay and his colleagues used rhetorical imagery to play on the self-image of rent recipients, calling this *rentier* class the *source* of France's wealth, with industry merely subsisting off the landed aristocracy's spending.

Characterizing industry and commerce as "sterile" (not directly producing the economic surplus) provided a logic for why landlords alone should bear the tax burden. Quesnay's ploy was to claim that the class that produces the surplus is the natural source of taxation. Depicting agricultural land as the ultimate source of surplus implied that all taxes would end up being paid out of it. Deeming manufacturing to be "sterile," merely working up the raw materials supplied by nature, meant that taxing industry or the labor it hired would raise the break-even cost that business needed to cover.

Any taxes on industry or labor would simply be passed on to the source of the surplus (agricultural landlords). In effect, the Physiocrats said: "Indeed you landowners are the source of our nation's wealth. That is why all taxes end up being paid by you, indirectly if not directly. Let us avoid the convoluted pretenses at work and tax you directly by our Single Tax instead of impoverishing French industry and commerce."

The Physiocrats' analysis of the economy's circular flow of revenue and spending enabled subsequent economists to analyze the net surplus (*produit net*), defined as income over and above break-even costs. They asked who ends up with it, and who ended up bearing the tax?

Quesnay's circular flow analysis describes what I call *rent deflation*. Like debt deflation to pay creditors, it is a transfer payment from agriculture, industry and commerce to rent recipients that do not play a direct and active role in production, but have the power to withhold key inputs needed for it to take place, or from consumers.

Adam Smith broadens Physiocratic rent theory

Adam Smith met Quesnay and *Les Économistes* on his travels in France during 1764–66. He agreed with the need to free labor and industry from the land rent imposed by Europe's privileged nobilities: "Ground-rents and the ordinary rent of land are ... the species of revenue which can best bear to have a peculiar tax imposed on them."[13] But in contrast to the Physiocratic description of industry being too "sterile" to tax, Smith said manufacturing was productive.

In his lectures at Edinburgh a decade before he wrote *The Wealth of Nations*, Smith generalized the concept of rent as passive, unearned income – and used the labor theory of value to extend this idea to finance as well as land ownership:

The labour and time of the poor is in civilized countries sacrificed to the maintaining of the rich in ease and luxury. The landlord is maintained in idleness and luxury by the labour of his tenants. The moneyed man is supported by his exactions from the industrious merchant and the needy who are obliged to support him in ease by a return for the use of his money. But every savage has the full enjoyment of the fruits of his own labours; there are no landlords, no usurers, no tax gatherers.[14]

Failure to tax this rent burden shifted taxes onto commerce and industry, eroding its profits and hence capital accumulation. In addition to bearing the cost of land rents, populations had to pay excise taxes levied to pay interest on public debt run up as a result of the failure to tax landlords.

The major focus of value and price theory remained on land rent throughout the 19th century. In 1848, John Stuart Mill explained the logic of taxing it away from the landlord class: "Suppose that there is a kind of income which constantly tends to increase, without any exertion or sacrifice on the part of the owners: those owners constituting a class in the community." Rejecting the moral justification that Locke provided for landownership – that their land owed its value to their own labor – Mill wrote that landlords

grow richer, as it were in their sleep, without working, risking, or economizing. What claim have they, on the general principle of social justice, to this accession of riches? In what

[13] Smith, *Wealth of Nations*, Book 5, Ch.2, Pt.2., Art.1. He elaborated: "Both ground rents, and the ordinary rent of land are a species of revenue, which the owner in many cases enjoys, without any care or attention of his own. Though a part of this revenue should be taken from him, in order to defray the expenses of the State, no discouragement will thereby be given to any sort of industry." Ricardo endorsed this passage (*Principles of Political Economy and Taxation* [1817], *Works*, Vol. I, p. 203).

[14] Smith, *Lectures on Jurisprudence*, ed. R. L. Meek and D. D. Raphael (Oxford 1978), pp. 340f. In 1814, David Buchanan published an edition of *The Wealth of Nations* with a volume of his own notes and commentary, attributing rent to monopoly (Vol. III, p. 272n), and concluding that it represented a mere *transfer of value* rather than actually adding to wealth. High rents enriched landlords at the expense of food consumers – what today's economists call a zero-sum game, meaning that one party simply gains at another's expense.

would they have been wronged if society had, from the beginning, reserved the right of taxing the spontaneous increase of rent ... ?[15]

The value of land rose as a result of the efforts of the entire community. Mill concluded that rising site value should belong to the public as the natural tax base rather than leaving it as "an unearned appendage to the riches of a particular class."

Mill justified taxing land rent on grounds of national interest as well as moral philosophy. The aim was to avoid taxing labor and industry, but on income that had no counterpart in labor. In time the labor theory of value was applied to monopoly rents.

The remainder of the 19th century was filled with proposals as to how best to tax or nationalize the land's economic rent. Patrick Dove, Alfred Wallace, Herbert Spencer, Henry George and others provided an enormous volume of journalistic and political literature. Short of nationalizing the land outright, these land taxers followed Mill's basic logic:

> The first step should be a valuation of all the land in the country. The present value of all land should be exempt from the tax; but after an interval had elapsed, during which society had increased in population and capital, a rough estimate might be made of the spontaneous increase which had accrued to rent since the valuation was made. ... [A]n approximate estimate might be made, how much value had been added to the land of the country by natural causes; and in laying on a general land-tax ... there would be an assurance of not touching any increase of income which might be the result of capital expended or industry exerted by the proprietor.[16]

When Britain's House of Commons finally legislated a land tax in 1909-10, the House of Lords created a constitutional crisis by nullifying it. The procedural rules were changed to prevent the Lords from ever again rejecting a Parliamentary revenue bill, but the momentum was lost as World War I loomed and changed everything.

Ricardo throws the banking sector's support behind commerce and industry

Every economic class seeks to justify its own self-interest. Even rent-extracting sectors claim to contribute to the host economy's wellbeing. Nowhere is this clearer than in the debate between David Ricardo, the leading spokesmen for

---

[15]   Mill, *Principles of Political Economy, with Some of their Applications to Social Philosophy* (1848), Book V, ch. II §5. William Gladstone called land rent "lazy income." By the late 19th century the popular term was "unearned increment."

[16]   *Ibid.*

Britain's banking interests, and Reverend Thomas Robert Malthus defending
the landlord class and its protectionist Corn Law tariffs that raised food prices
(and hence the rental value of farmland).

Hoping to strengthen Britain's position as workshop of the world, Ricardo
pointed out that its competitive power required keeping down food prices and
hence the subsistence wage. Urging the nation to buy its grain in the cheapest
markets rather than remaining self-sufficient in grain and other food production, he developed what remains orthodox trade theory explaining the (supposed) virtues of global specialization of labor. Ricardo's logic reflected the
self-interest of his banking class: Globalization promoted commerce, which
was still the major market for bank lending in the early 19th century.

The crux of his argument was that labor's cost of living, headed by food,
represented the main production expense for industrial employers. Ricardo's
solution was to replace the Corn Laws with free trade so as to buy crops and
other raw materials more cheaply abroad, from regions with more fertile land
and other natural resources. This meant convincing Britain not to abandon
the self-sufficiency in food production achieved during the Napoleonic Wars
that ended in 1815

In Ricardo's hands, the labor theory of value served to isolate the land rent
obtained by owners of allegedly more fertile soils, who were able to sell their
crops at prices set at the high-cost margin of cultivation. (He applied the same
concept of differential rent to mines and natural resources.) Attributing fertility
to "the original and indestructible powers of the soil," he claimed (unscienti-
fically) that no amount of capital investment, fertilizer or other action could
alter the *relative* fertility of lands.[17] The landlord's capital investment thus could
not avert the steady rise in *differential* land rent – the cost advantage obtained
by farmers on the richest and most fertile lands.

Even further, Ricardo claimed, diminishing returns were inevitable as
population growth forced cultivators onto inherently poorer soils. Rising food
prices set by these "last," presumably poorer soils taken into cultivation would
provide a widening margin of rental income over and above costs, a windfall
price umbrella for owners of more fertile lands. It followed that these sites did
not require more capital investment by the landlord to obtain a rising share of
national income. They did not need to do anything.

---

[17]   Malthus retorted that Ricardian differential rent was more a theoretical than a real
       phenomenon, "very much more limited than has been supposed" *Principles of Political
       Economy* (London: 1820), pp. 208f.

Ricardo's pessimistic agricultural assumptions failed to take into account the revolution in agricultural chemistry that was vastly increasing farm productivity. He insisted that even if fertilizer and capital improvements did increase yields, fertility *proportions* among soils of varying grades would remain unchanged. The best land thus would retain its edge even after capital was applied – and diminishing returns would still occur, forcing up food prices as more capital was applied to the land.

The logic Ricardo outlined for why land rents would rise as populations grow applies much better to the rent of location for urban sites. The desirability of sites in good neighborhoods is enhanced by public infrastructure investment in transportation and other improvements, combined with the general level of prosperity – and most of all in recent times, by bank credit on easier (that is, more debt-leveraged) lending terms. Owners enjoy a price rise without having to invest more of their own money – the situation Ricardo described with regard to agricultural landowners.

Malthus's focus on how landlords invest their gains and spend on consumption

At issue was whether landlords used the rents they received in ways that helped the economy, or whether high rents were an unjustified burden. Malthus put forth two arguments to defend highly protected land rents. First of all, if landlords earned more, they would act like industrial capitalists and plow their gains back into their farms to earn still more revenue by producing more. Instead of being the unearned passive income that Smith had described, high rents enabled more investment to raise yields.[18]

Malthus credited the high crop prices protected by Britain's Corn Laws for enabling landlords to invest more in the land to raise output per acre. He pointed out that when trade in food was suspended during the war with France (1798-1815), landlords had responded to higher prices by raising farm productivity enough meet domestic demand.[19] The technology of artificial fertilizers and mechanization promised to further spur farm productivity.

Assuming that protected income would be invested productively, Malthus chided Ricardo for treating the landlord's rent as the economy's deadweight

---

[18] There is a logic to this claim. However irrational the price supports of American agriculture since the 1930s often have seemed, they helped finance large and prolonged productivity gains.

[19] *Ibid.*, pp. 222f., 207. In his notes on this book, Ricardo wrote that this assertion was "wholly unfounded" (*Works*, Vol. II: *Notes on Malthus* [1951:205]).

loss when buyers of bread had to pay more. Contrary to Ricardo's description of rent as "a transfer of wealth, advantageous to the landlords and proportionally *injurious* to the consumers," Malthus countered that new capital investment in the land could not be afforded without high crop prices: "rent, and the increase of rent, [as] the necessary and unavoidable condition of an increased supply of corn for an increasing population."[20] This assumption that higher prices would mean more capital investment to increase productivity has been the argument for tariff protection for many centuries, including by American industrialists urging tariffs to support "infant industry" investment.

Malthus's second point concerned consumer spending by landlords. Far from draining the economy, he argued, such spending was needed to save it from unemployment. Landlords were what today's One Percent call themselves: "job creators" who hired coachmen, tailors and seamstresses, butlers and other servants, and bought coaches, fine clothes and furnishings. So even when rent recipients spent their revenue on luxuries, they augmented the demand for labor.

This argument failed to recognize that if workers did not have to pay such high food prices, they could spend more on the products of industry – or, if they still earned only the subsistence wage (as Ricardo assumed), industrial profits would be higher at the expense of land rent. The real choice thus was between luxury consumption by the landed aristocracy or higher living standards for the rest of the population and more industrial investment.

John Maynard Keynes applauded Malthus's emphasis on spending by landlords (or by government, financiers or any other class) as showing the importance of consumer demand.[21] But what Malthus described is best characterized as *rentier* demand by the One Percent. He was justifying what the late 19th-century cartoonist Thomas Nast depicted: Wall Street plutocrats dressed in finery and so fat from gluttonous over-eating that the buttons on their jackets nearly burst.

---

[20] Malthus, *Principles*, p. 149. That book was published three years after Ricardo's *Principles of Political Economy and Taxation* appeared in 1817.

[21] Keynes wrote (*Essays in Biography*, Norton, 1963): "One cannot rise from a perusal of this correspondence [between Ricardo and Malthus] without a feeling that the almost total obliteration of Malthus's line of approach and the complete domination of Ricardo's for a period of a hundred years has been a disaster to the progress of economics. Time after time in these letters Malthus is talking plain sense, the force of which Ricardo with his head in the clouds wholly fails to comprehend."

The threat of rising land rent to impose austerity

Ricardo won the day. Despite the fact that his theory of differential soil fertility and his belief in diminishing agricultural returns were diametrically at odds with the empirical experience of his time, his logic defining economic rent as the excess of price over costs of production shaped subsequent conceptualization of rent theory.

Free trade ideology also involved persuading foreign countries not to protect their industry with tariffs and subsidies. The principle of buying in the cheapest market meant that they would rely on Britain for their manufactures – and for their bank credit as well. After Parliament repealed the Corn Laws in 1846, Britain negotiated free trade pacts with foreign countries to refrain from protecting their own manufacturing in exchange for free entry into the British market for their food and raw materials. Ricardo's trade theory depicted this as a mutual gain. The problem, of course, is that buying in the cheapest market leaves the economy dependent on foreign producers. The long-term risk of dependency on imported food and basic consumer goods escaped Ricardo's attention, as did the problem of financing trade deficits by foreign debt.

Ricardo elaborated his concern that without such free trade, rising domestic food prices would push up the subsistence wage into a long-term pessimistic forecast: "The natural tendency of profits then is to fall; for, in the progress of society and wealth, the additional quantity of food required is obtained by the sacrifice of more and more labor" on the marginal soils.[22] Falling profits resulting from higher prices for labor's subsistence would bring

> an end of accumulation; for no capital can then yield any profit whatever, and no additional labour can be demanded, and consequently population will have reached its highest point. Long indeed before this period the very low rate of profits will have arrested all accumulation, and almost the whole produce of the country, after paying the labourers, will be the property of the owners of land and the receivers of tithes and taxes.[23]

In the end, Ricardo argued, landlords would obtain all the surplus income over and above the economy's bare subsistence wages. Industrial capital formation would stop:

> The farmer and manufacturer can no more live without profit, than the labourer without wages. Their motive for accumulation will diminish with every diminution of profit, and will cease altogether when their profits are so low as not to afford them an adequate

---

[22]   Ricardo, *Principles of Political Economy and Taxation*, Ch. 6: "On Profits," (3rd ed., 1821), pp. 120f.

[23]   *Loc. cit.*

compensation for their trouble, and the risk which they must necessarily encounter in employing their capital productively.[24]

Marx called this scenario "the bourgeois 'Twilight of the Gods' – the Day of Judgement."[25] Importing lower-cost food from abroad could only postpone economic Armageddon. As the American diplomat Alexander Everett observed, Ricardo's logic implied that diminishing returns would occur in one country after another as populations grew.[26] Soil fertility in outlying lands ultimately would decline, forcing up food prices and hence the cost of labor, squeezing industrial profits and hence capital accumulation.

From rent deflation to debt deflation

Ricardo's labor theory of value sought only to isolate land rent, not the payment of interest. As Parliamentary spokesman for his fellow financiers, he accused only landlords of draining income out of the economy, not creditors. So his blind spot reflects his profession and that of his banking family. (The Ricardo Brothers handled Greece's first Independence Loan of 1824, for instance, on quite ruinous terms for Greece.)

Seeing no parallel between paying interest to bankers and paying rents to landlords, Ricardo sidestepped Adam Smith's warning about how excise taxes levied on food and other necessities to pay bondholders on Britain's war debt drove up the nation's subsistence wage level.[27] His one-sided focus on land rent diverted attention from how rising debt service – the financial analogue to land rent – increases break-even costs while leaving less income available for spending on goods and services. Treating money merely as a veil – as if debt and its carrying charges were not relevant to cost and price levels – Ricardo insisted that payment of foreign debts would be entirely recycled into purchases of the paying-nation's exports. There was no recognition of how paying debt service put downward pressure on exchange rates or led to domestic austerity.

In Parliament, Ricardo backed a policy of monetary deflation to roll back the price of gold (and other commodities) to their prewar level in 1798.[28] The

---

24   *Ibid.*,p. 123.
25   Marx, *Theories of Surplus Value*, Vol. II, p. 544 discussing the passages quoted here.
26   I review Everett's, E. Peshine Smith's and Simon Patten's critiques of Ricardo and Malthus in *America's Protectionist Takeoff: 1815-1914* (ISLET 2011).
27   Smith, *Wealth of Nations*, Book V.
28   I discuss Ricardo's Bullionism and claim that how foreign debt-payments do not cause problems in *Trade, Development and Foreign Debt* (2009), Chapter 13, and *The Bubble and Beyond* (2012), Chapter 3: "How Economic Theory Came to Ignore the Role of Debt."

reality is that keeping debts on the books while prices decline enhances the value of creditor claims for payment. This polarization between creditors and debtors is what happened after the Napoleonic Wars, and also after America's Civil War, crucifying indebted farmers and the rest of the economy "on a cross of gold," as William Jennings Bryan characterized price deflation.

The financial sector now occupies the dominant position that landlords did in times past. Debt service plays the extractive role that land rent did in Ricardo's day. Unlike the rental income that landlords were assumed to spend into the economy for luxuries and new capital investment, creditors recycle most of their receipt of interest into new loans. This increases the debt burden without raising output or living standards.

Ricardo's critique of rent extraction was used first to oppose tariff subsidies for Britain's landlords, and then by "Ricardian socialists," such as John Stuart Mill, to advocate taxing away their land rent. But *rentiers* have always fought back, rejecting any analysis depicting their income as imposing an unearned, parasitic overhead charge on labor and industry (not to mention leading to austerity and depression).

Today, banking has found its major market in lending to real estate and monopolies, adding financial charges to land and monopoly rent overhead. The financial counterpart to diminishing returns that raise the cost of living and doing business takes two forms. Interest rates rise to cover the growing risks of lending to debt-strapped economies. And the "magic of compound interest" extracts an exponential expansion of debt service as creditors recycle their interest income into new loans. The result is that debts grow more rapidly and inexorably than the host economy's ability to pay.

4

The All-Devouring "Magic of Compound Interest"

That terminator is out there. It can't be bargained with. It can't be reasoned with. It doesn't feel pity, or remorse, or fear. And it absolutely will not stop, ever, until you are dead.

Kyle Reese, describing the character of "The Terminator" (1984)

Driven by the mathematics of compound interest – savings lent out to grow exponentially – the overgrowth of debt is at the root of today's economic crisis. Creditors make money by leaving their savings to accrue interest, doubling and redoubling their claims on the economy. This dynamic draws more and more control over labor, land, industry and tax revenue into the hands of creditors, concentrating property ownership and government in their hands. The way societies have coped with this deepening indebtedness should be the starting point of financial theorizing.

Money is not a "factor of production." It is a claim on the output or income that others produce. Debtors do the work, not the lenders. Before a formal market for wage labor developed in antiquity, money lending was the major way to obtain the services of bondservants who were compelled to work off the interest that was owed. Debtors' family members were pledged to their creditors. In India, and many other parts of the world, debt peonage still persists as a way to force labor to work for their creditors.[29]

In a similar way, tempting landholders to go into debt was the first step to pry away their subsistence lands, beaching archaic communalistic land tenure

---

[29] Piotr Steinkeller reviews the details in "Money-Lending Practices in Ur III Babylonia," in Michael Hudson and Marc Van De Mieroop, eds., *Debt and Economic Renewal in the Ancient Near East* (2002): 109-38. Following Moses Finley, "Debt-bondage and the Problem of Slavery" (1981), he answers Finley's question "as to why a lender would be willing to advance loans to impoverished peasants, whose economic capacity to repay such loans was virtually nonexistent." It was not to make a profit, but "to obtain more dependent labour, rather than as a device for enrichment through interest."

systems. In this respect creditors are like landlords, obtaining the labor of others and growing richer in the way that J. S. Mill described: "in their sleep," without working.

The problem of debts growing faster than the economy has been acknowledged by practically every society. Religious leaders have warned that maintaining a viable economy requires keeping creditors in check. That is why early Christianity and Islam took the radical step of banning the charging of interest altogether, even for commercial loans. It is why Judaism placed the Jubilee Year's debt cancellation at the core of Mosaic Law, based on a Babylonian practice extending back to 2000 BC, and to the Sumerian tradition in the millennium before that. Calculating how money lent out at interest doubles and redoubles was taught to scribal students in Sumer and Babylonia employed in palace and temple bookkeeping.

Mesopotamia's standard commercial interest rate from around 2500 BC through the Neo-Babylonian epoch in the first millennium was high – the equivalent of 20 percent annually.[30] This rate was not reached in modern times until the prime loan rate by U.S. banks peaked at 20 percent in 1980, causing a crisis. Yet this rate remained stable for more than two thousand years for contracts between financial backers and commercial traders or other entrepreneurs. The rate did not vary to reflect profit levels or the ability to pay. It was not set by "market" supply and demand, but was an administered price set as a matter of mathematical convenience by the initial creditors: the Sumerian temples and, after around 2750 BC, the palaces that gained dominance.

A mina-weight of silver was set as equal in value to as "bushel" of grain. And just as the bushel was divided into 60 "quarts," so a mina-weight of silver was divided into 60 shekels. It was on this sexagesimal basis that temples set the rate of interest simply for ease of calculation – at 1 shekel per month, 12 shekels in a year, 60 shekels in five years.

The exponential doubling and redoubling of debt

Any rate of interest implies a doubling time – the time it takes for interest payments to grow as large as the original principal. A Babylonian scribal exercise circa 2000 BC asks the student to calculate how long it will take for a

---

[30] I explain the logic underlying this rate and that of subsequent Greece and Rome in "How Interest Rates Were Set, 2500 BC – 1000 AD: *Máš, tokos* and *fænus* as metaphors for interest accruals," *Journal of the Economic and Social History of the Orient* 43 (Spring 2000):132–161.

mina of silver to double at the normal simple interest rate of one shekel per mina per month. The answer is five years, the typical time period for backers to lend money to traders embarking on voyages. Contracts for consignments to be traded for silver or other imports typically were for five years (60 months), so a mina lent out at this rate would produce 60 shekels in five years, doubling the original principal. Assyrian loan contracts of the period typically called for investors to advance 2 minas of gold, getting back 4 in five years.[31]

The idea of such exponential growth is expressed in an Egyptian proverb: "If wealth is placed where it bears interest, it comes back to you redoubled."[32] A Babylonian image compared making a loan to having a baby. This analogy reflects the fact that the word for "interest" in every ancient language meant a newborn: a goat-kind (*mash*) in Sumerian, or a young calf: *tokos* in Greek or *foenus* in Latin. The "newborn" paid as interest was born of silver or gold, not from borrowed cattle (as some economists once believed, missing the metaphor at work). What was born was the "baby" fraction of the principal, $1/60$ each month. (In Greece, interest was due on the new moon.) The growth was purely mathematical with a "gestation period" for doubling dependent on the interest rate.

The concept goes back to Sumer in the third millennium BC, which already had a term *mashmash*, "interest (*mash*) on the interest." Students were asked to calculate how long it will take for one mina to multiply 64 times, that is, 2^6 – in other words, six doubling times of five years each. The solution involves calculating powers of 2 ($2^2 = 4$, $2^3 = 8$ and so forth).[33] A mina multiplies fourfold in 10 years (two gestation periods), eightfold in 15 years (three periods), sixteenfold in 20 years (four periods), and 64 times in 30 years. The 30-year span consisted of six five-year doubling periods.

Such rates of growth are impossible to sustain over time. Automatic compounding of arrears owed on debts was not allowed, so investors had to find a new venture at the end of each typical five-year loan period, or else draw up

---

[31]   The example comes from a Berlin cuneiform text VAT 8528. Karen Rhea Nemet-Nejat, *Cuneiform Mathematical Texts as a Reflection of Everyday Life in Mesopotamia* (New Haven 1993 = AOS Series Vol. 75) provides a bibliography of schoolbook exercises and applications.

[32]   Miriam Lichtheim, *Ancient Egyptian Literature*, II:135.[33] This arithmetic exercise comes from VAT 8525. It is discussed by Hildagard Lewy, "Marginal Notes on a Recent Volume of Babylonian Mathematical Texts," *Journal of the American Oriental Society* 67 (1947):308 and Nemet-Nejat, *op. cit.*: 59f.

[33]   This arithmetic exercise comes from VAT 8525. It is discussed by Hildagard Lewy, "Marginal Notes on a Recent Volume of Babylonian Mathematical Texts," *Journal of the American Oriental Society* 67 (1947):308 and Nemet-Nejat, *op. cit.*: 59f.

a new contract. With the passage of time it must have become harder to find ventures to keep on doubling their savings.[34]

Martin Luther depicted usurers scheming "to amass wealth and get rich, to be lazy and idle and live in luxury on the labor of others." The growing mass of usurious claims was depicted graphically as a "great huge monster ... who lays waste all ... Cacus." Imbuing victims with an insatiable desire for money, Cacus encouraged an insatiable greed that "would eat up the world in a few years." A "usurer and money-glutton ... would have the whole world perish of hunger and thirst, misery and want, so far as in him lies, so that he may have all to himself, and every one may receive from him as from a God, and be his serf for ever. ... For Cacus means the villain that is a pious usurer, and steals, robs, eats everything."[35]

The mathematical calculation of interest-bearing debt growing in this way over long periods was greatly simplified in 1614 by the Scottish mathematician John Napier's invention of logarithms (literally "the arithmetic of ratios," *logos* in Greek). Describing the exponential growth of debt in his second book, *Robdologia* (1617), Napier illustrated his principle by means of a chessboard on which each square doubled the number assigned to the preceding one, until all sixty-four squares were doubled – that is, 2^{63} after the first doubling.

Three centuries later the 19th century German economist, Michael Flürscheim, cast this exponential doubling and redoubling principle into the form of a Persian proverb telling of a Shah who wished to reward a subject who had invented chess, and asked what he would like. The man asked only "that the Shah would give him a single grain of corn, which was to be put on the first square of the chess-board, and to be doubled on each successive square," until all sixty-four squares were filled with grain. Upon calculating 64 doublings of each square from the preceding, starting from the first gain and proceeding 1, 2, 4, 8, 16, 32, 64 and so on.

---

[34] Michael Hudson and Mark Van De Mieroop, eds., *Debt and Economic Renewal in the Ancient Near East* (CDL Press, Bethesda, Md., 2000), on which much of the following discussion is based.

[35] The passage occurs in Luther's 1540 Wittenberg pamphlet, *An die Pfarrherren wider den Wucher zu predigen* ["That the priests should preach against interest"]. Marx footnoted this passage in *Capital* (Vol. I, London 1887:604 and Vol. III, ch. xxiv:463f.), but it is missing from Vol. 45 of Luther's works (Fortress Press, 1962) dealing ostensibly with his economic writings. That so important a denunciation of interest would be omitted attests to the cognitive dissonance with which denunciations of interest strike modern secular and religious minds.

Figure 1:
The miracle of compound interest

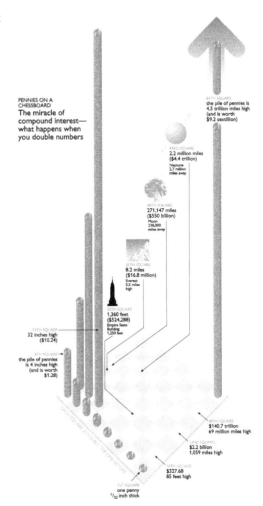

PENNIES ON A
CHESSBOARD
The miracle of
compound interest—
what happens when
you double numbers

64TH SQUARE
the pile of pennies is
4.5 trillion miles high
(and is worth
$9.2 sextillion)

43RD SQUARE
2.2 million miles
($4.4 trillion)
Neptune
2.7 million
miles away

40TH SQUARE
271,147 miles
($550 billion)
Moon
238,000
miles away

25TH SQUARE
8.2 miles
($16.8 million)
Everest
5.5 miles
high

20TH SQUARE
1,360 feet
($524,288)
Empire State
Building
1,250 feet

11TH SQUARE
32 inches high
($10.24)

8TH SQUARE
the pile of pennies
is 4 inches high
(and is worth
$1.28)

48TH SQUARE
$140.7 trillion
69 million miles high

32ND SQUARE
$2.2 billion
1,059 miles high

16TH SQUARE
$327.68
85 feet high

1ST SQUARE
one penny
1/32 inch thick

At first the compounding of grain remained well within the physical ability of the kingdom to pay, even after twenty squares were passed. But by the time the hypothetical chessboard was filled halfway, the compounding was growing by leaps and bounds. The Shah realized that this he had promised "an amount larger than what the treasures of his whole kingdom could buy."[36]

The moral is that no matter how much technology increases humanity's productive powers, the revenue it produces will be overtaken by the growth of

---

[36]   Michael Flürscheim, *A Clue to the Economic Labyrinth* (Perth and London 1902): 327ff.

debt multiplying at compound interest. The major source of loanable funds is repayments on existing loans, re-lent to finance yet new debts – often on an increasingly risky basis as the repertory of "sound projects" is exhausted.

Strictly speaking, it is savings that compound, not debts themselves. Each individual debt is settled one way or another, but creditors recycle their interest and amortization into new interest-bearing loans. The only problem for savers is to find enough debtors to take on new obligations.

The Rule of 72

A mathematical principle called the "Rule of 72" provides a quick way to calculate such doubling times: Divide 72 by any given rate of interest, and you have the doubling time. To double money at 8 percent annual interest, divide 72 by 8.

The answer is 9 years. In another 9 years the original principal will have multiplied fourfold, and in 27 years it will have grown to eight times the original sum. A loan at 6 percent doubles in 12 years, and at 4 percent in 18 years. This rule provides a quick way to approximate the number of years needed for savings accounts or prices to double at a given compound rate of increase.

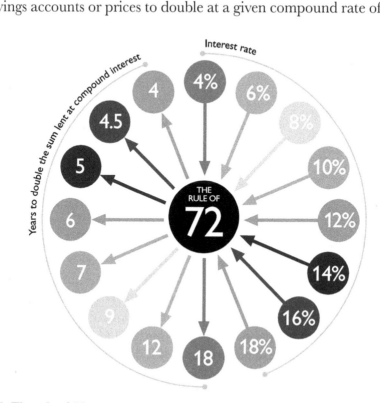

Figure 2: The rule of 72

The exponential growth of savings (= other peoples' debts)

One of Adam Smith's contemporaries, the Anglican minister and actuarial mathematician Richard Price, graphically explained the seemingly magical nature of how debts multiplied exponentially. As he described in his 1772 *Appeal to the Public on the Subject of the National Debt*:

> Money bearing compound interest increases at first slowly. But, the rate of increase being continually accelerated, it becomes in some time so rapid, as to mock all the powers of the imagination. One penny, put out at our Saviour's birth at 5% compound interest, would, before this time, have increased to a greater sum than would be obtained in a 150 millions of Earths, all solid gold. But if put out to simple interest, it would, in the same time, have amounted to no more than 7 shillings 4½d.[37]

In his *Observations on Reversionary Payments*, first published in 1769 and running through six editions by 1803, Price elaborated how the rate of multiplication would be even higher at 6 percent: "A shilling put out at 6% compound interest at our Saviour's birth would … have increased to a greater sum than the whole solar system could hold, supposing it a sphere equal in diameter to the diameter of Saturn's orbit."[38]

Rather naïvely, Price suggested that Britain's government make use of this exponential principle to pay off the public debt by creating a public fund that itself would grow at compound interest (called a sinking fund). The idea had been proposed a half century earlier by Nathaniel Gould, a director of the Bank of England. Parliament would set aside a million pounds sterling to invest at interest and build up the principal by reinvesting the dividends annually. In a surprisingly short period of time, Price promised, the fund would grow large enough to enable the government to extricate itself from its entire debt. "A state need never, therefore, be under any difficulties, for, with the smallest savings, it may, in as little time as its interest can require, pay off the largest debts."

What Price had discovered was how the exponential growth of money invested at interest multiplies the principal by plowing back the dividends into new saving. Balances snowball in the hands of bankers, bondholders and other savers, as if there always will be enough opportunities to find remunerative projects and credit-worthy borrowers to pay the interest that is accruing.

The moral is that the economy's ability to produce and earn enough of a surplus to pay exponentially rising interest charges is limited. The more it is

---

[37] Richard Price, *Appeal to the Public on the Subject of the National Debt* (London, 1772), p. 19.
[38] Price, *Observations on Reversionary Payments* (London, 1769), p. xiii, fn a.

stripped to pay creditors, the less able it is to produce and pay as a result of unemployment, underutilization of resources, emigration and capital flight.

In the two thousand years since the birth of Christ, the European economy has grown at a compound annual rate of 0.2 percent, far lower than the level at which interest rates have stood. Yet financial fortunes have crashed again and again – in part because interest payments have absorbed the revenue that otherwise would have been available for new direct investment.

The inability of productive investment opportunities to keep pace with the expansion of credit is the Achilles heel of finance-based growth. How can compound interest be paid? Who will end up paying it? Who will receive it, and what will they do with it? If banks and a creditor class receive this money, will they spend it domestically to maintain balance, or will they drain the economy's income stream and shift it abroad to new loan markets, leaving the economy strapped by the need to pay interest on the growing debt? If the state accrues this money, how will it recirculate it back into the economy?

"The Magic of Compound Interest" vs. The Economy's Ability to Pay

1. Neither money nor credit is a factor of production. Debtors do the work to pay their creditors. This means that interest is not a "return to a factor of production." Little credit is used to expand production or capital investment. Most is to transfer asset ownership.

2. If loan proceeds are not used to make gains sufficient to pay the creditor (productive credit), then interest and principal must be paid out of the debtor's other income or asset sales. Such lending is predatory.

3. The aim of predatory lending in much of the world is to obtain labor to work off debts (debt peonage), to foreclose on the land of debtors, and in modern times to force debt-strapped governments to privatize natural resources and public infrastructure.

4. Most inheritance consists of financial claims on the economy at large. In antiquity, foreclosure for non-payment was the major lever to pry land away from traditional tenure rights inheritable within the family. (Early creditors got themselves adopted as Number One sons.) Today, most financial claims are on the land's rent, leaving ownership "democratized" – on credit.

5. Most interest-bearing debt always has been predatory, apart from lending for commerce. Carrying a rising debt overhead slows material investment and economic growth.

6. The rate of interest never has reflected the rate of profit, the rise in physical productivity or the borrower's ability to pay. The earliest interest rates were set simply for ease in mathematical calculation: 1/60 per month in Mesopotamia, 1/10 annually in Greece, and 1/12 in Rome. (These were all the unit fractions in their respective fractional systems.) In modern times the rate of interest has been set mainly to stabilize the balance of payments and hence exchange rate. Since 2008 it has been set low to re-inflate asset prices and bank profits.

7. Any rate of interest implies a doubling time for money lent out. See the Rule of 72 (*e.g.*, five years in Mesopotamia).

8. Modern creditors avert public cancellation of debts (and making banks a public utility) by pretending that lending provides mutual benefit in which the borrower gains – consumer goods now rather than later, or money to run a business or buy an asset that earns enough to pay back the creditor with interest and still leave a profit for the debtor.

9. This scenario of productive lending does not typify the banking system as a whole. Instead of serving the economy's production trends, the financial sector (as presently organized) makes the economy top-heavy, by transferring assets and income into the hands of an increasingly hereditary creditor class.

10. The exponential growth of debt shrinks markets and slows and investment, reducing the economy's ability to pay debts, while increasing the debt/output and debt/income ratios.

11. The rising volume of debt changes the distribution of property ownership unless public authorities intervene to cancel debts and reverse expropriations. In antiquity, royal "Jubilee" proclamations liberated bondservants and restored lands that had been foreclosed.

12. Cancelling debts was politically easiest when governments or public institutions (temples, palaces or civic authorities) were the major creditors, because they were cancelling debts owed to themselves. This is an argument for why governments should be the main suppliers of money and credit as a public utility.

Financial vs. industrial dynamics, and the One Percent vs. the 99 Percent

European and North American public debts appeared to be on their way to being paid off during the relatively war-free century of 1815–1914. The economy's debt burden seemed likely to be self-amortizing by being linked to industrial capital formation. Bond markets mainly financed railroads and canals (the largest ventures usually being the most corrupt), mining and construction. Wall Street was interested in industry mainly to organize it into trusts and monopolies. Yet most economic writers limited their focus to the promise of rising technology and productivity, assuming that finance and banking would be absorbed into the industrial dynamic.

The threat of interest-bearing claims growing so exponentially as to subvert industrial progress was analyzed mainly by critics from outside the mainstream, many of whom were socialists. Two of the earliest books warning that financial dynamics threatened an economic crisis were published by the Chicago co-operative Charles H. Kerr, best known for publishing Marx's *Capital* and Gustavus Myers' *History of the Great American Fortunes*. In 1895, J. W. Bennett warned of a *rentier* caste drawing the world's wealth into its hands as the inventive powers of industry were outrun by the mathematics of compound interest, "the principle which asserts that a dollar will grow into two dollars in a number of years, and keep on multiplying until it represents all of the wealth on earth."[39]

Although not much noticed at the time, Bennett was one of the first to recognize that financial recycling of interest receipts into new lending was the driving force of the business cycle. Despite the rising role of industry, "financial systems are founded on rent and interest-taking," and "interest-bearing wealth increases in a ratio which is ever growing more and more rapid," leaving few assets unattached by debt. The exponential growth of debt makes business conditions more risky, because "there are not available assets to meet [creditor] demands and at the same time keep business moving."[40] Bankers call in their loans, causing a crash followed by "a trade depression every ten years or oftener and panics every twenty years."

The mathematics of compound interest explain "the extremely rapid accumulation of wealth in the hands of a comparatively few non-producers," as well as "the abject poverty of a large percentage of the producing masses."[41]

---

[39] J. W. Bennett, *A Breed of Barren Metal* (Chicago 1895), p. 87.
[40] *Ibid.*, pp. 49 and 93.
[41] *Ibid.*, p. 80.

Non-producers receive "much the largest salaries," despite the fact that their "income is often in inverse ratio to the service which [they do for their] fellow men."[42] As a result, Bennett concluded: "The financial group becomes rich more rapidly than the nation at large; and national increase in wealth may not mean prosperity of the producing masses."[43] All this sounds remarkably modern. The same basic criticisms were made after the 2008 crash, as if the discovery of predatory finance was something new.

Bennett's contemporary John Brown (not the abolitionist) argued that compound interest "is the subtle principle which makes wealth parasitic in the body of industry – the potent influence which takes from the weak and gives to the strong; which makes the rich richer and the poor poorer; which builds palaces for the idle and hovels for the diligent."[44] Only the wealthy are able to save up significant amounts and let sums simply accumulate and accrue interest over time. Small savers must live off their savings, drawing them down long before the mathematics of compound interest become truly significant.

What is remarkable is that this principle of compound interest has come to be viewed as a way to make populations richer rather than poorer. It is as if workers can ride the exponential growth of financial debt claims, by saving in mutual funds or investing in pension funds to financialize the economy. This rosy scenario assumes that the increase in debt does not dry up the growth in markets, investment and employment in much the way that Ricardo imagined landlords and their rent would stifle industrial capitalism.

---

[42] *Ibid.*, p. 111.
[43] *Ibid.*, p. 102.
[44] John Brown, *Parasitic Wealth* (Chicago 1898), pp. 81f.

5

How the One Percent Holds the 99 Percent in Exponentially Deepening Debt

[W]hat Smith and Marx shared, critically, was the belief that it was entirely possible for an activity to be revenue- and profit-generative without actually contributing to the creation of value. There was no paradox. (Or rather, for Marx at any rate, the paradox was not that banks made profits without producing value, but that industrial capitalists allowed them to do so.)[45]

J. P. Morgan and John D. Rockefeller are said to have called the principle of compound interest the Eighth Wonder of the World. For them it meant concentrating financial fortunes in the hands of an emerging oligarchy indebting the economy to itself at an exponential rate. This has been the key factor in polarizing the distribution of wealth and political power in societies that do not take steps to cope with this dynamic.

The problem lies in the way that savings and credit are lent out to become other peoples' debts without actually helping them earn the money to pay them off. To the financial sector this poses a banking problem: how to prevent losses to creditors when loan defaults occur. Such defaults prevent banks from paying their depositors and bondholders until they can foreclose on the collateral pledged by debtors and sell it off. But for the economy at large, the problem is bank credit and other loans loading the economy down with more and more debt, "crowding out" spending on current output. Something has to give– meaning that either creditors or debtors must lose.

Politicians thus face a choice of whether to save banks and bondholders or the economy. Do they simply reward their major campaign contributors by giving banks enough central bank or taxpayer money to compensate losses on bad loans? Or do they restructure debts downward, imposing losses on large

45 Brett Christophers, "Making finance productive," *Economy and Society*, 40 (2011), pp. 112–140.

bank depositors, bondholders and other creditors by writing down bad debts so as to keep debt-strapped families solvent and in possession of their homes?

It is politically convenient in today's world to solve the banking dimension of this problem in ways that please the financial sector. After the 1907 crash hit the United States harder than most economies, the Federal Reserve was founded in 1913 to provide public back-up credit in times of crisis. The assumption was that debt problems were merely about short-term liquidity for basically solvent loans whose carrying charges were temporarily interrupted by crop failures or a major industrial bankruptcy.

The exponential growth of debt was not anticipated to reach a magnitude that would bring economic growth to a halt. That worry has faded almost entirely from mainstream discussion for the past century.

The 1929–31 financial crash, of course, led the Yale economist and progressive Irving Fisher to analyze debt deflation (reviewed below in Chapter 11) and Keynes to urge government spending to ensure enough market demand to maintain full employment. In 1933 the New Deal created federal deposit insurance up to specific limits (rising to $100,000 before the 2008 crash, and $250,000 right after it, in order to stop bank runs). Banks paid a levy to the Federal Deposit Insurance Corporation (FDIC) to build up a fund to reimburse depositors of institutions that failed. The low fees reflected an assumption that such failures would be rare. There was no thought that the biggest banks would act in a reckless and unregulated manner.

The Glass Steagall Act, also passed in 1933, separated normal banking from the risky speculation until 1999, when its provisions were gutted under Bill Clinton. Banks were regulated to make loans to borrowers who could provide sound collateral and earn enough to carry their debts.

On paper, it seemed that the business cycle's ebb and flow would not derail the long-term rise in income and asset values. Adopting Wesley Clair Mitchell's theory of "automatic stabilizers" popularized in his 1913 *Business Cycles*, the National Bureau of Economic Research assumed that crises would automatically bring revival. The economy was idealized as rising and falling fairly smoothly around a steady upward trend.

The mathematics of compound interest should have alerted regulators to the need "to take away the punch bowl just as the party gets going," as McChesney Martin, long-term Federal Reserve Chairman (1951–70) famously quipped. But the combination of New Deal reforms and soporific economic theory (assuming that economies could carry a rising debt burden *ad infinitum*) led regulators to lower their guard against the strains created by banks and bondholders lending on increasingly risky terms at rising debt/income and debt/asset ratios.

Alan Greenspan promised the public before the 2008 crash that a real estate implosion was impossible because such a decline would be only local in scope, not economy-wide. But by this time the pro-Wall Street drive by the Clinton Administration's orchestrated by Treasury Secretary Robert Rubin (later to chair Citibank, which became the most reckless player) had opened the floodgates that led rapidly to widespread insolvency. Nearly ten million homes fell into foreclosure between 2008 and mid-2014 according to Moody's Analytics. Cities and states found themselves so indebted that they had to start selling off their infrastructure to Wall Street managers who turned roads, sewer systems and other basic needs into predatory monopolies.

Across the board, the U.S. and European economies were "loaned up" and could not sustain living standards and public spending programs simply by borrowing more. Repayment time had arrived. That meant foreclosures and distress sales. That is the grim condition that the financial sector historically has sought as its backup plan. For creditors, debt produces not only interest, but property ownership as well, by indebting their prey.

The debt buildup from one financial cycle to the next

The business cycle is basically essentially a financial cycle. Its "recovery" phase is relatively debt-free, to the extent that a preceding crash has wiped out debt (and thus the savings of creditors), while prices for real estate and stocks have fallen back to affordable levels. This was the stage in which the U.S. economy found itself when World War II ended in 1945. The economy was able to grow rapidly without much private sector debt.

New homebuyers were able to sign up for 30-year self-amortizing mortgages. Bankers looked at their income to calculate whether they could afford to pay each month to pay up to 25 percent of their wages each month to pay off ("amortize") the mortgage over the course of their working life. At the end of thirty years, they would be able to retire debt-free and endow their children with a middle-class life.

Wages and profits rose steadily from 1945 to the late 1970s. So did savings. Banks lent them to fund new construction, as well as to bid up prices for housing already in place. This recycling of savings plus new bank credit into mortgage lending obliged homebuyers to borrow more as interest rates rose for 35 years, from 1945 to 1980. The result was an exponential growth of debt to buy housing, automobiles and consumer durables.

Financial wealth – what the economy owes bankers and bondholders – increases the volume of debt claims from one business cycle to the next. Each business recovery since World War II has started with a higher debt level.

Adding one cyclical buildup on top of another is the financial equivalent of driving a car with the brake pedal pressed tighter and tighter to the floor, slowing the speed – or like carrying an increasingly heavy burden uphill. The economic brake or burden is debt service. The more this debt service rises, the slower markets can grow, as debtors are left with less to spend on goods and services because they must pay a rising portion of income to banks and bondholders.

Markets shrink and a rising proportion of debtors default. New lending stops, and debtors must start repaying their creditors. This is the debt deflation stage in which business upswings culminate.

By the mid-1970s entire countries were reaching this point. New York City nearly went bankrupt. Other cities could not raise their traditional source of tax revenue, the property tax, without forcing mortgage defaults. Even the U.S. Government had to raise interest rates to stabilize the dollar's exchange rate and slow the economy in the face of foreign military spending and the inflationary pressures it was fueling at home.

Deterioration of loan quality to interest-only loans and "Ponzi" lending

Hyman Minsky has described the first stage of the financial cycle as the period in which borrowers are able to pay interest and amortization. In the second stage, loans no longer are self-amortizing. Borrowers can only afford to pay the interest charges. In the third stage they cannot even afford to pay the interest.[46] They have to borrow to avoid default. In effect, the interest is simply added onto the debt, compounding it.

Default would have obliged banks to write down the value of their loans. To avoid "negative equity" in their loan portfolio, bankers made new loans to enable Third World governments to pay the interest due each year on their foreign debts. That is how Brazil, Mexico, Argentina and other Latin American countries got by until 1982, when Mexico dropped the "debt bomb" by announcing that it could not pay its creditors.

Leading up to the 2008 financial crash, the U.S. real estate market had entered the critical stage where banks were lending homeowners the interest as "equity loans." Housing prices had risen so high that many families could

---

[46]   Hyman P. Minsky, "The Financial Instability Hypothesis," Levy Institute Paper No. 74, May 1992. For a summary of Minsky's theories see Dimitri B. Papadimtriou and L. Randall Wray, "The Economic Contributions of Human Minsky," Levy Institute Working Paper No. 217, December 1997.

not afford to pay down their debts. To make the loans work "on paper," real estate brokers and their banks crafted mortgages that automatically added the interest onto the debt, typically up to 120 percent of the property's purchase price. Bank credit thus played the role of enticing new subscribers into Ponzi schemes and chain letters.

Over-lending kept the economy from defaulting until 2008. Many credit-card holders were unable to pay down their balances, and could only pay the interest due each month by signing up for new credit cards to stay current on the old ones.

That is why Minsky called this desperate third stage of the financial cycle the Ponzi stage. Its dynamic is that of a chain letter. Early players (or home-buyers) are promised high returns. These are paid out of the proceeds from more and more new players joining the scheme, *e.g.*, by new homebuyers taking out ever-rising mortgage loans to buy out existing owners. The newcomers hope that returns on their investment (like a chain letter) can keep on expanding *ad infinitum*. But the scheme inevitably collapses when the inflow of new players dries up or banks stop feeding the scheme.

Alan Greenspan was assisted by the mass media in popularizing an illusion that the financial sector had found a self-sustaining dynamic for the exponential growth of debt by inflating asset prices exponentially. The economy sought to inflate its way out of debt through asset price inflation sponsored by the Federal Reserve. Higher prices for the houses being borrowed against seemed to justify the process, without much thought about how debts could be paid by actually earning wages or profits.

Banks created new credit on their keyboards, while the Federal Reserve facilitated the scheme by sustaining the exponential rise in bank loans (without anyone having to save and deposit the money).[47] However, this credit was not invested to increase the economy's productive powers. Instead, it saved borrowers from default by inflating property prices – while loading down property, companies and personal incomes with debt.

The fact that price gains for real estate are taxed at a much lower rate than wages or profits attracted speculators to ride the inflationary wave as lending standards were loosened, fostering lower down payments, zero-interest loans and outright fictitious "no documentation" income statements, forthrightly called "liars' loans" by Wall Street.

---

[47] Modern Monetary Theory focuses on how banks create this "endogenous" credit. See L. Randall Wray, *Understanding Modern Money* and *Modern Money Theory*, as well as Steve Keen, *Debunking Economics* and his *Debtwatch* blog, and the UMKC economics department website *New Economics Perspectives*.

But property prices were bound to crash without roots in the "real" economy. Rental incomes failed to support the debt service that was owed, inaugurating a "fourth" phase of the financial cycle: defaults and foreclosures transferring property to creditors. On the global plane, this kind of asset transfer occurred after Mexico announced its insolvency in 1982. Sovereign governments were bailed out on the condition that they submit to U.S. and IMF pressure to sell off public assets to private investors.

Every major debt upswing leads to such transfers. These are the logical consequence of the dynamics of compound interest.

Table B.100 from the Federal Reserve's flow-of-funds statistics shows the consequences of U.S. debt pyramiding. By 2005, for the first time in recent history, Americans in the aggregate held less than half the market value of their homes free of debt. Bank mortgage claims accounted for more than half. By 2008 the ratio of home equity ownership to mortgage debt had fallen to just 40 percent.

Bank mortgages now exceed homeowners' equity, which fell below 40% in 2011.

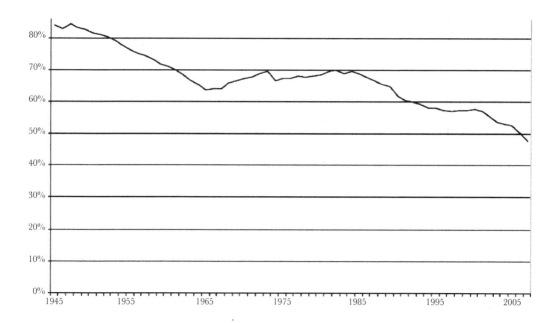

Figure 3: Home owners' equity as percentage of household real estate

What happens when the exponential buildup of debt ends

During the financial upswing the financial sector receives interest and capital gains. In the fallback period after the crisis, the economy's private- and public-sector assets are expropriated to pay the debts that remain in place.

A "Minsky moment" erupts at the point when creditors realize that the game is over, run for the exits and call in their loans. The 2008 crash stopped bank lending for mortgages, credit cards and nearly all other lending except for U.S. government-guaranteed student loans. Instead of receiving an infusion of new bank credit to break even, households had to start paying it back. Repayment time arrived.

This "saving by paying down debt" interrupts the exponential growth of liquid savings and debt. But that does not slow the financial sector's dominance over the rest of the economy. Such "intermediate periods" are free-for-alls in which the more powerful *rentiers* increase their power by acquiring property from distressed parties. Financial emergencies usually suspend government protection of the economy at large, as unpopular economic measures are said to be necessary to "adjust" and restore "normalcy" – finance-talk for a rollback of public regulatory constraints on finance. "Technocrats" are placed in control to oversee the redistribution of wealth and income from "weak" hands to strong under austerity conditions.

This aftermath of the bubble's bursting is not really "normalcy" at all, of course. The financial sector simply changes gears. As debt deflation squeezed homeowners after 2008, for instance, banks innovated a new financial "product" called reverse mortgages. Retirees and other homeowners signed agreements with banks or insurance companies to receive a given annuity payment each month, based on the owner's expected lifetime. The annuity was charged against the homeowner's equity as pre-payment for taking possession upon the owner-debtor's death.

The banks or insurance companies ended up with the property, not the children of the debtors. (In some cases the husband died and the wife received an eviction notice, on the ground that her name was not on the ownership deed.) The moral is that what is inherited in today's financialized economy is creditor power, not widespread home ownership. So we are brought back to the fact that compound interest does not merely increase the flow of income to the *rentier* One Percent, but also transfers property into its hands.

Financialization at the economy's expense

The buildup of debt should have alerted business cycle analysts to the fact that as debt grows steadily from one cycle to the next, economies veer out of balance as revenue is diverted to pay bankers and bondholders instead of to expand business.

Yet this has not discouraged economists from projecting national income or GDP as growing at a steady trend rate year after year, assuming that productivity growth will continue to raise wage levels and enable thrifty individuals to save enough to retire in affluence. The "magic" of compound interest is held to raise the value of savings as if there are no consequences to increasing debt on the other side of the balance sheet. The internal contradiction in this approach is the "fallacy of composition." Pension funds have long assumed that they and other savers can make money financially without inflicting adverse effects on the economy at large.

Until recently most U.S. pension funds assumed that they could make returns of 8.5 percent annually, doubling in less than seven years, quadrupling in 13 years and so forth. This happy assumption suggested that state and local pension funds, corporate pension funds and labor union pension funds would be able to pay retirees with only minimal new contributions. The projected rates of return were much faster than the economy's growth. Pension funds imagined that they could grow simply by increasing the value of financial claims *on* a shrinking economy by extracting a rise in interest, dividends and amortization.

This theory simply wrapped Richard Price's "sinking fund" idea in a new guise. It is as if savings can keep accruing interest and make capital gains without shrinking the economy. But a rate of financial growth that exceeds the economy's ability to produce a surplus must be predatory over time. Financialization intrudes into the economy, imposing austerity and ultimately forcing defaults by siphoning off the circular flow between producers and consumers.

To the extent that new bank loans find their counterpart in debtors' ability to pay in today's bubble economies, they do so by inflating asset prices. Gains are not made by producing or earning more, but by borrowing to buy assets whose prices are rising, being inflated by credit created on looser, less responsible terms.

Today's self-multiplying debt overhead absorbs profits, rents, personal income and tax revenue in a process whose mathematics is much like that of environmental pollution. Evolutionary biologist Edward O. Wilson demonstrates how impossible it is for growth to proceed at exponential rates without encountering a limit. He cites "the arithmetical riddle of the lily pond. A lily pod is placed in a pond. Each day thereafter the pod and then all its descendants double. On the thirtieth day the pond is covered completely by lily pods, which can grow no more." He then asks: "On which day was the pond half full and half empty? The twenty-ninth day," that is, one day before the half the pond's lilies double for the final time, stifling its surface.[48] The end to exponential growth thus comes quickly.

The problem is that the pond's overgrowth of vegetation is not productive growth. It is weeds, choking off the oxygen needed by the fish and other life below the surface. This situation is analogous to debt siphoning off the economic surplus and even the basic needs of an economy for investment to replenish its capital and to maintain basic needs. Financial *rentiers* float on top of the economy, stifling life below.

Financial managers do not encourage understanding of such mathematics for the public at large (or even in academia), but they are observant enough to recognize that the global economy is now hurtling toward this pre-crash "last day." That is why they are taking their money and running to the safety of government bonds. Even though U.S. Treasury bills yield less than 1 percent, the government can always simply print the money. The tragedy of our times is that it is willing to do so only to preserve the value of assets, not to revive employment or restore real economic growth.

Today's creditors are using their gains not to lend to increase production, but to "cash out" their financial gains and buy more assets. The most lucrative assets are land and rent-yielding opportunities in natural resources and infrastructure monopolies to extract land rent, natural resource rent and monopoly rent.

The inability of economies to sustain compound interest and a rising *rentier* overhead for any prolonged time is at the root of today's political fight. At issue is whose interests must be sacrificed in the face of the incompatibility between financial and "real" economic expansion paths. Finance has converted its economic power into the political power to reverse the classical drive to tax away property rent, monopoly rent and financial income, and to keep potential rent-extracting infrastructure in the public domain. Today's financial dynamics are leading back to shift the tax burden onto labor and industry while banks and bondholders have obtained bailouts instead of debts being written down.

This is the political dimension of the mathematics of compound interest. It is the pro-*rentier* policy that the French Physiocrats and British liberals sought to reverse by clearing away the legacy of European feudalism.

---

[48] Edward O. Wilson, *Consilience* (1998), p. 313.

6

Rentiers Sponsor Rent-Free National Income Statistics

The people of Goldman Sachs are among the most productive in the world.
Lloyd Blankfein, Goldman Sachs chief executive, November 10, 2009.[49]

The question is, productive of *what*? To Goldman Sachs, it is productive of profits and speculative gains. Neoliberals such as Gary Becker (discussed below) define the firm's high salaries and bonuses as returns to "human capital." The National Income and Product Accounts (NIPA) depict all this charge as adding an equal value to the nation's "product" of financial services. It all seems to be what Mr. Blankfein notoriously euphemized on another occasion as "doing God's work" of raising productivity.

At issue is whether today's widening inequality between the wealthy and wage earners is justified or not. This question has been catapulted to the forefront of the news by the statistical research of Thomas Piketty and Emmanuel Saez showing the increasing concentration of income in the hands of the richest One Percent.[50] The main remedies they propose are a wealth tax (especially on inherited estates) and a return to steeper progressive income taxation.

The idea of taxing higher income brackets more without regard for whether their gains are earned "productively" or in extractive *rentier* ways represents a victory in dissuading critics from focusing on the policy aim of Adam Smith and other classical economists: preventing "unearned" income

---

[49] Quoted by Greg Farrell, "Goldman chief defends employees' pay," *Financial Times*, November 11, 2009.

[50] Thomas Piketty, *Capital in the Twenty-First Century* (Harvard, 2013), and Emmanuel Saez, "Income Inequality: Evidence and Policy Implications," UC Berkeley, January 2013. For related statistics on wealth and income distribution, see also "WEALTH: Having it All and Wanting More," Oxfam Issue Briefing, January 2015: "In 2014, the richest 1% of people in the world owned 48% of global wealth, leaving just 52% to be shared between the other 99% of adults on the planet," citing Credit Suisse (2013 and 2014 respectively) "Global Wealth Databook, https://www.credit-suisse.com/uk/en/news-and-expertise/research/credit-suisse-researchinstitute/publications.html..

from being obtained in the first place. As Chapter 3 has described, they recognized not only that *rentier* revenue (and capital gains) is earned in a predatory and unproductive way, but also that land rent, monopoly rent and financial charges are mainly responsible for the rising wealth of the One Percent as compared to that held by the rest of society.

The turn of the 20th century saw wages rising, but most of the increasewas paid to landlords via higher housing costs, and to monopolists, bankers and financiers. These *rentier* charges prevented wage earners from benefiting from wage gains that flowed through their hands to the Finance, Insurance and Real Estate (FIRE) sector. What ultimately is important is how much remains for discretionary spending *after* meeting payments for real estate, debt service and other basic needs. What is most unequal is the share in the economic surplus *net* of break-even subsistence costs. To the extent that labor or businesses only break even while income is concentrated in the hands of the FIRE sector and monopolies, the degree of inequality is much more pronounced than gross statistics indicate.

Instead of treating *rentier* overhead as a charge against production and consumption, today's NIPA depict rent-extracting activities as producing a "product." FIRE sector revenue appears as a cost of producing an equivalent amount to Gross Domestic Product (GDP), not as unearned income or "empty" pricing. And neither the NIPA nor the Federal Reserve's flow-of-funds statistics recognize how the economy's wealthiest financial layer makes its fortunes by land-price gains and other "capital" gains. A cloak of invisibility thus is drawn around how FIRE sector fortunes are amassed.

J. B. Clark denies that *rentier* income is unearned

The foundation myth of pro-*rentier* economics is that everyone receives income in proportion to the contribution they make to production. This denies that economic rent is unearned. Hence, there is no exploitation or unearned income, and no need for the reforms advocated by classical political economy.

In America the rejection of classical analysis was spearheaded by John Bates Clark (1847–1938). Like nearly all American economists of the late 19th century, he had studied in Germany where he absorbed the Historical School's emphasis on public policy to shape markets. But upon returning to the United States, Clark became a critic of labor and socialism, finding his ultimate academic home at Columbia University (1895–1923), a natural center for the reaction against classical rent theory. The journalist Henry George had attracted a large following among New York City's large Irish population (driven out of its home country by the depredations of British landlords), and almost was elected mayor in 1885 by proposing a land tax and public owner-ship of railroads and similar natural monopolies. Other immigrant commu-nities brought Marxism and an advocacy for labor unionization with them to the States. The fight against absentee landlords merged naturally with denun-ciations of Wall Street.

By the time Clark wrote *The Distribution of Wealth* in 1899 he was a full-fledged defender of *rentier* interests. His core message was that everyone earns what they deserve, in proportion to their contribution to production. "It is the purpose of this work," he wrote in its introduction, "to show that the distribu-tion of the income of society is controlled by a natural law, and this law, if it worked without friction, would give to every agent of production the amount of wealth which that agent creates."[51] The revenue of each recipient (euphe-mized as a "factor of production") is assumed to be equal to the value they add to the product being sold, whether it takes the form of wages, profits, rents or interest. Robber barons, landlords and bankers are depicted as part of the production process, and prices are assumed to settle at their cost of production, defined to include whatever *rentiers* manage to obtain.

This closed logical circle excludes any criticism that markets may work in an unfair way. To Clark and other "free market" economists, "the market" is simply the existing status quo, taking for granted the existing distribution of wealth and property rights. Any given distribution of property rights, no matter how inequitable, is thought of as part of economic nature. The logic is that all income is earned by the recipient's contribution to production. It follows that there is no free lunch – and also that There Is No Alternative to the extent that the existing distribution of wealth is a result of natural law.

Treating any revenue-yielding asset as capital conflates financial and *rentier* claims *on* production with the physical means *of* production. The vantage point is that of financiers or investors buying land and real estate, oil and mineral deposits, patents, monopoly privileges and related rent extraction opportunities without concern for whether economists classify their returns as profit or as rent. Today's tax laws make no such distinction.

Clark's most trenchant critic was Simon Patten, the first economics pro-fessor at America's first business school, the Wharton School at the University of Pennsylvania.[52] "The defect of the reasoning of Professor Clark," he

---

[51] John Bates Clark, *The Distribution of Wealth* (New York, 1899, Macmillan), p. v.
[52] I give a biography in *America's Protectionist Takeoff, 1815-1914: The Neglected American School of Political Economy* (ISLET, 2010), and "Simon Patten on Public Infrastructure and Economic Rent Capture," *American Journal of Economics and Sociology* **70** (October 2011), pp. 873–903.

observed, was his failure to distinguish manmade capital from property rights that did not involve any necessary or intrinsic cost of production.[53] The result, Patten said, was to conflate profits earned on tangible industrial capital investment with land and monopoly rent. To real estate investors or farmers buying properties on mortgage, the financial and monopoly charges built into their acquisition price appear as an investment cost. "The farmer thinks that land values depend on real costs" because he had to pay good money for his property, explained Patten, "and the city land speculator has the same opinion as to town lots."

This individualistic view is antithetical to the socialist and Progressive Era reforms being introduced in the late 19th century. That is what makes classical concerns with the economics of national development different from the financialized investor's-eye view of the world. At issue was what constitutes the cost of production in terms of real value, as distinct from extractive *rentier* charges. Freeing economies from such charges seemed to be the destiny of industrial capitalism.

"Institutionalist" and sociological reformers retained rent theory

Patten pointed out that land sites, like mineral rights provided by nature and financial privileges provided by legal fiat, do not require labor to create. But instead of describing their economic rent as an element of price without real cost or labor effort, Clark viewed whatever amount investors spent on acquiring such assets as their capital outlay and hence as a market cost of doing business. "According to the economic data he presents," Patten wrote, "rent in the economic sense, if not wholly disregarded, at least receives no emphasis. Land seems to be a form of capital, its value like other property being due to the labor put upon it."[54] But its price simply capitalizes property rights and financial charges that are not intrinsic.

"Professor Clark has a skillful way of hiding land values by subserving them under the general concept of capital," Patten observed elsewhere, but "if the doctrine of physical valuation is once introduced the public will soon be educated to the evils of watered land values"[55] and railroad rates. By "doct-

53   Patten, "Another View of the Ethics of Land Tenure," *International Journal of Ethics*. **1** (1890), p. 363. John Henry analyses Clark's development of marginal productivity theory in "God and the Marginal Product: Religion and the Development of J. B. Clark's Theory of Distribution," *Research in the History of Economic Thought and Methodology*, **13** (1995), pp. 75-101.
54   *Ibid.*, p. 356.
55   "The Political Significance of Recent Economic Theories," reprinted in Patten, *Essays in Economic Theory* ed. Rexford Guy Tugwell (New York: 1924) ,p. 254.

rine of physical valuation" he meant the classical analysis of real costs of production, in contrast to what his contemporaries called "fictitious" costs such
as land rent, watered stocks and other political or institutional charges unnecessary for production to take place.

"Rent is obtained by owners of land, not as a right based on economic
considerations," because land and monopoly rights are not real factors of production, but are claims for payments levied as access charges to land, credit or
basic needs, that is, ultimately "from the lack of supply of some needed
article," Patten explained. "Although the case of land is not the only example
where there is an unearned increment, because the price of food is always
more than its cost of production on the best land, yet it is the best example,
and hence is the one in common use as an illustration."[56]

For national economies, the problem is that and land rent and natural
resource rent are taken at the expense of wage earnings as well as from industrial profits. "It seems to me," Patten wrote,

> that the doctrine of Professor Clark, if carried out logically, would deny that the laborers
> have any right to share in the natural resources of the country. ... All the increase of
> wealth due to fertile fields or productive mines would be taken gradually from workmen
> with the growth of population, and given to more favored persons ... When it is said that
> the workingman under these conditions gets all he is worth to society, the term 'society,'
> if analyzed, means only the more favored classes ... They pay each laborer only the utility
> of the last laborer to them, and get the whole produce of the nation minus this amount.[57]

This is why Patten's contemporary reformers urged that land, natural resources
and monopolies be kept in the public domain, so as to minimize the rake-off
of national patrimony "given to more favored persons." The idea of unearned
income as a subtraction from the circular flow of income available for labor
and industry as wages and profits has vanished from today's post-classical
NIPA. Now, whatever is paid to *rentiers* is considered a bona fide cost of doing
business as if it embodies intrinsic value for a product.

Clark's claim that no income is unearned defines all economic activities as
being productive *in proportion to how much income they obtain*. No one way of
making money is deemed more or less productive than any other. Everyone
earns just what he or she deserves. Natural law will proportion income and
wealth to their recipients' contribution to production, if not "interfered" with.

Today's highest paying occupations are on Wall Street, running banks,
hedge funds or serving as corporate Chief Financial Officers. In Clark's view

---

[56] "Another View of the Ethics of Land Tenure," pp. 356f.
[57] *Ibid.*, pp. 364ff.

they earn everything they get, and everyone else only deserves whatever is left over. Gary Becker, the University of Chicago economist, followed this logic in justifying such incomes as being earned productively, warning that progressive taxation would discourage their enterprise and hence productivity: "A highly progressive income tax structure tends to discourage investment in human capital because it reduces take-home pay and the reward to highly skilled, highly paid occupations."[58]

Rentier income, inherited wealth, landlords and monopolies making money off the economy is thus interpreted as "earnings" on one's "human capital," the neoliberal catchall residual to absorb whatever cannot be explained in terms of actual labor effort or cost. It replaces what former economists called unearned income. It is as if the One Percent and the FIRE sector do not make money off the property they have (either inherited or built up far beyond what anyone's individual labor and enterprise could explain), but out of their own human talents. Finance capital, *rentier* capital, land and monopoly rights are all conflated with "capital."

To depict an economy bifurcated between earned and unearned income, it is necessary to distinguish interest and economic rent from wages and profit, to trace the flow of payments from production and consumption to the FIRE sector and other *rentier* sectors. This discussion recently has been revived as it applies to banking.

Siphoning off the circular flow of production and consumer spending

All national income accounts since the *Tableau Économique* are based on the idea of circular flow: recognition that one party's spending is another person's revenue. Since Keynes, discussion of the circular flow of spending and consumption has been framed in terms of "Say's Law," named for the facile French economist, Jean-Baptiste Say. His "law of markets" is standard textbook teaching, usually paraphrased as "production creates its own demand." Workers spend their paychecks on the goods they produce, while industrial employers invest their profits on capital goods to expand their factories and employ more labor to buy yet more products.

---

[58] Gary Becker, Edward P. Lazaer and Kevin McMurphy, "The Double Benefit of Tax Cuts," *Wall Street Journal*, October 7, 2003, cited in "The Wisdom of Gary Becker," *ibid.*, May 5, 2014 as an obituary. Like Clark, Becker also taught at Columbia University, and in 1967 he won the American Economics Association's annual John Bates Clark medal, awarded to the most promising economist under the age of forty. In a September 2, 2011 *Wall Street Journal* editorial he blamed Fannie Mae and government regulation for the 2008 financial crash, not the fraudulent mortgages and financial junk that rewarded its creators so highly.

But buying a property, stock or bond does not involve hiring labor or financing production. Neither Say's Law nor national income accounts distinguish between spending on current production and asset markets, or between productive and unproductive labor, earned and unearned income. Today's NIPA thus fail to address how financial and allied *rentier* overhead imposes austerity. Say's Law simply states the precondition for economies to operate without business cycles or debt deflation draining income to pay a *rentier* class. The reality is that debt service and rent payments rise, extracting income from markets and preventing them from buying what they produce.

Most economics professors discuss Say's Law simply to explain why it doesn't work to maintain full employment. Keynes worried that as economies grew richer, people would save a larger proportion of their income instead of spending on consumption. This drain from the circular flow would lead to depression, unless governments compensated by infusing money into the economy, hiring labor for public works.

Keynes depicted saving simply as hoarding – withdrawing revenue from the spending stream of production and consumption. But what actually happens is that the savers lend to debtors while banks create new "endogenous" credit at interest. When repayment time arrives – when consumers have to start paying down their credit card balances and homeowners pay down mortgages without taking out new loans – "saving" takes the form of reducing debt. A negation of a negation is counted as a positive – and in this case, negating debt is defined as "saving." This sets in motion an exponentially rising rake-off of financial returns from the "real" economy.

Value-free monetary theory of prices

Mainstream monetary theory likewise has narrowed to exclude transactions in assets and payments to the FIRE sector. All money (M), credit and income as assumed to be spent only on goods and service transactions (T), not on buying more real estate, stocks and bonds or being lent out to indebt the economy. Economics students are taught the MV=PT tautology.

(Money × Velocity = Prices × Transactions)

But by far most money and credit (M) is spent on real estate, stocks, bonds and bank loans. Every day an entire year's worth of GDP passes through the New York Clearing House and the Chicago Mercantile Exchange for such asset transactions. Assuming that changes in the money supply only affect commodity prices and wages ignores this fact that T only refers to transactions in current output, not assets. When this fails to work in practice, any errors and omissions are swept up into V (Velocity of turnover, whatever that means), a residual determined by whatever M, P and T leave out of account.

There always is an economic gain for some party in sponsoring bad theory. Many erroneous economies can be traced to policies endorsed by the bad theorists. Leaving *rentier* income and spending out of the equation enables anti-labor economists to demand monetary austerity and a balanced government budget as their knee-jerk policy response. The narrow-minded MV=PT tautology enables economists to blame wages for inflationary pressures, not the cost of living being pushed up by debt-leveraged housing prices and other FIRE sector expenses, or by the rising corporate debt service built into the pricing of goods and services.

In reality, asset prices rise or fall at a different rate from commodity prices and wages. This is a result precisely of the fact that the Federal Reserve and other central banks "inject" money into the economy via Wall Street, the City of London or other financial centers, by buying and selling Treasury securities or providing commercial bank reserves, *e.g.,* in the post-2008 waves of Quantitative Easing.

Monetary injections affect asset prices by influencing the interest rate. Central bank purchases of government bonds bid up their price. The higher price lowers the interest yield (i) on government securities (or whatever the central bank may buy), and this affects asset prices in general. The interest rate is used to "discount" the income flow of a bond, rental property or dividend-paying stock. At a 5% rate of interest, the income-yielding asset would be 20 times earnings; at 4%, 25 times earnings, and so forth.

National income accounts exclude rent extraction and financial drains

The NIPA were created in the 1930s and World War II to help keep inflationary pressures in check by comparing wages and profits to the flow of output, not to focus on the *rentier* dynamics weighing down modern economies. Failure to isolate the FIRE sector and *rentier* overhead has led national income accounting into a quandary. Instead of estimating economic rent, the NIPA counts it as "earnings" for making a contribution to Gross Domestic Product (GDP). *Rentiers* appear to earn their income by producing a "product" equal in value to the rents they collect. If landlords charge more rent, real estate product rises correspondingly. If Goldman Sachs and other bankers charge their clients more for financial services, or make money by winning arbitrage bond trades against them or other counterparties so as to pay themselves more, their financial "product" is counted as rising accordingly. The assumption is that people only receive income for what they produce.

This assumption rests on a tunnel vision that reflects the ideological victory that landlords and vested financial interests achieved in the late 19th century against the classical drive to tax economic rent. The effect of excluding land rent, natural resource rent and monopoly rent – the drain of income from producers and consumers to pay landlords, privatizers, monopolists and their bankers – is to deter measurement of what I call rent deflation. That is the analogue to debt deflation – the diversion of income to pay debt service.

There also is no measure of criminal income, smuggling or fictitious accounting for tax avoidance. No category of spending is counted as overhead, not even pollution cleanup costs or crime prevention, not to mention financial bailouts. Economists dismiss these as "externalities," meaning external to the statistics deemed relevant. Yet despite the rising proportion of spending that takes the form of rent extraction, environmental pollution cleanup costs, debt pollution and its bailout costs, GDP is treated as a an accurate measure of economic welfare. The result confuses healthy growth with that of a tumor on the body politic. Taken together, these omissions deter the kind of systemic analysis that would have alerted policy makers and voters to the distortions leading up to the 2008 crash.

Treating economic rent as "earnings"

The word "rent" appears only once in the NIPA (Table 2.1, line 12), and it reflects neither what most people imagine rent to be nor the classical concept of economic rent. In fact, it is not even any transaction that actually is paid or received. It is "imputed homeowners' rent" – the amount that homeowners would have to pay if they rented their own homes. No cash changes hands in this valuation. The NIPA include this imputed non-payment because enjoying one's home is part of the economy's product – less than 2 percent of GDP and falling.

This is not classical economic rent. Rental income obtained by commercial investors and natural resource owners is called "earnings" on a par with profits and wages. This diverts attention away from how fortunes are made without labor or out-of-pocket production costs. It also requires a convoluted reorganization of statistics to discover how large the actual cash-flow return to absentee real estate ownership is, given the heavy component of interest and the "just pretend" economic category of over-depreciation.

Fred Harrison, the British economics journalist, summarizes how economists have confused the burgeoning land rent with the much more modest imputed homeowners' self-rental estimate. The successful strategy at euphemistic confusion has made its way into today's leading textbooks as if it represents land rent for the economy as a whole. The most famous school text of its day, *Economics* by Paul Samuelson and William D. Nordhaus, reports that "Rent income of persons" is less than 2 percent of Gross National Product – and falling steadily over the past half-century.[59] A more recent textbook by Paul Krugman and Robin Wells states that "rent" constitutes only 1 percent of U.S. national income.[60]

This obviously would be too trivial for a century of classical political economy to have bothered to analyze, not to mention urging that it serve as the tax base. Land rent appears to have disappeared into the Orwellian memory hole. It is as if commercial real estate investors and owners receive no land rent at all.

This terminological sleight of hand helped divert attention from how bank over-lending led to the real estate bubble that burst in 2008. It also trivializes international trade theory, by failing to recognize how capitalizing land rent into mortgage loans raises the cost of housing and other debt-leveraged prices.

What the NIPA do make clear is that most real estate rental income is paid to the banks as interest (Chart 6.1).[61] NIPA accountants find real estate and banking are so intertwined in the symbiotic FIRE sector that for many years

---

[59]   Paul Samuelson and William D. Nordhaus, *Economics*, 12th ed. (New York, (1985), p. 115, cited in Fred Harrison, "Ten Theses, #4: Moral Taxes or a Life of Liberty," http://www.sharetherents.org/thesis/mortal-taxes-life-liberty/.

[60]   Paul Krugman and Robin Wells, *Economics* (New York, 2006), p. 283, cited in Harrison, *ibid*. Harrison points out the political effect of such confusion: In 1963, Richard Lipsey's textbook assured students that "an effective tax on economic rent would finance only a tiny portion of government expenditures." Besides, there was a grave problem with the proposal: "The policy implications of taxing rent depends on being able in practice to identify economic rent. At best, this is difficult; at worst, it is impossible." Richard G. Lipsey, *Positive Economics*, 5th ed. (London, 1979), pp. 370f.

[61]   I provide a technical discussion and chart the statistics in *The Bubble and Beyond*, chapter 8: "The Real Estate Bubble at the Core of Today's Debt-Leveraged Economy." The rental cash flow (ebitda: earnings before interest, taxes, depreciation and amortization) of landlords and other real estate investors (divided into corporate investors and partnerships, the latter being the form in which most real estate business is organized), occurs in the lines for real estate earnings (non-corporate and corporate, Tables 6.12 and 6.17), interest (Table 6.15) depreciation (Tables 6.13 and 6.22), taxes paid at the state and local level (Table 3.3), as well as individuals (Table 2.1). This cash flow includes revenue from real estate as a whole – buildings and capital improvements as well as land. To estimate how much of this is land rent and how much is actually profit on capital improvements, it is necessary to impute how much of the price of a property consists of land and how much of buildings, as well as the valuation resulting from lower interest rates increasing the amount of credit that can be borrowed against a given flow of income. Similar calculations can be made for oil and mining, as well as for industrial monopoly profits.

financial and real estate income was not separated in the statistics. The activities of mortgage brokers and real estate agents seem to belong to Finance, Insurance or Real Estate in common.

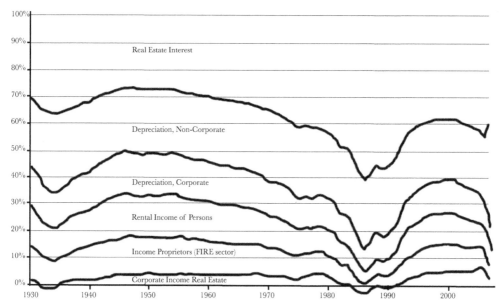

Figure 4: Composition of real estate cash flow

The NIPA also show how the tax fiction of over-depreciation (writing off a building more than once, over and over again) offsets otherwise taxable earnings for commercial real estate, enabling commercial real estate, oil and mining companies to operate decade after decade without a reportable taxable profit. An army of accountants has been backed by political lobbyists to write "loopholes" (a euphemism for distorting economic reality) into the tax code to make it appear that landlords and oil companies *lose* money, not make it! According to the NIPA, real estate earnings do not cover the rate at which landlords pay interest as a cost of production and buildings depreciate.

Depreciation and the rate of return

For industrial capital that wears out or obsolesces (becoming high-cost as a result of improving technology, *e.g.*, computers that quickly get out of date even though they remain in working order), depreciation is a return of capital, and hence not part of surplus value strictly speaking.

But this is not the case in the real estate, because buildings do not wear out – and rather than their technology becoming obsolete, older buildings tend to have much more desirable construction, or else have been renovated as a result of the ongoing maintenance repairs that typically absorb about 10 percent of rental income (or a property's equivalent rental value). So for real estate, depreciation is largely a fictitious category of income designed to make rental revenue tax-free. The same building can be depreciated all over again – at a rising price – each time the property is sold to a commercial investor. (Homeowners are not allowed this tax subsidy.) Thus, despite the pretense by accountants that real estate is losing its value, the land's site value (and the decline in interest rates) actually is increasing its value. Reality and seemingly empirical statistics tell opposite stories.

No wonder the wealthiest One Percent have widened their wealth gap over the rest of the economy, defending this just-pretend statistical picture as if it is empirical science and therefore objective simply because its deception has decimal points.

Classical economics is free of such pretenses and *rentier* tax favoritism. What actually happens is that landlords, oil and gas companies, mining companies, monopolies and banks charge rents for access to the land, natural resources and credit needed for production to take place. These payments drain the circular flow of spending between producers and consumers, shrinking markets

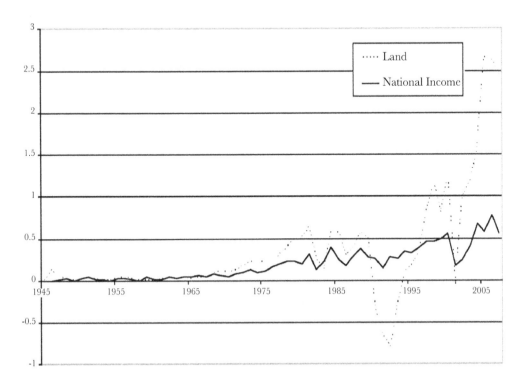

Figure 5: Annual Land-Value Gains Compared to Growth in National Income

and causing unemployment. *Rentiers* spend their income not only to hire labor and buy its products (as Malthus described, and as Keynes applauded) but also to buy financial assets and more property. Banks use their revenue to make more loans. This creates yet more debt while bidding up asset prices, obliging new homebuyers to borrow even more for ownership rights.

Figure 5 traces real estate price gains. These reflect rising site values for land, magnified by bank credit at rising debt-leveraging ratios, "capitalizing" rental value into mortgage loans at falling rates of interest. These price gains far overshadow actual rental income, and are taxed at much lower rates than wages and profits. Yet the Federal Reserve's flow of funds accounts have no statistics for price increases for real estate, stocks and bonds; or, for that matter, for speculative winnings by arbitrageurs and other gamblers. (Chapter 11 will discuss debt-financed asset-price inflation in detail.) Without a measure of such price gains, one cannot calculate "total returns," defined as current income plus asset-price gains. Each year's growth in Land Value far exceeds the growth in National Income.

In short, the NIPA are not really a model of how economies work and how fortunes are made in today's world. Instead, the NIPA provide a cloak of invisibility for rent-extracting activities. The vested interests have won the fight against creating more relevant statistical categories. Their hope evidently is that if exploitative activities are not seen or quantified, they are less likely to be taxed or regulated.

Does the financial sector produce a "product," or a subtrahend from GDP?

Today's major *rentier* sector is banking and high finance. Most bank loans are geared not to produce goods and services, but to transfer *ownership rights* for real estate, stocks (including those of entire companies) and bonds. This has led national income theorists to propose treating the revenue of such institutions as *transfer payments*, not payments for producing output or "product." Australian economist Bryan Haig has called this "the banking problem." "If financial services were treated like other industries," he writes, "the banking sector as a whole would be depicted as making a negligible, or perhaps even negative, contribution to national economic output as being, effectively, unproductive."[62]

---

[62] Bryan Haig, "The treatment of interest and financial intermediaries in the Economy and Society," *Review of Income and Wealth*, Vol. 32 (1986), p. 409, cited in Christophers, "Making Finance Productive."

Updating this discussion of how best to describe financial services in the national income accounts, Brett Christophers asks: "What 'service', if any, is actually being rendered by the banks here?" At issue are "situations where payments are made but production is not considered to have taken place." As Britain's 2006 National Accounts reports noted, such payments "do not represent 'any addition to current economic activity."[63]

The Clark-like neoclassical view assumes that if someone pays a fee, they must be getting a product in return. Treating bank payments as a subtrahend or simply as a cost of transferring wealth without affecting production is anomalous to today's mainstream. The concept of unproductive labor or unearned income that was at the core of classical economics has disappeared. As Christophers explains:

> … national accounts economists of the mid- to late-twentieth century could not see anything but paradox in the notion that such a prosperous industry as banking, with such self-evident utility, either detracted from the national output or added only marginal value to it; a negative or nil output was unacceptable because, from the neo-classical perspective, it literally made no sense.

Raising "the banking problem" thus poses a threat to post-classical economic doctrine. There is no category in the NIPA for income obtained *without* contributing an equivalent amount to "national product." Finance and rent seeking appear as *part of* the economic growth process, not parasitic and external to it.

This explains why the NIPA exclude "capital" gains from rising prices for land and other real estate, stocks and bonds. They have the same *effect* as income – raising the net worth of owners, and are mainly responsible for building up fortunes over the past half-century, especially since 1980. But they are incompatible with the facile "income = product" assumption used to rationalize and justify *rentier* income (so as to save it from being taxed as classical economists urged). Making asset-price inflation statistically invisible helps deter public pressure to tax real estate and financial gains at the same rate as normal income, as originally was the case in the U.S. tax code.

Today's economic accounts ignore the classical economic focus on *rentier* overhead. Keynesian macroeconomics traces the circular flow among sectors, without analyzing intrinsic value or the classical concern for "invested labour"

---

[63] Brett Christophers, "Making finance productive," *Economy and Society*, **40** (2011), http:// dx.doi.org/10.1080/03085147.2011.529337 (elaborated in *Banking across boundaries: Placing Finance in Capitalism* (Wiley-Blackwell, 2013), citing *United Kingdom National Accounts: The blue book 2006* (Basingstoke: Palgrave Macmillan), p. 21.

or *how* revenue is obtained. Instead, a seemingly empirical statistical picture pretends that the FIRE sector plays a productive role in helping economies grow and prosper.

Here's the problem: If all income is obtained as part of the production process and spent on buying goods and services, as Clark and his followers claimed, there is no diversion of spending away from economic growth. But what about income spent on assets, loans or debt payments?

At issue is what constitutes "economic growth" – in reality vs. under today's measurement concepts. A rising portion of economic activity does not have to do with production (investment and output) *or* consumption, but with buying and selling property already in place: primarily real estate (the largest asset), natural resources, stocks and bonds. A recent book, *G.D.P.: A Brief but Affectionate History*, notes how irrational this measure is for the financial sector. In view of "the negative output of an imaginary segment of the economy," the GDP's measure "greatly exaggerate[s] the importance of financial services to overall economic output. Perversely, in the final quarter of 2008, Britain's banking industry showed its fastest growth on record, almost matching manufacturing in size, just as the money markets all but froze."[64]

Treating the creation of largely fictitious, unpayably high financial claims on the economy as if this adds to output and wealth leaves out of account the massive public bailouts needed to sustain the banking sector. The "external economic" costs are a form of debt pollution. "When someone confidently quotes the contribution of financial services to national income," writes *Financial Times* columnist John Kay, "you can be sure they have no understanding of the esoteric concept of 'financial services indirectly measured' (don't ask). Only a few people in the depths of national statistics offices do. This problem casts doubt on the validity of reported growth rates both before and after the crisis."[65] In a similar vein Yves Smith notes the effect "of periodic crises. Andrew Haldane of the Bank of England, using a simple back-of-the-envelope analysis, concluded that there was no way for banks to even remotely pay for all the damage they produce in terms of lost output. …"

The GDP's report of the financial sector's economic contribution in "services"

---

[64]   Diane Coyle, *G.D.P.: A Brief but Affectionate History* (Princeton, 2014).

[65]   John Kay, "GDP is flawed – just not in the way most people think," *Financial Times*, March 16, 2014. He adds: "It values expenditure on war and nursing care on the same basis. It records the despoliation of the environment only by reference to the amount spent despoiling it, and then includes the amount spent to clean it up." This includes the cleanup costs of debt pollution.

"doesn't account for risk. Before the 2008 crisis, banks' increased risk-taking and leverage was counted as 'growth' in GDP. Since then studies have shown that adjusting for risk-taking would reduce financial sector contributions to GDP by 25-40%." … As a result, "the financial sector contribution to GDP is largely a statistical mirage …"[66]

The resulting system of seemingly empirical statistics leads to confusion about what actually is happening to the economy. As Alan Greenspan summarized, if you just look at GDP statistics you miss the bubble altogether:

> So, the question is if you can't stop a bubble, what do you do? Fortunately most bubbles are not toxic. The dot-com boom when it collapsed, you can't find it in the GDP figures in 2001, 2002. It didn't happen. The 1987 crash, which was really the most horrendous thing, I defy you to find that in the GDP numbers. It's not there. Yes, there were huge capital losses, but to the people who made the capital gains, essentially.[67]

What a realistic set of national accounts should show is that instead of using their wealth to invest in producing more to raise living standards, the One Percent lend out their savings at interest to extract revenue from wage earners, real estate, industry and government, shrinking the economy instead of expanding it.

Most financial transactions now take place with other financial institutions, largely in the form of computerized bets ("derivatives") calculating risks on which way interest rates and exchange rates or stock and bond prices will move. One party's gain is another's loss, and the overall system ends up needing to be bailed out by government. But instead of simply creating the money to pay everyone off, central bank managers insist that labor and industry must pay, by raising taxes on the "real" economy to pay for the financial sector's losses, on the pretense that the financial sector is what is making the economy richer, not poorer, and that austerity (poverty for the 99 Percent) will be a "cure" – a cure mainly for the fact that the One Percent do not yet control *all* the wealth.

The guiding principle of today's official statistical models seems to be that if people don't see unearned wealth explicitly labeled as overhead, if there is no measure of how much output the FIRE sector and monopolies siphon off, voters will be less likely to advocate regulating or taxing it. The concept of parasitic activity, in which one party's gains are another's loss, is cynically excluded from government accounting formats. This numbing of the obvious has enabled the vested interests to gain control of society's statistical sensory system that is supposed to guide its economic planning, tax policy and resource allocation.

---

[66] Yves Smith, "Yes, Virginia, Banking Contributes a Lot Less Value Than You are Lead to Believe," *Naked Capitalism*, March 4, 2014, citing Coyle, *op. cit.*

[67] Alan Greenspan, interview with Justin Fox at the *Harvard Business Review*, cited by Izabella Kaminska, "Greenspan, the Keynesian," http://ftalphaville.ft.com/. January 9, 2014.

So we are brought back to the strategy of financial parasitism: In order to extract the economy's surplus in the form of rent and interest, it is necessary to convince people that the FIRE sector makes a contribution to the real economy in keeping with the income its recipients get. The NIPA defend land rent, interest and other financial rents and monopoly rents as contributing to output, not extraneous to the "real" economy extracting parasitic *transfer payments*. The *rentier* "free lunch" is depicted as a contribution to national income and product, not as a subtrahend, that is, a transfer payment from the 99 Percent to the One Percent. The idea that interest, rent and price gouging are a burdensome overhead disappears.

Little of this financial revenue is spent back into the "real" economy of production or consumption. Most is simply recycled into the acquisition of yet more property, financial securities or new loans. The banking system creates credit mainly to finance the purchase of rent-yielding assets, headed by real estate, oil and mineral resources, and monopolies. Banks lend out their receipt of interest as yet more mortgage credit to buyers of rent-yielding resources. The effect is to turn economic rent into a flow of interest payments, which expands exponentially, inflating asset prices but also draining debt service from the economy. Paying land rent as interest leaves it unavailable as the tax base, so labor and industry must bear the burden, raising the economy's cost of living and doing business.

This wasn't how the financial sector was expected to evolve when the Industrial Revolution was gaining momentum. And it doesn't have to be the way today's post-industrial finance capitalism develops. Alternatives were advocated in the 19th century to mobilize finance to fund capital investment in production and public infrastructure. But after World War I, financial interests joined with property interests to shift the tax burden off themselves onto labor and industry by promoting an illusion that rent and interest are payments for productive services, and even deserved special breaks.

7

The Failed Attempt to
Industrialize High Finance

Activism has caused companies to cut R&D, capital investment and, most significantly, employment. It forces companies to lay off employees to meet quarterly earnings. It is a disaster for the country.

Martin Lipton, inventor of the "poison pill" for corporate defense.[68]

Every economy is planned in some way or another. Feudal economies were planned by the heirs of the warlord bands that conquered the land, living off their rents and taxing the economy to pay for more military conquests. The Industrial Revolution led merchants and industrialists to fight against the landed interest and its associated military adventurism that loaded nations down with public debts and the taxes levied to carry their interest charge.

Throughout history the wealthiest families have seeded economic and political institutions with leaders to defend their interests, typically using banks as their center of power. The Medici supplied Popes Leo X (1513–21), Clement VII (1523–34), Pius IV (1559–65) and Leo XI in 1605. Elsewhere in feudal Europe, landed aristocrats ran economies for their own interest. Yet despite the Industrial Revolution, few global managers today are drawn from industry. Most economic decision-makers have been trained in business schools to view companies primarily as vehicles to produce financial gains (as Chapters 8 and 9 will illustrate).

National policy in today's world is planned mainly by financial loyalists to serve financial interests. Central bank and U.S. Treasury officials are on loan from Wall Street, above all from Goldman and Citigroup. Goldman Sachs's roster of CEOs in public service is hallmarked by Treasury Secretaries Robert Rubin (1995–99, at Goldman 1966–92) and Hank Paulson (2006–09, at Goldman from 1974 to 2006). At Treasury, Paulson was aided by Chief of

---

68   Martin Lipton, interviewed by Joe Nocera, "The Battle Over DuPont," *The New York Times*, May 9, 2015.

Staff Mark Patterson (Goldman lobbyist 2003–08), Neel Kashkari (Goldman Vice President 2002–06), Under-Secretary Robert K. Steel (Vice Chairman at Goldman, where he worked from 1976 to 2004), and advisors Kendrick Wilson (at Goldman from 1998–2008) and Edward C. Forst (former Global Head of Goldman's Investment Management Division).[69] Goldman Sachs kept Paulson's successor Tim Geithner, a protégé of Robert Rubin, close by with the usual reward tactic of paying lucrative speaking fees.[70]

Federal Reserve Bank of New York Chairman Stephen Friedman (2008–09) was former Co-Chairman at Goldman Sachs, where he had worked since 1966. Its president after 2009 was William Dudley (at Goldman from 1986 until 2007). Former New York Fed President Gerald Corrigan (1985–93) "descended from heaven" to work at Goldman Sachs, as did former Treasury Secretary Henry Fowler. Other Goldman Sachs alumni in high positions include White House chief of staff Joshua B. Bolten and World Bank president Robert B. Zoellick.

In Europe, Goldman Sachs Vice Chairman Mario Draghi (2002–05) left to become Bank of Italy Governor (2006–11) and later President of the European Central Bank. Italian Prime Minister Romani Prodi served Goldman Sachs from 1990–93 and acted as a consultant when not in office. Former Italian prime minister and finance minister Mario Monti is an international adviser to Goldman Sachs. Bank of Canada Governor Mark Carney (2008–13 moving to the Bank of England in 2013) joined Goldman Sachs in 1995 and worked there for thirteen years. Antonio Borges, head of the IMF's European division in 2010 and main administrator for Portugal's privatization program, was Goldman Sachs's International Vice Chairman 2000-08, and Carlos Moedas, Portugal's Secretary of State to the Prime Minister, worked at Goldman Sachs on mergers and acquisitions. The list could go on and on.

Robert Rubin provides the most important link, leaving the Clinton Administration to head Citigroup in 1999, receiving over $120 million in compen-

---

[69] For a recent list see Paula Reid, "Goldman Sachs' Revolving Door," *CBS Investigates*, April 8, 2010. http://www.cbsnews.com/news/goldman-sachs-revolving-door/.
[70] Robert Scheer, "Geithner and Goldman, Thick as Thieves," *Truthdig*, May 31, 2011: "Geithner's priorities were all too obvious from his days in the Clinton administration's Treasury Department when he worked first under former Goldman honcho Robert Rubin and then Lawrence Summers, who took six-figure speaking fees from Goldman and other banks while he was an adviser to candidate Obama. It was the recommendation of Rubin and Summers that landed Geithner the job as president of the New York Fed, where he faithfully followed the policy lead of Goldman-CEO-turned-Treasury-Secretary Henry Paulson." http://www.truthdig.com/report/item/geithner_and_goldman_ thick_as_ thieves_20110531/.

sation during his tenure over the next decade. He was helped by future Treasury Secretary Jack Lew during 2006–08 (and earlier by Stanley Fischer during 2002–05, President Obama's nominee for Vice-Chairman of the Federal Reserve in 2014). This team dug the hole that ran Citigroup into the ground, but its political influence led the U.S. government to "pump in $45 billion in equity, made $300 billion in asset guarantees, and the Fed chipped in over $2 trillion in below market rate loans to the listing shipwreck."[71]

The way in which these managers of U.S. Government policy obliterated Citigroup's net worth prompted FDIC Chair Sheila Bair to characterize Citigroup as a former commercial bank "hijacked by an investment banking culture that made profits through high-stakes betting." Calling it the worst run bank in the United States, having "bought into all the gimmicks to generate short-term profits: poorly underwritten loans, high-risk securities investments, and short-term, unstable liquidity," Bair wrote that it was wrecked under Rubin and his hand-picked successor Vikram Pandit, who "wouldn't have known how to write a loan if his life depended on it. But he was the guy Rubin wanted."[72]

The Goldman Sachs story has been well-told by Matt Taibbi, describing the company as "a great vampire squid, wrapped around the face of humanity, relentlessly jamming its blood funnel into anything that smells like money."[73] The behavior of Goldman Sachs, Citigroup and other giant banks is extractive, charged with fine after fine for repeated civil frauds perpetrated against their counterparties and clients. Much like Russia's "Seven Bankers," who gained control of that nation's natural resources, land and infrastructure monopolies under Boris Yeltsin's insider privatizations of the mid-1990s, Goldman Sachs managers squeeze out fees, interest, financial and commodity speculation at the economy's expense. Their idea of a free market is non-enforcement of regulatory checks on investment bankers who view new technology and privatization of the public domain mainly as opportunities to make underwriting and management fees, and enormous stock price gains. Toward this end, financial lobbyists and the politicians whose campaigns they underwrite demand veto power over the appointment of regulators, central bankers and Treasury officials.

---

[71] Pam Martens, "Fed Nominee Stanley Fischer Has a Citigroup Problem," Wall Street on Parade, March 4, 2014. http://wallstreetonparade.com/2014/03/fed-nominee-stanley-fischer-has-a-citigroup-problem/

[72] Sheila Bair, *Bull by the Horns* (2012), p. 122.

[73] Matt Taibbi, "The Great American Bubble Machine, *Rolling Stone*, July 9, 2009. For a less rhetorical description see William Cohan, *Money and Power: How Goldman Sachs Came to Rule The World* (2011).

It didn't have to be this way. While rent theory was refined to tax or natio-nalize the takings of landlords and monopolies in the 19th century, a parallel financial reform movement flowered in France and Germany. Having less capital available than England, these countries could not afford the predatory practices of British merchant banking. Inspired largely by the French reformer Henri de Saint-Simon, advocates of industrialization developed a strategy to restructure financial systems to promote industry. Saint-Simon, along with early socialists and the large German banks that flowered in the Bismarck era, designed more productive banking systems to overtake Britain's head start by coordinating industrial investment with state-sponsored investment and planning.

But the past century has shown that financial systems do not automatically evolve to optimize society's technological potential. Instead of steering savings, credit and industrial profits into new tangible capital investment, employment, research and development, today's banks and money managers are diverting savings and lending *away* from financing productive enterprise, while finding their major loan market in rent extraction opportunities at the expense of eco-nomic growth.

How debt service raises costs and prices

It seems remarkable how much more clearly 18th and early 19th-century writers discussed the way in which debt service raises costs and prices, compared to today's economists. Eight centuries of warfare with France had driven Britain deeply into debt. Parliament issued new bonds to finance each new conflict, with a new excise tax levied to pay its interest charge. Most such taxes were levied on consumer essentials, raising the cost of living and hence the price of labor. Costs were further increased by the high prices charged by trading monopolies that governments created and sold to investors to retire their bonds. The tax and monopoly problems thus were basically a byproduct of the public debt problem.

In 1744, Mathew Decker, a merchant and director of the East India Com-pany, attributed the deterioration in Britain's industrial competitiveness to the taxes imposed on food and other essentials to pay the interest charges on its public debt. Much like private-sector interest charges today, these taxes pushed up the subsistence wage that employers had to pay, and hence the prices they had to charge as compared to those of less debt-ridden economies. In the pre-face to his *Essay on the Causes of the Decline of the Foreign Trade*, Decker wrote that by imposing a "prodigious artificial Value ... upon our Goods to the hindrance of their Sale abroad," these debts and taxes threatened to price British exports out of world markets.[74]

Funding wars by running into debt instead of on a pay-as-you-go basis was called Dutch financing because, as Adam Smith explained, "the Dutch, as well as several other foreign nations, [hold] a very considerable share of our public funds."[75] In fact, they held more than half of the securities of the major British Crown corporations, including the East India Company and Bank of England. The interest and dividends Britain dished out to these foreign investors absorbed much of its trade surplus. "As Foreigners possess a Share of our national Funds," Smith explained, "they render the Public in a Manner tributary to them, and may in Time occasion the Transport of our People, and our Industry."

As early as 1757, the English commercial sage Malachy Postlethwayt decried the remittance of interest, dividends and capital to Dutch investors. He estimated that the Seven Years War (1757–63) cost Britain £82 million. In the year the conflict broke out, his pamphlet on *Great-Britain's True System* explained that the outflow of bullion drained money needed to employ labor, leaving Britain with little domestic market for its own products. Even if all the debt were held at home, he warned, "it would not upon that account be less pernicious."[76] The taxes levied to service the public debt increased the price of necessities and hence the cost of labor and overall costs by "at least 31 per Cent. of the annual Expense of the whole People of England."[77]

What Britain might win militarily, it would lose commercially as a result of royal military ambitions. "The more the Nation runs into Debt, the more Money will be locked up in the Funds, and the less will there be employed in Trade."[78] Economies would gain more power by investing their savings productively at home than by going into debt to finance their military adventures. "Before such Debt took Place, every body possessed their whole Gains," Postlethwayt pointed out. Taxing the population to pay interest to creditors drained money that otherwise could be used for private investment. "If the present public Debt instead of being encreased, was paid off, the Profits of the Manufacturers, Tradesmen and Merchants, &c. would be all their own," doubling their rate of profit. By avoiding wars and their debts Britain could

---

[74] Mathew Decker, *Essay on the Causes of the Decline of the Foreign Trade* (1744), preface. Decker had emigrated from Holland to settle in London in 1702.

[75] Adam Smith, *The Wealth of Nations*, V, iii (Cannan ed., p. 452).

[76] Malachy Postlethwayt, *Great-Britain's True System* (1757), p. 21.

[77] *Ibid.*, p.165.

[78] *Ibid.*, 20f.

"undersell our Neighbours. ... new Arts and new Manufactures would be introduced, and the old ones brought to greater Perfection."[79]

To make matters worse, Postlethwayt added, bondholders spent their revenue unproductively, creating monopolies and sponsoring financial bubbles. In a message that could well describe the 2001–08 bubble, he described how the financial maneuverings of his day created monopolies and tricked investors out of their savings. "Funding and Jobbing too often ... introduces Combination and Fraud in all Sorts of Traffic. It hath changed honest Commerce into bubbling; our Traders into Projectors; Industry into Tricking; and Applause is earned when the Pillory is deserved." This Postlethwayt might have been speaking of today's economies in warning that, "while there is more to be got by Jobbing, than by dischargeing our Debts, all Arts will be used to encrease the new Debts, not to redeem the Old."[80]

The protestations by Decker and Postlethwayt (and later by Smith) against the sale of public monopolies anticipated today's complaints that monopoly charges, interest and other financial charges push up the prices that labor and industry must pay, as well as emigration of their labor in order to find work. The great political economist James Steuart, author of *An Inquiry into the Principles of Political Economy*, warned in 1767: "if we suppose governments to go on increasing, every year, the sum of their debts upon perpetual annuities, and appropriating, in proportion, every branch of revenue for the payment of them; the consequence will be, in the first place, to transport, in favour of the creditors, the whole income of the state ..."[81]

Indeed, for the typical year of 1783, the historian Leland Jenks has calculated that Britain's government paid out some three-fourths of its tax revenue to bondholders: "Nine million pounds ... when the entire annual turnover of British foreign trade did not exceed thirty-five millions."[82] By 1798, in the wake of the American and French Revolutions, William Pitt's policy of borrowing instead of paying on a tax-as-you-go basis, imposed interest charges so heavy that "the nation was mortgaged to a new class of society, the *rentiers*, the fundholders, for an annual sum of thirty million pounds, three times the public revenue before the revolutionary wars. The bulk of this sum was being collected in customs, excise and stamp duties, and constituted an engine by which wealth was transferred from a large consuming public to the much smaller

---

[79] *Ibid.*, pp. 52f.
[80] *Ibid.*, pp. 22f.
[81] James Steuart, *Principles of Political Œconomy* (1767), Vol. II, pp. 349ff.
[82] Leland Jenks, *The Migration of British Capital to 1875* (1927), pp. 14ff.

number who owned consols." These were government bonds with no fixed maturity, paying interest for as long as the bonds were not redeemed.

Adam Smith spelled out the geopolitical implication: wars eroded rather than built British power. Higher debts and the taxes to pay the interest charges on Britain's war debts threatened to increase its production costs and hence its export prices, impairing its balance of trade and draining its bullion abroad.

If today's trade theory has little to say about how debt or *rentier* charges affect domestic and international prices, it is largely due to David Ricardo's lobbying on behalf of financial interests, arguing that debt levels and payment of interest to foreigners did not matter – as if such payments would be automatically self-correcting. His writings and Parliamentary testimony lay the groundwork for two centuries of narrow-mindedness down through Milton Friedman and the Chicago School, crowding out the more sophisticated analysis developed by critics of Ricardo's banking class.

Saint-Simon and French industrial reform

Although Britain was the home of the Industrial Revolution, it was French and German writers who took the broadest perspective in theorizing about how banking and credit systems could best be organized to fund industry. The French had a particular reason to focus on banking reform. Their financial system had not evolved much since the pre-Revolutionary *ancien regime*. To catch up with Britain and other nations' advancing technological potential, Count Claude-Henri de Saint-Simon (1760–1825) and his followers provided the guiding philosophy to create an industrial credit system.

Like many well-born aristocrats, Saint-Simon came to attack the inherited privileges of his class as a useless *rentier* burden on society. At the age of sixty, in 1819, he published a satire, *Parabole politique*, depicting France's governing aristocracy as living off inherited wealth, collecting rent and interest without performing a productive function. The French Revolution had overthrown this hereditary feudal nobility politically but not economically.

In this respect Saint-Simon was a market reformer. What made him more radical than today's free marketers was his treatment of inherited wealth as a market imperfection. His followers depicted the rent, interest and dividends from land ownership, bonds and stocks as a vestigial post-feudal overhead. They were tributary claims on society's income and output, a legacy of the dead hand of the past.

Saint-Simon's key reform was to replace debt financing with equity ownership shares. If loan proceeds are invested to produce a profit, he argued, the borrower can pay interest out of the venture's proceeds, as dividends from its earnings. Dividends on equity capital – literally, an ownership share – can be cut when profits decline. But bank loans and bonds bear interest that must be paid regardless of the fortunes of the debtor. Missing a debt payment may lead to default and forfeiture of assets when creditors foreclose. Saint-Simon laid out the logic for banks to take ownership shares in their customers rather than making straight loans.

Hoping to train a meritocracy of industrial engineers, Saint-Simon's followers transformed government's role away from supporting idle *rentier* aristocracies. Assuming that talent was best able to show its abilities in industry, they sought to create a new type of industrial capitalist (*travailleur*). In contrast to the "projectors," adventurers and pirates of John Law's day, the banks would invest directly in industry, not merely for speculative or mercantile gains.

Within the ranks of capitalists, bankers were glorified as the future organizers and promoters of industry. According to the 1831 *Religion Saint-Simonienne, Economie politique et Politique*, "the banks perform the role of capitalists in their transactions with those *travailleurs*, to whom they loan money," enabling "industrious people" to obtain financing for their enterprise.[83]

As the spirit of early industrial and banking reform gained momentum, the Saint-Simonian reformers attracted supporters ranging from socialists to investment bankers, and won government backing for their policies under France's Third Empire. They went further than British and American land-taxation advocates, such as Adam Smith and John Stuart Mill, by placing heavier emphasis on the need for financial reform. Their ranks included the social theorist Auguste Comte, the economist Michel Chevalier, the socialist Pierre Leroux, the engineer Ferdinand de Lesseps (whose plans for canals elaborated ideas initiated by Saint-Simon) and the brothers Emile and Isaac Pereire, who founded the Crédit Mobilier in 1852 to give institutional expression to Saint-Simon's banking ideals.

It was left to Emile Pereire (1800–1875) to begin putting Saint-Simon's ideals into effect. In the 1830s, Pereire built France's first railway line (from Paris to St. Germain), and later developed other routes. In 1852 he formed the *Société Génerale du Crédit Mobilier* as a joint-stock bank with his younger

---

[83] *Religion Saint-Simonienne, Economie politique et Politique* (Paris: 1831), pp. 98 and 45. Marx quotes these passages in *Capital* III (Chicago 1909), p. 714. Charles Pecqueur's *Theorie Nouvelle d'Economie Sociale et Politique* (Paris 1842, p. 434) urged that production be ruled by what the Saint-Simonians called the *Systeme general des banques*.

brother Isaac (1806–1880).[84] Their guiding principle was to provide low-cost long-term credit that would enable industrialists to expand production.

Instead of extending loans directly to its customers, the Crédit Mobilier invested in stocks and bonds issued by these companies. Returns were expected to be higher than the rate of interest it paid depositors. "The institution was in effect a gigantic holding company engaged in financing and managing industrial enterprises," notes George Edwards. "The securities of the controlled companies were used as assets on which the Crédit Mobilier issued its own securities, to be sold to the public. For a number of years the Bank was highly successful, and performed notable service in promoting railroads and public utilities."[85]

But this freer supply of long-term equity capital and bond financing proved to be the bank's undoing. A downturn comes over the course of every business cycle. When profits declined and stock prices crashed in 1866, the Crédit Mobilier suffered both as banker and as stockholder. It could not turn these investments into immediate cash to pay depositors, or write down or delay payment on what it owed. Matters were aggravated by the bank's "crony capitalism" links to Louis Napoleon's government. Insider speculation drove Crédit Mobilier bankrupt in 1867 and into liquidation in 1871.

Financial scandals were endemic to the 19th century's largest international investments, headed by the Suez and Panama Canal schemes (both were early St. Simonian ideas), and almost wherever governments were involved. The most notorious were America's railroad land grants to robber barons, whose stock and bond waterings (diluting shares by simply printing more and giving them to directors, insiders and the politicians being bribed) helped give high finance its bad name. As aggregations of finance capital grew larger and more closely linked to government, banking systems became prone to such dealings.

Saint-Simon's influence on Marx and other socialists

The ideal of mobilizing banking to finance industry soon spread beyond France. Saint-Simon's influence extended to John Stuart Mill, Karl Marx and Christian Socialists, as well as to industrialists. The common denominator of this broad political spectrum was recognition that an efficient industrial credit system was needed.

---

[84]   Emile contributed a number of essays to the Saint-Simonian *Revue Encyclopedique*, collected in his 1832 *Considérations sur les Finances de la France et des États Unis*. Isaac Pereire explained the Crédit Mobilier's financial philosophy in *Le Rôle de la Banque de France et l'Organisation du Crédit en France* (1864) and *La Politique Financière* (1879).

[85]   George W. Edwards, *The Evolution of Finance Capitalism* (1938), p. 51.

Engels wrote that Marx spoke "only with admiration" of Saint-Simon's "genius and encyclopedic brain."[86] However, Marx wrote sarcastically of his "world-redeeming credit-phantasies" and believed that followers such as Charles Fourier and Auguste Comte were utopian in their hope to reconcile the interests of capital and labor. What Marx shared with Saint-Simon was an optimism that the banking and credit system would evolve in a way that "signifies no more and no less than the subordination of interest-bearing capital to the conditions and requirements of the capitalist mode of production."[87]

Marx contended that any conflict of interest between financial and industrial capital would be settled in favor of the latter. "This violent fight against usury, this demand for the subordination of the interest-bearing under the industrial capital" was a prerequisite for grounding "capitalist production in the modern banking system, which on the one hand robs usurer's capital of its monopoly by concentrating all fallow money reserves and throwing them on the money-market, and on the other hand limits the monopoly of the precious metals themselves by creating credit-money."[88]

Marx described usury as an ancient practice independent of the mode of production, growing by its own compound interest dynamics in ways that historically had been parasitic. Usurer's capital "does not confront the laborer as industrial capital," but "merely impoverishes this mode of production, paralyzes the productive forces instead of developing them." Usury transfers ownership of assets to usurers, making life harder for the laborer and serving as a brake on industrial capitalism, preventing the social productivity of labor from developing. "Usury centralises money wealth ... It does not alter the mode of production, but attaches itself as a parasite and makes it miserable. It sucks its blood, kills its nerve, and compels reproduction to proceed under even more disheartening conditions."[89]

Reliance on usurers for credit, Marx granted, would persist for needy individuals, "such persons or classes ... as do not borrow in the sense corresponding to the capitalist mode of production."[90] But the great financial achievement of industrial capitalism would be to create a superior outlet for saving than the consumer usury and war lending that characterized pre-industrial banking. Usury-capital no longer would be able to block society from achieving

---

[86]   *Capital*, Vol. III (Chicago 1909), p. 710, fn 116.
[87]   *Ibid.*: 704 f.
[88]   *Ibid.*, p. 707.
[89]   *Ibid.*: 699 f.
[90]   *Ibid.*, pp. 704 f..

its technological potential once an industrial banking system came into being to provide low-interest credit to be invested productively.

Marx expected increasingly capital-intensive production to require more credit. The question was how to supply it. Given his faith in the driving force of technological evolution, Marx asserted that the destiny of industrial capitalism was to modernize finance, turning usurious lending into productive industrial banking. Financial institutions would become society's means of planning the future as banks reinvested their interest revenue in new loans to expand the means of production and pay interest out of profits.

As matters turned out, Marx proved too optimistic. In fact, nobody of his epoch was so pessimistic as to anticipate banking to behave the way it does today, stripping capital and adding financial overhead to the cost of production. Expecting industrial capitalists to shape financial systems to serve their needs, Marx assumed that the most productive banking systems would survive to serve the industrial host and, in due course, to socialize finance. And indeed this seemed to be occurring in Germany, where Bismarck's "state socialism" found its financial expression in the Reichsbank and other large industrial banks that became part of the "trinity" of banking, heavy industry and government.

The emergence of German industrial banking

The German Historical School of economists was among the most optimistic in expecting finance to promote industrial prosperity. Wilhelm Roscher pointed to the fact that interest rates tended to fall steadily with the progress of civilization; at least, rates had been falling since medieval times.[91] A more socially productive credit system was replacing the age-old usury problem. Credit laws were becoming more humanitarian as debtors' prisons were being phased out throughout Europe, while more lenient bankruptcy laws were freeing individuals to start afresh with clean slates.

Lacking the funds necessary to expand on a large scale, German industry relied on banks for a broad range of long-term investment and short-term financing. Recognizing that reinvesting profits in expanding production limited the ability to pay interest, banks willingly accepted part of their return in higher-yielding equity shares, that is, in stock rather than as interest on outright loans. This Saint-Simonian ideal was followed simply as the most pragmatic and remunerative practice.

---

[91] I summarize the optimistic views of Roscher and his contemporaries in "Roscher's Victorian Views on Financial Development," *Journal of Economic Studies* 22 (Spring 1995):187–208.

In Germany, bank owners were the most important source of capital, not depositors as was the case in Britain. (A middle class of German savers emerged only gradually.) This focus on owner's equity prompted German banks to resist the speculative excesses found in American finance of the period. Loans and bond issues were kept "to the actual cash value of the property of the corporation being financed."[92]

At the other end of the debt/equity spectrum, U.S. financiers engaged in stock waterings that overfunded companies by bond issues far beyond their needs or capacity to carry. The difference was pocketed by the directors of these corporations, a practice that led much honest industry to stay clear of Wall Street. Fraud was almost built into the system. A distinguishing feature of America's Gilded Age proved to be the ability of insiders to prevent financial checks from being legislated, and to render attempts along these lines ineffective in practice.

It was not industry but railroads (which European countries kept in the public domain) that provided the basis for America's stock market, which was used largely to create trusts and monopolies. Its heroes were insiders gaining fortunes by stock market raids, politicking for land giveaways, manipulating stock prices and issuing bonds to themselves (and friendly politicians and lawmakers). As matters have turned out, this is the financial system that has won the struggle for survival.

The World War I debate over German vs. Anglo-Dutch banking

When war broke out in 1914, Germany's rapid victories over France and Belgium seemed to reflect the superior efficiency of its financial system. To the German priest-politician Friedrich Naumann and the English economist H. S. Foxwell, the Great War appeared as a struggle between rival forms of financial organization to decide who would rule Europe and, beyond that, whether the continent would have a laissez faire or a more state-socialist economy. In 1915, shortly after fighting broke out, Naumann summarized the continental banking philosophy in *Mitteleuropa*, from which Foxwell drew for his argument in two highly influential essays: "The Nature of the Industrial Struggle," and "The Financing of Industry and Trade."[93] In particular, Foxwell cited Naumann's contention that "the old individualistic capitalism, of what he calls the English type, is giving way to the new, more impersonal, group form; to the discipline, scientific capitalism he claims as German."

---

[92]   Edwards, *Evolution of Finance Capitalism*, p. 68.
[93]   *Economic Journal* **27** (September and December 1917), pp. 323–27 and 502–15.

Germany recognized that the industrial technology required to catch up with Britain needed long-term financing in addition to government support. In the emerging integration of industry, banking and government, Foxwell observed that finance was "undoubtedly the main cause of the success of modern German enterprise."[94] Holding equity capital as an ownership share of profits instead of straight debt, banks took the lead in much of the planning that guided Germany's development. Bank staffs were forging industrial policy into a science, becoming engineers under the new industrial philosophy of how public policy should shape credit markets. In America, Thorstein Veblen soon voiced much the same theory in *The Engineers and the Price System* (1921).

The political connections of German bankers gave them a decisive voice in formulating international diplomacy, making "mixed banking ... the principal instrument in the extension of her foreign trade and political power."[95] German bank officials sat on their boards, and extended loans to foreign governments on condition that German clients would be named as the chief suppliers in major public investments. It seemed that the dynamics of economic history were leading toward this kind of symbiosis between national planning and large-scale financing of heavy industry.

The short time frame of loans and liquidity characteristic of England's merchant bankers ill suited them for this task. By focusing on trade financing rather than long-term industrial development, English bankers preferred to lend against collateral in place and available for liquidation in the event of default: inventories, money due on bills for goods in transit and sold to customers but not yet paid for, and real estate. This prompted Foxwell to warn that British manufacturers of steel, automobiles, capital equipment and other heavy industry were in danger of becoming obsolete, largely because the nation's bankers failed to perceive the need to extend long-term credit and increase equity investment.

British bankers paid out most of their earnings as dividends, instead of investing in the shares of the companies that their loans supposedly were building up. They also pressed their industrial clients to pay out the maximum proportion of earnings as conditions for the loan. This short time horizon forced borrowers to remain liquid rather than giving them the leeway to pursue long-term strategies. By contrast, German banks paid out dividends (and expected such dividends from their clients) at only half the rate of British banks, preferring to retain earnings as capital reserves to build up equity.

---

[94] *Ibid.*, p. 514.
[95] *Ibid.*

So two kinds of banking vied against each other: extractive Anglo-Dutch-American collateral-based lending against existing real estate and orders on hand vs. productive long-term credit to fund tangible capital formation and infrastructure.

Although Britain was the home of the Industrial Revolution, little manufacturing was financed in its early stages by bank credit. Most innovators were obliged to raise money privately. Britain's stockbrokers were no more up to the task of financing industry than were its banks, having an equally short-term frame of reference. Stock markets were dominated by railroads, canals and large public infrastructure utilities. After earning their commissions on one issue, they moved on to the next without much concern for what happened to investors who had bought the earlier securities. "As soon as he has contrived to get his issue quoted at a premium and his underwriters have unloaded at a profit," complained Foxwell, "his enterprise ceases. 'To him,' as the *Times* says, 'a successful flotation is of more importance than a sound venture.'"[96]

In sum, the aim of British and American banks was to maximize their own short-run advantage, not to create a better and more productive economy by planning for the future. Most banks favored large real estate borrowers, along with railroads and public utilities whose income streams easily could be forecast. Manufacturing only obtained significant bank and stock market credit once companies had grown fairly large.

Veblen's analysis of financial distortions of industrial capitalism

Describing the financial class as ascendant, Thorstein Veblen the machinations of high finance, stock watering and debt pyramiding by Wall Street stock manipulators who dominated the Gilded Age of his day. His Theory of Business Enterprise (1904) emphasized the divergence between productive capacity and "pecuniary" gains from inflating stock-market prices over and above cost-value ("book value"; today's jargon calls this premium the Q ratio). To Veblen this pecuniary gain was the aim of Wall Street operators. The upshot of this economic game, as Veblen put it, was not capital investment in plant and equipment to produce profits by employing labor, but speculative "capital" gains in asset prices – an exercise in promotion and collusion not unlike land speculators puffing up the market.

Emphasizing how financial "predation" was hijacking the economy's technological potential, Veblen described the manner in which industry was becoming financialized in ways that put financial gains ahead of production.

[96] *Ibid.*

Meanwhile, the Finance, Insurance and Real Estate (FIRE) sectors were joining forces to fuel property speculation. Bank credit inflated asset prices by lending primarily to buy shares and real estate, not to produce more. This finance-driven practice was imposing a debt overhead that threatened to end in corporate bankruptcy and liquidation.

Yet Veblen was as optimistic as Marx when it came to industrial capitalism's potential to uplift society – if it enacted social reforms to check the predatory behavior of banks, absentee property owners and monopolists. But Veblen saw that while technological innovation was trimming costs, it also was breeding monopolies. The fruits of rising productivity were being appropriated by robber barons, who had no better use of their wealth than to create trusts to dictate high prices and extract economic rent.

Veblen's description of the dynamic that has led financial managers to use profits not to invest but to pay out as dividends or buy up their company's stock (raising the value of their stock options) has been largely vindicated. Hedge funds have become notorious for stripping assets and loading companies down with debt, leaving bankrupt shells in their wake in what George Akerlof and Paul Romer have characterized as looting.[97] Lending and debt are becoming more usurious and less productive. The end result is to impose austerity regimes rather than promote growth, tangible capital formation and rising living standards.

Will financial pessimism trump industrial optimism?

After World War I, banking throughout most of the world adhered to the Anglo-Dutch model. Germany not only lost the war, but also saw the post-war leaders of Europe reject its philosophy of industrial banking and the warnings against predatory finance. Instead of governments coordinating industrial planning, finance has taken over corporate and also government policy making. Bankers and financial managers are indebting economies without putting in place new means of production to pay off their mushrooming debt overhead. Industry has been financialized and planning has been centralized in Wall Street, London, the Paris Bourse and Frankfurt, instead of in public hands as socialists expected or those of industrial engineers as Veblen forecast. Stock and bond markets have been transformed into arenas for debt leveraging as the post-industrial means of appropriating property. The major financial

---

97   George Akerlof and Paul Romer, "Looting: The Economic Underworld of Bankruptcy for Profit," *Brookings Papers on Economic Activity*, Vol. 1993, No. 2 (1993):1-73, also published as *NBER Working Paper No. R1869* (April 1994).

innovations have been corporate junk bonds in the 1980s, junk mortgages and complex financial derivatives in the 2000s.

Even though rising productivity lowered the direct costs of production, prices have continued to rise, mainly as a result of the steady buildup of financial charges (interest, fees and insurance), as well as real estate rents and monopoly pricing. These charges have risen not by increasing the money supply, but by the way in which the financial system adds to the debt overhead. Interest and debt repayment has been engineered into the cost of doing business, and increasingly as a cost of living, at the expense of spending on goods and services, investment and employment. The price rise is aggravated by rent-extracting privatization of public infrastructure to create private *rentier* fortunes by predatory pricing for essential services.

The aim of a financialized economy is to make money for a narrow financial layer by establishing a credit stranglehold on industry and labor, and on the government itself. This reverses the direction in which classical political economy seemed to be moving to propel governments out of the feudal era by reforming the way society employs and accumulates wealth. In a modern version of the feudal epoch's "primitive accumulation" by military seizure, financial dynamics serve to concentrate wealth by means of debt leveraging and privatization loading down industry, real estate and infrastructure with debt.

Part II

Wall Street as Central Planner

8
The Stock Market as a Predatory Arena

It is rare, one is told, for an American to invest, as many Englishmen still do, "for income"; and he will not readily purchase an investment except in the hope of capital appreciation. … he is, in the above sense, a speculator. Speculators may do no harm as bubbles on a steady stream of enterprise. But the position is serious when enterprise becomes the bubble on a whirlpool of speculation. When the capital development of a country becomes a by-product of the activities of a casino, the job is likely to be ill-done.

John Maynard Keynes, *The General Theory of Employment, Interest and Money* (1936), Chapter 12, §vi.

Wall Street paints its activities in as positive a light as possible, as if to justify its enormous salaries being earned productively rather than at the economy's expense. This smiley-face picture also serves to rationalize its tax breaks and, most recently, its bailouts. Academic models echo a view of the stock and bond markets raising funds mainly for new industrial investment, innovation and employment, while making savers richer.

Yet finance rarely ever in history has played a productive role funding capital formation in industrial plants and equipment, research and development. Since antiquity, workshops and factories, farms and other capital assets traditionally have been self-financed. Until the early Industrial Revolution the means of production were owned outright.[98] The idea of productive credit to finance *new* investment in means of production was an alien concept down through the mid-19th century, and even then the investment was mainly for railroads and canals, not industry. Credit arrangements were used to bridge the time gap between production and sale, between planting and harvesting, and especially for commerce over large distances. But *not* to invest in manufacturing.

---

[98] I survey the early evolution of financial practice, industrial enterprise and the focus on land ownership in "Entrepreneurs: From the Near Eastern Takeoff to the Roman Collapse," in David S. Landes, Joel Mokyr, and William J. Baumol, eds., *The Invention of Enterprise: Entrepreneurship from Ancient Mesopotamia to Modern Times* (Princeton University Press, 2010):8-39.

This strategy remains in effect today. Most U.S. and European corporations pay for their capital investment out of their current earnings, not by borrowing from bondholders or banks. The financial system extends credit mainly to buy property already in place, from real estate (the focus of most bank lending today) to entire companies. This shift in ownership adds to debt without increasing output, merely transferring ownership. Existing stockowners are bought out by new owners who issue high-interest bonds and borrow takeover loans from banks. And corporations borrow increasingly to buy up their own stock, and even to pay dividends, creating gains by inflating asset prices.

Apple is a case in point. In 1980 the computer company went public with a $100 million Initial Public Offering of shares. The largest U.S. IPO since that of Ford Motor Company in 1956 a quarter-century earlier, the stock sale set a record by making 300 instant millionaires within its own ranks, including 40 employees and early investors for their three years of work to build up the company before it went public.[99]

Founded in 1977, Apple required funds to invest in more production facilities and to buy companies with complementary patents that it needed to expand. However, Apple only received a portion of the proceeds of this stock issue. Its underwriters, headed by Morgan Stanley and Hambrecht & Quist, initially priced the stock at only $14 a share, but enough orders poured in to price it at $22 by the opening bell. Being oversubscribed (given the underwriters' low pricing), Apple's price rose by 32 percent to $29 a share, valuing the company at $1.8 billion by the end of the day.

A first-day jump means that a company's stock is worth more than the underwriter promises to raise. This underestimation of the market enables early subscribers – so-called preferred customers, usually institutional investors and a few prominent individual players – to make a killing. Giving them a chance to buy low-priced shares to turn around and sell at a price gain during the first few hours of hectic trading helps the underwriter attract a loyal following of investors. The bigger the hit-and-run windfall the underwriter can offer these clients, the larger a client base it builds up for future offerings. This investor base is permanent; most companies issuing new stock are only one-time hits, so underwriters low-ball their promises to companies going public. The result is that financial speculators make more than the companies that actually create real value.

---

[99] See Daniel Eran Dilger, "Apple, Inc. stock IPO created 300 millionaires 33 years ago today," *Apple Insider*, December 12, 2013. http://appleinsider.com/articles/13/12/12/apple-inc-stock-ipo-created-300-millionaires-33-years-ago-today.

Underwriters thus have a conflict of interest with the companies whose stock they float. In addition to charging their underwriting fee (as high as 7 percent for new businesses), the more they understate what a company is worth, the bigger the gains they and their favored customers quickly make by flipping its shares to a later buyer at the more reasonable market price established by the end of the first trading day or week.[100] A "successful" issue is one where the stock price may double from the opening to the closing bell. Company officers, venture capitalists and other initial long-term holders will see the value of their shares rise, but the company itself receives only the opening sales price. The underwriter and its clients may end up making as much on the sale that it orchestrates as the company and its founders receive for all the years of effort that they put into creating the business.

Yet in this case there was so much money to be made selling computers that Apple viewed being exploited by its underwriters simply as the price of doing business on Wall Street. That is how the financial world works. Apple went on to become immensely profitable – but this success led to yet another example of how the financial sector's interests have become antithetical to those of industry over the past generation.

Apple's plague of activist shareholders (formerly known as corporate raiders)

Once a company has issued stock to the public, financial managers and "activist shareholders" jump into the game to turn it into a cash cow. Instead of plowing profits back into the corporation to expand the business by new long-term investment, research and development, the company is urged to pay out its earnings as dividends and buy back its stock to bid up its price. The aim is to enable speculators to make trading gains. Toward this end, activist shareholders have even tried to force Apple and other cash-rich companies to take on debt they do not need for productive investment, merely to spend on stock buybacks.

---

[100] Such underpricing strategy was heaviest in Britain when Margaret Thatcher sought to encourage privatization by deliberately underpricing shares of British Telephone and subsequent public utilities, for which their customers were given vouchers to buy on partial down payment. First day gains to buyers – money that BT did not receive – were strong, as was the case with subsequent privatization sell-offs. The idea was to give everyone the idea that they could get rich off the stock market, especially by privatizing state-owned utilities. Britain's economy was rapidly de-industrialized while the City of London – the nation's financial center – became the economy's dominant sector and policy maker.

At issue is a conflict that was characterized a century ago as being between industrial capitalism and finance capitalism. Apple CEO John Sculley chose to spend $1.8 billion in the late 1980s and early 1990s to buy back its own stock to support its price. "That was money it could have really used when the company then stumbled and needed to issue junk bonds – and issue $150 million in convertible preferred stock to Microsoft – just to survive."[101]

Many other companies found themselves similarly squeezed by buying up their stock at high prices, only to see prices later fall. In effect, their earnings were stripped and new capital investment or expansion foregone simply to make temporary gains for stockholders. This is the strategy that "activist shareholders" have been urging Apple and other companies to do today – to use their earnings to buy its stock instead of making new tangible investment, and even to go into debt to finance stock buybacks.

Why should a company as cash-rich as Apple take on debt? If ever a company has not needed to borrow to fund new research and development, hire more employees or invest in new plant and equipment, it would seem to be Apple. As of August 2013, the company was sitting on a $137 billion mound of cash. Yet despite having become the highest-valued U.S. company by 2012 ($626 billion, with annual sales of $156 billion), Apple has become one of the leading targets of such short-term financial predation.

By 2013, Apple's soaring earnings attracted speculators like hyenas to raw meat. Activist shareholder Carl Icahn, a leading corporate raider since the 1980s, bought over $1.5 billion of Apple shares and mobilized a group of fellow financiers to demand a debt-leveraging ploy that he forecast would raise Apple's stock price above its 2012 level of $525 – by amassing enormous debt to engineer strictly financial gains.

Icahn had made his first fortune by raiding TWA in 1985. He paid off the debts that he took on to buy the airline by carving it up and leaving it bankrupt. By 2013 he had done this kind of financial smash-and-grab exercise often enough to create a vast pool of hedge fund capital, which he wielded to attack companies and make money off money.

Speculators such as Icahn search for cash-rich companies as the most lucrative targets for making a quick gain by using whatever is in the corporate treasury to bid up their stock price with share buybacks. The operation is purely financial, not involving any new business investment or other production advantage such as went into the creation of Macintosh computer, IPhones,

---

[101] Joe Nocera, "Carl Icahn's Bad Advice," *The New York Times*, October 25, 2014.

IMacs, IPods and ITunes. No information technology or sales strategy is involved. It is simple financial engineering: low-interest loans at 3% to buy company stock, bidding up its price. "This is a no-brainer to go buy stock in a company that can go borrow," Icahn explained.[102] The lower the interest rate, the larger amount of debt (new borrowing) that any given earnings flow can carry – and Apple's earnings were immense.

Apple's management had no particular need to pay out more dividends to establish a basis for future stock offerings. Its production and research are self-financed out of its earnings, and its capital reserves are large enough to fund any acquisitions it might need to make.[103] Maintaining its growth calls for using its capital reserves and earnings to acquire companies that owned complementary information technology patents or marketing power, and also to expand its own production facilities and long-term research and development. That is what a growth company does. Paying out earnings as dividends or using them to buy back a company's own stock, does not facilitate future sales or profit. All it does is leave fewer shares outstanding, so that earnings per share (and hence potential dividend payouts) will be higher.

That is what Icahn promised would raise Apple's stock price, so that "even without earnings growth, we think it ought to be worth $625."[104] Indeed, Apple's stock price rose 5 percent simply on the news of his buying into the company. It was a signal to Wall Street that a financial feeding frenzy was about to begin.

In September 2013, Icahn increased his stake in Apple by half a billion dollars, to more than $2 billion – about 0.5% of Apple – and demanded that the company spend $150 billion to buy back its shares. He had a large enough following among Apple shareholders and speculators that after he sent out a tweet that he had spoken to its CEO Tim Cook to suggest this, Apple's shares rose 2.2 percent (to $487.12), producing a one-day gain of $40 million for Icahn alone.[105]

---

[102] Ian Sherr and David Benoit, "Icahn Pushes Apple on Buyback," *Wall Street Journal*, August 14, 2013.

[103] As of January 2014, Apple's market capitalization was $456 billion. The decline from 2012 reflected a lower price/earnings multiple for the company's slower earnings growth in the slowing U.S. and global economy. In February 2014, Apple's market valuation lead was overtaken by Google.

[104] Sherr and Benoit, *op. cit.* See also "Bold attempt to unlock tech treasure chests," *Financial Times*, February 8, 2013.

[105] "Icahn beats the drum for $150bn Apple buyback," *Financial Times*, October 2, 2013.

The company already had promised to pay $100 billion in dividends and undertake the largest buyback any company had ever announced – $60 billion over the next three years. But while this "may seem like a large buyback," Icahn wrote, "it is simply not large enough given that Apple currently holds $147 billion of cash on its balance sheet."[106]

By February 2014, Icahn ended his efforts, claiming to have won the battle inasmuch as Apple had stepped up its stock repurchases "so close to fulfilling our requested repurchase target": $40 billion over the preceding twelve months (a record for U.S. companies), with $14 billion in just the two weeks preceding its quarterly earnings report.[107] Apple's earnings were slowing and the stock price fell back, but not by as much as would have occurred without this $40 billion removal of shares from the market. As a coda, on April 29, despite holding $150 billion in cash, Apple borrowed $12 billion and used the entire sum to buy back its stock (having borrowed $17 billion in the bond market the preceding April).

Its stock nonetheless fell $1.76 the next day to $592, valuing the company at $512 billion. The moral is that stock prices rise and fall, but only tangible capital assets and debt remain in place. But the financial world lives in the short run, not the long run. And Icahn's "barbarians at the gates" took their gains and ran.

Financial vs. industrial engineering

Stock buybacks are changing the character of industrial capitalism. Using earnings to repurchase a company's stock bids up its price, but diverts earnings away from being invested to expand the business. During the 1990s, for instance, IBM typically spent $10 billion of its earnings each year to buy its own stock. The company also borrowed – so in effect it was borrowing to bid up its stock price instead of to expand research and development. This policy led it to outsource research and development for its software, leaving Bill Gates

---

[106] David Benoit, "Carl Icahn Continues to Push Apple for $150 Billion Stock Buyback," *Wall Street Journal*, October 24, 2013. "A lot of critics are just keep saying why doesn't Icahn just leave our companies alone," he said. "To me that like saying: Why didn't Teddy Roosevelt leave the monopolies alone when they were strangling our economy."

[107] Ben Fox Rubin, "Icahn Ends Apple Stock Buyback Campaign," *Wall Street Journal*, February 10, 2014. There was plenty of criticism in the financial press. Michael MacKenzie and Nicole Bullock, "Money well spent?" *Financial Times*, October 13, 2014, notes: "Apple epitomises the US companies selling cheap debt and then ploughing the proceeds back into enormous purchases of their own stock to pay chunky dividends to shareholders… It lags behind only Exxon Mobil and IBM in terms of such largesse since the start of 2009."

and Microsoft to make the fortune that IBM would have obtained if it had used its earnings for in-house investment instead of buying back shares that it had long since issued.

IBM continued this policy during 2000–2014. It spent

> some $108 billion on its own shares ... It also paid out $30 billion in dividends. To help finance this share-buying spree, IBM loaded up on debt. While the company spent $138 billion on its shares and dividend payments, it spent just $59 billion on its own business through capital expenditures and $32 billion on acquisitions ... All of which is to say that IBM has arguably been spending its money on the wrong things: shareholders, rather than building its own business.
>
> "IBM's financials make it self-evident that its stock-rigging strategy is not about value creation through investment'," David A Stockman, the director of the Office of Management and Budget under President Ronald Reagan ... "IBM is a buyback machine on steroids that has been a huge stock-market winner by virtue of massaging, medicating and manipulating" its earnings per share.[108]

Basically, the company's share buybacks announced to the world that IBM was no longer a growth company and could not think of a new avenue to develop in-house that would be more remunerative than using its flow of earnings to liquidate its share ownership. It ended up selling its laptop personal computers to Lenovo in China, concentrating on its traditional large-hardware market.

This is not a long-term growth strategy, but it enriches financial speculators during the period in which the company is burning up its shares. The key to creating wealth in this purely financial manner is simple mathematics: interest-rate arbitrage. The idea is to borrow at a low rate (*i.e.*, the 3% at which Icahn claimed Apple could obtain credit) and buy shares yielding a higher return on equity (say, 10%), and pay out the difference to shareholders. Debt replaces equity.

This is why debt/equity ratios have risen for corporate America. It is symptomatic of the economy's overall rise in debt/income and debt/GDP ratios. By 2004, Standard and Poor's reported that the S&P 500 companies spent $197 billion on buying back their own shares. The pace of buybacks accelerated to over $100 billion a quarter by 2006, by which time "268 of the companies in the S&P 500 bought back shares in the first quarter, with nearly 110 of them cutting their diluted shares outstanding by at least 4% from a year earlier. ... Exxon Mobil Corp., Microsoft Corp. and Time Warner Inc. were the biggest buyers of their own shares during the first quarter, spending $14.37 billion combined," prompting a *Wall Street Journal* report to conclude:

---

[108] Mike Whitney, "Do Tumbling Buybacks Signal Another Market Crash?" *Counterpunch*, October 23, 2014.

A company that aggressively buys its own shares on the market can give investors a skewed picture of its earnings growth. When a company reduces its shares outstanding, it will report higher earnings per share, even if its total earnings don't grow by a penny, simply because those profits are spread across fewer shares. Exxon Mobil's net income rose 6.9% in the first quarter, but that turned into a 12.3% earnings-per-share increase after share buybacks, according to S&P."[109]

Creating financial wealth by debt leverage instead of new tangible investment

A recent *Harvard Business Review* article calculated that for the decade 2003-2012, the 449 companies publicly listed in the S&P 500 index "used 54% of their earnings – a total of $2.4 trillion – to buy back their own stock" – even more than the 37% paid as dividends.[110] This left only 9% of earnings available for new capital investment. Summarizing the article's statistics, a *Financial Times* columnist noted: "seven of the top 10 largest share re-purchasers spent more on buybacks and dividends than their entire net income between 2003 and 2012. In the case of Hewlett-Packard, which spent $73bn, it was almost double its profits. ... Others, such as Microsoft (125 per cent), Cisco (121 per cent) and Intel (109 per cent) were even more extravagant."[111]

This management strategy created financial wealth by elevating the stock price, not by producing more goods. Earnings per share rose not because companies actually earned more, but because there were fewer shares outstanding among which to spread the earnings. Many of the companies downsized and outsourced their employment and production.

The immediate beneficiaries were corporate officers exercising their stock options. These accounted for 42% of executive compensation (with a further 41% coming from payment in the form of stock awards) for the 500 highest-paid executives in 2012. This averaged out to $30.3 million each, with over 80% coming from stock options and bonuses tied to their price performance. In effect, companies were buying up the stocks created to reward these execu-

---

[109] "Big Companies Put Record Sums Into Buybacks. Repurchases Aim to Bolster Shares but They Also Signal Hesitancy to Invest in Growth," *The Wall Street Journal*, June 12, 2006. Cisco Systems "approved the repurchase of an additional $5 billion of its own stock, on top of a $35 billion repurchase plan it announced five years ago. The week before, Tribune Co. announced a $2 billion buyback, to be financed by debt, in a decision that sparked controversy on the company's board, with representatives of the Chandler family, one of the company's biggest shareholders, objecting to the massive outlay."

[110] William Lazonick, "Profits Without Prosperity," *Harvard Business Review*, September 2014. He is an economics professor at the University of Massachusetts (Lowell campus).

[111] Edward Luce, "The short-sighted US buyback boom," *Financial Times*, September 22, 2014.

tives, supporting their cash price. And the executive rewards themselves were linked to the stock price! No wonder management pursued this easy self-enrichment policy. Many executives even pushed up their stock price by borrowing to buy up their shares and hence earning higher performance bonuses tied to the price rise.

"The debt incurred will have to be serviced by future earnings," Paul Craig Roberts pointed out. "This is not a picture of capitalism that is driving the economy by investment."[112] Why should investors buy into a company that isn't investing in its own business?

The explanation is that financial engineering has replaced industrial engineering. Stocks of companies whose managers use earnings for share buybacks have outperformed those of old-fashioned industrial companies that reinvest their earnings in tangible capital formation and new hiring to expand sales.

Unlike the corporate raiders of the 1980s – infamous as barbarians at the gate "leveraging other people's money to fund takeovers," today's corporate executives raid their own company's revenue stream. They are backed by self-proclaimed shareholder activists. The result is financial short-termism by managers who take the money and run. The management philosophy is extractive, not productive in the sense of adding to society's means of production or living standards.

The Federal Reserve's policy of Quantitative Easing implemented in 2008 (creating more bank reserves to lend out to buy assets) has made it increasingly profitable to borrow from banks at a low interest rate, buy stocks whose dividends yield a higher return, and pocket the difference. This interest/dividend arbitrage pushes up stock prices, by steering more bank credit to enough capital gains to cover what is paid in dividends and bank interest. Since its post-crash low of March 2009, the S&P 500 stock index nearly tripled – while average wages and other economic indicators stagnated in the wake of the debt overhead left in the wake of the financial crisis.

But in the process, the stock market and indeed the corporate sector becomes more highly indebted – the same scenario that ravaged the real estate market. This is not new. As early as 1910, Rudolf Hilferding's *Finanzkapital* described high finance as extractive: "Property ceases to express any specific relation of production and becomes a claim to the yield, apparently unconnected with any particular activity."[113] The effect of financialization is to divert

---

[112] Paul Craig Roberts, "Illusionary Growth," *Counterpunch*, October 3-5, 2014
[113] Letter of Mr Philip Pilkington, Political Economy Research Group, Kingston University, *Financial Times*, September 28, 2014.

corporate cash away from investment and job creation. In the wake of this debt deflation (described below in Chapter 11), Federal Reserve Chairman Janet Yellen said: "it speaks to the depth of the damage that, five years after the end of the recession, the labor market has yet to fully recover."[114] Such recovery is not the aim of financial engineering. Most corporate strategists view low wages as a benefit, not a detriment.

Yet as far as academic economics is concerned, higher dividend payouts should not matter. The Modigliani-Miller theorem (named for Nobel Prize-winning Franco Modigliani and Merton Miller) deems dividends irrelevant by "proving" mathematically (in the way that economists do) that payout ratios make no difference in stock valuation, because investors are smart enough to treat the rise in book value stemming from capital re-investment on the same plane as dividend payouts. This principle that dividend yields make no difference in stock pricing is mainstream business school teaching.

If the academics are right and high finance is all knowing and a wise allocator of resources, would corporate raiders exist? The Modigliani-Miller portrait of investors ignores the financial maneuvering to raise stocks in the short run to reward hit-and-run speculators and managers whose bonuses are tied to stock prices. Investors may be smart, but are they really interested in taking the long-term planning role that academic economists wish they would do? Or, do they want to liquefy assets, take the money and run?

A company's cash position does not improve from higher stock prices unless it plans to issue new equity at the higher price – which has not been happening. Also, rising price/earnings ratios mean *lower* dividend yields for *new* buyers. The investment focus shifts away from investing to expand business and earn more, to seeking capital gains.

These asset-price gains from financialization do not increase tangible wealth. They are leveraged by rising debt levels. And because interest payments are tax-deductible, turning profits into interest payments has the fiscal effect of deepening government budget deficits. At the 50 percent corporate tax rate of the early 1980s, companies were able to pay out twice as much of their earnings in the form of interest to creditors than they could pay in dividends to stockholders. This tax-deductibility of interest led stockholders to be replaced by bondholders – especially junk-bond holders. Equity was replaced by debt.

The tax subsidy for debt over stock market financing is a major catalyst to debt-leveraged buyouts (LBOs) and share buybacks. The new breed of corpo-

---

[114] Janet L. Yellen, "Labor Market Dynamics and Monetary Policy," speech at the Federal Reserve Bank of Kansas City Economic Symposium, Jackson Hole, Wyoming, August 22, 2014.

rate raiders and "financial engineers" pay themselves interest and produce capital gains with the profits hitherto shared with federal, state and local tax collectors. The government budget deficits deepens, and the Treasury issues more bonds (and looks to raise taxes from labor and consumers). The entire economy becomes more debt-leveraged, paying income to creditors – headed by the One Percent – instead of investing it or spending to raise living standards. This phenomenon is the major theme of this book.

**

This is not how financial systems were expected to evolve a century ago. The Industrial Revolution inspired a long debate over how best to mobilize banking and finance to fund capital investment: by debt or by issuing equity stock? Debt takes the form of interest-bearing loans or bonds. The interest payment is stipulated in advance, regardless for how much the business earns. The alternative is equity ownership in the form of saleable partnership slices. Stocks usually pay higher returns, because dividends may be cut back when business turns down. That is what makes equity ownership claims safer for the company to issue.

Debts require interest to be paid at a stipulated pace without regard for what the debtor earns. If a payment is missed, creditors have the right to foreclose on whatever assets are pledged as collateral. To protect themselves, debtors keep a liquid savings cushion on hand to cover the risk of declining income. Paying interest and amortization thus leaves less available to spend. The virtue of financing companies by issuing shares is that companies free of debt can use their income for whatever they wish, without having to first pay the bank or other debts. Also, shares in equity ownership – stocks in a company – are as long-term as the company remains in business or until the company buys them back. But bank loans are extended for relatively short periods or take the form of a line of credit (like a credit card) that bankers can call in at their discretion.

Banks hesitate to finance new ventures. They prefer to lend against collateral on which they can foreclose if debtors cannot meet their scheduled payment. This obliges debtors to keep liquid savings on hand, leaving less for current spending. In antiquity, debtors who could not pay fell into bondage to their creditors. That is the original literal meaning of bond: a fetter imprisoning the debtor. Now that debtors' prisons have been phased out, creditors have recourse to the debtor's property and future earnings. Homeowners pledge their real estate to back their mortgage debts, companies pledge their assets, and clients of payday loan sharks pledge their kneecaps.

The problem is that instead of raising capital to fund new capital investment and avoid debt, the stock market has been turned into a vehicle for debt-financed takeovers, replacing equity with debt. Starting with the high-interest "junk" bonds issued from 1977 onward, a class of raiders and "buyout kings" like Carl Icahn emerged to become Wall Street's most lucrative market. Financial empire builders borrowed from banks and institutional bond buyers to buy out existing stockholders.

Takeover financing pays an interest rate premium because of the relatively high risk that the process will drive targeted companies bankrupt, or at least will strip their capital and slow their growth by raising their debt/equity ratio. The process is called debt leveraging. It has been welcomed as "wealth creation," as if it enriches the economy rather than leaving less for new investment and hiring.

Chapter 9 explains how the stock market has evolved, and how today's financial system has become parasitic and diverged from the path that was expected a century ago, to focus on rent extraction instead of industrial finance, and to "create wealth" by financial engineering to create short-term capital gains rather than by enhancing the economy's production and viability.

9

From the Stock Market's Origins to Junk Bonding

Researchers at Stanford University have concluded that pressure to meet quarterly earnings targets may be reducing research and development spending, and cutting US growth by 0.1 percentage points a year. Others have found that privately held companies, free to take a longer-term approach, invest at almost 2.5 times the rate of publicly held counterparts in the same industries. This persistent lower investment rate among America's biggest 350 listed companies may be reducing US growth by an additional 0.2 percentage points a year.

Much of the problem stems from the way the vast majority of asset owners pay the people who manage their money. On average, 74 per cent of remuneration is paid in cash, and tied to outperforming an annual stock market benchmark. The result is an obsession with next quarter's earnings rather than the next 10 years'.

Financial Times, April 1, 2015[115]

The idea that banking and finance should fund new direct investment in means of production is an ideal of the Industrial Revolution, by economists thinking about how to create a better role for banking, a better way to mobilize peoples' savings. Chapter 7 has described how hope that banking might be industrialized began to be realized in Germany, but faded away after World War I. The idea was absent from the initial four thousand years of financial history. It remains elusive today. So rather than being an aberration, the evolution of predatory finance in Wall Street and the City of London are simply continuing an age-old trajectory.

Origins of modern banking and the stock market

The origins of banking, financial partnerships and shares in enterprises are to be found in the temples and palaces of the ancient Near East at the inception of the Bronze Age (3200–1200 BC). From the time interest-bearing debt was

---

[115] Dominic Barton and Mark Wiseman, "Short-term profit can cost shareholders dear," *Financial Times*, April 1, 2015.

innovated in Mesopotamia to finance commerce and provide agricultural credit around 3000 BC, there is no trace of borrowing to manufacture goods in workshops, and rarely to buy land. Business credit came into the picture initially to consign temple handicrafts or commodities to seafaring merchants and caravans for long-distance commerce.

By classical antiquity wealthy individuals were producing pottery, metalwork, textiles and other products for sale. There was little business debt except for trade partnerships, where debt financing served as a kind of maritime insurance. The wealthy used their profits from this commerce and money lending to buy land, which was the major determinant of social status and economic patronage throughout antiquity. (What modern historians call "banks" were family or public lenders using mainly their own money, not deposits.) Purchases of real estate and other assets were for cash.

Even in modern times it has been rare for banks to finance investment in industrial production. Until the 19th century most business loans were to fund the sale (usually exportation) of goods *after* they were produced, not to put workshops and factories in place. Banks thus found their major market in international trade, which helps explain why the British bank spokesman David Ricardo advocated an international specialization of labor instead of national self-sufficiency in food and other basic needs.[116]

European banking in its modern form dates from the Crusades, catalyzed by the vast infusion of silver and gold looted from Constantinople. (The Doge of Venice financed the conquest in exchange for a quarter of the spoils – an equity investment, not a debt claim.) As in antiquity, temples took the lead in developing contractual banking practice over far-flung networks. The largest Church banking orders were the Knights Templar and the Order of St. John, also known as the Knights Hospitallers. The indebted rulers of France and England grabbed the Templars' wealth in 1306, when King Phillip of France conveniently accused the order of heresy and sodomy, the traditional metaphor for "sterile lending" and abusive anti-social behavior.[117]

---

[116] I explain how self-serving free trade theory and a global division of labor is to the financial class in *Trade, Development and Foreign Debt: A History of Theories of Polarization v. Convergence in the World Economy* (2nd ed., ISLET 2010 [1992]).

[117] For a discussion see G. Legman, *The Guilt of the Templars* (New York, 1966), p. 37; and Norman Cohn, *Europe's Inner Demons* (New York, 1975), pp. xi, 41, 85. Raymond Oursel, *Les Proces des Templiers* (Paris, 1955) gives a transcript, and Michael Goodrich reviews the analogy between sodomy and unproductive debt, see, *The Unmentionable Vice: Homosexuality in the Later Medieval Period* (Santa Barbara, 1979), p. 9.

Their practices were emulated by private bankers, headed by those close to the papacy. Charging interest was legitimized by the fact that lenders and the main borrowers were at the top of the social pyramid. Bankers lent to rulers to pay Peter's Pence (originally a levy of a penny per household in a kingdom) and other tribute to the papacy, and increasingly to fight wars. But warfare is not usually a paying proposition, and if the sinews of war are money, this usually meant credit. Hopes of profiting from military conquest quickly gave way to running into debt.

Christian sanctions against charging interest were strong enough so that banks focused on charging *agio*, ostensibly a fee for converting currency and transferring payments. Until the 19th century the focus of banking remained international, starting in the 14th century with Italian bankers taking the lead in organizing a triangular flow of goods and money. To meet papal demands for contributions, Britain exported wool to Flanders, where it was woven into textiles and sold mainly to the Italians.

Historically, most lending to governments has focused on war borrowing. When the Habsburgs and other rulers had trouble paying their debts, bankers pressed for payment in the form of a transfer of ownership of mines and other natural resources in the public domain. Rulers also created commercial monopolies to privatize: the East and West Indies Companies of Holland, Britain and France, and similar exclusive privileges (literally "private law") to trade with specific regions or similar. These Crown Corporations paid dividends out of monopoly rent extraction, not profits from industrial manufacturing.

From royal war debts to the stock market

Stock markets in their modern form were created largely to sell shares in these new royal monopolies, taking payment in government bonds. This is how Britain created the East India Company in 1600, the Bank of England in 1694 (with its monopoly on bank-note issue) and similar commercial trading privileges with particular regions or other monopoly rights to be sold off, mainly to bondholders.

To maximize what they received for these monopolies, governments promoted stock markets as a speculative vehicle. The "madness of crowds" always has required fanning by public officials and the opinion makers. To maximize what they could get from bondholders, the British and French governments sponsored financial bubbles, aiming to free themselves from the need to levy taxes to pay interest. What made the Mississippi and South Sea bubbles of the 1710s different from earlier sales of royal monopolies in the stock market was that they were not worth anywhere near what the public was convinced to pay. Yet the experience helped catalyze the stock market as a popular investment vehicle. Its appeal – and that of financial bubbles – has always been hopes to make quick and easy gains, usually involving debt leveraging.

The tactics were refined by John Law, the Scottish economist who served as Comptroller General of France under the Duke of Orleans in the early 1700s. To dispose of France's royal debt, he created the Mississippi Company to develop plantation slavery in what later was called the Louisiana territory (named for Louis XIV). Britain emulated the scheme, hoping to retire its war debts by privatizing the *asiento* slave trade monopoly its navy had won from Spain. This treaty became the sole asset of the newly incorporated South Sea Company, named for the South Atlantic across which slaves were shipped from Africa to the New World. Together, these two government-sponsored bubbles promised enormous wealth from 18th century's the major growth sector: the African slave trade, that century's version the dot.com bubble of the 1990s. The beneficiaries were the French and British governments, along with insiders who became part of what today is called a pump and dump operation.

The French and British governments accepted payment for stock in these companies in their own bonds – at full par value. This provided a giveaway to bondholders, because the bonds could be bought at a steep discount, reflecting widespread doubt that they could actually be paid. Bond prices rose as new buyers used them to buy shares in the Mississippi and South Sea companies.

Almost no money raised by these companies was actually invested to undertake business and generate a profit. What was sold was hope – shares in purely potential gains. Investors only needed to put down about 10 percent of the purchase price of the stock to subscribe. By the time the second payment was due, the stock price may have been bid up by at least that amount, doubling the initial down payment. This debt leveraging – buying on credit with only a small down payment – magnifies gains and losses in asset prices on both the upside and downside.[118] It was the strategy Margaret Thatcher used to popularize the privatization of British Telecom and subsequent selloffs of government assets, providing quick speculative gains to early buyers with small down payments.

The government tactic was to sell stocks in order to retire its bonds instead of defaulting on them, by persuading bondholders to swap their bonds for

---

[118] If an investor only needs to put down 10 percent of the purchase price of a stock (or a home), the overall market price need rise only by 10 percent to double the equity that the investor has paid. But if the price of a stock or real estate asset falls by 10 percent, the entire down payment is wiped out – a 100% loss.

shares in the new companies. When the swap was completed, the stock price was allowed to plunge. The government shed crocodile tears at the "madness of crowds" that it itself had encouraged! It was a carefully orchestrated madness. Insiders avoided loss by selling out in time.

Making stock market gains from financial leverage and rent extraction

The privatization of monopolies, canals or national railroad systems always has been associated with insider dealing and fraud, ending with latecomer buyers holding a collapsing financial bag. Yet despite insider manipulations and subsequent collapse, the idea of making capital gains while putting down only a fraction of the purchase price seized the public imagination. It offered the temptation of outsiders making the huge gains that insiders tended to monopolize. It also is as if the stock market bubble was producing gains by playing a productive role in funding new capital investment. But since its inception, stock prices have been pushed up more by financial engineering than by new capital investment.

The irony of the stock market is that corporations were created to replace short-term partnerships for voyages and other such ventures. Instead of having to divide up profits at the end of each voyage or upon the death of major partners, corporations have been given a permanent existence, divided into shares that were transferable.

Yet the financial time frame is still short-term. This is especially true of bankers, who did little to finance the Industrial Revolution. The economic historian George W. Edwards has found that Britain's "investment banking houses had little to do with the financing of corporations or with industrial undertakings. The great investment houses bitterly opposed the numerous corporate issues which were floated in 1824 and 1825," hoping to control industry by bank credit. "The investment houses for a long time refused to take part even in the financing of the British railways."[119]

Banks and other lenders advanced credit to industry only if proprietors could show orders for their products, or bills falling due for sales. Most of all, banks financed shipments of goods, spanning the time gap between production, delivery and receipt of payment by the customer, usually payable after 90 days. This financing involved foreign exchange fees for the banks as well as interest. But it was a short-term business.

---

[119] George W. Edwards, *The Evolution of Finance Capitalism* (1938), pp. 16f.

Mortgage credit was available against whatever real estate or easily marketable assets could be pledged as collateral and taken in case of non-payment. But the Industrial Revolution's leading entrepreneurs could obtain bank credit only after investing their own funds to get production underway. From James Watt's steam engine in the late 18th century to Henry Ford's automobile in the early 20th century, banks were not in the foresight business.

Stock markets really began to take off in the 19th century for railroads and canals, other basic infrastructure, monopolies and trusts. These undertakings were rife with financial fraud, headed by the Panama and Suez Canal schemes. America's stock market consisted mainly of railroad stocks during its early years, which transferred enormous sums of British and other European savings to the United States. Wall Street operators skimmed off much of the inflow. A favorite tactic was "stock watering," a practice of proprietors issuing stock to themselves, "diluting" the ownership of existing shareholders.

Banks favored railroads and public utilities whose income streams could be easily forecast, and large real estate borrowers with land pledged as collateral. Manufacturing enterprises only obtained significant bank and stock market credit after companies had grown fairly large with stable earnings. Growth potential hardly qualified. By the 1920s, Britain's banks were broadly criticized for their failure to finance industry, and for favoring international clients rather than domestic ones.[120]

Apart from infrastructure speculation, the stock market was mainly a vehicle for manipulators to buy ownership rights of natural monopolies and rent-seeking privileges, especially to create large trusts such as U.S. Steel and Standard Oil. Banks, pension funds and other financial institutions have lent increasingly for speculation in stocks and bonds, including today's debt-leveraged buyouts for mergers, acquisitions and outright raids.

Trade financing was evolving into investment banking, focusing on real estate, oil and other natural resources, and funding speculation in stocks, foreign bonds and currencies. These high-risk activities held consumer and business deposits hostage to financial gambling and raiding, leading to the 1929 crash and the Great Depression. The economic wreckage made it obvious that

---

[120] Lloyd George called them "the stronghold of reaction" (see Thomas Johnston, *The Financiers and the Nation* [London 1934:138]). Ernest Bevin, G. D. H. Cole and other members of the British Labour Party criticized banks in *The Crisis* (London 1931). See also G. D. H. Cole, *The Socialisation of Banking* (London 1931), and John Wilmot, *Labour's Way to Control Banking and Finance* (London 1935). The Labour Party's proposed solution was to nationalize the Bank of England, and in 1933 to recommend socializing the joint-stock banks as well. Keynes was sympathetic in "A New Economic Policy for England," *Economic Forum*, Winter 1932–33:29–37.

the U.S. financial system needed to be insulated from such speculation. Congress passed the Glass-Steagall Act in 1933 to isolate financial speculation from personal and basic business banking. Other New Deal reforms included creation of the Securities and Exchange Commission (SEC), the Federal Deposit Insurance Corp. (FDIC) and a shift to 30-year home mortgages instead of the short three-year time frame.[121] These reforms succeeded in stabilizing banking through the 1940s up to the 1970s.

The junk-bonding of American industry: replacing equity with high-interest debt

The 1980s saw a reversal in the stock market's role. Instead of raising funds for industry by issuing shares to finance new capital investment, the market has become an arena to *retire* stocks by replacing them with bonds. Raiders and ambitious empire-builders raise money to buy out stockholders by borrowing from banks, institutional investors, hedge funds and bond investors. Over the past three decades more stocks have been bought back than new shares have been issued. This has shifted the stock market's role as an alternative to debt, to buying out stockholders by borrowing. Buyouts are "leveraged" (or in British jargon, "geared") to replace stocks with bonds and bank debt. The aim is to make money financially.

A review of the post-1980 financial changes supports Federal Reserve Chairman Paul Volcker's quip that the ATM cash machine is the only positive innovation to come out of the past generation. From the junk bond takeovers of the 1980s (the first hostile takeovers were financed in 1983, by Drexel Burnham Lambert) to the dot.com bubble of the 1990s mutating into the "activist shareholder" and hedge fund proliferation of the 2000s, high finance has promoted debt at the expense of equity, and used it to make short-term financial returns rather than funding new capital investment.

The result is that despite 20th-century reformers' hopes to see the stock market promote industrial capital formation, it has become a vehicle for loading companies down with debt and cutting back their long-term investment. Unlike dividends to shareholders, interest charges on debt cannot be reduced when sales and earnings turn down. Companies that replace equity with debt lose economic flexibility and must live on short financial leashes.

---

[121] Until the 1930s, mortgage loans typically were for only three years. When depositors began to pull out their funds, banks stopped rolling over their loans. Few homeowners had the cash or marketable assets to pay off the balance. If they did not protect themselves by keeping a high amount of savings, they risked losing their homes when the banks foreclosed. This prompted the innovation of 30-year mortgages to avoid such risk.

Replacing stocks with bonds and other debt makes corporate business more fragile and risky, and crowds out funds available for new capital investment. And when downturns come, control passes to creditors.

The term "junk bonds" was coined to reflect high-interest bonds issued to corporate raiders and takeover kings to buy companies with borrowed credit (or, less negatively, to finance smaller new business without a track record or deemed too risky to obtain normal bank credit). Catalyzed by Michael Milken at Drexel Burnham, this financial takeover of industry required a legal trans-formation, and Drexel's tactics were shaped largely by the law firm of Skadden Arps.[122] Perfecting the technique of hostile takeovers along lines hitherto shunned by "white shoe" lawyers, the new mentality is reflected in a *New York Times* piece published in the obituary of the law firm's rainmaker Joe Flom:

He was rejected by Manhattan firms where he hoped to work because he was Jewish … Mr. Flom and Skadden became specialists at counseling about bet-your-company deals because the old-style white-shoe firms initially spurned the work. … The verb Skaddenize was coined to describe its aggressive style. … "We've got to show the bastards that you don't have to be born into it," Mr. Flom exhorted colleagues.[123]

The result of mergers by "a renegade law firm serving the nation's fortunes movement," a biographer of the firm concludes, "was widespread financial distress, business failure, and corporate bankruptcy."[124] These transfers of rev-enue to corporate raiders were squeezed out "from employees of the target company (through layoffs and wage cuts); from pensioners (through so-called reversions, or seizures, of pension funds); from bondholders (through the decrease in the value of their bonds); from governments (through the loss of tax revenues); and from other so-called corporate stakeholders to whom exec-utives were responsible."[125]

From 1981 the pace of leveraged buyouts financed by junk bonds doubled approximately every year, from $1.2 billion in 1981 to reach a $31 billion

---

[122] The story is told in Connie Bruck, P*redators' Ball: The Inside Story of Drexel Burnham and the Rise of the Junk Bond Raiders* (1988), Bryan Burrough and John Helyar, *Barbarians at the Gate: The Fall of RJR Nabisco* (1989) and a host of other popular treatments. Nabisco's $25 billion takeover, the largest of its day back in 1988, was advised by the law firm of Skadden Arps. See Lincoln Caplan, *Skadden: Power, Money, and the Rise of a Legal Empire* (1993).

[123] Lincoln Caplan, "Joe Flom," *The New York Times*, February 27, 2011. For Flom's role in developing the tactics of raids, mergers and acquisitions, see Malcolm Gladwell, *Outliers: The Story of Success*, (2008).

[124] Caplan, *Skadden*, p. 227.

[125] Caplan, *Skadden*, p. 220.

plateau by 1986.[126] Raiders made themselves billionaires, and justified becoming so rich by claiming that this reflected how much more efficiently they were running the companies and "squeezing the fat" out of them. Along similar lines, "activist shareholders" claimed that bringing pressure on management to inflate stock prices would increase the economy's wealth by streamlining lazy or inefficient managers. The reality is that instead of improving under-performing companies, corporate raiders focus on well-financed companies – like Apple – with available cash or real estate ("fat") to empty out. Also deemed "fat" is profit used for new capital investment or to build up a cash cushion against risk. This cash flow is turned into a financial diet to be devoured by raiders, vulture funds, and a broadening range of institutional investors seeking higher income as fast as they can get it. And the fastest way is to dismantle industrial production and live in the financial short run.

Pumpers and Dumpers

While finance had little direct interface with industrial investment prior to modern times, at least it did not interfere. Matters changed in the 1980s when aggressive "junk bond" financing and leveraged buyouts began to lay waste to the industrial economy rather than funding its growth. Industry has been starved of capital spending not to make it more efficient but merely to make earnings statements, dividend payouts and stock prices more attractive in the short run. Vast new fortunes were made simply by "pumping and dumping" companies.

Carl Icahn was the king of "pumpers and dumpers." His fight in 2005–06 to carve up Time Warner pressed predatory finance to new limits. The company was still recovering from the shock of what has been dubbed the "biggest mistake in corporate history": its disastrous merger with AOL. Time Warner became the object of financial maneuverings by Icahn and other "activist shareholders" seeking arbitrage gains by pushing up stock prices for a fillip lasting long enough to enable the interlopers to take their winnings and run.

In November 2005 Icahn bought over 3 percent of the company's stock. Other hedge funds controlling a similar amount joined him in what was then the largest proxy fight in U.S. corporate history. Icahn's investment bank, Lazard, also set a precedent. The bank's client base traditionally consisted of large blue-chip companies. Then Lazard broke the gentleman's agreement – their upper class consciousness – by advising predatory attackers. Lazard's Bruce Wasserstein produced a 343-page report urging Time Warner to

---

[126] *Ibid.*, p. 212.

quadruple its pace of annual stock buybacks from $5 billion to $20 billion to bid up its stock price. The company also was asked to break itself into four parts and sell them off to pay quick dividends to stockholders.

Around the same time, William Ackman's Pershing Square Capital hedge fund bought options on 4.9 percent of McDonald's. Vornado Realty Trust bought another 1.2 percent, T2 Partners some more, and a few other funds joined in to mount a proxy contest for control of McDonald's. This was the second fast food company that Ackman had attacked. Earlier he had cornered 9.3 percent of Wendy's stock – enough to force it to spin off its Horton's coffee-shop division and pay out the proceeds as a special dividend.

Ackman's plan for McDonalds was along the same lines, but much bolder. He wanted the company to sell two-thirds of the restaurants it owned for $3.3 billion, and raise $9 to $15 billion more by mortgaging its real estate to the hilt, using the proceeds to buy back its shares. It would break off its wholly owned restaurants into a distinct property company (McOpCo) and lease the sites back to McDonald's franchise holders. Ackman forecast that these policies would create an income stream enabling the new company to sell 20 percent of its shares to raise a further $1.3 billion, enabling McDonald's to triple its dividend payouts to stockholders from 67 cents to $2 per share.[127]

These carve-ups were projected to raise McDonald's stock price by about 10 percent (around $2 to $4 per share), despite reducing the company's net worth by paying out the value of its assets. For Ackman's plan to work, buyers of McDonald's shares would focus on the company's dividend yield, not its long-term prospects. McDonald's officers pointed out that this would strip its assets and leave it deeply indebted. Characterizing Ackman's plan as "financial engineering,"[128] the company's Chief Financial Officer Matthew Paull warned that it would discourage new franchise purchases by raising the threat that the proposed real estate affiliate might increase rents, siphoning off the restaurant's profits.

But as the *Wall Street Journal* observed: "In the hedge-fund world, 'financial engineering' isn't a pejorative." However, it acknowledged, sometimes "companies live to regret share-repurchase decisions. In the late 1990s, both General

[127] "Investor urges McDonald's to sell off restaurants," *Financial Times*, Nov. 14, 2005. Whitney Tilson, whose T2 Partners hedge fund joined Ackman's raid, earlier had urged Wal-Mart to buy back its stock and "take advantage of the low interest-rate environment and take on debt, allowing it to both expand and buy back shares." Demands for share buybacks thus were becoming the new norm.
[128] Alan Murray, "Attack on McDonald's Heralds a New Order," *Wall Street Journal*, November 23, 2005.

Motors Corp. and Ford Motor Co. had large cash positions, which investors saw as 'lazy assets' that the companies would spend foolishly ... The companies responded with large share-repurchase programs, buying stock at much higher price levels than now with cash that would have helped them in their current straits."[129] Ackman's strategy would have made McDonald's more financially fragile and set it along the ruinous path that had led General Motors to survive only by the 2008 public bailout.

It was not as if McDonald's needed rescuing. It already had raised its dividend by 185 percent since 2002, tripling its share price at a time when most stock market averages were drifting downward. None of the hedge-fund proposals involved changing the restaurant's management or supplying innovations in production or sales. The aim was pure debt leveraging – borrowing against property and paying out the loan proceeds to shareholders. This would spark a price jump, brief but sufficient to enable the hedge funds to dump their shares for a quick killing, leaving the company deep in debt.

By the time the dust settled in February 2006, Icahn and Ackman both had failed in their takeover attempts. Time Warner and McDonald's remained in one piece. Icahn was unable to convince most shareholders that he could improve significantly on Time Warner's stock market performance. Its shares remained stuck around $18, far from the $26 level he claimed his policies would justify. Lazard, which had negotiated a fee of $5 million for every $1 increase in Time Warner's share price, also lost.[130] Still, the attack had its effect: It forced Time Warner to quadruple its share buybacks to $20 billion annually, and to slash operating expenses by $1 billion. This prompted Fitch Ratings to downgrade the company's bonds a notch, from BBB+ to BBB.

Ackman did better with McDonald's. His hedge fund leveraged its purchase of shares by debt-financed options at a low interest rate, and cleaned up when the shares jumped by 11 percent by January 2006. But taken together, these two episodes show how little this kind of hit-and-run finance has to do with industrial capital formation.

By 2006, hedge funds – collections of wealth for raiders to use as a basis for borrowing to take over companies – were accounting for nearly half the trades on the London and New York stock exchanges, and their share is substantially higher today. Although they only control a small percentage of equity, their aggressive behavior has gained support from pension funds and other

---

[129] Justin Lahart, "Cash-Rich Firms Urged to Spend," *Wall Street Journal*, Nov. 21, 2005
[130] "Icahn Plan For a Split Gets a Push," *The New York Times*, February 8, 2006.

investors that join them in subordinating the industrial economy to financial managers. "Even the very best management teams aren't safe in today's free-for-all corporate environment," one report described the new financial perspective. "Holding so much [cash] is inefficient: companies reduce their return on equity by having too little debt. That makes the smaller ones targets for private equity funds."[131]

Google's strategy to avoid the stock market's financialization threats

The Internet search company Google sought to avoid the underwriting practices that had left Apple and other companies with only a portion of what they proved to be worth within just a few hours of early trading. Google's founders had started by selling 10-percent partnerships to two venture capital firms, Sequoia Capital and Kleiner Perkins Caufield & Byers, for $12.5 million each in 1999. The value of these holdings soared to nearly $40 billion when Google went public in 2004 – a 1,600-fold return on the venture capitalists' five-year investment.

This valuation was largely the result of the company adopting a strategy to price its initial public offering at what its stock normally would be worth at the end of the first day of trading, not at the opening insiders' price. Sidestepping the most obvious traps, Google limited the underwriting commission for investment bankers to just 3 percent, less than half the 7 percent rake-off that had become common for information technology companies.

The rationalization for this high fee is that it is hard to forecast sales and profits for untested new technology in today's rapidly evolving world. The reality is that most technology analysts and brokers serve merely as salesmen with only crude and often fanciful projections, as the collapse of the dot.com bubble in 2000 showed.

To avoid the usual rapacious underpricing of its shares, Google hired Morgan Stanley and Credit Suisse First Boston to hold a "Dutch auction," in which prospective buyers were invited to submit bids. The auction started with a high price and then lowered it until reaching a level that cleared the market. This method of bidding gave all buyers within the bidding range an opportunity to buy shares at the moment the issue was offered, instead of the standard practice of giving speculators the first low-priced picks so that they could turn around and make a windfall gain by flipping the stock to later buyers.

---

[131] Alan Murray, "Attack on McDonald's Heralds a New Order," *Wall Street Journal*, Nov. 23, 2005.

In a letter included with the "Owners Manual" for their stock offering, Google's founders, Larry Page and Sergey Brin, spelled out their rationale for avoiding the usual financial policy yielding management control to Wall Street financiers. To make sure that speculators would not have an opportunity to "jeopardize the independence and focused objectivity that have been most important in Google's past success and that we consider most fundamental for its future," Google limited voting power in its publicly traded shares to only one-tenth of that of the shares kept by the company's founders. Most important of all, they explained: "If opportunities arise that might cause us to sacrifice short-term results but are in the best long-term interest of our shareholders, we will take those opportunities. ... We will not shy away from high-risk, high-reward projects because of short-term earnings pressure."[132]

Wall Street recoiled. "Let's hope this doesn't become a precedent," one banker remarked.[133] A hedge fund manager told the *New York Times* that he thought "shareholders should punish Google for its failure to give new investors the same rights as its founders. Once a company goes public, its founders must understand and accept that they are responsible to public shareholders and are no longer fully in control."[134]

But this was precisely what Google sought to avoid. Its aim was to free the company from financial techniques designed to generate gains for Wall Street rather than for the industries that produced and sold actual goods and production services. At issue was using corporate profits to expand the business rather than giving quick hit-and-run returns to the wealthiest One Percent that own the hedge funds and most bank bonds.

But it did set a precedent. A decade later Michael Dell explained his logic: "My partners at Silver Lake Management and I successfully took Dell private a year ago in the largest corporate privatization in history." The problem was that "Shareholders increasingly demanded short-term results to drive returns; innovation and investment too often suffered as a result. Shareholder and cus-

---

[132] "Excerpts from 'Owner's Manual' Included With Offering," *The New York Times*, April 30, 2004. Contrary to Wall Street tradition, they announced, they would not make quarterly earnings estimates but would focus on the long run. They would not use accounting techniques to "smooth" reported quarterly earnings, but would report actual current earnings and expenses even as these zigzagged. Given the fluid state of information technology, the letter continued, there was no way that Google could "give earnings guidance in the traditional sense" by predicting "our business within a narrow range for each quarter.

[133] "An Egalitarian Auction? Bankers Are Not Amused," *The New York Times*, April 30, 2004.

[134] "Google Says To Investors: Don't Think of Flipping." See also Frank Norris, "Google May Have Pre-empted Regulators on Public Offerings," *The New York Times*, May 4, 2004.

tomer interests decoupled. … As a private company, Dell now has the freedom
to take a long-term view. No more pulling R&D and growth investments to
make in-quarter numbers. No more having a small group of vocal investors
hijack the public perception of our strategy."[135]

The great disconnect that needs to be explained – and reversed

Corporate takeovers, management buyouts and company share buybacks typically are bought with borrowed credit. The theory is simplicity itself: Borrow
cheap to buy companies with a higher yield. If the interest rate is lower than
the profit or dividend rate, it pays raiders to buy these companies on credit –
and companies themselves to borrow cheap and buy up their own higher-
paying shares. At least, that is the theory.

The logical end of this process is for companies (or speculators) to buy up
all the real estate and industry, mines and public utilities in the world that yield
more than the going interest rate. And interest rates have plunged steadily to
only nominal levels today.

Given the ability of banks to create credit electronically, why should they
not create enough credit to buy up every stock in the world – and for that
matter, all the housing and commercial real estate – and pocket the excessive
typical yield of real estate (about 6 percent) or of dividend-paying stocks (3 to
7 percent) over this borrowing rate?

The end result would replace equity with debt, which would be backed by
the income of industry and real estate. Along the way, leveraged buyouts would
bid up stock market and property prices, generating enormous capital gains
up to the point where companies and other properties were so high-priced that
interest charges would totally absorb their profits and rents.

This debt-for-equity arbitrage would make the world's corporate raiders
rich, along with their bankers. But it would not leave revenue available for new
direct investment, research and development or other expenses that are not
quickly reflected in profit streams. Hiring would slow, consumer spending and
hence markets would shrink, causing profits to fall – resulting in defaults on
the debt service that is owed.

This is the bubble economy's financialization dynamic along which the
world's economies were moving until 2008. The trend is now being resumed.
Economies throughout the world are moving back into debt, corporate buyouts

---

[135] Michael Dell, "Going Private Is Paying Off for Dell," *Wall Street Journal*, November 25,
      2014.

and stock buybacks are accelerating and a veritable bubble is re-inflating in junk bond financing.

The question is, can economies prosper through debt leveraging alone? So far, its main critics come from Wall Street, not from the political left or from academia, whose curriculum has little room to analyze debt dynamics. As for the mainstream media, the stock market is the world's most widely watched sporting event. Television news shows and the printed press tend to treat debt and prospects of defaults as a downer story that loses audience interest compared to the success stories of financial celebrities.

Most capital investment in the U.S. and other economies has been paid for out of retained corporate earnings or initially self-financed, not by borrowing from banks or bondholders. This correlation between capital investment and corporate profits reflected the fact that the main way to make more profits was to invest more in the long 35-year upswing in the return to peace after World War II. "Profits and overall net investment in the US tracked each other closely until the late 1980s, with both about 9 per cent of gross domestic product," noted a *Financial Times* report.[136] But then "the relationship began to break down." By 2012 the National Income and Product Accounts (NIPA) were reporting that pre-tax corporate profits had risen to a record 12 per cent-plus of GDP, "while net investment is barely 4 per cent of output."

Rising profits thus are not leading to new tangible investment, employment or output. Corporate profits have soared (although some 40 percent today are registered by the banking and financial sector, not industry) but capital investment has stagnated.

Adam Smith long ago remarked that profits often are highest in nations going fastest to ruin. There are many ways to commit economic suicide on a national level. The major way throughout history has been by indebting the economy. Debt always expands to reach a point where it cannot be paid by large swaths of the economy. That is the point where austerity is imposed and ownership of wealth polarizes between the One Percent and the 99 Percent.

Today is not the first time this has occurred in history. But it is the first time that running into debt has occurred deliberately, applauded as if most debtors can get rich by borrowing, not reduced to a condition of debt peonage.

Hardly by surprise, it is mainly lawyers defending companies against LBOs that have spoken up. At the Tulane legal conference in New Orleans, Martin Lipton singled out Carl Icahn and Pershing Square's Bill Ackman as the

---

[136] Robin Harding, "Corporate investment: A mysterious divergence," *Financial Times*, July 24, 2013.

activists that he most disliked. "[They are] looking to create immediate profit for themselves. Granted, it creates immediate profit for all shareholders but it does not benefit the shareholders of all companies," Mr. Lipton said. "Activism has a huge effect on the strategies companies follow in order to avoid being attacked by a Carl Icahn or a Bill Ackman. ... There is something terribly wrong about businesses borrowing money to buy back stock."[137]

What is unique is that indebting companies to pay bondholders financing corporate buyouts, or simply to buy back corporate stock, is being backed by academic theorists, as we shall explain in the following chapter. This asset stripping is occurring within companies, by their own management following tactics taught in America's leading business schools.

---

[137] Ed Hammond, "Top M&A lawyer attacks activist investors," *Financial Times*, March 28, 2014.

10

Finance vs. Industry: Two Opposite Sides of the Balance Sheet

Last year, the corporations in the Russell 3000, a broad U.S. stock index, repurchased $567.6 billion worth of their own shares – a 21% increase over 2012 … That brings total buybacks since the beginning of 2005 to $4.21 trillion – or nearly one-fifth of the total value of all U.S. stocks today.

Jason Zweig, "Will Stock Buybacks Bite Back?" *Wall Street Journal*, March 22, 2014.

Today's financial sector is raiding what was expected a century ago to be the social functions of capital: to expand output and employment. Economies are slowing in the face of exponentially growing financial claims (bank loans, stocks and bonds) that enrich the One Percent at the expense of the 99 Percent. This polarization leads to unemployment and also to corporate underinvestment by leaving companies too cash-strapped to undertake new capital spending to raise productivity.

Business schools teach today's new breed of managers that the proper aim of corporations is not to expand their business but to make money for shareholders by raising the stock price. Instead of warning against turning the stock market into a predatory financial system that is de-industrializing the economy, they have jumped on the bandwagon of debt leveraging and stock buybacks. Financial wealth is the aim, not industrial wealth creation or overall prosperity.

The result is that while raiders and activist shareholders have debt-leveraged companies from the outside, their internal management has followed the post-modern business school philosophy viewing "wealth creation" narrowly in terms of a company's share price. The result is financial engineering that links the remuneration of managers to how much they can increase the stock price, and by rewarding them with stock options. This gives managers an incentive to buy up company shares and even to borrow to finance such buybacks instead of to invest in expanding production and markets.

Since 1985, U.S. corporations on balance have been net buyers of stock (to retire it), not sellers.[138] The effect is to raise debt/equity ratios (more debt, less equity). Instead of issuing equity to invest and expand the business and its long-term prospects, companies run into debt to buy their own stock or that of other companies. The result functions like a debt-financed takeover from within. Companies become more dependent on banks and bondholders, which press for short-term gains to maximize their own performance measures every three months.

The traditional corporate aim was to build up the value of plant and equipment, real estate and other investments over and above a company's debts. According to textbook theory, stock prices reflect prospects for earning profits and paying dividends. Managers are supposed to increase earnings to build up the enterprise's value in the form of tangible means of production. But the new aim is to use corporate profits for stock buybacks or to pay higher dividends to shareholders, or to pledge to creditors for more loans to create stock-price gains. The major factors raising stock prices since 1980 have been the decline in interest rates, easier credit (especially high-interest junk bonds for corporate takeovers and management buyouts), and falling taxes on business.

Under these conditions, more credit at lower interest rates has a different effect from what economics textbooks describe. Conventional wisdom throughout the 20th century described low interest rates as spurring new investment and employment by lowering the cost of borrowing, and hence supposedly the cost of new investment. But few bank loans or bonds are for this purpose. Instead, low interest rates provide easier credit for raiders to attack companies, or simply for mergers and acquisitions.

On an economy-wide level, asset-striping can be sustained mainly by asset-price inflation, that is, increasing prices for real estate, stocks and bonds simply by lending more bank credit against them, at a falling interest rates and on easier (more reckless) credit terms. This debt leveraging ends up increasing the break-even cost of doing business, until the corporate sector collapses under the debt burden.

---

[138] For statistics on stock market issues less retirements, see Federal Reserve Board, Flow of Funds Report, Table F.213 ("Corporate equities"). For current statistics by industry see Buyback Quarterly, published by Factset, http://www.factset.com/websitefiles/PDFs/buyback/buyback_12.17.13. By 2013 many companies were buying back as many shares as they were issuing to employees. See http://seekingalpha.com/article/1334571-more-bad-news-for-stock-buybacks.

Business school endorsement of financialization and debt leveraging

The financial strategy of tying executive pay and bonuses to their companies' share price seemed radical in 1976 when Michael Jensen of the Harvard Business School and William Meckling at the University of Rochester applauded it in an academic paper, entitled "Theory of the Firm: Managerial Behavior, Agency Costs and Ownership." Along with a follow-up 1990 *Harvard Business Review* article by Jenson and Kevin J. Murphy, "CEO Incentives: It's Not How Much You Pay, But How," the new theory argued that companies should get their managers to act as "agents" for stockholders.

Jensen and his colleagues had a particular problem in mind when they encouraged corporations to aim at producing capital gains. They were concerned with empire builders whose objective was simply to expand their business – and egos – by mergers and acquisition. Jensen's point was that expanding without adding to profits just to satisfy the CEO's own glory did not help stockholders. The hope was that making the stock's price the criterion for performance would curtail this merger mania.

Stock prices can indeed be increased by practices that have nothing to do with long-term production or higher corporate earnings. They can be bid up temporarily by spending profits on stock buybacks or paying out more as dividends. As matters turned out, CEOs with stock options engaged in activities that Jensen later admitted had backfired by depleting corporate liquidity, leaving less to invest in long-term projects.

President Reagan's 1985 *Economic Report of the President* endorsed a combination of tax subsidy and deregulation for leveraged buyouts, on the grounds that whatever generates the highest return is the most efficient use of resources: "contests for corporate control are part of a larger merger and acquisition process that plays an important role in the economy's adjustment to changing market circumstances," the economic advisors concluded; "there is no economic basis for regulations that would further restrict the ... process."[139]

Many prominent business leaders have warned against corporate raiders loading industry down with junk bonds and other debt leveraging, and against paying corporate managers in stock options. Henry Kaufman resigned from the board of directors of Salomon Brothers (and later from the firm itself) to protest its underwriting of debt-for-equity swaps. Felix Rohatyn, of Lazard Frères, also warned of the risks in burdening balance sheets with heavy interest payments. The lawyer Martin Lipton developed the defensive tactic of "poison pills" to counter the threat of hostile buyouts, and wrote a public letter in 1986

---

[139] *Economic Report of the President*, 1985.

to Senator William Proxmire, Chairman of the Senate Banking Committee, defending companies against financial raiding:

> These takeovers move assets into hands that profit by cutting off … research and development and capital improvements and instead divert those revenues to paying the debt incurred to acquire the assets. One can analogize the situation to a farmer who does not rotate his crops, does not periodically let his land lie fallow, does not fertilize his land and does not protect his land by planting cover and creating wind breaks. In the early years he will maximize his return from the land. It is a very profitable short-term use. But inevitably it leads to a dust bowl and economic disaster. … Day after day the takeover entrepreneurs are maximizing their returns at the expense of future generations that will not benefit from the research and development and capital investments that takeover entrepreneurs are forcing businesses to forego.[140]

But in 1993, Wall Street used this "agency theory" to persuade Congress to give tax deductibility for firms to pay management in the form of stock options (Section 162(m) of the U.S. Internal Revenue Code). Industrial capitalism turns into what Hyman Minsky called money-manager capitalism, sacrificing long-term growth by running down the business to generate stock gains.

The British financial analyst Andrew Smithers criticized such "stockbroker economics" in his 2013 book *The Road to Recovery*. Explaining to Martin Wolf at the *Financial Times* how the "bonus culture" aggravates post-industrialization in England and the United States, Smithers said, "if you have these bonuses, you will want to put up the return on equity or earnings per share. And how do you do that? You push profit margins up more than you would otherwise and you underinvest … So what we've done is to increase the conflict between the short-term interests of management and the long-term interests of the company."[141]

Bleeding companies and the economy at large

The economy at large suffers from these tactics as well as companies. Yves Smith points out that financial managers typically cut back "paying suppliers, honoring terms of warranties, complying with environmental, product, and workplace safety laws, paying creditors (bondholders, banks, owners of rental

---

[140] *American Lawyer*, May 1986. For a discussion of the techniques of corporate takeovers, poison pills and other defenses see Gregg A. Jarrell, "Financial Innovation and Corporate mergers," Boston Federal Reserve, pp. 52-73. https://www.bostonfed.org/economic/conf/conf31/conf31c.pdf.

[141] Martin Wolf, "Lunch with the FT: Andrew Smithers," *Financial Times*, March 1, 2014.

property), paying taxes, and for public companies, fulfilling their obligations under state and Federal securities laws."[142]

One sees the self-defeating effects in nearly every sector. Despite being warned that badly designed ignition keys might result in sudden engine shutdowns causing accidents and deaths, General Motors chose not to spend a few cents more per key. Retailers and credit-card companies chose to save a quarter-dollar per card by not putting in the encryption protection that Europeans do. This facilitated the massive computerized stealing from Target over the 2013 Christmas shopping season that led customers to avoid Target stores because they feared identity theft.

The effect of financial interlopers buying a company and making it appear more profitable in the short run by "bleeding" its balance sheet (hoping to find a buyer who will believe that the company has been "streamlined," not depleted) is like a landlord stinting on maintenance and repairs, paying bills more slowly, and letting the property deteriorate by laying off doormen and other niceties. The property is left debt-ridden, with a stagnating rent roll unable to cover the mortgage.

If we view industry as part of the economic and social environment, today's breed of corporate raiders and shareholder activists are strip-mining companies, causing debt pollution, clear-cutting industry and leading to economic drought. Such short-termism is much like a debt-strapped family having to rely on a junk-food diet in order to make ends meet, leading to long-term medical costs and shorter lifespans. Living in the short run does not help make economies lower-cost and more productive. The aim is simply to report bigger profits so that managers and stockholder "activists" can exercise their stock options at a higher price.

Michael Jensen, the academic catalyst for paying managers in stock options, expressed his second thoughts in a 2005 interview:

They look for legal loopholes in the accounting, and when those don't work, even basically honest people move around the corner to outright fraud. If they hold a lot of stock or options themselves, it is like pouring gasoline on a fire. They fudge the numbers and hope they can sell the stock or exercise the options before anything hits the fan.[143]

---

[142] Yves Smith, "Why the 'Maximizing Shareholder Value' Theory of Corporate Governance is Bogus," *Naked Capitalism*, October 21, 2013. She adds: "I've been getting reports from McKinsey from the better part of a decade that they simply can't get their clients to implement new initiatives if they'll dent quarterly returns."

[143] Claudia H. Deutsch, "An Early Advocate of Stock Options Debunks Himself," *The New York Times*, April 3, 2005.

By this time, the policy of attacking one company after another and loading each one down with debt had won Wall Street's applause, echoed by the mainstream media. A 2006 *Financial Times* article noted: "With pressure on institutional investors to deliver short-term gains, corporate hell-raisers – once vilified as 'vultures' and 'speculators' – have become champions of better governance."[144]

Short-termism accelerates as new managers arrive, seeking to win bonuses by slashing expenses even further, running down inventory even more, delaying even longer in paying suppliers, and not replacing retirees but working the remaining labor force more intensively, short-changing contributions to the corporate pension fund, and cutting back on employer contributions to health care. Projects with long lead times, headed by research and development, are the first to be cut back. Focusing on the financial bottom line turns corporate management into a race to the bottom, without acknowledging how much long-term growth is sacrificed by driving companies to increase stock prices by means of share buybacks, debt leveraging and higher dividend payouts instead of capital formation.

Money manager capitalism replaces industrial capitalism

The easiest way to increase earnings is to do what Professor Jensen noted: "fudge the numbers." Profits can be whatever the chief financial officer (CFO) tells the accountant to report, aiming at targets set by brokerage houses and money managers. It is difficult even for well-managed companies to resist this focus on financial short-termism, which Hyman Minsky called money-manager capitalism. Instead of prizing growth as traditional long-term investors did, companies find themselves obliged to defend against raiders and activist shareholders. Cash-rich, low-debt companies take self-imposed "poison pills," running into debt to buy their own stock or that of other companies so as to leave less profit for prospective raiders to borrow against to take them over. Martin Lipton, credited with refining the "poison pill" to defend companies against such debt-financed takeovers, explained why giving activist shareholders the power to raid is dangerous:

> Excessive stockholder power is precisely what caused the short-term fixation that led to the current financial crisis. As stockholder power increased over the last 20 years, our stock markets also became increasingly institutionalized. The real investors are mostly professional money managers who are focused on the short term. It is these shareholders

---

[144] "Raiders rolling back the years," *Financial Times*, August 16, 2006.

who pushed companies to generate returns at levels that were not sustainable. They also made sure high returns were tied to management compensation. The pressure to produce unrealistic profit fueled increased risk-taking.[145]

Despite criticism of these trends a generation ago, corporate raiders gained enough political power to block regulation and tax penalties for their debt leveraging. It took until March 2013, thirty years after the trend gained momentum, for the Federal Reserve and the Office of the Comptroller of the Currency (OCC) to announce guidelines for leveraged buyouts, advising banks to "avoid financing takeover deals that would put debt on a company of more than six times its earnings before interest, taxes, depreciation and amortization, or Ebitda." Their suggestion did not prove effective. "So far in 2014, 30% of new U.S. leveraged buyouts have been financed at a debt-to-ebitda ratio of more than six times ... The most recent peak was in 2007, when the percentage reached 52%."[146]

The financial distortion of industrial capitalism

Even the public sector has adopted financial management criteria to squeeze out a positive cash flow. Governments are reducing their budget deficits by cutting back on maintenance and repair of bridges, roads and other infrastructure, and selling off public real estate and other assets. The effect is to inject less purchasing power and employment to support economic recovery. In academia, universities have replaced tenured professors with part-time adjuncts and treat each department as a profit-center, cutting back classes and programs that do not show a financial return.

An internal contradiction afflicting this financialization strategy is that engineering capital gains by more debt at falling interest rates lowers *current* returns on pension funds assets. This requires companies, states and localities to set aside more revenue if they are not to default on their retirement promises. Pension funds try to avoid this squeeze by engaging in risky speculation organized by Wall Street's investment banks. Many funds have become desperate to earn the 8.5 percent annual return widely assumed as needed to pay retirees

---

[145] Martin Lipton, Jay W. Lorsch and Theodore N. Mirvis, "Schumer's Shareholder Bill Misses the Mark," *Wall Street Journal*, May 12, 2009.

[146] Gillian Tan, "OCC Has 'No Exceptions Policy' for Financing Takeover Deals, Official Says," *Wall Street Journal*, March 20, 2014. The reporter notes that the most highly leveraged buyout during the preceding year was by Bain Capital, headed by 2012 Republican Presidential candidate Mitt Romney. See Gillian Tan, "What's Next for LBOs Amid Crackdown?" *Wall Street Journal*, January 22, 2014.

without raising what companies and public bodies need to set aside. As interest rates and yields fell below this level, many financial managers sought higher returns by backing raiders and financing LBOs. But by supporting financial-ization, pension funds contributed to a dynamic that undercut the economy's markets for goods and services, sales, profits and employment.

The hope was that financial engineering would create enough capital gains to pay the retirement incomes promised to pensioners, without expanding the industrial base. The dream was to live by finance alone, not by bread and other basic needs. The financial sector promised to inaugurate a postindustrial economy in which bank customers could make money from borrowed credit created on computer keyboards without a need for industrial capital formation or employment.

What actually happened was that financial engineering painted the economy into a corner by increasing corporate debt without parallel growth in underlying assets and earnings. Creating more credit (other peoples' debt) and lowering interest rates to bid up real estate, bond and stock prices leaves the economy more debt-ridden and fragile by increasing the economy's car-rying charges while leaving less available to invest and hire labor.

Communities suffer when raiders or other financial managers make short-term gains by downsizing the work force. Jobs are lost and employees who for-merly paid taxes end up collecting unemployment insurance. Paying out earnings in the form of tax-deductible interest to bondholders, instead of after-tax dividends, also widens public budget deficits, creating political pressure to raise taxes on labor and consumers.

It doesn't have to be this way. As Chapter 7 has shown, banking was on its way to becoming a public utility in the years leading up to World War I. If this trend had continued, much of the world might have credit cards, deposit banking services and loans provided at cost or at subsidized rates instead of today's fees and penalties. Business credit funded industrial engineering more than financial engineering, and public banking would be less likely to extend credit for the asset-stripping and asset-price inflation that characterizes today's financial system.

Most futurists a century ago believed that public regulation was needed to keep predatory finance and rent-seeking in check. But bankers and financiers successfully instituted a deregulatory economic philosophy and have seized control of governments to use its money-creating power to subsidize high finance, while leaving creditors "free" to stifle the economy's real growth with debt deflation.

Today's financial interests denounce public regulation and *rentier* taxes as socialism. But "socialism" was not initially a term of invective for classical theorists. John Stuart Mill was called a Ricardian socialist because classical economists were moving toward reforms they themselves characterized as social – and hence, as socialist. Most reformers referred to themselves as socialists of one kind or another, from Christian socialists to Marxist socialists and reformers across the political spectrum. The question was what *kind* of socialism "free market" capitalism would evolve into.

The Reform Era leading up to World War I expected the natural evolution of industrial capitalism to steer savings, wealth, credit and new money creation productively. Like other natural monopolies or special privileges, finance was to become a public utility, situated in the public domain or at least alongside a public banking option. Instead, the past century's expansion of predatory credit has been reinforced by de-taxing interest, land rent, financial speculation, debt leveraging and "capital" (asset-price) gains.

At issue is what the economy does with the surplus of productive capacity and savings over and above its break-even needs. Industrial profits are being diverted away from new capital investment to support stock market prices and enrich the One Percent. Instead of using financialized wealth to build up the economy, managers are diverting corporate income and bank lending mainly to increase the market price of their assets, and to build up their financial claims *on* the economy in the form of debts owed to banks and bondholders.

Central bank support for financial bubbles

Managers pay themselves enormous sums ostensibly for inflating the price of their stock. But the overall surging level reflects the Federal Reserve's wave of money creation more than actions by most companies. The financial sector is riding this wave of Quantitative Easing and tax cuts, thanks largely to its control of the Treasury and Federal Reserve, and capture of the regulatory agencies originally meant to steer credit along more productive lines.

The key to making money "from money" is for creditors to lend it at interest. Most families today simply seek to break even each month while carrying their home mortgage, student loan, and an auto loan if they need to drive to work. Merely avoiding further credit-card debt is a victory in coping with their immediate economic demands.

More affluent borrowers hope to realize speculative gains from real estate, and the economy's wealthiest layer uses hedge funds to raid corporations or, more recently, to buy real estate at distress prices. The common hope is to ride the wave of asset-price inflation for real estate, stocks or bonds bought on credit. A financial bubble is the kind of inflation that Wall Street loves, in contrast to wage and commodity price inflation. A bubble raises the price of financial assets and property relative to living labor, and the power of inheritance over non-heirs.

Asset-price inflation is the primary dynamic explaining today's polarization of wealth and income. Yet most newscasts applaud daily rises in the stock averages as if the wealth of the One Percent, who own the great bulk of stocks and other financial assets, is a proxy for how well the economy is doing.

What actually occurs is that financing corporate buyouts on credit factors interest payments and fees into the prices that companies must charge for their products. Paying these financial charges leaves less available to invest or hire more labor. Likewise for the overall economy, the effect of a debt-leveraged real estate bubble and asset-price inflation is that interest payments and fees to bankers and bondholders leave less available to spend on goods and services. The financial overhead rises, squeezing the "real" economy and slowing new investment and hiring. Wealth created by rising asset prices fueled by interest-bearing debt thus sucks income out of labor and industry.

The Bubble Economy vs. classical industrial growth

The stock market is not the largest part of the economy whose prices are inflated by bank credit. As the biggest asset category, real estate is by far the largest market for debt. The Federal Reserve's quarterly Flow of Funds statistics show that by 2007–08, about 80 percent of new bank loans were real estate mortgages. Most such loans are to buy property already in place, just as most stock market transactions are for shares long since issued.

The effect is twofold: it inflates asset prices ranging from real estate to entire companies, and yields banks interest that imposes a carrying charge on buyers. That is what makes bubble economies high-cost. Housing prices are inflated, requiring mortgage debtors to pay more. Companies borrow to buy other companies, increasing the volume of corporate debt simply to finance ownership changes. And education is financialized, enabling students to afford higher tuition costs by committing to pay monthly debt service out of what they earn after they graduate.

The resulting financial overhead consists of claims *on* the economy's actual means of production. Yet most people think of these bonds, bank loans and stocks and creditor claims as wealth, not its antithesis on the debit side of the balance sheet. This inside-out doublethink is a precondition for the bubble economy to be applauded by the mass media, keeping its corrosive momentum expanding.

From the corporate sphere and real estate to personal budgets, the distin-guishing feature over the past half-century has been the rise in debt/equity and debt/income ratios. Just as debt leveraging has hiked corporate break-even costs of doing business, so the cost of living has been increased as homes and office buildings have been bid up on mortgage credit. "Creating wealth" in a debt-financed way makes economies high-cost, exacerbated by the tax shift onto labor and consumers instead of capital gains and "free lunch" rent. These financial and fiscal policies have enabled financial managers to siphon off the industrial profits that were expected to fund capital formation to increase productivity and living standards.

The financial disconnect from the industrial economy

Most capital investment in the U.S. and other economies normally is self-financed out of retained corporate earnings, not by borrowing from banks or bondholders. During the 35-year upswing spanning the return to peace after World War II until the late 1980s, "profits and overall net investment in the US tracked each other closely ... with both about 9 per cent of gross domestic product," noted a recent *Financial Times* report.[147] But this correlation between capital investment and corporate profits "began to break down" in the Reagan/Thatcher era. By 2012 the National Income and Product Accounts (NIPA) were reporting that pre-tax corporate profits had risen to a record 12 per cent-plus of GDP, "while net investment is barely 4 per cent of output."

Although corporate profits have soared in recent years, they are not leading to new tangible investment, output or employment. The explanation for this disconnect is financialization. Some 40 percent of profits are now registered by the banking and financial sector, not industry. In the manufacturing sector, managers increase reported profits by cutting back basic spending, letting their physical investment run down, and replacing long-term skilled employees with less highly paid new recruits, while using the remaining corporate profits increasingly for share buybacks and higher dividend payouts.

These practices have decoupled financial management from investment in new means of production. The idea that economies can get rich mainly from the debit side of the national balance sheet reflects the degree to which creditor interests have taken over the economy's brain. Finance capitalism is based on exponentially growing debts owed to creditors. Industrial capitalism is based on expanding tangible capital investment, employment and markets. When

---

[147] Robin Harding, "Corporate investment: A mysterious divergence," *Financial Times*, July 24, 2013.

personal and business income is diverted from production and consumption to pay debt service and/or bid up asset prices, the "real" economy cannot expand. And when the debt bubble overhead grows to a point where the economy cannot pay any more, the financial sector demands payment for the debts run up, imposing austerity. Chapter 11 describes this bubble sequence from asset-price inflation to debt deflation.

11

The Bubble Economy: From Asset-Price Inflation to Debt Deflation

The new aristocracy of finance, a new sort of parasites in the shape of promoters, speculators and merely nominal directors … demands … precisely that others shall save for him.

Marx, *Capital*, Vol. III, pp. 519f.

September 2008 was not a typical business cycle peak. The economy had excess debt and peak real estate prices, but interest rates were falling and real wages had remained fairly stagnant for three decades. So did consumer prices. Not even residential rent was rising, thanks to the fact that speculators were desperately seeking renters to cover the carrying charges on properties they had acquired in hope of reselling at a capital gain.

The fact that wages, interest rates and consumer prices were not overheating prompted economists to applaud the "Goldilocks" economy, neither too hot nor too cold, but just right. For bankers, the economy did seem just right, as their loans were soaring, and their bonuses followed suit. Mainstream economists called the 1990–2007 era the Great Moderation. But then, bankers were in charge of naming it (in this case, David Shulman of Salomon Brothers).

In reality it was the Great Indebtedness, leading to the Great Polarization that paved the way for today's Great Austerity. When the bubble crashed, Wall Street blamed "the madness of crowds." This blame-the-victim view depicted borrowers as being immoderate and greedy, and it seemed only moral that the "mad crowd" should now pay the price for its reckless indebtedness, not the creditors. So the most reckless banks were bailed out, as if it were not they and the Federal Reserve that were mad and immoderate.

What made this period immoderate was deregulation of the financial sector. By 2004, the FBI reported that the greatest wave of financial fraud since the S&L scandals was in full swing. The Justice Department looked the other way. Also immoderate was economic polarization. Not since the 1920s had the One Percent pulled so far ahead of the 99 Percent. What was deemed "moderate" was the fact that the population at large did *not* receive higher wages or a rising share of income and wealth. The Great Moderation was

Wall Street's euphemism for debt pyramiding and polarization between creditors and debtors.

To new homebuyers, housing prices rose so high that by 2008 taking out a
mortgage to buy a home meant cutting back consumption and living standards
– unless one ran up credit-card debt and other borrowing. Many homeowners
took out home equity loans ("second mortgages"), using their homes as an
ATM to draw against a bank account. Paying interest on this rising debt left
less for consumption, so the position of normal citizens worsened as they sank
deeper into debt.

Every economic recovery since 1945 has started with a higher debt level
than the one before it, and each successive recovery has been weaker. The
rising debt overhead explains why the bank bailout that resolved the 2008
financial crisis has failed to yield a real "recovery." To banks and other creditors, recovery means keeping the debts on the books, and indeed, re-inflating
prices for homes by creating yet new debt. The bankers' "solution" is to extend
a new wave of credit to bid real estate, stock and bond prices back up.

But debt is the problem. What is depressing today's economies is that the
debts have been kept in place, acting as a financial brake blocking a business
upswing. The "solution" that banks offer is austerity: Most of the economy is
geared to work off its debts, not write them down to levels that can be paid
without pushing the economy into austerity. Austerity is Wall Street's (and the
Eurozone's) new definition of "moderation."

Creditors and debtors thus have naturally opposing worldviews. Labor
("consumers") and industry are obliged to pay a rising proportion of their
income in the form of rent and interest to the Financial and Property sector
for access to property rights, savings and credit. This leaves insufficient wages
and profits to sustain market demand for consumer goods and investment in
new means of production (capital goods). The main causes of economic austerity and polarization are rent deflation (payments to landlords and monopolists) and debt deflation (payments to banks, bondholders and other creditors).

To the banks, "moderation" simply means not defaulting. From the 1990s
to 2007, this eventuality was postponed by consumers running deeper into
debt to pay their scheduled debt service and other *rentier* charges. Banks created
enough new credit to finance rising personal budget deficits by lending mortgage credit and home equity loans to a widening segment of the population,
without much regard for their ability to pay. Supplemented by soaring credit-
card debt, this bank credit enabled consumers to support the living standards
that their wages were unable to cover. The hope was that somehow they would
come out ahead, as long as bank credit continued to bid up prices for real
estate, stocks and bonds.

This circular flow of bank lending to inflate asset markets suffered a break in the chain of payments when the Production and Consumption sector no longer could pay the interest falling due. Speculators stopped buying, and banks stopped lending the money for debtors to pay what they owed. Real estate prices fell below the mortgages attached to them – the definition of negative equity.

Somebody had to bear the loss – the gap between what was owed and what debtors could afford to pay. To the Federal Reserve and Treasury, the sectors that needed to be saved were not labor and industry, but bank balance sheets – claims *on* the economy. So the Fed and Treasury government absorbed the losses by their constituency, the One Percent.

Wall Street made an ideological about-face to applaud what it had long attacked: rising government debt and deficit spending. Its endorsement of central bank money creation was inspired not by charitable feelings toward the economy, but by self-interest. Government deficits are deemed "good" as long as they are spent to bail out banks and bondholders. They are only "bad" when they are spent on labor and the "real" economy. Federal Reserve credit ("Quantitative Easing") is good if it helps inflate asset prices for the One Percent and improves bank balance sheets. But public money creation is deemed "irresponsible" if it spurs recovery in employment and wages, helping the 99 Percent break even and recover its former share of national income and wealth. Rising asset prices for real estate, stocks and bonds are "good" because they increase the power of the One Percent *over* the rest of the economy. Rising wages and commodity prices are deemed bad, because they threaten to erode this power of debt over the economy.

The financial sector's greatest trick has been to convince the 99 Percent that "the economy" can be judged by how well it benefits the One Percent. Mainstream media echo Federal Reserve speeches to convince the public that saving the banks meant saving the indebted economy – by giving banks a large enough bailout to start lending again. It was as if what labor and industry needed to survive was more borrowing to pay their debt service, not a debt writedown.

Most people saw the obvious need to write down mortgage debts, student loans and other personal debts in keeping with the ability to be paid. At the very least, the fictitious inflated prices that banks had recklessly assigned for highly mortgaged property needed to be brought in line with the falling market price of real estate.

But that is not what the One Percent wanted in 2008. Their solution to the crisis was to further impoverish economies with debt deflation. Until a new wave of credit and debt creation takes off, returning to "normal" means forcing the economy to pay down the debt overhead built up since 1980.

After 2008, new lending dried up. Consumers had to start paying down their credit card balances. Homeowners had to pay down their mortgages rather than "cashing out" on the debt-inflated "equity" value of their homes. This net repayment has become the new definition of "saving." It increases net worth not by building *up* assets and real wealth, but by paying *down* the debts that have been taken on. In accounting terms, it is a negation of a negation. (Hegelians and Marxists will appreciate the philosophical inversion at work.) But it is not debtors that enjoy the liquidity from this saving; it is the creditors who receive the loan amortizations.

For many, of course, foreclosure time arrived. Debtors who couldn't pay defaulted. Only student loans continued to rise, thanks to government guarantees of subsidized interest premiums to the banks, leading to today's heavy default rates. Western economies entered a period of debt deflation hitherto suffered only by Third World countries under IMF (de)stabilization plans. Opportunities for upward mobility gave way to a debt-ridden austerity, shrinking markets and leaving even less income available to pay debts.

The key to understanding how Asset-Price Inflation leads inexorably to Debt Deflation is to recognize that there are, in fact, two economies. Wall Street pretends that its financial gains are infused *into* the economy (much as Malthus described British landlords two centuries ago), creating jobs and financing new factories and other means of production. The reality is that bank loans do *not* fund direct investment and employment. They extract debt service while inflating asset prices to provide "capital" gains. This makes homes more expensive to buy, requiring new owners to take out larger mortgage loans. That is the Asset-Price Inflation phase of the financial cycle.

At some point, repayment time arrives. Paying off debts absorbs income that otherwise would be available for spending on the goods and services that labor produces. This is the Debt Deflation phase. Each business upswing leaves a higher level of debt, diverting a rising proportion of income to pay debt service. The post-2008 bailout and imposition of austerity aimed to squeeze out enough income to carry the debt claims. But austerity generates even more defaults and a deeper crash.

Asset-Price Inflation

By far the fastest growing category of wealth is asset-price gains for real estate, stocks and bonds, not profits made by producing goods and services. Until 2008 these gains outstripped the rise of income, making them the main source of new "wealth creation." They are taxed at a much lower rate than wages or profits, and over three quarters of such gains are reaped by the One Percent.

These beneficiaries evidently are so embarrassed by this fact that they have drawn a cloak of invisibility around wealth in property and financial assets, discouraging official statistics from estimating such gains. As Chapter 5 has explained, they appear nowhere in the national statistics – neither in the NIPA nor in the Federal Reserve's flow-of-funds report on the economy's balance sheet. Yet on an economy-wide level, capital gains (or since 2008, losses) often overshadow the entire change in national income or GDP. The most important aim of investors in today's financialized economy has been shielded from public scrutiny: the *total returns* at which today's investors aim, defined as current income (interest, dividends and rent) *plus* capital gains.

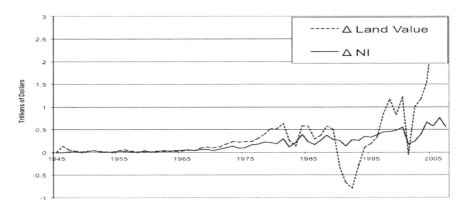

Figure 6: Annual Land-Value Gains compared to Growth in National Income

I prefer the term Asset-Price Gains to avoid confusion with what tax account-ants mean by "capital gains," referring only to what is declared on income-tax filings as *realized* gains.[148] No taxes are paid on gains when they are transferred upon the death of asset owners, or when real estate gains are plowed into new purchases.

---

[148] This explains why Piketty's charts do not show the economy polarizing much more when "capital gains" are taken into account alongside earned income. His statistics do not explain the price rise for assets that are not sold and hence are not subject to a capital gains tax. Only the rise in assets can explain these gains (after subtracting what can be explained by current new construction and tangible capital formation).

Real estate is the focus of this bubble dynamic because about 80 percent of asset-price gains are for real estate; the balance is for bonds and stocks.[149] The resulting price gains are not really "capital" gains. Land and other rent-yielding assets are not "capital" in the classical sense of the term – manmade means of production whose value reflects an actual cost of production. Land has only a market cost of acquisition, and that is based on how much banks will lend against it. Some 80 percent of new bank loans are mortgages, so the rise in bank credit creation is felt mainly in property prices.

In contrast to industrial profits, capital gains are the product largely of the wave of asset-price inflation – that is, the wave of bank credit on easier terms for debt leveraging. Since interest rates began their 30-year decline in 1980, a financial wave of credit has enabled borrowers to buy these assets and their flow of incomes with higher amounts of low-interest credit. Price/earnings ratios rise when interest rates fall (described below). Making such gains therefore is different from earning them by labor and enterprise. These profits are what 19th-century writers called the "unearned increment," especially when they accrue for the land's rising site value.

The ten dynamics that led the Bubble Economy to focus on asset-price gains

1. Rising site-value for land from prosperity, infrastructure spending and population growth
2. The exponential growth of credit
3. Declining interest rates raise "capitalization rates"
4. Pension fund investment in the stock market and real estate
5. Tax favoritism for capital gains and inherited wealth
6. Lower amortization payments, culminating in interest-only loans
7. Lower down payments
8. "Teaser" interest rates, with charges exploding in three years
9. A secondary market for non-bank mortgage buyers
10. Outright fraud ("Liars' loans" and other toxic financial waste)

---

[149] I describe the details in *Real Estate and the Capital Gains Debate* (with Kris Feder), The Jerome Levy Economics Institute of Bard College, Working Paper No. 187 (March 1997).

A combination of population growth and urbanization, prosperity (with homes being the most important status indicator), public spending on transportation and other infrastructure, and the rising political power of property owners to lower tax rates has increased the price of land and its rental value. Within these long-term trends, financial cycles raise and lower interest rates asset prices and asset prices. The Bubble Economy increased asset prices by purely financial factors, mainly by driving down interest rates from their 1980 peak of 20%, while loosening lending terms to increase how much banks would lend against income and property valuations (culminating in out right "liars' loans").

1. *Rising site value of land from prosperity, population growth and public spending*

Chapter 3 has traced how classical economics explained why prices for land sites, mineral deposits and other natural endowments rise for reasons that do not involve an expenditure of labor or enterprise by their owners. Public investment in roads and other transportation, schools and parks, water and other infrastructure is provided freely or at prices subsidized by taxpayers as a whole. The result is that taxpayers as well as rent-payers end up paying to create wealth for landlords – enabling them to borrow more or obliging new homebuyers to borrow more to obtain ownership of such sites. To the extent that rental values are paid to the banks as interest, landlords as well as taxpayers end up creating revenue and wealth for the financial sector.

2. *The exponential growth of credit*

Capital gains are fueled mainly by debt leveraging – buying with as little of one's own money as possible. As financial wealth mounts up, banks compete for new business by loosening their lending terms. The process becomes self-feeding as property prices rise. Speculators and homeowners are willing to pay their banks the rental value, hoping to get a capital gain. The logical end is reached at the point where the financial carrying charges absorb all the rental income or profits. This willingness of borrowers to pay all the rental income to creditors is the driving force behind asset-price bubbles.

3. *Declining interest rates raise "capitalization rates"*

The capitalization rate is the reciprocal of the interest rate. At 5% interest, a $1 million net annual rent will support a $20 million interest-only mortgage. At 4% it will support a $25 million mortgage. So as interest rates fall, a given flow of rental income will support a larger loan. As the U.S. banking system's prime rate declined from 20% in 1980, banks were willing to lend more to prospective property buyers and investors.

4. *Pension fund investment in the stock market and real estate*

Since the 1950s most retirement saving has been steered into the stock market. Bidding up stock prices was applauded as pension-fund capitalism (sometimes called pension-fund socialism). Pension funds diversified into junk bonds in the 1980s, and into packaged mortgages after the dot.com bubble burst in 2000. Mortgages became the highest-yielding form of security, steering pension savings into the real estate market by providing banks with a market for loans they originated.

5. *Tax favoritism for capital gains and inherited wealth*

When the U.S. income tax was inaugurated in 1913, capital gains were taxed as normal income. The logic was that a price gain for a stock, bond or real estate builds up the owner's net worth just as do savings out of wages or profits. But by 1921, financial and real estate lobbyists succeeded in getting taxes on capital gains lowered to $12\frac{1}{2}\%$ for assets held at least two years. In 1934 the capital gains tax was further reduced, and the Eisenhower administration cut the rate to 25% in 1954, where it remained through 1967. The Reagan-Bush Administration eased it yet more, especially for real estate. Landlords were allowed to pretend that their buildings depreciated in just over seven years, creating a fictitious charge that offset the rental income. This made commercial and absentee real estate basically income-tax free.

Real estate gains are not taxed if they are re-invested in new property acquisition. Many European countries do not tax capital gains at all. British landlords can evade taxes by holding their property in an Isle of Man account or other tax-avoidance enclave. This favoritism has enabled real estate fortunes to be built up largely free of income and capital gains taxes. When owners die, all tax liability is forgiven and the heirs can continue the buildup. No wonder the One Percent now controls the lion's share of U.S. wealth and income!

6. *Lower amortization payments, culminating in interest-only loans*

Until the 1980s the standard home mortgage was for 30 years. Paying off a loan at $^1/_{30}$ per year is the equivalent of paying 3.3 percent of the principal each year. "Freeing" borrowers from having to pay this percentage enables it to be capitalized into a larger loan value. At 5% interest, a no-amortization loan raises the mortgage potential by $^2/_3$ (that is, 3.3 divided by 5). At 6% interest, a loan principal can increase by 55%.

By the time the real estate bubble peaked in 2008, interest-only loans had become increasingly widespread. Banks prefer loans not to be repaid but simply rolled over, yielding interest year after year. Homeowners who paid all they could afford just in interest were not able to pay down the mortgage, having stepped onto a perpetual debt treadmill.

7. *Lower down payments*

New lending practices called forth a new financial vocabulary. Providing 100% mortgages broadened the market to "subprime" borrowers in the years leading up to 2008. Lending even more than 100% – up to 110% – enabled borrowers to obtain not only the property but enough credit to pay the brokerage and closing fees, bank fees and perhaps leaving enough to repaint and furnish the hope. Who could say "No" under these tantalizing giveaway deals? The result of a zero down payment was an infinite debt/equity ratio.

8. *Low "teaser" interest rates, with charges exploding in three years*

Banks wrote mortgages with initial interest charges low enough for low-income borrowers to sign up, but which "exploded" to high-risk rates in a few years. Alan Greenspan downplayed the danger of such contracts by pointing out that many Americans move after three years, so the debtors could escape by selling their home to the proverbial greater fool. This worked until even fools stopped buying in 2008 – or at least, banks stopped lending to fools. The game was up.

9. *A secondary market for non-bank mortgage buyers*

Mortgages traditionally were held by the savings banks, S&Ls and commercial banks that made the loans. Holding these mortgages as a source of revenue over and above interest payments to depositors made these institutions prudent enough not to over-lend against real estate that might lose value and cause the bank's portfolio to fall below what was owed to depositors and bondholders.

Fannie Mae and Freddie Mac were created to foster a government-insured market for packaged mortgages sold to institutional investors – pension funds, insurance companies, and even for German Landesbanks. The aim was to make mortgages liquid, that is, salable among institutions. More "liquidity" meant a larger flow of savings to be lent out to inflate property prices. Much as pension funds had bid up stock prices since the 1950s, they repeated this experience in mortgage lending by the late 1980s.

10. *Outright fraud, "liars' loans" and toxic financial waste*

When a bank makes money by selling the mortgage loans it has originated rather than keeping these on its own books, its interest in avoiding default disappears. It is much like a fly-by-night retailer selling the cheapest products it can buy at the highest price so as to maximize its profits as quickly as possible.

Some stores will buy substandard merchandise and try to sell it as genuine, from patent medicine to food coloring that turns out to be poisonous. Such fraud can be cured only by public regulation and quality control.

A home or office building, stock or bond is worth whatever a bank will lend against it. The limit traditionally was set by the ability of the asset's income to cover the debt service. If that rule had been followed in the bubble economy leading up to 2008, there would have been little solvency problem or need for bailouts, except perhaps for short-term emergency credit in a normal downturn. But "liars' loan" mortgage applications were doctored to report fictitious income, and banks employed property assessors who gave fictitiously high property valuations. Loans and hence home prices lost reference to the ability to pay or rental value.

How financial bubbles raise the break-even cost of labor

Rent and interest add to the cost of living, while diverting revenue away from the circular flow of production and consumption spending. These financial charges thus simultaneously deflate market spending while adding to the break-even cost of living.

What makes American labor so high-cost is the monthly "nut" that wage earners must spend to carry their debts and pay for housing, taxes and health insurance. Prior to 1980 the rule of thumb was that bankers should approve mortgage loans only if the cost of housing did not exceed 25 percent of the borrower's income. But the new Fannie Mae/FHA guidelines permit mortgages to be guaranteed if they absorb all the way up to 43 percent of household income.

In the realm of tax policy, FICA wage withholding for Social Security and medical care is now over 7.5%. State, local and federal taxes, plus health insurance may absorb another 15 percent.[150] Typical household budgets show non-mortgage debt service absorbing another 10 percent of wage income.[151]

---

[150] For 2014, the FICA tax rate is 6.2% on the first $117,000 wages paid. Employers pay a matching 6.2%. The Medicare tax rate is 1.45% on the first $200,000 and 2.35% above $200,000 under sections 1401, 3101, and 3111 of the Internal Revenue Code. In Europe, the OECD average for income tax and social security contributions is 35.2 per cent of labour costs – and in Austria it is 48.4 per cent, according to the Austrian Institute of Economic Research. See James Shotter, "Freedom party exploits unease in one of Europe's strongest economies," *Financial Times*, May 21, 2014.

[151] Statistics by income cohort are published every three years in the Federal Reserve's *Survey of Consumer Finances*.

Together these payments to the FIRE sector (and the tax shift off it onto consumers) absorb roughly two-thirds of many blue-collar family budgets, leaving only about a third available to spend on current output:

Rent or home ownership costs (incl. property tax):	35 to 40 %
Other debt service (credit cards, student loans etc.):	10%
FICA wage withholding (Social Security and Medicare):	7.5%
Other taxes (income and sales taxes and health insurance):	10 to 15 %
TOTAL	about **67 %**

There is no way for an economy with such high debt service, real estate and tax charges to compete with less financialized economies where housing is not so debt-leveraged, where family budgets do not have such high debt carrying charges, and where taxes have not been shifted so regressively off the FIRE sector onto labor and industry.

Debt Deflation

Meanwhile, the *rentier* overhead leaves consumers with less to spend on current output. This imposes deepening austerity as asset-price inflation gives way to debt deflation:

Phase 1

Consumer Demand = wages + new borrowing (that is, increase in debt)

Paying back the rising debt taken on prior to 2008 led to the Debt Deflation phase of the credit cycle:

Phase 2

Consumer Demand = wages *minus* debt service.

Asset-price inflation turns into debt deflation when paying amortization and interest (not to mention late fees) drains income from the economy's circular flow of production and consumption spending ("Say's Law" discussed in Chapter 3). This slows growth. The economy tapers off while the volume of credit and debt grows exponentially.[152] Carrying this rising debt leaves less available to spend on goods and services, while government tax revenues and new money creation are paid to bondholders instead of being spent on public infrastructure, education, health and other social programs.

---

[152] I provide a technical discussion in "Saving, Asset-Price Inflation and Debt Deflation," in *The Bubble and Beyond*, ch. 11 (ISLET 2012), pp. 297–319, first published in L. Randall Wray and Matthew Forstater, eds., *Money, Financial Instability and Stabilization Policy* (Edward Elgar, 2006), pp. 104–24.

The term Debt Deflation was coined in 1933 by Irving Fisher to explain how bankruptcies stemming from the inability to pay debts were wiping out bank credit and spending power, and hence the ability of economies to invest and hire new workers.[153] Federal Reserve Chairman Ben Bernanke failed to understand this. In his view, debt service simply transfers purchasing power from debtors to creditors, with no effect on overall spending on current output. This assumes that creditors will spend the debt service they receive on consuming as much as indebted consumers and workers would have done.

No economist prior to the 1980s anticipated that government budget deficits would take the form of transfer payments to the banks in the form of bailouts and cheap Federal Reserve credit. But since 2008 the rise in public debt and central bank credit has not been created to increase employment or consumer demand. The aim is to help Wall Street's liquidity, not that of consumers. Chairman Ben Bernanke's helicopter dropped money only over Wall Street, for banks to lend yet more to the already debt-ridden economy. The Fed's idea of "recovery" has been to fund a new financial bubble and bid prices back up for existing real estate, stocks and bonds, as if this will revive the industrial economy instead of simply weighing it down with yet more debt.

Bernanke's denial that rising debt levels do not reduce overall market demand for goods and services is reminiscent of Malthus's argument that landlords spend their rents back into the economy. In trying to absolve the financial sector from causing austerity, Bernanke claimed that "debt-deflation represented no more than a redistribution from one group (debtors) to another (creditors). Absent implausibly large differences in marginal spending propensities among the groups, it was suggested, pure redistributions should have no significant macroeconomic effects."[154] In other words, if creditors (or real estate moguls) spend the same proportion of their income and capital gains on consumer goods and investment goods as do average wage earners, there would be no debt deflation or general spending shortfall, but simply a transfer of purchasing power from debtors to creditors and their fellow *rentiers*.

But the whole point is that "spending propensities" *do* differ between the One Percent and the 99 Percent, between *rentiers* on the one hand, and con-

---

[153] Fisher, "The Debt-Deflation Theory of the Great Depression," *Econometrica* (1933), p. 342. Available at http://fraser.stlouisfed.org/docs/meltzer/fisdeb33.pdf

[154] Ben Bernanke, *Essays on the Great Depression* (Princeton, 2000), p. 24, quoted by Steve Keen Debtwatch No. 42 (http://www.debtdeflation.com/blogs/), "The case against Mr. Bernanke." In *Debunking Economics,* Prof. Keen expands his criticism of economists who fail to understand endogenous credit creation, that is, the fact that bank lending creates deposits. This understanding lies at the heart of Modern Monetary Theory.

sumers and producers on the other. As Keynes emphasized in his *General Theory*, wealthier people spend a *lower* proportion of their income on consumption. And when today's Wall Street financiers *do* spend their multi-million dollar salaries and bonuses money on themselves, it is largely on fine art trophies, luxury apartments that already have been built, on yachts and high fashion – largely imported, as was noted already in Malthus's day. But most important, the super-rich lend out most of their gains, indebting the rest of the economy to themselves.

Endorsing President Roosevelt's spending and New Deal policies in 1933, Fisher believed that more monetary and credit creation would be able to cure the depression. "When over-indebtedness … is counteracted by inflationary forces (whether by accident or design), the resulting 'cycle' will be far milder and far more regular."[155] He anticipated that suppressing debt deflation by an easy-money policy would revive employment, wages and commodity prices. But President Obama and Republicans sought to *reduce* the government's budget deficit, not spend more money into the economy. For Bernanke, monetary inflation after 2008 was limited to providing easy Federal Reserve credit money for banks.

He expressed the hope that they would extend credit to the real estate, stock and bond markets to re-inflate asset prices. The "real" economy was left to suffer debt deflation. But more debt overhead involves carrying charges that drain consumption and investment spending. And paying down the debt overhead intensifies the austerity. This transforms the character of "saving" to mean a pay-down of debt, not money in the bank.

Saving by paying down debt

Leading up to 2008, the U.S. saving rate fell to zero. The much-discussed number seemed to suggest that no saving was taking place – as if the entire economy were making a choice to be profligate and live for today, not tomorrow.

There actually was as much overall saving as ever. *Gross* savings remained high – about 18 percent of national income. But the rise in debt was keeping pace. *Most savings were lent out to become other peoples' new debt*, not invested in tangible capital formation. Homebuyers, industrial companies, consumers, and even local and federal government had run so deeply into debt that their borrowing fully absorbed the savings, producing a zero *net* saving rate. In fact, the

---

[155] Fisher, *op. cit.*, p. 344.

domestic U.S. savings rate was actually a *negative* 2%. The overall rate was rescued from negative territory by foreign central banks (mainly in China, Japan
and Germany) recycling their export surpluses into U.S. Treasury bonds. This
"foreign savings inflow" is counted as part of the U.S. savings rate.

When the banks stopped lending in 2008, the savings rate rose to 7 percent
of GDP by May 2009. *The New York Times* applauded that "many people were
putting that money away instead of spending it."[156] The *Wall Street Journal*
reported that Social Security recipients of one-time government payments
"seem unwilling to spend right away."[157] But this saving was not taking the
form that most people think of as saving. It did not mean that prudent behavior
had returned and people were keeping more money in the bank to withdraw
on a rainy day. It took the form of paying down debts, not liquid money available for spending by the former debtors, who found that they needed to run
down whatever liquid savings they had. They simply were spending their
income to pay down the debt they had taken on earlier.

The "saving" in question was an accounting entry in the national income
accounts – a negation of a negation, and hence a positive. The only way these
savings were "money in the bank" was that they were paid *by* debtors *to* their
banks and credit card companies.

This debt deflation shows how false the image is of using one's home like
the proverbial piggy bank. Running up a debt is not at all like withdrawing
cash from a savings account. Bankers euphemize taking out equity loans (borrowing more against the property's rising market price) as "cashing out" on
one's equity, as if this does not leave a legacy of debts, which constrain future
spending by diverting more income to pay creditors.

The more the "savings rate" rose in the post-2008 world, the *less* money
"savers" had to spend. Debtors ate cheaper foods and ran *down* whatever liquid
savings they had. This "upside down" saving led to debt deflation.

The rentier sector's economic overhead

Today's post-bubble debt deflation is not a cyclical downturn that will return
to normal as a result of "automatic stabilizers." Leaving present debt trends
in place will polarize the economy further between the financial sector and the
rest of the economy. To restore prosperity, the way the economy operates must
be changed – mainly by writing down the debt overhead.

---

[156] Jack Healy, "As Incomes Rebound, Saving Hits Highest Rate in 15 Years," *The New York
Times,* June 27, 2009.
[157] Kelly Evans, "Americans Save More, Amid Rising Confidence," *Wall Street Journal,* June
27, 2009.

Piketty and Saez have documented the extent to which just One Percent of the population owns most of the stocks and bonds in the banks and other firms, and receive their surplus in the form of dividends, profits, interest, rent and capital gains. A realistic model or picture of how the economy operates would require separating the "wealthy" households from the wage earners that live by their own labor rather than on dividends, rents, interest and capital gains.

There is no way for markets to maintain full employment and grow in the face of debt deflation and regressive tax systems that have reached today's magnitudes. The economic Armageddon that Ricardo worried would befall industrial capitalism from tax favoritism for the *rentier* landlord class is now being imposed by the financial sector. Today's mortgage bankers ride on the landlords' shoulders, receiving the rent as interest, as well as industrial cash flow and a broad chunk of personal income from employees.

Industrial capitalism was revolutionary in seeking to free itself from the *rentier* burdens of landlordship, banking and monopolies inherited from feudalism. But instead of classical reforms succeeding, the financial sector has captured government policy to subordinate industrial capitalism to finance capitalism and its *rentier* allies.

The political problem is that bankers and bondholders do not want to lose what they have, even when their gains cannot be maintained without plunging economies into austerity, because that is the only way they can collect the debts they have promoted. The following chapters describe how this inversion of economic democracy and prosperity was achieved from the United States to Europe.

12

The Bankers Saw It Coming, But Economists Averted Their Eyes

Most mainstream macroeconomic theoretical innovations since the 1970s ... have turned out to be self-referential, inward-looking distractions at best. Research tended to be motivated by the internal logic, intellectual sunk capital and aesthetic puzzles of established research programmes, rather than by a powerful desire to understand how the economy works—let alone how the economy works during times of stress and financial instability. So the economics profession was caught unprepared when the crisis struck.

Willem Buiter[158]

When Queen Elizabeth visited the London School of Economics on November 4, 2008, shortly after the financial meltdown had spread from Wall Street to the City of London and on to the Paris Bourse, Frankfurt and Tokyo, she famously asked, "Did nobody see this coming?"

A wave of self-righteous testimony arose from Wall Street to the City of London claiming that nobody reasonably could have foreseen the crash. Such protests were all for show. Bankers and hedge fund managers knew quite well what was coming, and they had the foresight to put in place a political strategy to make the government bail them out when the crash did hit. But for the losses to be borne by "taxpayers," the collapse had to seem as if it all were a surprise, an act of nature rather than bad policy and outright fraud.

The *Financial Times* cited numerous economists for having diagrammed the dynamics that led up to the crash.[159] (I was among them.) But the pretense

---

[158] Willem Buiter, "The Unfortunate Uselessness Of Most 'State Of The Art' Academic Monetary Economics", Maverecon, 3 March 2009, http://blogs.ft.com/maverecon. This blog was organized by the Financial Times. Since 2010 Buiter has been Chief Economist for Citigroup, which his blog earlier had called "a conglomeration of worst practice from across the financial spectrum."

[159] Dirk Bezemer, "Why some economists could see the crisis coming," *Financial Times*, September 7, 2009. For a roster of financial Cassandras see Alphaville, *Financial Times*, July 13, 2009: "Who saw it coming and the primacy of accounting," posted by Tracy Alloway. Michael Lewis's *The Big Short* (2010) gives examples of those who "saw it coming" and put their money where their mouths were.

of ignorance became the basis for Wall Street's claim that nobody could be found guilty of negligence, not to mention fraud. The breakdown was said to be part of the natural functioning of the economy, not a result of warped policy and insider corruption.

Any lingering doubts about how many people saw the 2008 crash looming can be dispelled by looking the jargon coined by Wall Street and the financial press new to describe the junk mortgage boom based on "liars' loans." The liars were the real estate brokers, appraisers, bankers, mortgage packagers and ratings agencies lending to NINJA borrowers (No Income, No Job, No Assets) at interest rates that "exploded" after the initially low teaser rates expired.

Financial markets were deemed "fragile," techno-talk for the pyramid scheme that was unfolding. Backed by fictitious property appraisals, Wall Street packaged mortgages into collateralized debt obligations (CDOs), paying ratings agencies fortunes for pinning AAA labels attesting that the toxic financial waste was as risk-free as Treasury bonds. When sued, the agencies claimed that their grades were only "opinions," not culpable analysis.

Two well-subsidized and broadly popularized fictions kept the bubble going. Homebuyers had to believe that running deeper into debt peonage would make them rich, not paint them into a financial corner. And gullible investors had to believe that AAA ratings meant secure investments, not packaged lies.

Regulators such as Brooksley Borne, chairperson at the Commodity Futures Trading Commission, warned of the impending danger in 1999. Her agency was charged with overseeing speculation in options and futures contracts, which were at the core of the collapse. But Clinton Treasury Secretary Robert Rubin (1995-99) and his successor Larry Summers (1999-2001) backed Greenspan's claim that no regulation was needed. "We always have to be watchful with respect to anything that can affect our system," Rubin whistled in the dark. "But I don't know of anything in that area that rises to the level of a systemic risk to our economy at this time."[160]

Eager to deregulate Wall Street, the three officials led the fight to repeal the Glass-Steagall Act that had saved retail deposit banking from being merged with the investment banking that was turning Wall Street into an increasingly reckless casino. None of these three ever apologized for having sponsored the ensuing disaster – mainly because they continued to prosper in its wake. Rubin left the Clinton administration to become head of Citibank, where he oversaw

---

[160] Robert Rubin quote database, http://www.successories.com/iquote/author/6194/robert-rubin-quotes/2

its descent into insolvency and financial fraud (for which it later was fined tens of billions of dollars).

Summers went on to become president of Harvard, where he lost $1 billion in derivatives speculation, and then President Obama's chief economic advisor. This position helped him shepherd Rubin's circle of Tim Geithner as Treasury Secretary, Jack Lew as his successor, Sylvia Matthews Burwell as director of the Office of Management and Budget, and other the pro-bank economists connected with the pro-austerity Hamilton Project. The latter neoliberal organization also provided Obama with Gene Sperling and Jason Furman to run the White House National Economic Council.[161]

Congress and the White House rewarded their leading campaign contributors by letting Wall Street put its defenders in charge of the key regulatory committees. Whistle-blowers who complained to the Securities and Exchange Commission and other agencies were harassed, ridiculed and forced to resign. The Department of Justice buried the few cases where the SEC recommended that it bring criminal prosecution. Another new term was coined: "regulatory capture," referring to staffing oversight agencies with representatives of the banks they were supposed to supervise. The whole purpose of regulatory capture was to *disable* regulatory protection against the bubble economy.

A similar dynamic was unfolding in the City of London's financial center. Gordon Brown's notoriously "light touch" led Wall Street banks and insurance companies to shift their most speculative operations there. Iceland's "Viking bankers" gambled a sum as large as that nation's entire GDP. The financial police retreated from the world's financial centers, announcing that a deregulated free market finally had arrived – and with it the most pervasive fraud and over-lending in a century.

AIG's London office, AIG Financial Products, charged unrealistically low fees for insuring bets (derivatives) on fictitiously valued mortgages. Its managers simply paid themselves the revenue coming in, not setting aside anything like the risks being insured. Back in the United States, Angelo Mozilo saw the 2008 crash coming, writing a memo warning his Countrywide Financial staff about the rise in fraud, as if it were not centered in his own institution. He had the foresight to sell $406 million of his stock, and protect his $100 million-plus salary and bonuses from being clawed back by future prosecutors.

Across the banking sector the organizers of what would become a vast insolvency took the money and ran, leaving shell institutions in their wake. The most reckless bank was Citigroup, which Rubin had joined in 1999 after

---

[161] Damian Paletta, "Tracing Budget Team's DNA," *Wall Street Journal*, March 5, 2013.

his "descent from heaven" at Clinton's Treasury. Under Rubin's direction Citigroup wove its speculative activities into so complex a veil of tiers that when Federal Deposit Insurance Corp. (FDIC) regulators thought of taking it over in 2008, they found it impossible to untangle the maze to find out who owed how much to whom, and how to evaluate the complex derivatives at the heart of Citigroup's loss.

Nobody could know in advance precisely when the crescendo of speculation would peak. The endgame often is triggered by an embezzlement or bankruptcy that freezes markets. "When the music stops, in terms of liquidity, things will be complicated," explained Charles Prince, Rubin's successor at Citigroup, in a July 2007 interview with the *Financial Times* a year before the crash. "But as long as the music is playing, you've got to get up and dance. We're still dancing."[162] With their salaries and bonuses reflecting their performance every three months, money managers are afraid to jump off the trend before it has run its course. Seeing that a market is over-valued is not enough. One has to keep riding the trend as long as the proverbial "greater fools" keep buying into it.

For public consumption, Prince parroted Wall Street's claim that the financial system had built-in stabilizers. "The depth of the pools of liquidity is so much larger than it used to be that a disruptive event now needs to be much more disruptive than it used to be," he assured investors. But he knew that the game had to end. "At some point," he acknowledged, "the disruptive event will be so significant that instead of liquidity filling in, the liquidity will go the other way." Across Wall Street, money managers positioned themselves to run for the exit as soon as the expected crash occurred.

To insure government support for when this day arrived, Wall Street lobbied to place its managers in control of the Federal Reserve, Treasury and key Congressional committees, as well as the European Central Bank, who duly bailed out creditors at full taxpayer expense after 2008.

The largest banks, brokerage houses and money managers have no interest in promoting popular understanding that what they are touting as a road to prosperity is really a path to their own gains. Consequently, they back academic theory reassuring people that every crash ("self-correcting cyclical downturn") leads to a recovery that will carry homeowners and other debtors to new heights – as long as the 99 Percent retain "confidence" (a euphemism for gullibility) in the system and let Wall Street insiders jump ship first.

---

[162] Michiyo Nakamoto and David Wighton, "Citigroup chief stays bullish on buy-outs," *Financial Times*, July 9, 2007.

How junk economics paved the way for 2008

Why haven't democracies been able to convince politicians to subordinate the financial sector to serve industrial prosperity instead of siphoning off its gains? What happened to the century of classical economics that created policies to avert this fate?

Something like *trahison des économistes* has fallen subject to what Erasmus called "learned ignorance" and Veblen "trained incapacity" to cope with the most pressing problems at hand. Decorated with complex mathematics as if it were an objective natural science, mainstream economics has become a lobbying effort to dismantle government power to regulate and tax *rentiers*. Well-subsidized models promote a trickle-down rationalization for the status quo, as if it were produced by inexorable economic laws. "Free market" ideologues then reason backward to construct a logic "proving" that economies become lower-cost and more efficient by lowering wage levels, removing taxes on wealth, cutting back public spending and privatizing infrastructure monopolies.

In the resulting symbiosis between bankers and other *rentiers*, debt is created mainly to purchase rent-extracting privileges and other rent-yielding properties, turning their economic rent into interest and related financial fees. Nearly all new credit since 1980 has been extended to the FIRE sector – credit to transfer ownership of assets while running the economy into debt, not to create new wealth.

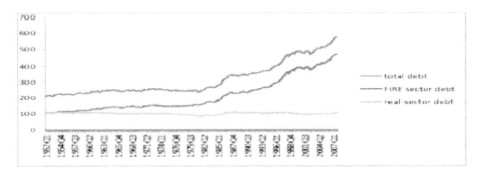

Figure 7: US Flow of funds (Source: Bezemer (2012) based on US flow of fund data, BEA 'Z' tables.)

The fatal assumption is that making money by debt leveraging or kindred engineering is as productive as investing in new means of production. The intended effect is to leave financial management to "technocrats," who turn out to be bank lobbyists toting around a few academics as useful idiots embedded in well-subsidized "think tanks." Much as the oil industry subsidizes

Junk Science to deny how carbon emissions contribute to global warming, so Wall Street subsidizes Junk Economics to deny that debt pollution plunges economies into chronic austerity and unemployment. Their conclusion is that no public regulation is needed, and no cleanup charges to compensate for the damage being caused.

Questions that a relevant economic theory needs to answer

Today, years after the 2008 financial crisis, the most pressing task for economic theory should be to explain why employment and consumption spending have not recovered. The Federal Reserve has given banks $4 trillion and the European Central Bank €1 trillion in Quantitative Easing to help the financial layer atop the economic pyramid, not to write down debts or revive the "real" economy by public spending. This enormous act of money creation could have enabled debtors to free themselves of debt so that they could resume spending to keep the circular flow of production and consumption in motion. Instead, governments have left the economy debt-strapped, creating money only to give to financial institutions.

Orwellian rhetoric is invoked to describe governments running budget deficits and creating central bank credit to help banks and bondholders but not employment and production. This is called "preserving the system." However, what is intended to be preserved is not the indebted economy, but the debt overhead owed to the financial sector. Central banks assiduously avoid any attempt to quantify how far wages, profits and tax revenue can be diverted to pay creditors without causing economic collapse and insolvency. Today's crisis is dismissed as an anomaly, ruled out by assumptions made at the outset. This blind spot is a precondition for steering economies down the road to debt deflation.

The radical reversals since 1980 in interest rates, asset prices and wages

The radical changes in financial and fiscal dynamics that led to the 2008 crash were sponsored by Margaret Thatcher in Britain and Ronald Reagan during the 1980s. The key trend they sought to reverse was that of interest rates. Their 35-year rise from 1945 to 1980 reached an unsustainable distress peak of 20% for loans to prime corporate borrowers. By tightening the money supply to slow the rate of inflation, Federal Reserve Chairman Paul Volcker (1979-87) made credit more expensive, stopping the boom in financial and property markets. Prices fell for bonds already issued (and which paid lower interest rates), while stocks and real estate followed suit. After 1980 rates declined steadily.

Also reversed was the trend in wages. From the Vietnam War and its "guns and butter" policy through the early 1970s, wages had risen faster than overall prices. But since the late 1970s, they have hardly moved. Consumer prices also have stabilized over the past thirty years. What *have* risen are asset prices, fueled by a tidal wave of bank credit inflating the greatest bond market rally in history. More money has been made in the stock market, bonds and real estate than by employing labor to produce goods for sale.

Structural changes in global economics and politics since the 1980s
Deregulation leads to an explosion of fraud

Pre-1980	Since 1980
1. *Interest rates, which determine prices for bonds, stocks and real estate*	
Steady rise to a peak of 20%, causing bond prices and other asset prices to fall.	Falling interest rates fuel a bull market in bonds that extends to stocks and real estate.
2. *Wage levels*	
Steady rise in real wages and living standards, especially under "guns and butter" policy.	Stagnant real wages, with more being paid for debt service, housing and Social Security taxes.
3. *Political philosophy*	
Social democratic policy: a rising government role, and "Keynesian" public spending as counter-cyclical stabilization.	Neoliberal deregulation and privatization, dismantling social spending programs and public infrastructure investment.
4. *Tax philosophy*	
Progressive income taxation, and taxing of real estate and financial wealth.	Tax shift off real estate and other FIRE-sector wealth and high incomes onto wage earners (heavier FICA tax) and consumers (sales taxes and value-added tax).
5. *Wealth and income distribution*	
Trend toward more equal distribution of wealth and income.	Widening polarization of wealth and income in the hands of the One Percent.

6. *Bank regulation*

Separation of retail banking and speculative investment banking under Glass Steagall.

Repeal of Glass Steagall in 1999 lets Wall Street create holding companies to absorb commercial banks, savings banks and S&Ls. From Chile to the post-Soviet Union, bank subsidiaries control industrial affiliates in *grupos* and conglomerates.

7. *Law enforcement*

Prosecution of financial fraud and crime, especially after the S&L crisis of the 1980s.

Decriminalization of financial and accounting fraud, esp. under Eric Holder.

8. *Pension planning*

Wages deferred in the form of defined-benefit pension plans to provide retirement security, mainly by investment in the stock market. (Pension-fund finance capitalism.)

Pension plans downsized into defined-contribution plans or wiped out in bankruptcy. Money managers invest pensions in LBOs and financial speculation.

9. *Accounting and the quality of statistics*

Strong government regulation ensures accurate financial and economic statistics. Arthur Andersen closed down for its role in Enron's fraud.

"Mark to model" accounting and off-balance-sheet subsidiaries ("Enron-style") make corporate statistics increasingly unrealistic in order to avoid taxes.

10. *Debtor/creditor legislation*

Increasingly humanitarian treatment of debtors via lenient bankruptcy laws and debt forgiveness.

Personal bankruptcy is made more difficult as the debt overhead rose for households, business and government. Indebted governments are coerced to privatize the public domain by selling it to rent-extracting private buyers.

11. *International trade and finance*

The trade balance normally reflects competition based on relative prices and costs of living.

Costs for labor and industry increasingly reflect interest, land rent, monopoly rent and other FIRE-sector dynamics, not direct production costs.

As Chairman of the Federal Reserve from 1987 to 2006, Alan Greenspan blocked attempts by board members to rein in crooked debt practices and put deregulators in charge of understaffed oversight agencies. By 2004 the FBI was warning about the explosion of financial fraud.[163] But by not distinguishing between free markets and outright deception, Greenspan cleared the way for junk mortgage lending.

Instead of protecting economies from danger, the disabled regulatory system protected bankers from being prosecuted. Fines were paid by their companies (and hence, "stockholders") or their insurance policies, without acknowledging criminal liability. After Bank of America bought Countrywide Financial, its insurers paid the $20 million fine for the "liars' loans" dumped into the financial system by Angelo Mozilo. Citigroup, JP Morgan Chase, Goldman Sachs and other banks paid billions of dollars in corporate fines to settle hundreds of billions of dollars of fraud by their managers.

President Obama's future Attorney General Eric Holder set the benevolent tone for financial felons under President Clinton in 2000 when he negotiated the pardon of Marc Rich for his billions of dollars of theft. The deal looked suspiciously like a payoff for Rich's ex-wife lavish funding of the Clinton Library. Former officials and insiders are now stepping forward to show how crooked the regulatory system has become in refusing to prosecute the behavior that led up to 2008.[164] But the Justice Department still refrains from holding

---

[163] "From 2000 to 2007, [appraisers] ultimately delivered to Washington officials a petition; signed by 11,000 appraisers…it charged that lenders were pressuring appraisers to place artificially high prices on properties. According to the petition, lenders were 'blacklisting honest appraisers' and instead assigning business only to appraisers who would hit the desired price targets." (*Financial Crisis Inquiry Commission* 2011, p. 18.) Commenting on this passage, William K. Black explains: "The CEO of lenders that follow the fraud 'recipe' can count on three 'sure things.' The lender will report exceptional income in the near term. The controlling officers will promptly be made wealthy by modern executive compensation. The lender will (later) suffer severe losses. … This turns market forces perverse and makes accounting control fraud surge." "Two Sentences that Explain the Crisis and How Easy it Was to Avoid," *New Economic Perspectives* [UMKC Economics Department blog], July 9, 2013.

[164] See http://www.law.columbia.edu/media_inquiries/news_events/2013/march2013/financial-fraud-panel for a link to the Columbia Law School presentation on February 26, 2013 on "Rent-Seeking, Instability and Fraud," with UMKC Prof. Bill Black, SEC chief accountant Lynn E. Turner and former SEC commissioner Harvey J. Goldschmid. For supporting documentation see Turner's statement Before the Senate Committee on Banking, Housing, and Urban Affairs On Enhancing Investor Protection and the Regulation of the Securities Markets, "The Economic Crisis—Bad Loans, Bad Gatekeepers, and Bad Regulation," March 10, 2009, http://www.banking.senate.gov/public/index.cfm?FuseAction=Files.View&FileStore_id=16e2bab5-2d77-4f6e-a471-933a438f6cac.

specific individuals responsible or making them surrender the money they have taken. Apart from the economics profession not wanting to deal with debt or financial fraud, the essence of Wall Street's regulatory capture is to make sure that the agencies charged with regulating banking and the stock market is staffed with non-regulators.

The junk mathematics behind junk economics

Myron Scholes and Robert Merton won the Swedish Central Bank's 1997 "Nobel" Economics Prize for refining a mathematical formula for pricing options, based on a paper that Scholes and Fischer Black wrote in 1973.[165] As a larger reward, Scholes and Merton were invited to put their math into practice by running the Long-Term Capital Management hedge fund. Nine months after the prize was awarded, LTCM lost $4.6 billion and went bankrupt. Over $1 billion was lost in just two days of the September 1998 crisis it instigated, when the stock market plunged 508 points.

The fund should have been called Short-Term Debt-Leveraged Management because its risk formulae assumed that any price changes would be merely marginal squiggles. In *The Black Swan* (2007) Nicholas Taleb described LTCM's strategy to be like "picking up pennies in front of a steamroller," a series of probable small gains with only minimal expectation of a large loss. Such wipeouts always happen when bad lending occurs, but this inevitability was assumed to lie at the far tip of the bell-shaped probability curve.

Nearly all of the major Wall Street firms were asked to contribute to LTCM's bailout to prevent a serious financial rupture in the web of computerized bets in which it had enmeshed the major Wall Street investment banks. Lehman Brothers refrained, for which it was duly punished in 2008. By that time the largest bets hinged on whether and when the junk mortgage market would collapse. (Lehman kept playing too long.)

---

[165] "LTC bailout reassures," CNN Money, Sept. 24, 1998. http://money.cnn.com/1998/09/24/companies/ltc/ Merton had written his doctorate at MIT under Paul Samuelson. Scholes studied at the neoliberal University of Chicago. Seemingly incorrigible, he started yet another hedge fund, Platinum Grove Asset Management, soon after LCTM crashed. Managing $4.5 billion, the company had an average annual return of 9.4 percent while the "What, me worry?" economy soared without fear of risk up to 2008. But from the start of 2008 through October 15, the company's Contingent Master fund lost 38 percent, wiping out the preceding four years' gains. Investors were soon blocked from withdrawing their money, showing that hedge fund pyramiding works fine when markets are rising, but are wiped out when zigs turn into zags.

Wall Street insiders saw the crisis coming – and sought to profiteer from it

There was plenty of warning in the year leading up to the September 2008 crisis.

> The world changed on August 9, 2007. That's when French bank BNP Paribas announced that it wouldn't let investors withdraw money from its subprime funds anymore. It couldn't value them, because nobody wanted to buy them.
>
> It was a mistake, but it was nothing like the one that was to come. Hawks had convinced themselves that the financial crisis had been going on for so long that it wasn't one anymore. That banks had had more than enough time to cut their exposure to troubled firms. That one bankruptcy, say Lehman's, wouldn't cause a cascade of others. Or, as St. Louis Fed president James Bullard put it, that "the level of systemic risk has dropped dramatically, and possibly to zero."[166]

Regulators not only turned a blind eye to reckless lending and fraud; they also sought to suppress warnings, which threatened to lower the prices and profitability of bubble securities. Protecting the top Wall Street losers was the Rubin acolyte Tim Geithner, who had joined with Wall Street billionaire and austerity promoter Pete Peterson, who recommended the young Geithner for the presidency of the New York Federal Reserve Bank. As Geithner wrote in his memoir *Stress Test*: "I basically restored the New York Fed board to its historic roots as an elite roster of the local financial establishment."[167] In a classic case of regulatory capture, Geithner reorganized its Board to include a virtual rogues gallery of Wall Street players, "including Lehman Brothers CEO Dick Fuld; JPMorgan Chase CEO Jamie Dimon; former Goldman Sachs Chairman Steve Friedman, who was still on the firm's board of directors; and General Electric CEO Jeff Immelt."

His position enabled Geithner to rescue Rubin's Citigroup and its bondholders from public takeover by bailing it out, pretending that the alternative would be chaos for the economy at large. When nominated for to be Treasury Secretary in 2009 he assured his Congressional questioner, Ron Paul of Texas, that he had fought *against* regulation:

---

[166] Matthew O'Brien, "How the Fed Let the World Blow Up in 2008," *The Atlantic*, February 26 2014. http://www.theatlantic.com/business/archive/2014/02/how-the-fed-let-the-world-blow-up-in-2008/284054/

[167] Matt Stoller, "THE CON-ARTIST WING OF THE DEMOCRATIC PARTY," *The Vice Reader*, June 4, 2014, http://www.vice.com/read/tim-geithner-and-the-con-artist-wing-of-the-democratic-party.

I have never been a regulator, for better or worse. And I think you are right to say that we have to be very skeptical that regulation can solve all these problems. We have parts of the system which are overwhelmed by regulation…It wasn't the absence of regulation that was a problem. It was, despite the presence of regulation, you got huge risks built up.[168]

Geithner was much more than a mere deregulator. He defended the bubble and the New York bankers who engineered it against their critics. After Bear Stearns collapsed on March 18, 2008, he assured the Federal Open Market Committee that there was no need for investment banks to set aside higher reserves: "It is very hard to make the judgment now that the financial system as a whole or the banking system as a whole is undercapitalized." For Geithner, the real danger seemed to be not junk mortgages, speculation on derivatives or other debt leveraging, but the economists who were warning the public to get out of the market. "There is nothing more dangerous in what we're facing now," Geithner accused, "than for people who are knowledgeable about this stuff to feed these broad concerns about our credibility and about the basic core strength of the financial system."[169]

Geithner will play a major role in nearly all the remaining chapters of this book for his unrelenting moves to block any policy that might not benefit or might even curtail the power of the major New York banks. Acting as special protector of the rogue operations at Citigroup and Goldman Sachs (in its claims against AIG), Geithner has been called to the Albert Speer of the Obama administration, an apparatchik installed by Rubin and Summers to run interference against regulators and critics.

Whether in Las Vegas or on Wall Street, the economics of a casino operate outside the logic of industrial capitalism. It is a zero-sum game, in which fortunes are made from bets with counterparties and customers. Wealth is redistributed to winning bettors, not created. Indeed, the "product" is a pool of toxic mortgages. Timing in such markets is based on the moody winds of the trading floors in New York and Chicago. This is the time horizon of bank robbers – and of robber banks. The idea is to get out safely before the peak is reached, because crashes occur quickly and sharply.

[168] Quoted in Pam Martens and Russ Martens, "As Citigroup Spun Toward Insolvency in '07- '08, Its Regulator Was Dining and Schmoozing With Citi Execs," *Wall Street on Parade*, January 7, 2014.
[169] Gretchen Morgenson, "A New Light on Regulators in the Dark," *The New York Times*, February 23, 2014, summarizing transcripts of the March 18, 2008 FOMC meeting at the New York Fed.

All such crashes are triggered by fractures in the chain of payments. The fraud, embezzlement or reckless gambling that trigger these breaks erupt like aneurisms where the debt-leveraged financial surface is stretched most thin. The highest debt leverage comes when there are no real assets at all behind the debt, Ponzi- or Madoff-style, as in the 2008 crash. But the Fed was more concerned about rising wages than about prices rising for real estate and financial securities. Asset-price inflation was applauded; rising wages feared.

The crisis was the inevitable result of the mathematics of compound interest and fictitious financial valuations. From January through mid-March of 2008, banks and brokerage stock prices fell by about 40 percent. But as long as the dancing was speeding up toward a final frenzy like Ravel's *Boléro*, standing on the sidelines would have meant letting rival money managers report better returns. The goal was to take the money and run. As one trader told me, "You only need to make a fortune once in a lifetime." For most players, this was that fortune moment, fueling the greedy turmoil leading up to 2008, after which housing prices would plunge by about 30 percent.

***

Bear Stearns went broke on March 17, 2008. A tentative sale was arranged to JPMorgan Chase for $2 a share, but the Federal Reserve felt such compassion for Bear Stearns' stockholders that it stepped in to absorb $29 billion of "toxic waste" losses so that they could receive five times as much. But when Lehman Brothers collapsed half a year later, on September 15, Treasury Secretary Hank Paulson told reporters that there was no way the investment bank could be saved. Stuck with the junk mortgages Lehman Brothers had hoped to sell to pension funds and German Landesbanks, it would have been a travesty to reward stockholder faith in the firm's reckless behavior.

Bear Stearns and Lehman were not like the banks where regular people keep their checking and savings accounts. They dealt with other financial institutions and the One Percent. Until 1999 the Depression-era Glass Steagall Act had insulated retail banking from such wholesale high finance in order to minimize risk to depositors. But Bill Clinton's brazen dismantling of this financial firewall enabled Citigroup, Bank of America and commercial banks to become holding companies that included investment houses, insurance and mortgage servicing firms, stockbrokers and real estate brokers.

The facile promise of deregulation was that by letting banks do whatever they wanted, the financial system would operate more efficiently. The reality is that speculation and outright dishonest dealings have become interwoven with retail banking, shifting the risk onto what had been relatively risk-free banks prior to 1999. The losses were concentrated among Wall Street's Too

Big To Fail high rollers, too politically connected to be constrained by regulators. Even banks with the most reckless or outright fraudulent operations were
protected and bailed out. Subsidizing Citibank, AIG and other institutions
that lost so heavily that they otherwise were unable to pay the winning bettors
and speculators kept the Wall Street casino afloat, at public expense.

Attorney General Eric Holder and Lanny Breuer refused to charge the
banks' real estate departments and mortgage brokers with falsifying documents. The "liars' loan" epithet was applied only to the low-income borrowers
who put their signature on the mortgage applications filled out by Countrywide
and other toxic financial polluters. The ten million homeowners whose debt
soared in excess of the market price of their homes ("negative equity") received
no leniency such as the banks received. They were subjected to a wave of foreclosures by robo-signed documents hitherto illegal under U.S. law, but which
were permitted simply because the practice was so pervasive that to have
enforced the law would have brought down the system.

"The system" was precisely what *should* have been brought down! The
financial high-jinks on Wall Street was not "the economy." It was the banksters,
pretending that their interest coincided with that of the economy at large. It
was as if keeping debts in place preserved real wealth and employment rather
than destroying them.

A full-court press was mounted to drive home the message that saving Wall
Street's super-rich was necessary to save the banks' everyday role of processing
checks and facilitating payments for the 99 Percent. But insured depositors
were never in danger of losing their funds. Nor were ATMs threatened with
running out of folding money. The bailout was deftly constructed to save these
large creditors, not the bread-and-butter economy. Declaring bad banks insolvent would have left their *uninsured* depositors, bondholders and stockholders
to absorb the losses from their bad loans.

Self-serving declarations that the crash was not foreseen led to a pro-Wall
Street response orchestrated under emergency conditions and public obfusca-
tion. Bad debts and "liars' loans" were kept in place instead of writing them
down to their inherent market valuations. This saved banks and their bondholders in a way that has imposed debt deflation and austerity from the United
States to Europe.

The assertion that keeping the debt burden in place was necessary to promote recovery is a textbook case of Orwellian doublespeak. The banks and
their customers were saved at the economy's expense. The middle class is being
crushed while markets are shrinking. Today's post-2008 austerity is the result.
Debt service is being squeezed out via mortgage debt, student loan debt and

credit card debt. Real wages and "markets" are stagnating because consumers have little left to spend after paying larger proportion of their income as debt service.

Neoliberal economists claim that debt is not a problem and can be ignored because (as the saying goes) "we owe it to ourselves." According this chop-logic, it all cancels out into a net zero balance in which one person's debt is treated as another's asset. This simplistic and misleading view neglects the who/whom dimension: Most of the net debt is owed *by* the 99 Percent *to* the One Percent (Wall Street's "ourselves"). The credit that banks create adds to *rentier* charges, not to price and income stability.

Thirty years of neoliberal junk economics has prepared the ground for imposing mass unemployment, emigration and privatization selloffs. The pre-tense is that public budget deficits cause inflation. But inflation has largely remained in check for the past few decades. What critics of government spending really oppose is public funding of Social Security, Medicare and other social programs out of the general budget, including progressive taxes paid by the wealthiest classes. The hypocrisy becomes apparent when Wall Street praises public debt creation as governments create money to bail out banks.

This asymmetrical pattern of debt creation is destroying our industrial economy and widening the inequality of wealth and income. It also is cor-rupting the economics discipline by suppressing awareness that today's finan-cial and fiscal austerity is based on the deception that financial and other *rentier* free lunchers are part of the host economy rather than intrusive and predatory, and that today's austerity is neither inherently natural nor inevitable. It is a result of financial policy that has almost fully captured the workings of gov-ernments. The remainder of this book therefore describes how the financial system has gained control of government policy throughout the world since 2008, "freeing" itself from public control and decoupling itself from industrial investment, except to finance corporate asset stripping.

13

The Coup of 2008: Bailing Out the Banks, Not the Economy

Sometimes I think people in the financial sector don't want you to understand the issues. Of course, if Main Street voters are confused or don't feel they understand the problems, they are unlikely to exert political influence to correct those problems. That only serves the purposes of the bad actors, who do not want meaningful government protections against their risk taking.

Sheila Bair, *Bull By the Horns* (2012), p. 323.

The financial sector mobilized its forces in the 2008 banking crisis to convince the world that bailing out insolvent banks would restore prosperity. The deeper aim was to reverse the progressive tax system and financial regulation that had guided the economy since the New Deal. This sophisticated political con game has enabled the One Percent to monopolize the recovery since 2008, widening their wealth and income advantage over the rest of the population.

This wealth gap is not the result of any irreducible economic law of nature. It reflects the system of subsidies, tax favoritism and bailouts crafted by lobbyists and banking elites to counter most people's sense of what is fair. The 2008 crisis afforded an opportunity to grab vast sums and subsidies by threatening that the alternative was chaos.

There *was* an alternative, of course. It was for banks, bondholders and other One Percenters to take their losses as bad loans to be written off the balance sheets. But Congress kept the bad debts on the books, surrendering to the false threat of empty ATM machines and losses even on insured bank accounts.

Pretending that it was not waging financial warfare, the Federal Reserve's idea of reviving prosperity was to re-inflate a new bubble by providing nearly free credit to banks. While the Fed effortlessly facilitated trillions of dollars in Quantitative Easing for Wall Street, the Obama Administration warned that Social Security must be cut back to balance future budgets. New money was to be spent only on financial securities, not tangible investment.

While the debt overhead's interest, amortization and penalties reduced consumer spending and industrial investment, the banks foreclosed and transferred assets from debtors to creditors. This fostered a fiscal crisis, backed by a chorus calls from Wall Street to solve it by privatizing public infrastructure and Social Security, cutting social spending and scaling back pensions.

Whichever way economies go from here, they cannot return to the pre-2008 normalcy. So there can be no talk of "recovery" of the past, given the overgrowth of debts that cannot be paid. Going forward, there are two alternatives: Either (1) banks and bondholders will lose if debts are written down; or (2) the economy will face a generation of austerity as debt deflation and privatization smother growth and upward mobility. In that case the One Percent will inherit wealth, while the 99 Percent inherit debt bondage.

The financial sector's political mission is to replace democratically elected governments and public planning with technocrats appointed by the banks. The first six years of Quantitative Easing saw the Federal Reserve create money to bail out Wall Street but not to finance tangible growth or demand writedowns of the household debt and the junk mortgages that triggered the breakdown.

The broad strategy of the banksters is to use economic distress as an opportunity to grab assets from the public domain, along with the government's taxing and money-creating ability. Instead of taxing *rentier* wealth and spending to rebuild infrastructure, federal and local governments are being pressed to sell public roads for buyers to turn into toll roads, much as they have transformed the health care system into rent-extraction opportunities.

How resolving the 2008 crisis differed radically from past resolutions

For a century, bank crises followed a well-understood pattern. Bad debts and investments were wiped out. Deposits in banks that made bad loans were reduced to whatever residual value remained after foreclosures and distress sales swept away debt-inflated prices. Herbert Hoover's Treasury Secretary, Andrew Mellon, summarized the process in advising the president in November 1929:

> Liquidate labor, liquidate stocks, liquidate the farmers, liquidate real estate. It will purge the rottenness out of the system. High costs of living and high living will come down. People will work harder, live a more moral life. Values will be adjusted, and enterprising people will pick up from less competent people.[170]

---

[170] Reported in Herbert Hoover, *Memoirs*, Volume 3: *The Great Depression, 1929–1941* (1952). Hoover didn't take Mellon's advice. But Chicago Boys and the IMF have advocated it for the past generation.

Until 2008 almost nobody expected that the largest Wall Street banks, such as Citigroup and Bank of America, would comprise the "less competent people." But financial lobbyists insisted that special favoritism to these institutions was needed to prepare the way for renewed prosperity.

Until 2008, financial crashes had a silver lining: to wipe away the debt overhead so that economies *can* recover. Debt relief through bankruptcy traditionally forced housing prices to fall back to more affordable levels. But the Fed's aim was (and remains) to preserve the economic power of the One Percent and revive bank balance sheets by *preventing* housing, stock market or bond prices from falling. Instead of the bad debts built up prior to 2008 being wiping out, they have been kept in place. In conjunction with cutting back public spending programs, this shrinks the domestic market, and wages fall instead of the housing and other asset prices being supported. The banks were bailed out, not the economy.

Starting with the Troubled Asset Relief Program (TARP) in the United States, banks throughout the world demanded that governments save large uninsured depositors and bondholders from losses, and let managers of the broken banks keep the bonuses and gains they had paid themselves. Ireland's government followed European Union advice to bail out uninsured creditors of Anglo-Irish Bank at taxpayer expense. In Greece, the European "troika" – the IMF, European Commission and European Central Bank – saved bondholders by extending enough bailout credit to pay them in full for loans made to governments without any reference to the ability to be paid without plunging its economy into a worse depression than the country had suffered in the 1930s. Bondholders and bank depositors took their money and ran, foreign debts to be paid by burdening populations with enormous taxes on a scale hitherto suffered only in war emergencies.

The 1929–31 crash had led to government regulation and control over banking. The Federal Deposit Insurance Corporation (FDIC) was created in 1933, the Glass-Steagall Act separated commercial banking from speculative Wall Street investment banking, and other reforms were passed. But from 1987 to 2006, Fed Chairman Greenspan led the fight to dismantle the New Deal, disabling the regulatory oversight designed to keep bank loans in line with the borrower's ability to pay. After 2008 the bailouts preserved the most reckless and "criminogenic" megabanks, headed by Citigroup and Bank of America, instead of letting them go under. A brief regulatory attempt, the Dodd-Frank Bill, was undone by bank lobbyists who bought control of politics, supporting politicians who promoted regulatory capture to a point where financial fraud was essentially decriminalized.[171] Instead of prosecuting financial law-breaking, the largest banks have been let off the hook, on the premise that enforcing laws against fraud would drive them under.

Much as the key to the Sherlock Holmes crime story "The Hound of the Baskervilles" was that the dog *didn't* bark, the most revealing aspect of the 2008 bailout was that contrary to what the Federal Reserve and Treasury avowed, the agencies did not follow the century-old "Bagehot Rule." Their emergency lending to commercial banks was *not* limited to the traditional "good securities at penalty rates of interest."

Bank-friendly economists depicted this loosening of loan terms under emergency conditions as an effort to restore normalcy. But it was abnormal not to prosecute wrongdoers as was done in the S&L scandals of the 1980s, when many bank executives were sent to jail. It also was a break from tradition to extend banks enough public credit to start lending again, without obliging them to wipe out shareholders and impose losses on their large uninsured depositors and bondholders. A financial coup d'état had occurred.

Walter Bagehot was editor of the *Economist* from 1860 to 1877. His influential book *Lombard Street: A Description of the Money Market* (1873) was required reading even when I was taking my PhD in the 1960s. It outlined the strict terms on which central banks should provide liquidity in times of crises. Seriously bad loans back then were only a small portion of the banking business. The main problem was a general crisis leading prompting nervous depositors to withdraw their money from banks whose loans were basically sound. These loans went to debtors who were able to keep paying the carrying charges, but which the banks could not readily convert into immediate cash to pay depositors. Governments naturally sought to prevent economic crises resulting from banks having to call in their loans and drive their customers into insolvency.

However, central banks were not supposed to save *insolvent* institutions that had made bad loans to borrowers who could not carry their debts. Support for banks was supposed to be made on sufficiently onerous terms so as not to give them an opportunity to make speculative and predatory gains in times of distress. But by 2008, bad loans accounted for more than the entire net worth

---

[171] Former S&L prosecutor Bill Black describes the details in *The Best Way to Rob a Bank is to Own One* (2005) and in his contributions to New Economic Perspectives and to The RealNews Network. He emphasizes that the 2001 "Nobel" Economics Prize was given to George Akerlof for his 1993 article with Paul Romer: "Looting: The Economic Underworld of Bankruptcy for Profit."

of some banks. Many of these loans were fraudulent, for which banks would pay hundreds of billions of dollars in civil penalties. As a Levy Institute study describes:

> Government response to a failing, insolvent bank is supposed to be much different than its response to a liquidity crisis: government is supposed to step in, seize the institution, fire the management, and begin a resolution. … Normally, stockholders lose, as do the uninsured creditors – which would have included other financial institutions. … However, rather than resolving institutions that were probably insolvent, the Fed, working with the Treasury, tried to save them – by purchasing troubled assets, recapitalizing them, and by providing loans for long periods.[172]

After banks had gained control of the Fed and Treasury they turned Bagehot's Law upside down. Henry Paulson's easy loan terms, like those of subsequent Federal Reserve lending, were a radical departure from the Bagehot Rule. The Fed did not impose a penalty charge for being insolvent. The Fed, Congress and Treasury provided credit at giveaway rates to Wall Street's investment houses as well as to normal commercial banks. The terms were so favorable that banks became the most profitable sector in the aftermath of the crisis.

The Fed also lent against junk mortgages, derivatives and credit-default swaps at face value, or accepted them for "non-recourse" loans at prices far above what the market would have paid. The government absorbed the risk instead of banks, bondholders and financial speculators. Quantitative Easing (low-interest credit to banks) tailored toward making speculation profitable enough so that banks could make enough money to compensate for their losses on junk mortgages and risky speculations gone bad. It amounted to the largest American giveaway of wealth to favored beneficiaries since the Yazoo land fraud of the mid-1790s.

FDIC Chair Sheila Bair insisted that even the two most reckless insolvent lenders, Citibank and Bank of America, had enough reserves and sound loans to cover their FDIC-insured deposits, even when the government more than doubled the insurance limit from $100,000 to $250,000. But Wall Street's strategy was to frighten depositors that they might have to absorb the losses if Wall Street banks and speculators were not paid immediately in full, with no "haircuts" for the bondholders. As late as 2014, six years after the crash, former Treasury Secretary Geithner continued to claim that his insider giveaways saved bank customers from the alternative – ATMs running out of money.[173]

---

[172] *The Lender of last Resort: A Critical Analysis of the Federal Reserve's Unprecedented Intervention After 2007*, Levy Institute, April 2013 (prepared mainly by Randall Wray), p. 7.

[173] Timothy F. Geithner, "The Paradox of Financial Crises," *Wall Street Journal*, May 13, 2014: "Because two presidents were willing to put politics aside and deploy a massive and

This combination of a bailout of lenders while keeping bad debts in place was very far removed from a market-based solution. It shows that banks hate free markets when they lose – and demand that the economy needs to rescue them, not their debtors. That is why banks feel that they must control the government, turning it into a fail-safe for their biggest blunders by absorbing their losses and serving their interests. Bankers also hate going to jail, and insist that any fines for crooked behavior be paid by the banking institutions (*i.e.*, stockholders), not the managers responsible for the transgressions.

The Federal Reserve and Treasury provided credit under the guise that recovery requires banks to rebuild their depleted net worth so that they can make yet *more* interest-bearing loans to the already debt-ridden economy – pushing housing and stock prices back up, as if this is what prosperity means. And by yearend 2010 the financial sector did indeed recoup its heavy losses from 2008 to register "about 30% of all operating profits" despite accounting "for less than 10% of the value added in the economy."[174] By mid-2013 the banking system's share of corporate profits had risen "to 42 percent … and the Fed expects them to keep rising."[175]

But as Chapter 5 has explained, the consequence of this policy is that debt keeps growing exponentially until it engulfs the economy. Paying more interest and amortization on yet more debt leaves less to be spent on current output. What the debt-ridden economy actually needed was write-downs – at the *expense* of bankers and other creditors. This was the great opportunity that government decision-makers (vetted by the banks) spurned in 2008. Banks recovered in a way that bled the non-financial host economy with austerity.

Bailing out bondholders, not the debtors

The bailout process began on September 7, 2008 when the Federal Housing Finance Agency took over the $5.3 trillion of mortgage obligations held by Fannie Mae and Freddie Mac.[176] Founded as public agencies in 1938, these

---

creative rescue, we prevented economic catastrophe and got the economy growing again in about six months. We kept the ATMs working, saved the auto industry, fixed the broken credit channels so that the economy could grow …" This theme was elaborated in his fanciful apologia *Stress Test* (2014). In short, There Was No Alternative.

[174] Kathleen Madigan, "Like the Phoenix, U.S. Finance Profits Soar," *Wall Street Journal*, March 25, 2011.

[175] Richard Eskow, "The 'Bankization' of America," *Common Dreams*, August 16, 2013. http:// www.commondreams.org/view/2013/08/16.

[176] For background leading up to this, see Mike Whitney, "Swan Song for Fanny Mae," *CounterPunch*, July 18, 2008, and Peter J. Wallison, "There Is No Reason to Panic," *Wall Street Journal*, July 14, 2008.

mortgage insurance institutions were privatized in 1968, but their presumed semi-public character led most investors to view their debt as implicitly having a public guarantee against default. This enabled Fannie and Freddie to borrow at interest rates nearly as low as the Treasury had to pay, while buying mortgages yielding a much higher rate.

By buying, insuring and packaging these mortgages, Fannie and Freddie made them easily liquid and tradable for pension funds, insurance companies and other institutional investors, who got higher interest rates than were available on Treasury bonds. Even foreign central banks were advised to hold Fannie Mae bonds in their dollar reserves.

These investors assumed that Fannie and Freddie did the basic lending oversight. But in their managers' zeal to expand this business – and keep their market share as Countrywide Financial and Washington Mutual led a race to the bottom – Fannie and Freddie increasingly bought fraudulent mortgage loans.

It turned out to be easier to make profits without doing any due diligence at all, but simply to buy mortgages with no questions asked. Fraud usually is immensely profitable in the short run. Stock prices for Fannie and Freddie soared, and their managers paid themselves correspondingly high salaries and bonuses. Even investors who did not fully trust these institutions at least assumed that the government would pick up the losses from reckless lending. The government did end up on the hook for what turned out to be junk mortgages, although nowhere near as junky as the "toxic waste" packaged by investment banks such as Bear Stearns and Lehman Brothers.

The mortgage market finally caved in when Lehman Brothers' filed for bankruptcy on September 15, 2008. To save bondholders of Fannie and Freddie from bearing losses on defaults that threatened to wipe out the net worth of these two privatized institutions, the Treasury invested up to $100 billion in each to cover the losses on the "liars' loan" junk mortgages they had bought from Countrywide and other fraudsters. In exchange, the Treasury received warrants (that is, options) to buy 79.9 percent of each company's common stock.[177]

---

[177] For a discussion of the political maneuvering around these options, see Peter J. Wallison, "How Paulson Would Save Fannie Mae," *Wall Street Journal*, September 12, 2008, James R. Hagerty and Jessica Holzer, "U.S. Move to Cover Fannie, Freddie Losses Stirs Controversy," *Wall Street Journal*, December 26, 2009, and David Skeel, "Now Uncle Sam Is Ripping Off Fannie and Freddie," *Wall Street Journal*, Feb. 28, 2014, and Wikipedia, "Federal takeover of Fannie Mae and Freddie Mac."

The CEOs and boards of directors of these two companies were dismissed, but there was no clawback to recapture the outsized salaries, bonuses and stock options their managers had awarded themselves. The government also refused to risk the ire of stockholders by returning the two companies into public ownership. Instead of a takeover, the government's action amounted to a giveaway to save bondholders from suffering a loss. This was euphemized as saving the economy from "socialism."

But this was merely a dress rehearsal for the $750 billion TARP bailout in Congress. TARP was a total victory for Wall Street over Congress. "It was all about the bondholders," Sheila Bair summed up when the dust had settled. The Treasury

> did not want to impose losses on bondholders, and we did. We kept saying: 'There is no insurance premium on bondholders,' you know? For the little guy on Main Street who has bank deposits, we charge the banks a premium for that, and it gets passed on to the customer. We don't have the same thing for bondholders. They're supposed to take losses.[178]

But it was financiers and investment bankers who were rescued, not homeowners, other debtors and pension funds.

Panicking Congress to pass the TARP bailout with no conditions attached

Treasury Secretary Paulson submitted a terse three-page plan for the Troubled Asset Relief Program (TARP) on September 20. Republicans voted against it, accusing it of being a move toward bigger government. Paulson's initial version left no room for Congressional oversight, and Section 8 of his plan called for the money to be handed out without being subject to question by elected officials or the courts. "Decisions by the Secretary pursuant to the authority of this Act are non-reviewable and committed to agency discretion, and may not be reviewed by any court of law or any administrative agency." As economist Willem Buiter summarized Paulson's demand: "I want $750 bn. I want it now. I will use these funds for good works, but I cannot tell you what these will be. Don't ask any questions. And you cannot sue me."[179]

---

[178] Joe Nocera, "Sheila Bair's Bank Shot," *The New York Times Magazine*: July 10, 2011. This was the interview she gave upon stepping down from the FDIC.

[179] "Slaughtering sacred cows: it's the turn of the unsecured creditors now," *Financial Times*, March 18, 2009.

Paulson asked for unlimited Treasury authority to buy or sell mortgage-backed securities up to $700 billion at any given time. The figure reflected Paulson's guess as to what homeowners owed the banks over and above their ability to pay – and above the market price for property pledged as collateral. The Treasury was to use the money to buy mortgage-backed securities, on whatever terms the Treasury Secretary wanted – not only with commercial banks but also with investment banks, hedge funds and investment companies, "without regard to any other provision of law regarding public contracts."

The market for these securities was collapsing. Interest rates on adjustable-rate mortgages were about to explode to "third year" or penalty rates far above the "teaser" rates that banks used to hook prospective homebuyers. Instead of seeing market prices for their property rising above their mortgage, these debtors were losing their hoped-for free lunch of asset-price inflation (what Alan Greenspan euphemized as "wealth creation"). Their negative equity position was deepening, leading to mortgage delinquencies and defaults threatening bank profits – and for some of the biggest institutions, insolvency. That was where the Treasury's main concern lay, not with homeowners or investors for the packaged junk mortgages Wall Street produced.

Pressuring Congress not to add measures that could slow passage, Paulson said in a Sunday interview on ABC's *This Week* on September 21: "We need this to be clean and to be quick." It would be hard to think of a blunter illustration of Naomi Klein's *Shock Doctrine: The Rise of Disaster Capitalism*. The crisis provided an opportunity for the tycoons of high finance to seize the initiative from Congress. On December 19, President Bush used his executive authority to declare that TARP funds could be spent on any program that the Treasury Secretary deemed necessary to alleviate the financial crisis.

In fact, not a penny of the $700 billion was expended on buying mortgage-backed securities. It was all a classic bait-and-switch exercise. The money was given to Wall Street banks and investment houses that filed legal papers to become "banks" in order to qualify for FDIC support and other government handouts aimed ostensibly at protecting retail depositors rather than the One Percent.

Only the bad-mortgage lenders needed a bailout. But to conceal Citigroup's identity as by far the worst offender, the Treasury demanded that each of the ten largest Wall Street institutions be gifted by a similar $25 billion sum. The money was lent on concessionary terms, without any voice by Congress or any public agency over what these institutions did with it.

Paulson warned that Congressional pressure to provide relief for homeowners facing foreclosure would slow the economy, not rescue it. "The biggest help we can give the American people right now is to stabilize the financial system," by which he meant his Wall Street constituency from suffering losses by having to sell their mortgages and other loans in the face of falling real estate prices. Some four million foreclosures were looming, prompting Moody's to forecast housing prices dropping by as much 40 percent over the next few years, leaving families with negative equity, owing much more than their homes were worth – and hence, more than should have been lent in the first place.

To rescue banks from suffering from the market forces devastating underwater homeowners, the Fed bought packaged mortgages at above-market prices. Instead of subsidizing homeowners, these "cash for trash" swaps saved banks from losing money. No significant mortgage relief was stipulated. Promises by incoming President Obama and other Democrats turned out to be just for show.

The Obama-McCain presidential debate sidesteps the TARP bailout

Making an end run to the left of the Democrats, Congressional Republicans refused to vote for the TARP bailout. But John McCain fought to turn the tide. On Friday morning, September 26, the day of his first presidential debate with Senator Barack Obama, McCain flew to Washington to announce that he was suspending his campaign to devote all his efforts to persuading Congress to approve Paulson's plan. But the senator soon stopped grandstanding and flew down to Oxford, Mississippi to join the evening debate.

Amazing as it may seem (and an index of how far the mainstream press failed to inform the public, no doubt to avoid enraging their audience) the TV questioners refrained from asking the candidates about the proposed bailout that had dominated the day's news! To fill the vacuum that the media's self-censorship had created, the Treasury issued a fact sheet that Saturday evening, promising: "Removing troubled assets will begin to restore the strength of our financial system so it can again finance economic growth." By "growth" it meant a new wave of debt. Hedge fund traders and banksters were depicted impersonally as "the financial system," while the euphemism "removing troubled assets" meant buying junk mortgages at prices far above current market levels. (This task ended up being performed by the Fed, not TARP.)

Senator McCain went on Sunday TV to explain that "It's not a bailout; it's a rescue." Insisting that no strings be attached, he saw his poll ratings plunge as his identity reverted from "maverick" label back to his role in the Keating Five, the senators who had demanded that the Federal Reserve not interfere with Charles Keating's thieving at California's Lincoln S&L. Suspending proper S&L regulation had cost the government $3 billion, an enormous sum back in 1989. As Wall Street consultant Yves Smith points out:

> Bailouts increase moral hazard by rewarding risky and reckless lending practices. And they are often the result of crony capitalism due to the power of the financial services lobby. ... So what we have here is a case of crony capitalism and kleptocracy, plain and simple – whether by design or not is immaterial.[180]

But with an MSNBC poll showing that 62 percent of Americans opposed the bill, Republicans (but not McCain) struck a populist note and voted with righteous indignation against Secretary Paulson's open-ended giveaway on Monday, September 29. "This legislation is giving us a choice between bankrupting our children and bankrupting a few of these big financial institutions on Wall Street that made bad decisions," said Texas Congressman John Culberson.[181] Denouncing the bailout as "lunacy," President George W. Bush's first Secretary of the Treasury (2001–02), outspoken Paul O'Neill, called it "crazy. ... The consequences of it are unbelievably bad in terms of public intrusion into the private sector."[182] Former Republican Treasury official Paul Craig Roberts complained: "Under the bailout plan, the troubled assets move from the banks' books to the Treasury's."[183]

In line with their rhetoric about free enterprise and self-reliance, they opposed "handouts from government" – that is, from officials on loan from their Wall Street management positions – as being socialist. But waves of lobbyists descended on the Capitol to pressure Republicans to join the Democrats in a new vote. House leaders were reported to be "bringing in the small business lobby and the banking lobby to buy the twelve Republican votes they need,"[184] convincing them that the TARP bailout was not really socialism after all. It was a case of "socializing the losses, privatizing the profits."

Mobilizing government to save Wall Street from losses on bad loans and gambles is the opposite of socialism. It is oligarchy – control of the government by the wealthy. They were the largest campaign contributors, and Congress

---

[180] Yves Smith, "The less optimistic view of Treasury's handling of the crisis," *Credit Write-downs.*" Nov. 6, 2009 (also at "Geithner and Summers as Obama's Cheney and Rumsfeld," *Naked Capitalism,* July 9, 2011).

[181] Chris Isidore, "Bailout plan rejected - supporters scramble," *CNNMoney,* September 29, 2008. Some Democrats voted against the bill for not doing enough to help taxpayers facing foreclosure or unemployment and accused proponents of moving too fast. "Like the Iraq war and Patriot Act, this bill is fueled by fear and haste," said Lloyd Doggett, D-Texas."

[182] Brendan Murray, "Paulson Bank Rescue Proposal Is 'Crazy,' O'Neill Says (Update1), Bloomberg, Oct. 1, 2008. http://www.bloomberg.com/apps/news?pid=20601087&sid=atJMmClVjevU&refer=home

[183] Paul Craig Roberts, "Why Paulson's Plan is a Fraud," *Counterpunch,* October 3, 2008.

[184] Richard C Cook, "'Grand Larceny' on a Monumental Scale: Does the Bailout Bill Mark the End of America as We Know It?" *Global Research,* October 2, 2008.

got the message. Denunciations of Big Government were appropriate only when public policy supported labor, not when it subsidized Wall Street.

Despite the Constitution's rule that revenue bills must originate in the House, which had rejected the bailout, the Senate took it up and passed it by a vote of 74-25 on October 1. Republican Sen. Jeff Sessions of Alabama emphasized the few concessionary tax cuts to distract attention from the enormous giveaways to the big banks and brokerage houses – which were allowed to call themselves "banks" in order to obtain Federal Reserve money creation. "This bill has been packaged with a lot of very popular things to give it even more momentum," so that (as *The New York Times* explained), "instead of siding with a $700 billion bailout, lawmakers could now say they voted for increased protection for deposits at the neighborhood bank, income tax relief for middle-class taxpayers and aid for schools in rural areas where the federal government owns much of the land."[185]

Two days later, Treasury Secretary Paulson called Sheila Bair to meet at his office with Federal Reserve Chairman Ben Bernanke, and New York Fed apparatchik Tim Geithner on the phone line. Bair recalls indignantly how Paulson asked her "to publicly announce that the FDIC would guarantee the liabilities of the banking system. ... they wanted me to stand up and say that the FDIC was going to be guaranteeing everybody against everything in the $13 trillion banking system."[186] These liabilities would have included all losses by banks, investment banks such as Goldman Sachs and their affiliates, which were quickly turning themselves into commercial banks to qualify for Federal Reserve loans as well as for the TARP giveaway.

The Treasury claimed that in order to preserve peoples' bank accounts it was necessary to rescue large uninsured depositors, along with mortgage brokers, insurance companies and investment banks. The implicit threat was to wreck the economy if lawmakers did not move quickly to save Wall Street. Bair rejected this policy. "Besides the risk it would have entailed, it would have also meant a windfall for bondholders, because much of the existing debt was trading at a steep discount."[187]

Bair's major adversary was Tim ("I have never been a regulator") Geithner at the New York Fed. Geithner "did not want creditors, particularly bondholders, in those large, failing financial institutions to take losses." She coun-

---

[185] Carl Hulse, "Senate Passes Bailout Plan; House May Vote by Friday," *The New York Times*, October 1, 2008.

[186] *Bull by the Horns*, p. 111.

[187] Joe Nocera, "Sheila Bair's Bank Shot," *The New York Times Magazine*: July 10, 2011. 'They should have let Bear Stearns fail,' Sheila Bair said.

tered: "We [the FDIC] do not have an insurance program for big bond investors. They are sophisticated and well heeled and can fend for themselves. There is no reason for the government to protect them."[188]

But the tide had turned. Later that same Friday, House Republicans put aside their rhetoric about free markets and gave the Democrats enough votes to save Wall Street – adding enormously to the federal debt over which they would soon shed crocodile tears. President Bush immediately signed TARP into law as the Emergency Economic Stabilization Act.

Keeping Wall Street's mortgage claims above water involved creating new public debt that, in due course, would become the excuse for incoming President Obama to yield to Wall Street demands to define "stabilizing the economy" as cutting the budget deficit in other areas, headed by Social Security. The TARP and other subsidies to Wall Street since 2008 thus created pressure for offsetting cuts to balance the federal budget in ways that have deepened austerity – the opposite of the Act's pretended stabilization. It meant instability for the indebted economy. Debtors seemed not to need rescuing, only creditors.

Leading the fight to promote TARP, the Democratic Congress refrained from introducing safeguards to protect the public interest. No politician asked Paulson to define just what his idea of stability was, or how Citigroup's, AIG's or other Wall Street losses threatened the nonfinancial economy. The hardest questions came from Ohio Congressman Dennis Kucinich:

> Why aren't we having hearings on the plan we have just received? ... Why have we not considered any alternatives other than to give $700 billion to Wall Street? Why aren't we asking Wall Street to clean up its own mess? Why aren't we passing new laws to stop the speculation, which triggered this? Why aren't we putting up new regulatory structures to protect investors? How do we even value the $700 billion in toxic assets?
>
> Why aren't we helping homeowners directly with their debt burden? Why aren't we helping American families faced with bankruptcy? Why aren't we reducing debt for Main Street instead of Wall Street? ... Is this the United States Congress or the board of directors of Goldman Sachs?[189]

Neil Barofsky, TARP's Special Inspector General (SIGTARP), made a similarly harsh criticism of how the Treasury ignored even the modest care for debtors victimized by Wall Street that Congress supposedly intended:

> The legislation that created TARP, the Emergency Economic Stabilization Act, had far broader goals, including protecting home values and preserving homeownership. ...

---

[188] *Bull by the Horns*, pp. 99f.

[189] "Kucinich Opposes Bailout and asks, 'Is this the United States Congress or the board of directors of Goldman Sachs?'" September 28, 2008, speech on the House floor.

Congress was told that TARP would be used to purchase up to $700 billion of mortgages, and, to obtain the necessary votes, Treasury promised that it would modify those mortgages to assist struggling homeowners. Indeed, the act expressly directs the department to do just that.

But it has done little to abide by this legislative bargain. Almost immediately, as permitted by the broad language of the act, Treasury's plan for TARP shifted from the purchase of mortgages to the infusion of hundreds of billions of dollars into the nation's largest financial institutions, a shift that came with the express promise that it would restore lending.

Treasury, however, provided the money to banks with no effective policy or effort to compel the extension of credit. There were no strings attached: no requirement or even incentive to increase lending to home buyers, and against our strong recommendation, not even a request that banks report how they used TARP funds.[190]

Yves Smith points out that as soon as Congress passed the TARP bill, Wall Street changed how the money was to be spent. "The focus on toxic mortgage paper, rather than the real intent, equity injections, was presumably to distract Congresscritters and the public from asking: 'Whoa, if we are providing equity, what control and upside do we get?' This was a way to avoid inconvenient questions like 'Why don't we cap pay? Fire the top executives? Replace the board?' and other things that are normally done with failing or failed institutions."[191]

The Treasury gave the biggest losers, Citigroup and AIG, enough bailout money to pay the winning counterparties on the other side of their financial gambles. Banks quickly became the economy's most profitable sector. The administration insisted that their bondholders and large non-insured depositors not suffer a loss, and that neither the FDIC nor Congress should nationalize ailing banks and run them as a public utility whose services might rival those of the private banking system.

Preventing China from saving AIG

Six years after 2008 the lawsuit brought by AIG's largest stockholder, Starr International (owned mainly by Hank Greenberg) finally went to trial. Testimony by subpoenaed Treasury and other officials revealed many options

---

[190] Neil M. Barofsky, "Where the Bailout Went Wrong," *The New York Times*, March 30, 2011.
[191] Yves Smith, "AIG Bailout Trial Bombshell III: Paulson Lied to Congress About TARP," *Naked Capitalism*, October 17, 2014, commenting that the testimony by Scott Alvarez, general counsel for the Federal Reserve Board of Governors, "makes clear that the plan was always to inject equity into the banks." She adds: "Never forget that Wall Street showed its gratitude to American taxpayers by paying itself record bonuses in 2009 and 2010."

and fateful decisions hitherto concealed from the public and Congress. Gretchen Morgenson of *The New York Times* found that "the case's significance lies in the information it unearthed about what the government did in the bailout – details it worked hard to keep secret."[192]

The most remarkable revelation concerned the eagerness by China's government to buy into AIG, on terms that would have made the Treasury's own $85 billion initial bailout (later expanded to $182 billion) unnecessary. Unnecessary, that is, to save AIG, but not its counterparties such as Goldman Sachs; that turned out to be the real problem.

Asian sovereign wealth funds had been looking to invest their nation's foreign exchange holdings in something preferable to U.S. Treasury securities – not only higher yielding, but also in line with national economic development strategy. Of such global funds, the largest was China Investment Corporation (CIC). It had lost heavily by buying into Blackstone Group's 2007 IPO. But AIG after all had been founded in China and hence offered that nation a chance to de-colonize its FIRE sector.

The Wall Street standby, *Institutional Investor*, describes how CIC officials approached the Treasury on September 16, 2008, proposing to invest as much as the Treasury's $85 billion initial funding to buy into AIG. At a trade and commerce meeting in Yorba Linda, California, they asked Taiya Smith, Paulson's deputy chief of staff and executive secretary, to have him call Chinese Vice Premier Wang Qishan. The trial's report of findings quotes her as saying: "All [the Chinese officials] wanted to talk about was AIG." In fact, "The document says Smith added that 'the Chinese were actually willing to put in a little more than the total amount of money required for AIG.'"[193]

Under Secretary for International Affairs David McCormick consulted with Paulson about the Chinese interest, and then told Smith "that Treasury 'did not want the Chinese coming in at this point in time on AIG.'" Paulson "did not return CIC's phone call, as requested by the Chinese government. A Treasury colleague was dispatched to tell the fund, in effect, to go away."

Commenting on this evidence, one money manager told *Institutional Investor*: "This was the epitome of crony capitalism. What happened was egregious, and the public doesn't get how egregious it was, and Congress doesn't understand how egregious it was." Geopolitics proved overwhelming. Accord-

---

[192] Gretchen Morgenson, "Fresh Doubt Over the Bailout of A.I.G.," *The New York Times*, December 21, 2014.

[193] Richard Teitelbaum," Hank Greenberg, AIG, CIC and the Backdoor Bailout," *Institutional Investor*, November 21, 2014.

ing to Duke University Law Professor James Cox: "The savior of the financial system would have been a communist, totalitarian country. The irony of the Chinese saving Wall Street would have been too much." The bottom line, Cox concluded, was a "sinister or cynical [way of] protecting the big banks against the yellow peril." So AIG was saved in a way that benefited Goldman, and kept U.S. control of its own FIRE sector, while insisting on controlling that of other countries.

The 2014 trial's big revelation was the degree to which the Treasury and New York Fed were more concerned with protecting Wall Street firms than with saving the government money or protecting the economy at large.

It was all about saving the counterparties, as Chapter 16 will show. Any private buyer would have rejected the bold claims by Goldman for payment, on the ground that the mortgage securities being guaranteed were fraudulent. Paulson's Treasury sacrificed AIG to Goldman as a kind of adjunct to TARP.

14

The Giveaways Get More Deeply Politicized and Corrupt

"There's this thing about hindsight and stuff. Many things that seemed prudent at the time turned out to be imprudent."

Tim Geithner, testifying at the 2014 AIG trial against the U.S. Government[194]

It sounds as if everything was just an accident, like the chronic IMF and European Central Bank miscalculations that austerity will bring recovery and prosperity if bondholders are paid enough, social programs and pensions cut back enough, and wages lowered enough to "restore confidence." The same mistake is made decade after decade. The post-2008 giveaway to Wall Street – without benefiting strapped mortgage debtors – was no accidental mistake. It was deliberate policy, over which politicians shed crocodile tears when it turned out that the public lost heavily while the wealthy One Percent-serving institutions gained so vastly. Yet this benefit for insiders and the One Percent is what has made the bailout a successful policy capture from Wall Street's vantage point.

"We didn't do it for the banks," claimed Geithner. "We did it to protect people from the failures of banks. It's very counterintuitive."[195] Indeed it was! It was the FDIC's job to protect depositors against failure, and Geithner worked like a demon to block the commission from performing this function by taking over the large and most reckless banks that he was protecting. This rationale that saving "the people" required saving the banks – the trickle-down idea that saving the 99 Percent required enriching the One Percent even more – became the umbrella for unlimited giveaways and concessions to the Treasury's and Fed's Wall Street constituency, much as bondholders used to hide behind "widows and orphans" whose trust funds presumably would be eroded

---

[194] Gina Chon, "Geithner clashes with lawyer for Greenberg over bailout of AIG," *Financial Times*, October 9, 2014.

[195] David Wessel, "Geithner: Post-Crash," *Wall Street Journal.MONEY*, Summer 2014, p. 14.

by inflation resulting from wage increases for the population having to work for a living.

President-elect Obama's refusal to help over-indebted homeowners

Barney Frank, Democratic chairman of the House Financial Services Committee, wanted banks to use some of the bailout money to scale down mortgage debts to payable levels. Homeowners would have received the benefit, and their mortgages would not have gone bad. "Paulson at first resisted that, he just wanted to get the money out," Frank said. "And after he got the first chunk of money out, he would have had to ask for a second chunk, he said, all right, I'll tell you what, I'll ask for that second chunk and I'll use some of that as leverage on mortgages, but I'm not going to do that unless Obama asks for it." But the president-elect rejected the proposal.

> This is now December, so we tried to get the Obama people to ask him and they wouldn't do it. During the critical period when the TARP was being administered, there was a vacuum of political leadership. And Obama at one point, when we were pressing him, said, 'Well, we only have one president at a time.'[196]

That was his way of saying "No." The problem was not so much a vacuum of leadership as one of continuity from the Clinton and Bush administrations. Obama quickly locked in the giveaways on pro-bank terms by naming Larry Summers as his chief advisor and promoting Geithner to take Paulson's place as Treasury Secretary. Summers and Geithner were in place to block moves that would not serve the "Rubinomics" wing that had risen to dominate the Democratic Party. Rubin, after all, had been Obama's major early sponsor.

Obama's refusal to press for debt writedowns or back any other conditions for the TARP left Democrats "owning" the bailout. They supported it without "conditionalities." The government did not even use its majority ownership in Citigroup and other Too Big To Fail banks to fire the officers responsible for bank losses. No civil and criminal charges were brought against personal malefactors in the "troubled" institutions.

In contrast to Britain's government forcing top executives to resign at RBS, Northern Rock, and Bradford and Bingley, neither the U.S. Treasury nor Congress asked for any say in the running of these rogue institutions. Vague talk by Congress of curtailing the high salaries and bonuses of individuals most responsible for the disaster soon dissipated without further action or follow-through. The fines that regulatory agencies ultimately levied on the banks were

---

[196] "In Conversation: Barney Frank," *New York Magazine*, April 23, 2012.

mostly covered by insurance policies, so shareholders bore the cost rather than the managers responsible for the infractions.

There was no attempt by the U.S. Government to use the $700 billion in TARP loans or the bailout of Citigroup to change the lending policies of Citi or other U.S. banks. There was no demand that banks scale back their dividend payouts to stockholders, or interest to bondholders or payments to counter-parties on bets gone bad. The Democratic leadership sought merely to "save the banks" by extending them trillions of dollars of Federal Reserve credit and subsidies unconditionally. The only parties obliged pay in full without subsidy were indebted homeowners, who remained on the hook even for liars' loans widely recognized as being rife with fraud.

Revising TARP's terms to give easier funding to Wall Street

On October 14, 2008, barely two weeks into TARP, Paulson made full use of the legislation's leeway giving the Treasury Secretary "broad authority to buy 'any other financial instrument' that he deems 'necessary to promote financial market stability.'"[197] Instead of buying mortgage-related securities – the program's "troubled assets" – the Treasury helped recapitalize bank balance sheets directly by buying $25 billion senior "preferred" non-voting stock and warrants from each of the ten largest American banks.

The label "preferred" confuses many casual readers. Bailing out the banks by buying preferred shares – instead of directly taking over the most reckless lenders – set the Treasury and Fed at odds with the FDIC's ability to protect depositors. An FDIC takeover would have wiped out the value of the government's preferred stock along with that of common stockholders. Although "preferred" stockholders are paid dividends before normal stockholders get their turn, they do not have legal priority over bondholders, or even over spec-ulators in collateralized swaps (CDOs) in case of bankruptcy. To preserve the government's investment position in bank "preferred" stock, Paulson's ploy hooked it into continuing support rather than letting the FDIC do its job.

The non-voting character of the TARP shares prevented the Treasury from exerting management policy over the banks that received funding. It also did not use its controlling creditor position to ask for seats on the bank boards, or for any voice in what the banks did with the TARP money, or with their deposits and credit-creating power.

---

197 Alan S. Blinder, "Missing the Target With $700 Billion," *The New York Times*, December 20, 2008.

To cap matters, the modified TARP's Capital Purchase Program provided banks with money at a concessionary rate of only 5%. As noted above, government loans are not supposed to be made to insolvent institutions, or on easy terms that enable banks to use the funds for speculation in a period of economic distress. But this is precisely what happened. The Congressional Budget Office estimated that the first $247 billion of securities purchased represented so large a premium over actual market valuation that it amounted to a 26 percent ($64 billion) subsidy to the banks receiving funds.[198] They were rewarded rather than punished for their reckless and even fraudulent lending.

This was the opposite of a penalty. It was a reward. It enriched banks for their irresponsibly loose lending, "liars' loans" and other financial junk. Warren Buffet, by contrast, obtained a 10% dividend plus stock options for his loan to Goldman Sachs.

A double standard was at work. Chris Dodd, chairman of the Senate Banking Committee, accused the Treasury of an "ad hoc and arbitrary" use of the funds by buying "stakes in banks, while the government's purchase of distressed mortgage securities – the plan's original centerpiece – was abandoned." He joined Barney Frank in charging that the Treasury was not following the "clear congressional intent" of the TARP law, warning that Congress would not release the remaining $350 billion of its $700 billion allocation "until 'at the very least' the Treasury agreed to use some of the funds to halt foreclosures."[199]

The threat had no effect, and seems to have been made mainly to assuage voter anger at the bailout. Once Obama took office, no more such complaints were heard from the Democrats in Congress, or from the government's financial agencies newly re-staffed by pro-Wall Street non-regulators.

Focusing $250 billion in TARP money on one rogue bank: Citigroup

Even the worst run banks held enough good assets to cover what they owed their insured depositors. So the problem was not whether to save everyday "vanilla" account-holders and customers. It was whether to use public funds to pay the high-stakes gamblers, the non-bank affiliates that had been merged into Wall Street conglomerate holding companies and brokerage houses.

---

[198] "The Troubled Asset Relief Program Report on Transactions Through December 31, 2008," CBO. January 16, 2009.
[199] Daniel Dombey and Joanna Chung, "Democrats threaten next Tarp disbursement," *Financial Times*, December 5, 2008.

The negative net worth threatened mainly their bondholders and the web of intra-bank bets on which way interest rates, currency exchange rates and packaged bank loans would move. "Bear Stearns should have been left to fail," Sheila Bair explained in the interview she gave upon stepping down as head of the FDIC in July 2011, because it wasn't a retail bank. That is why Bear Stearns didn't have an FDIC or Federal Reserve safety net. It was only "a second-tier investment bank." Such institutions "take higher risks, and they are supposed to be outside the safety net. If they make enough mistakes, they are supposed to fail."[200]

The bailout didn't have to be a giveaway to the wealthiest speculators, Bair explained. The FDIC had successfully wound down IndiMac, WaMu and other high fliers in the junk mortgage racket. That was the FDIC's task, after all. But Bair was not allowed to take on the big boys. As Joe Nocera noted in the report on his interview with her: "The F.D.I.C. had a wealth of experience, in part because it operated IndyMac for nine months until a buyer was found. It used that time to work on mortgage modifications with IndyMac borrowers and came up with a template for a program it felt could work nationwide."

In principle, speculative risk-taking subsidiaries of bank holding companies could have been isolated from the retail banking institutions, much as Glass-Steagall had organized back in 1933. The overall companies could have gone through normal bankruptcy, to be settled over the usual tedious process that insolvent corporations had to go through. Bair saw her opportunity when

> the president vented his frustration over the A.I.G. bonuses. "This doesn't happen with our process," she told the president. "We have a resolution process that we've used for decades, and when we put a bank into receivership, we have the right to break all contracts, we can fire people, we can take away bonuses and we don't get into this kind of problem."

But Bair's arguments lost out to those of Larry Summers and Geithner. What decided matters was the fact that one bank needed vastly more money than any other: Citigroup, whose alumni dominated the Democratic Party and its Treasury appointees. On December 12, 2014, Senator Elizabeth Warren summed up Citigroup's total regulatory capture of the Treasury and other key financial agencies. "Starting with former Citigroup CEO Robert Rubin, three of the last four Treasury Secretaries under Democratic presidents [Rubin, Larry Summers and Jack Lew] have had close Citigroup ties. The fourth [Tim Geithner] was offered the CEO position at Citigroup, but

---

[200] Joe Nocera, "Sheila Bair's Bank Shot," *The New York Times Magazine*: July 10, 2011.

turned it down."[201] President Obama also appointed from Citigroup the Federal Reserve's Vice Chairman Stanley Fischer, the U.S. trade representative and his deputy at Treasury, Nathan Sheets and Marisa Lago (responsible for much of the collapse as Global Head of Compliance at Citigroup during 2003-08). These links to what Bill Black has called a criminogenic institution should serve as fatal resume blots. Instead, they evidently qualified such officials for the highest positions, where they set to work to dismantle Dodd-Frank regulations and to continue the support and subsidies for Citigroup, much as the Republican Treasury had supported Goldman Sachs.

Rubin protégé Geithner had cultivated close ties to Citigroup. Its CEO Sandy Weill had offered Geithner the job of CEO after Charles Prince resigned in November 2007. "Instead of functioning as the tough cop on the beat in regulating Citigroup, Geithner hobnobbed, holding 29 breakfasts, lunches, dinners and other meetings with Citigroup executives," report Pam and Russ Martens.[202] Rumor had it that Geithner was prepared to move up from his $400,000 a year salary at the New York Fed, but then was asked to become Treasury Secretary in the incoming Obama administration to use his influence to protect Citigroup and its fellow Wall Street institutions as the crisis unfolded. Bair describes how Rubin's protégé Geithner duly lobbied to defend it by using "that familiar saw: if we didn't support Citi, it could destabilize the system."[203] As Bair summarized the pressure from Geithner and Paulson this way:

> They would bring me in after they'd made their decision on what needed to be done, and without giving me any information they would say, 'You have to do this or the system will go down.' If I heard that once, I heard it a thousand times. 'Citi is systemic, you have to do this.' No analysis, no meaningful discussion. It was very frustrating.[204]

The bank had long been notorious for "stretching the envelope," most of all when it merged with Travelers Insurance in 1998. Travelers had bought the brokerage firm Salomon Brothers the year before, so the merger created a conglomerate that was illegal under the Glass-Steagall Act, which separated retail deposit banking from investment banking. That acquisition made Glass-Steagall's nullification an urgent objective for Citibank.

---

[201] Remarks by Senator Warren on Citigroup and its Bailout Provision," floor speech opposing the "Citibank budget" and the nomination of Antonio Weiss to a high Treasury position," December 12, 2014, http://www.warren.senate.gov/?p=press_release&id=686.

[202] Pam and Russ Martens, "As Citigroup Spun Toward Insolvency in '07-'08, Its Regulator Was Dining and Schmoozing With Citi Execs," *Wall Street on Parade*, January 7, 2014, citing an April 26, 2009 *New York Times* article by Jo Becker and Gretchen Morgenson.

[203] Bair, *Bull by the Horns*, p. 105.

[204] Joe Nocera, "Sheila Bair's Bank Shot," *The New York Times Magazine*, July 10, 2011.

The Travelers merger created fierce pressure to revoke the signature 1933 act of Franklin Roosevelt. "Free market" lobbyists pressured the Clinton Administration to abolish the law Citigroup had blatantly violated. Rubin and Summers at Treasury led the deregulatory charge, with Alan Greenspan cheerleading at the Federal Reserve. In November 1999, Texas Republican Senator Phil Gramm, Iowa Republican Congressman Jim Leach and Virginia Republican Congressman Tom Bliley sponsored the Financial Services Modernization Act of 1999.

It was an Orwellian euphemism to characterize disabling the New Deal as "modernization." In the wake of the 1929-31 financial crisis, the idea of modernizing finance was to insulate retail consumer banking from Wall Street speculation. It took only a decade for the deregulation of mortgage credit and commercial lending to become tangled in a web of interbank speculation in casino "derivatives." Citigroup became the most reckless banking conglomerate making the worst financial bets.

Backed and applauded at the highest levels of government, the deregulatory environment created by reversing the array of New Deal controls proved the genesis of the 2008 crisis. Robert Rubin shepherded Wall Street's lobbying effort to deregulate banking and turn the financial system into a free-for-all to repeat the experience of the vast S&L frauds of the 1980s.

Having used his post at Treasury to help legalize Citigroup's 1999 merger with Travelers, Rubin joined Citigroup to exploit the new deregulated freedom, turning the bank into a Democratic Party version of Charles Keating's Lincoln S&L. But whereas Keating was jailed, Rubin's Citigroup alumni were handed the reigns of government, control of the Fed and exemption from prosecution for the mess they created at vast personal financial benefit to themselves.

At Citigroup CEO Rubin enjoyed the usual enormous salary boost that the Japanese call "descent from heaven" – over $10 million annually. Using the conglomerate's deposits and borrowed funds to gamble on mortgage-backed securities (MBS) and collateralized debt obligations (CDOs), he lost heavily, but kept raising Citigroup's bets, evidently hoping to cover his losses by making a killing somewhere else at someone else's expense.

This financial gaming dragged the bank's retail operations under, and matters got worse after 2007, when Rubin had hand-picked Vikram Pandit, a hedge fund manager from Morgan Stanley, to become the new CEO. "The selection of Pandit," Bair wrote, "simply reaffirmed that Citi was no longer a bread-and-butter commercial bank. It had been hijacked by an investment banking culture that made profit through high-stakes betting on the direction of the markets, in contrast to traditional banking, which focused on making loans to people based on their ability to repay."

As Citi's position worsened in 2008, Bair wanted the FDIC to "at least consider the feasibility of putting Citibank, Citigroup's insured national bank subsidiary, through our bankruptcy-like receivership process. That would have enabled us to create a good-bank/bad-bank structure, leaving the bad assets in the bad bank, with losses absorbed by its shareholders and unsecured creditors."[205]

The FDIC agreed to guarantee Citigroup's issuance of new debt, providing it was used for lending to help stimulate the economy. But the FDIC examiners discovered that "Citi was using the program to pay dividends to preferred shareholders, to support its securities dealer operations, and, through accounting tricks, to make it look as if funds raised through TLGP [Temporary Liquidity Guarantee Program] debt were actually raising capital for Citi's insured bank."[206]

Paulson and Geithner worried that singling out Citi for special aid would cause a loss of faith in Wall Street as a whole. Deeming the bank "systemically important" – meaning that it owed so much to other institutions on swaps and financial gambles that these counterparties would lose heavily if City went under – they warned that panic would spread if depositors and correspondent banks recognized how its managers had created a largely empty shell that in many ways resembled AIG's financial house of cards.

To cloak an emergency $25 billion loan to Citigroup, Paulson called the nine leading Wall Street bankers together and informed them that each of their banks would have to accept a $25 billion loan from the Treasury "whether they liked it or not," as part of the Capital Purchase Program announced on October 14. This scheme was designed to make Citigroup's subsidy appear to be part of "saving the system," by which they meant saving the deregulatory philosophy of] Greenspan, Rubin and Summers.[207]

Citigroup received hundreds of billions of dollars in bailout funding. Converting the Treasury's $25 billion loan into preferred stock alleviated its over-leveraged debt/equity ratio. The Treasury also extended the bank a $45 billion

---

[205] Bair, *Bull by the Horns.*, pp. 122f.
[206] Pam and Russ Martens, "As Citigroup Spun Toward Insolvency ..."
[207] Yves Smith, "Sheila Bair Gives Her Account of the Crisis, and (Quelle Surprise!) the Bailouts and Geithner Do Not Look Pretty," *Naked Capitalism*, September 26, 2012, notes that on Rubin's watch, 1999–2009, "the federal government was forced to inject $45 billion of taxpayer money into the company and guarantee some $300 billion of illiquid assets. Taxpayers ended up with a 27 percent stake in Citigroup, which was sold in 2010 at a cumulative profit of $12 billion. Rubin gave up a portion of his contracted compensation – and was still paid around $126 million in cash and stock during a tenure in which his serenity has come to look a lot more like paralysis."

credit line, and gave it a guarantee for $300 billion in "troubled assets," mainly junk mortgages whose market price had fallen by 60 to 80 percent. These actions saved the bank and its bondholders, but Citigroup stock plunged below a dollar by March 2009 as its equity value fell by more than 90 percent, to just $20 billion compared to $244 billion in 2006.

This was $5 billion less than the Treasury's TARP loan. The government had advanced more than the entire market value of the nation's most reckless and formerly largest bank. It is a sign of that bank's success in regulatory capture that public officials were able to resist taking control and running it in the public interest, or even changing its management, not to speak of making its counterparties and bondholders take a haircut for having enabled the bank's disastrous Rubinomics policy.

Paulson's TARP – plus the Treasury's decision to value Citigroup's assets at fictitiously high levels – saved the bank's stockholders from being wiped out, setting the stage for its stock to more than quadruple from under $1 in early March to over $4 a share. (It reverse-split 1:10 in May 2011, so its 2014-15 value of $49 a share represents $4.90 in former terms.) Troubled Bank of America also made enormous gains after being rescued from FDIC takeover (which would have been the *real* rescue).

The Fed backs the Treasury's bailout much more heavily

Stonewalling requests from Congress to find details about what junk mortgages and other "toxic waste" the Federal Reserve was accepting in exchange for its swaps, Chairman Bernanke claimed that politicians had no right to know how the public purse was being put at risk. Bloomberg filed a Freedom of Information Act request, and nearly three years later, in July 2011, the Government Accountability Office provided Senator Bernie Sanders with a report detailing $16 trillion of Fed loans and swaps.[208] It revealed how the officers of Wall Street's leading banks who sat on the New York Federal Reserve Board gave their own firms the fortune of a century to tide them over.

As widely rumored, Citigroup, Bank of America and the insurance conglomerate AIG were prominent among the financial institutions that turned over two trillion dollars worth of toxic mortgage packages and illiquid junk bonds to the Fed in order to avoid having to taking a loss in the open market, where demand for such packages had dried up once the widespread corruption was recognized.

---

[208] The details are in GAO-11-696, Report to Congressional Addressees. FEDERAL RESERVE SYSTEM, Opportunities Exist to Strengthen Policies and Processes for Managing Emergency Assistance, July 2011.

Taking the money and running, bankers emptied out the proceeds of government loans by paying bondholders, large depositors and counterparties in full. They even continued to pay dividends to stockholders. "Wall Street barely missed a beat with their bonuses," Bair noted. Bank-friendly writers and lobbyists fostered a myth that the economy needed its investment banks to remain solvent to keep the economy functioning.

But many former officials, including Bair, SIGTARP's Neil Barofsky, and Reagan Administration budget director David Stockman, rejected the claims that public guarantees for reckless bank loans was needed to protect insured depositors. Retail savings and checking accounts were never threatened by the bad gambles that banks made. But this myth had to be promoted in order for Paulson, Geithner Bernanke and other bank protectors to persuade Congress to overrule Bair and make government ("taxpayers") pay. Their aim was to save the banks from being nationalized, and to protect bankers from being prosecuted for fraud or reining in the exorbitant salaries and bonuses they had given themselves. No attempt was made to change the system that had led to the crash.

If the traditional bank reforms had been preserved, then the FDIC would have closed down Citigroup and the government would have regulated the derivatives market. If the legal system had worked, chief executives of Wall Street's major investment banks and the crooked brokerage companies that promoted and sold liars' loans would have landed in jail. Instead, banks paid civil fees – often covered by insurance policies – without their executives being prosecuted. Instead of "saving the system," the financial oligarchy made its move to end economic democracy. It saved its own future, not the existing status quo.

In addition to Citigroup, the vast pyramid based on debt-leveraged bets on financial securities was rescued. To resume paying out salaries and bonuses each year, banks had to repay their TARP loans. They did this by borrowing from the Federal Reserve, which provided credit without the restrictions that TARP credit had entailed. Over and above the TARP's $700 billion, the Fed extended $2 trillion in cash-for-trash swaps, which expanded to $4 trillion under the Quantitative Easing program through 2014.

Bailouts as a substitute for financial reform

The government could have created money to write down negative homeowner equity, as it had done with the banks. It could have bought bad mortgages at market prices and written down the debts more realistically, in keeping with the going rental value. Instead, the Treasury, Federal Reserve and

Congress left the debts in place. They remained a barrier to hopes for upward mobility (which already had been stifled since the 1980s). Wealth became much more concentrated at the top of the pyramid as the economy at large limped along after 2008. This polarization is one of the distinguishing features of *rentier* and financial wealth as compared to industrial wealth.

Under the pretense of restoring normalcy, the new financial oligarchy achieved a political coup to insure payment of debts owed mainly to the banks, bondholders and the One Percent behind them. Most people hardly realized that Congress, the Treasury and Federal Reserve had joined to endow bankers, bondholders and speculators with massive fortunes.

The closest parallel is Alexander Hamilton's commitment to pay off the "Continentals" – the paper money the American colonies fighting for their independence had used to pay militiamen and suppliers. The currency had lost nearly all its value, but was bought up by speculators, the "vulture funds" of their day.[209] Treasury Secretary Hamilton paid them off in full, ostensibly to show the fiscal dependability of the new U.S. Government. Speculators used their gains to buy up land in a follow-up series of frauds. Many of the nation's early fortunes thus were created at a stroke of the pen.

The process was repeated in 2008. It was applauded most loudly by the coterie of pro-financial economists calling themselves The Hamilton Project featuring leading Obama Administration figures Geithner, Summers, Rubin, Peter Orszag, and also Roger Altman.

Enriching a financial class rife with fraud and corrupt insider dealings inspired a long-standing mistrust of bankers and speculators at America's birth. This resentment inspired Andrew Jackson to close down the Bank of the United States in 1829, and to block creation of a real central bank for almost a century. But when the 2008 bailouts took bad debts onto the national balance sheet, the public accepted the giveaway – reluctantly, but under the false impression that there was little alternative.

For the Treasury, Federal Reserve and much of Congress, Wall Street *is* the economy. At least it is the sector from where financial officials are drawn, and from which politicians derive their largest campaign contributions. This makes it easy to believe that giving banks special tax breaks and privileges to "earn their way out of debt" is synonymous with saving the economy. The reality is that bailouts are being done at the expense of business, consumers and industry

---

[209] Stephen Zarlenga's *The Lost Science of Money* (2002) gives a good description of the Continentals.

The bailout was premised on the illusion that the financial problem was one of temporary illiquidity, not insolvency and the need for deep financial re-structuring. Assuming that there was only a liquidity problem, the infusion of money into the banks, their bondholders and uninsured depositors, was supposed to enable the banking system to start lending again – re-inflating housing prices and presumably the economy. But there was almost no chance of this really happening, because the legacy of bad loans left banks with little ability or desire to undertake the new lending.

So Washington's excuse for the TARP and the subsequent Treasury and Federal Reserve bailouts was based on deception. Banks did *not* start lending again to re-inflate real estate prices, because the market already was fully loaned up. Lending also dried up to the small and medium-sized companies that were responsible for most growth in job creation over the preceding decade. In the consumer market, banks scaled back their credit card exposure, as well as other consumer loans and business loans after 2008.

Refusal to admit the problem of insolvency – and how debt deflation would aggravate bankruptcy and unemployment – was a key factor for giving the banks the enormous subsidies they received since 2008, saving the claims of bondholders and large depositors on the economy. Erroneous economics thus proved highly purposeful and self-interested. Reviewing Geithner's fanciful memoir *Stress Test*, Paul Krugman pointed out: "the Obama administration never really tried to push the envelope on either fiscal policy or debt relief. And Geithner's influence was probably an important reason for this caution. … he believed that restoring that confidence by saving the banks was enough, that once financial stability was back the rest of the economy would take care of itself. And he was very wrong."[210]

Geithner was wrong because, Krugman continued: "Unlike a financial panic, a balance sheet recession can't be cured simply by restoring confidence: no matter how confident they may be feeling, debtors can't spend more if their creditors insist they cut back." But Geithner "never mentions the almost equally classic analysis of "debt deflation" by the American economist Irving Fisher." All he did was give the banks what they wanted, using "confidence" as a kind of rhetorical incantation as if it were a force in itself.

Keeping the pre-2008 buildup of debt in place suffocated the recovery. To make matters worse, the post-2008 debt deflation was reinforced by the Obama Administration's fiscal deflation. It tried to pay for the bailout's cost

---

[210] Paul Krugman, "Does He Pass the Test?" *New York Review of Books*, July 10, 2014. http://www.nybooks.com/articles/archives/2014/jul/10/geithner-does-he-pass-test/.

by cutting Social Security, health care and other programs, including federal revenue sharing with the state and cities.

Adding insult to injury, Wall Street's defenders adopted a "blame the victim" strategy. It was as if poor blacks and Hispanics – the targets most prone to be stuck with predatory liars' loans at exploding interest rates – were cheating Wall Street sharpies rather than the other way around. Reckless borrowers were blamed, not reckless lenders – except for Fannie and Freddie for trying to promote a rise in homeownership to those who evidently could not afford it.

The bailouts endowed a financial class that is evolving into an aristocracy, locking in its gains by shifting taxes off its wealth to push the U.S. and global economy into chronic austerity. This policy can only be defended by deception. Popular opinion in 2008 opposed subjecting ten million American homeowners to foreclosure. They did not cause the crisis, after all; banks did. No politician could have won re-election by coming right out and promising public giveaways to Wall Street and "labor market flexibility" (breaking union power, reducing wages and scaling back pensions). Meaningful democracy by informed voters had to be subverted. Using the 2008 financial crisis as their opportunity, financial elites set out to reverse the social democratic philosophy that had guided fiscal and monetary policy since 1945.

15

Wall Street Pretends to Insure Against the Crash

"Recognizing [Geithner's] tsunami of deceit is actually central to recognizing what happened during the bailouts. ... Geithner was hired to lie, steal, and cheat on behalf of bankers, and he did so. ... the Geithner era is increasingly seen as a time of betrayal and lies, not just disagreements over ideas."[211]

Matt Stoller, "The Con-Artist Wing of the Democratic Party" (2014)

The transition from the Bush to the Obama Administration was marked by an affair rife with conflict of interest between Treasury officials and Goldman Sachs. On the surface the scandal appeared to be a public takeover of American International Group (AIG), whose London office had insured junk-mortgage packages of Goldman and many European purchasers. Yet AIG's property and casualty insurance arms were not endangered, nor had it originated or packaged junk mortgages. The problem was that its Financial Products division (AIGFP) in London insured them, for only a tiny premium.

This trade in credit default swaps and related derivatives gave credence to the illusion that the mountain of bad mortgage debt could be carried without lenders or investors suffering a loss, simply by negotiating offsetting option and insurance contracts. In order to have "worked," the insurance premiums would have had to be large enough to build up reserves to pay for the trillions of dollars in losses that resulted from over-lending. Instead, risk models and ratings agencies said, "No risk from junk mortgages." Wall Street denied that a bubble existed, and AIG pretended to insure against its collapse.

The charade was made real by government intervention. But when Congress would not go beyond the TARP's $700 billion at the outset, the Fed and Treasury carved up AIG as a sacrificial lamb to save other financial giants from losses – and to preserve the illusion that financial asset prices were justified and that debts ultimately could be paid.

---

[211] Matt Stoller, "The Con-Artist Wing of the Democratic Party," *The Vice Reader*, June 4, 2014, http://www.vice.com/read/tim-geithner-and-the-con-artist-wing-of-the-democratic-party.

What was rescued was not AIG, but the illusion that Wall Street's deregulated financial system could make the economy richer rather than poorer. Tim Geithner's guiding principle upon being promoted to Secretary of the Treasury was that the financial sector's (and hence, the One Percent's) outsized profits and bonuses were a necessary condition for broader economic recovery. The reality was that the Federal Reserve's $4 trillion in Quantitative Easing helped support the debt burden by re-inflating asset prices. Coupled with debt deflation for the rest of the economy, this asset-price inflation – while keeping debt deflation for the 99 Percent – has polarized the distribution of wealth and net worth since 2008.

That this policy was deliberate is reflected in the deception and secrecy that the Treasury and Federal Reserve tried to maintain to hide its insider dealings rank with conflict of interest, while the Obama Administration used junk-accounting to pretend that "taxpayers" gained. Fiction was piled upon fiction to deter recognition of how unworkable the financially gerrymandered economy had become.

None of the players or public agencies in this episode are very attractive. In 2005, New York Attorney General Eliot Spitzer had forced AIG's board to depose its CEO, Morris Greenberg, for creating offshore entities and convoluted reinsurance transactions to avoid taxes. The Securities and Exchange Commission then brought civil charges. But the corrupt practices that took place in the wake of Greenberg's tenure proved much worse than tax dodges and misstated earnings. AIG's London office branched out into financial derivatives and credit default swaps (CDS) insuring "liars' loans" to which Wall Street institutions ascribed fictitiously high valuations and ratings agencies gave risk-free AAA appraisals.

To put matters bluntly, AIG and its counterparties were negligent in trusting Wall Street's banks and underwriters, trusting the bond ratings agencies pasting AAA labels on junk, trusting the U.S. Federal Reserve and other public agencies or Britain's Financial Services Agency to ensure honest dealings – and trusting neoliberal Larry Summers and investment bank *capo di tutti capi* Robert Rubin that financial markets were self-regulating and hence needed no "intrusion" from government that merely would "raise the cost of doing business." The cost of this misplaced trust added up to trillions of dollars. But the dynamics of this sophisticated con game never seem to appear in academic models purporting to explain how economies actually work in today's financialized world.

Wall Street financed the junk mortgage bubble largely by selling bad-loan packages to European banks, whose money managers (like their U.S. counterparts) were under pressure to find the highest short-term yields available. The

European banks bought U.S. mortgages, and compensated for the risk by purchasing credit default swaps (CDS). AIG London sold some three-quarters of
its CDS to European counterparties. "A.I.G.'s trading partners were not innocent victims here," blamed Senator Christopher J. Dodd (Democrat from Connecticut's insurance sector), presiding over a Congressional hearing on the
bailout. "They were sophisticated investors who took enormous, irresponsible
risks,"[212] pretending to protect themselves by taking out default insurance from
AIG without daring to ask whether the company had enough reserves to cover
the toxic financial waste it was insuring. Regulatory agencies from Britain to
America turned a blind eye. That often happens when banks are making a lot
of money quickly and capture the regulatory agencies by using political campaign contributions to influence policy or exploit the "revolving door" in which
bank managers are "loaned" to government agencies to defend their companies and class.

When the crash came, traditional policy would have let bad debts default,
leaving the courts to decide who owed what. AIG probably would have gone
bankrupt, and its default insurance payouts would have been scaled down to
its ability to pay the defrauded pension funds, German Landesbanks and other
investors for the junk mortgages they had bought from Wall Street. Or perhaps
AIG would have ridden the storm out and seen its derivative prices recover (as
later occurred) while holding onto its cash by accusing Goldman of misrepresentation.

Instead of letting this scenario unfold, the Treasury rushed to "save appearances" by making reality conform to Wall Street's self-serving Enron-style junk
"mark to model" accounting. It intervened to pay all parties, as if their financial
claims were honest and viable. The assumption was that reviving the Bubble
would enable the economy to recover by borrowing enough more to keep
paying the debt service mounting up.

The story trickled out slowly, with the most sordid details revealed in the
2014 trial where Greenberg and his company, Starr International, sued the
U.S. Government. Under oath, former Treasury Secretary Paulson and various
Federal Reserve officials explained why they had felt it necessary to find a

---

212 Mary Williams Walsh, "A.I.G. Lists Which Banks It Paid With U.S. Bailouts," *The New
York Times*, March 15, 2009: "Financial companies that received multibillion-dollar
payments owed by A.I.G. include Goldman Sachs ($12.9 billion), Merrill Lynch ($6.8
billion), Bank of America ($5.2 billion), Citigroup ($2.3 billion) and Wachovia ($1.5
billion). Big foreign banks also received large sums from the rescue, including Société
Générale of France and Deutsche Bank of Germany, which each received nearly $12
billion; Barclays of Britain ($8.5 billion); and UBS of Switzerland ($5 billion)."

major source of bailout money for Wall Street above and beyond what politicians were willing to commit. There was not enough TARP funding to pay, without spurring a political revolt. So AIG had to be emptied out to save them, by taking it over and giving it a quick $85 billion (later augmented to $182 billion) to rescue the actual beneficiaries, Goldman Sachs and other big investment banks.

Of course, AIG was by no means innocent. The prospect of more and more debtors taking on exponentially rising debt had created a huge market for writing default insurance contracts. AIG's London division won business by charging low fees for insuring many of the worst "liars' loans" being dumped onto U.S. and European markets. No attempt was made to build up enough reserves to cover the risks being underwritten. But until the collapse arrived, this underpricing of insurance fees enabled AIG's London managers to pay themselves enormous salaries and bonuses, as if they were making money on realistic risk assessment.

London as the global center for junk banking and fictitious insurance

AIG had already started writing credit default swaps through its London office by 1987. Finance Minister Gordon Brown's "light touch" Financial Services Authority was leading the global banking and insurance sectors' race to the deregulatory bottom. This prompted many U.S. and foreign banks to relocate to London. They were swiftly followed by Icelandic and Russian kleptocrats. By 2000, AIG's Financial Products division made credit default swaps its primary business, moving into the subprime area in 2003 and drawing up its first multi-sector CDS in 2004. "While many counterparties purchased these contracts to hedge or minimize credit risk, AIG essentially took the other side, a one-way, long-term bet on the U.S. mortgage market," the Congressional Oversight Panel noted in its 2010 report, *The AIG Rescue*. Federal Reserve Chairman Ben Bernanke described the affiliate as an undercapitalized "hedge fund, basically, that was attached to a large and stable insurance company."[213]

In the United States, local insurance regulatory agencies were largely vigilant in overseeing the safe investment of reserves. But AIG bought a small savings bank, which allowed it to choose as its national regulator the irrespon-

[213] Senate Budget Committee, Testimony of Ben S. Bernanke, chairman, Board of Governors of the Federal Reserve System, "Economic and Budget Challenges for the Short and Long Term" (March 3, 2009). AIG London entered into credit default swaps to insure $441 billion worth of securities rated AAA. Of these, $57.8 billion were "structured debt securities" backed by packaged subprime loans – the ones that Alan Greenspan and other financial gurus said that nobody could have foreseen would go bad.

sible Office of Thrift Supervision (OTS). The Congressional Oversight Panel's report notes that the OTS (cynically dubbed the Office of Theft Supervision for its deregulatory attitude in the S&L crisis of the 1980s) lacked anywhere near the resources needed to supervise AIG's far-flung operations. It showed little interest in AIG's complex bets on prices for junk mortgages.[214]

The Congressional Oversight Panel traced AIG's failure to the refusal of Geithner and his colleagues to regulate the web of proliferation of bad loans: "Everyone involved in AIG's rescue had the mindset of either a banker or a banking regulator," meaning deregulator or indeed, active protector of the financial sector. "It is unsurprising, then, that the American public remains convinced that the rescue was designed by Wall Street to help fellow Wall Streeters, with less emphasis given to protecting the public trust."[215]

Many regulatory agencies *could* have dealt with CDOs and CDSs on the grounds that they affected the solvency of banks, insurance companies and their counterparties. But credit default swaps are exempted from state gaming laws, so they are not deemed to be gambling. They also are not considered securities, so they are not regulated by the Securities and Exchange Commission. Nor are they regarded to be normal insurance, and so are not overseen by insurance regulators. So no regulatory agency seemed appropriate, leaving checks and balance nowhere to be found. In any event, Wall Street lobbyists make sure that Congress only approves officials drawn from the sectors they are supposed to regulate, acting as lobbyists for their sector and even for their own firms.

AIG's early default contracts contained clauses that protected its U.S. operations. But the company lost its AAA rating in March 2005. This meant that counterparties could contractually demand more collateral if the value of London's CDOs began to deteriorate. The division's head, Joseph Cassano, won more business (highly profitable for himself) by giving clients recourse to AIG as a whole. In effect he bet the firm!

This played out just as the FBI was warning of an unprecedented wave of mortgage fraud. Seeing mortgage underwriting standards erode, AIG stopped underwriting new contracts on subprime multi-sector CDOs. But many of the older contracts permitted portfolios to be updated as old loans matured, and clients substituted junk mortgages.

---

[214] Congressional Oversight Panel, *The AIG Rescue, Its Impact on Markets, and the Government's Exit Strategy* (June 9, 2010, on which the following pages are largely based): notes that OTS focused "primarily on the company's regulated thrift, which represented a small fraction of AIG's overall business, and accounted for well under 1 percent of the holding company's total assets." The actual ratio was only 0.14 percent.

[215] Congressional Oversight Panel, *The AIG Rescue,* June 9, 2010.

Precisely because "everyone" knew that the mortgage market was riven
with fraud, AIG raked in money. Fannie Mae and Freddie Mac saw their
profits soar as well, turning financial fantasies into high salaries and bonuses.
This easy money simply reflected the fact that default time had not yet
arrived.

While European financial institutions were buying mortgage packages
simply to obtain slightly higher than normal interest, Goldman sought to make
money from *losses* rather than gains! Hedge fund maven John Paulson became
a billionaire by getting Goldman Sachs to help him set up a fund of especially
fictitious mortgages, and taking out credit default insurance betting that they
would crash. Goldman sold this toxic waste to its clients, and took out bets for
billions of dollars with AIG London that a financial "accident" would happen.
This "sucker" portfolio formed the basis for its demand that AIG pay more
and more on an almost weekly basis as the mortgage market unraveled in 2008.

The insurance industry's role in the FIRE sector

Finance, insurance and real estate (FIRE) have had a symbiotic relationship
throughout history. Like Las Vegas casinos, insurance is all about arbitraging
probability curves, from lifespans to accidents and other casualties. Lloyds of
London was founded in 1688 at dockside coffee shops largely to insure
shipping. Life and casualty insurance emerged later in the 18th century, based
on probability computations for longevity and property-loss frequencies.

Today's banks oblige mortgage borrowers and other debtors to insure their
lives and property pledged as collateral against what they owe. Insurance companies invest their reserves and the funds they manage in the financial sector
and real estate. It was to create a closer synergy along these FIRE-sector lines
– the euphemism for an opportunity for self-dealing – that Citicorp merged
with Travelers Insurance in 1998, prompting its campaign to dismantle Glass
Steagall's banning of such vertical integration.

This act was repealed in 1999, followed on December 21, 2000 by the
Commodity Futures Modernization Act deregulating speculation in financial
derivatives. One of the Clinton Administration's final measures, this "modernization" turned high finance into speculation. Larry Summers, Tim Geithner and Alan Greenspan deemed secrecy – the antithesis to regulation – to
be necessary for the unfettered operation of "free markets." But without a regulated open market there is no way of knowing what derivatives are worth, or
how great a risk they may pose for banks that belong to conglomerates specu-
lating in derivatives.

This became clear by September 2008 when money managers ran for the exit and financial markets froze, recognizing the widespread fraud that had led to imbalance between what mortgage debtors owed, what insurance companies guaranteed to banks and speculators, and the economy's ability to pay. Nobody could know whether overnight loans to banks would be repaid. This was the inevitable result of regulators choosing not to regulate and markets using fictitious models "free" of reliable oversight.

Insurance companies had developed a market for risk arbitrage along similar lines to those they had developed to insure against property and casualty losses. But within a decade the outbreak of Collateralized Debt Obligations (CDOs) and credit default swaps (CDS) engulfed Wall Street's investment banks and AIG in webs of Black-Scholes probability curves. By insuring this toxic financial waste, London's "financial products" office thus did not make products in the classical sense of commodities produced by labor. It was a case of innovators combining Joseph Schumpeter's "creative destruction" with a race to the bottom. What was destroyed was the very idea of government regulation, along with the rule of law as formerly understood. Along with high finance in general, the insurance sector became an addendum to casino-capitalist gambling, calculating standard deviation ratios for changes in interest rates, stock prices and other financial variables. AIGFS in particular engaged in computerized modeling and speculation that had little to do with industrial and other capital investment, but with debt pyramiding on its rush to insolvency.

AIG's London "financial products" office charged unrealistically low fees to insure against the risk of nonpayment on junk mortgages. This underpricing attracted business whose premiums meant higher bonuses for managers. AIG projected this revenue stream from CDOs as "earnings," without accounting for the tens of billions of dollars in payouts soon to come. The investment banks that made or packaged junk-mortgages claimed not to be at risk because they were purchasing default insurance. This options trading enabled all players to make short-term gains – until the financial bolero abruptly stopped.

The illusion that insurance can cope with systemic collapse

Paying off all those bets would have required hundreds of billons of dollars to be kept in reserve – enough to equal the size of the meltdown. The magnitude of default was far beyond what AIG's London office had kept as reserves. Neither its counterparties nor the bond ratings agencies dared ask how much AIG was setting aside to back its default insurance policies. Judge Jed Rakoff called this "willful ignorance," and likened it to criminal negligence.[216] If not legally amounting to fraud, it was willfully reckless short-termism, evidently meant to enable all parties to claim plausible deniability when the collapse occurred.

Optimistic illusion is the handmaiden to irresponsible greed. Unacknowledged prospective losses mean higher rewards for managers, until the business finally blows up. Former bank regulator Bill Black quoted Jamie Diamond of JPMorgan to explain the strategy that led AIGFP's managers to attract enough business to pay themselves high salaries and bonuses: "Low-quality revenue is easy to produce, particularly in financial services. Poorly underwritten loans represent income today and losses tomorrow."[217]

What made AIG "systemically important" was the degree to which its London operations were interwoven with Wall Street's gambles on junk mortgages. The Federal Reserve and Treasury claimed that an economy-wide meltdown was imminent if AIG were not bailed out by enough to pay Goldman Sachs and other banks 100 cents on the dollar for the financial weapons of mass destruction they had planted in the company's London affiliate. Paulson even said that unemployment could have risen to 25 percent if AIG had not been bailed out. The alternative "was bankruptcy," he claimed, which "would have buckled our financial system and wrought economic havoc."[218]

Wall Street's casino ("the financial system") profits from the illusion that defaults can somehow be covered by private-sector insurance. It is as if everyone can buy options to avoid the systemic risk that results from over-lending. This illusion helped Wall Street shut its eyes to the looming convulsion that cost far more than any insurance company reserves ever would be able to pay for. Wall Street, the City of London and other financial centers had simply pretended to insure against the uninsurable.

The reality is that insuring against any economy's overall debt overhead is impossible in principle, because in the end the debts cannot be paid. It is magical to believe that money can be lent out as debts grow exponentially without limit. The Magic of Compound Interest leads in due course to debt deflation. The insurance obligation to "make losers whole" becomes unlimited, far beyond

---

[216] Yves Smith, "Judge Rakoff Blasts Breuer, Prosecution of Companies Rather than Individuals in Bar Speech," *Naked Capitalism*, November 14, 2013.

[217] Jamie Dimon, letter to JPMorgan shareholders, March 30, 2012, quoted in Bill Black, "The New York Times Authors the Most Ironic Sentence of the Crisis," *New Economic Perspectives*, October 24, 2013. Black adds that "poorly underwritten loans" produce fraudulently reported "income today" and losses that are not recorded until "tomorrow."

[218] Serena Ng and Michael R. Crittenden, "Geithner Defends Big AIG Payouts," *Wall Street Journal*, January 28, 2010.

the ability of default swaps or other financial insurance to cover the losses that stemmed from deregulation and financial fraud. Any scheme to protect against debt defaults is bound to be underinsured in the absence of regulatory agencies to prevent fraud.

The only way for these gambles to be paid in full when the insurance companies acting as "bookies" lack sufficient reserves is for the government to make up the gap. This is what happened in 2008. The Treasury and Fed picked up the tab, claiming that this was a necessary price to pay to "restore stability." By "stability" they meant preserving the fiction that much of the economy was not insolvent. What was "restored" was largely a state of denial regarding the underlying cause of the "financial products" crisis: the mathematical models of "efficient markets" and Black-Scholes regression analysis that presumably could make the junk-mortgage phenomenon risk-free at merely nominal cost. Ultimately, it took billions in public subsidies to "save the fiction" of the bankrupt deregulatory ideology.

The crash was what Charles Perrow terms a "normal accident" in the sense of being built into the financial system's design.[219] The bailout did not excise the cause of the inevitable "accident" by reversing the deregulation of banking and gambling. No banker was prosecuted, and the bailout terms did not even slow the explosion of financial salaries and bonuses. The government settled all the bets at 100 cents on the dollar when the insurance bookie went broke. There was no "haircut," thanks to the availability of AIG's solvent operations that could be seized to pay the financial casino's winners.

Bailing out Wall Street, not Main Street

It was all done under the distress sirens of imminent crisis. Every con man knows that the "mark" should not be given time to think things through. Speed is of the essence for high-pressure salesmanship. In September 2008, AIG's counterparties, headed by Goldman Sachs, wanted money fast. And they wanted to avoid taking a "haircut." Under the circumstances, only the government had enough to pay. Politicians rammed the bailout through with minimal discussion by crying havoc, warning that the economy would collapse if the government did not come to the rescue. What seems so ironic in the AIG affair is that the pressure involved an insurance company. Anyone who has tried to collect on a claim knows that the tactic of any insurance company is to stall as long as they can to avoid having to pay in full.

---

[219] Charles Perrow, *Normal Accidents: Living With High Risk Technologies* (1984, rev. ed. 1999, Princeton).

Wall Street Senator Charles Schumer, Democratic chairman of the Joint Economic Committee, wildly exaggerated when he warned: "If A.I.G. went down, it would affect Main Street more than Wall Street."[220] AIG was, after all, one of the largest providers of property and other forms of insurance. But its basic "vanilla" insurance business didn't need bailing out. Well regulated by local state agencies, it never faced a threat of insolvency, because its local offices for property and life insurance were well backed. In contrast to the public relations pretense for making AIG the hapless recipient of the first bailout, the Treasury's payments to AIG's Wall Street counterparties had nothing to do with saving Main Street's retail life insurance and casualty policyholders.

A *Wall Street Journal* editorial exposed the cover story as a sham: "The Treasury and the New York Fed appear eager to show that continuing to pour money into AIG is about saving Main Street, not just Wall Street. But … state laws segregate the assets needed to protect policyholders within the highly regulated insurance subsidiaries at AIG, and if they were to fail, state guarantee funds exist to ensure claims are paid."[221] New York State Superintendent of Insurance Eric Dinallo agreed: "If AIG had gone bankrupt, state regulators would have seized the individual insurance companies. The reserves of those insurance companies would have been set aside to pay policyholders and thereby protected from AIG's creditors." AIG's U.S. consumer and basic business policies were fully backed under state insurance agencies, just as the "plain vanilla" operations of Citibank and other U.S. banks were protected by the FDIC. To be sure, "AIG's insurance companies were [so] intertwined with each other and the parent company [that] policyholders would have been paid, but only after a potentially protracted delay."[222] But when are insurance payouts *not* tardy?

The threat that local AIG offices would run out of cash like ATM machines was a myth conjured up to pretend that the bailout was to protect normal policy holders, and only incidentally happened to pay Wall Street's high-rolling counterparties that had placed winning bets against AIG London. These gambling contracts had nothing to do with life insurance, property or casualty insurance. They were legally subordinate to AIG's normal retail and commercial insurance business.

---

[220] Eric Dash and Andrew Ross Sorkin, "Throwing a Lifeline to a Troubled Giant," *The New York Times*, September 17, 2008.

[221] "AIG's Black Box," *Wall Street Journal* editorial, March 3, 2009.

[222] Eric Dinallo, "What I Learned at the AIG Meltdown: State insurance regulation wasn't the problem," *Wall Street Journal*, February 3, 2010.

Rating agencies started to downgrade CDOs in 2007, prompting AIG London to write down its credit default swap portfolio by $11.5 billion. Further declines during spring and summer of 2008 enabled Goldman to demand more payments, using its models (that is, its own dice) to value the junk mortgages it had insured. The Congressional Oversight Panel reports that: "A battle of the models ensued between AIG and its counterparties, resulting in protracted discussions on valuations and corresponding collateral obligations." As a pair of *New York Times* reporters summarized the conflict: "The further mortgage securities' prices fell, the greater were Goldman's profits. In its dispute with A.I.G., Goldman invariably argued that the securities in dispute were worth less than A.I.G. estimated – and in many cases, less than the prices at which other dealers valued the securities. … The bank resisted, for example, letting third parties value the securities as its contracts with A.I.G. required. And Goldman based some payment demands on lower-rated bonds that A.I.G.'s insurance did not even cover."[223]

Goldman's abrupt demand for payment triggered AIG's collapse. Goldman insisted that AIG cover the losses that Goldman's own models predicted the mortgages would suffer. If the Treasury had not taken over AIG and made it pay everything Goldman asked for, Goldman would not have made a killing. Without a bailout for AIG, payoffs on the junk mortgage gambles would have had to be scaled back all across the board. Some of the world's largest banks would not have been able to collect their winnings. The Treasury's solution to save everyone from loss (of their bonuses as well as their firm's net worth) was to give Goldman Sachs an immediate $13 billion for its credit default insurance contracts with AIG, while Société Générale and Deutsche Bank were handed another $12 billion each.

There was no investigation of their claims, no haircut on any bill submitted. No wonder AIG's largest stockholder, Maurice Greenberg, brought a $25 billion lawsuit claiming that the Treasury had looted AIG to save Goldman and other firms from their own insolvency. AIG's lawyers could have insisted that Goldman exaggerated the valuation in its favor. Insurance companies contest claims all the time.

But Paulson and Geithner felt that Goldman and other big banks needed money quickly, being only days from insolvency. So on September 16 (the day after Lehman failed), the Treasury created a windfall for favored Wall Street institutions by taking over AIG and making good on whatever its counterpar-

---

[223] Gretchen Morgenson and Louise Story, "Testy Conflict With Goldman Helped Push A.I.G. to Edge," *The New York Times*, February 7, 2010.

ties said might be owed, starting with the $85 billion that rapidly ballooned to $182 billion. This intervention enabled Wall Street's pretenses to come true, paying sixteen investment banks every penny of what they claimed to be winning on their bets against AIG's London office on credit default swaps, as Chapter 17 will discuss.

16

Bailing Out Goldman Via AIG

"It's as if the New York Fed used A.I.G. as a front man to bail out big banks all over the world."
Senator Charles Grassley, summarizing his Congressional
Oversight Panel's findings, July 23, 2010.[224]

Much of the real motivation for seizing AIG was dragged out of witnesses in the lawsuit brought by Maurice Greenberg, whose Starr International was AIG's largest shareholder. When the six-week trial finally began in September 2014, former Treasury Secretary Hank Paulson acknowledged that popular anger at Wall Street's investment banks had made Congress unwilling to appropriate]more than the $700 billion in TARP funding. The money to cover investment bank losses had to be found elsewhere.

Next to Citigroup, Goldman seems to have been the most overstretched. But it managed to take charge of the bailout on all government levels. Former CEO Hank Paulson at Treasury said that he stood largely aside, but former Goldman CEO Stephen Friedman had become chairman of the New York Fed.[225] Most directly, Paulson appointed Goldman board member Edward Liddy as AIG's CEO. Liddy "had been a member of the board of Goldman Sachs since 2003 and head of its audit committee since 2007. He held 'a considerable amount of Goldman stock' when the bailout took place," a conflict of interest blunting AIG's ability to resist Goldman's demands. Pressed by Goldman officers to accept the position, Liddy "was appointed A.I.G.'s chief executive on Sept. 18. But he remained a Goldman director until Sept. 23,

---

[224] Quoted in Gretchen Morgenson, "An A.I.G. Failure Would Have Cost Goldman Sachs, Documents Show," *The New York Times*, July 24, 2010.

[225] Shah Gilani, Contributing Editor, *Money Morning*, "Warning: This is Not Another Wall Street Conspiracy Theory, These are the Facts," February 2, 2010: "Friedman subsequently resigned from his post at the New York Fed on May 7, 2009, in response to criticism of his December 2008 purchase of $3 million of Goldman stock, which added to his substantial holdings - a purchase made only after he had ushered through Goldman's approval to become a bank-holding company, enabling the firm to feed at the Fed's generous liquidity trough."

and he testified that he attended a Goldman board meeting by telephone on Sept. 21. ... Later that evening, Mr. Liddy led an A.I.G. board meeting [where he] urged the insurer's directors to accept the government's costly bailout."[226]

Costly to AIG that is; it proved to be a bonanza for Goldman. Goldman said, in effect: "We need this much," and asked Geithner at the New York Fed to make AIG pay it, and also to pay Merrill Lynch, Bank of America, Citigroup *et al*. This prompted Rep. Stephen F. Lynch, a Democrat from Massachusetts, to respond to Treasury Secretary Geithner at a Congressional committee hearing on January 26, 2010: "I think the commitment to Goldman Sachs trumped the responsibility that our officials had to the American people."[227]

One reporter found

> only two possible explanations for the overly solicitous treatment of Goldman and the others. The first is that their own financial position was so precarious that accepting anything less than the billions they expected from A.I.G. would have destabilized them, too. Which is to say, it really was a backdoor bailout of the banks — many of which, like Goldman, claimed they didn't need one. Alternatively, maybe Mr. Geithner simply felt that Goldman and the like had a more legitimate claim to billions of dollars in funds than the taxpayers who were footing the bill.[228]

The asymmetry in how AIG was treated, compared to Goldman, Citigroup *et al.*

In contrast to TARP and special loans made to Citigroup, Fannie Mae, Freddie Mac and Merrill Lynch at concessionary interest rates, the government charged AIG a high rate. Thomas C. Baxter Jr., the New York Fed's general counsel, described the 14 percent rate (and 8.5 percent on the credit line that AIG did not draw down) as "loan sharky."[229]

---

[226] Gretchen Morgenson, "Fresh Doubt Over the Bailout of A.I.G.," *The New York Times*, December 21, 2014.

[227] Mary Williams Walsh and Sewell Chan, "Under Fire, Geithner Says A.I.G. Rescue Was Essential," *The New York Times*, January 27, 2010.

[228] Noam Scheiber, "Finally, the Truth About the A.I.G. Bailout," *The New York Times*, September 28, 2014.

[229] Gretchen Morgenson, "Court Casts a New Light on a Bailout," *The New York Times*, September 28, 2014. She adds: "Banks tapping the government's Troubled Asset Relief Program, by contrast, paid only 5 percent interest. Banks lucky enough to borrow from the Fed's Primary Dealer Credit Facility — available only to institutions that were deemed trading partners of the Fed — paid just 2.25 percent on their loans. These fortunates received another perk: The Fed vastly loosened its collateral requirements, letting institutions post high-risk securities in exchange for cash," at fictitious higher-than-market valuations. See also Aaron M. Kessler, "A.I.G. Trial Witnesses Will Be Central Cast From 2008 Crisis," *The New York Times*, September 30, 2014.

The problem was not merely the high interest rate the government charged AIG for loans that it was forced to spend on paying Goldman and other counterparties. AIG had good reasons not to pay anywhere near what Goldman demanded, and even to contest payment on the grounds that Goldman misrepresented the junk mortgages it insured and then bet against. Early that year other insurance companies had started to negotiate CDO write-downs with their counterparties. "By the start of 2008, it was clear the insurance companies were running out of funds, so MBIA, Ambac and others then did what cash-strapped companies normally do: they settled with bond holders at a discount of between 10 per cent and 60 per cent of face value."[230] But in contrast to the writedowns that other insurance firms obtained from their counterparties, the former Goldman officials in charge of AIG did not let it impose haircuts on its derivatives contracts with Goldman or other counterparties.

Instead of bargaining with Wall Street bank overvaluations of their securities, the Fed blocked AIG from doing so, by taking 79.9 percent of its stock. This was the only financial institution over which the government took actual control. Its preferred stockholdings in Citigroup did not involve voting rights, and hence did not enable it to "interfere" with policy. But the Fed's takeover of AIG was done on terms that committed the company *not* to question any payments made, not to contest the demands of Goldman or other counterparties to write down what it had to pay them, and not to file for bankruptcy.

AIG was still solvent and current on its payments at the time of its takeover. Looking back at the fact that most junk mortgages were still being paid at a higher rate than pessimists had thought, *New York Times* journalist Gretchen Morgenson asked: "Why would those companies agree to pay out in full to a policyholder even if a fire had not occurred?"[231] Reviewing the details of the double standard imposed on AIG, Morgenson later suggested that perhaps "the government saw an opportunity in the insurer's liquidity crisis: It could become an enormous taxpayer-funded piggy bank from which the government could funnel billions to a throng of teetering banks. Remember, taxpayers were growing increasingly outraged by bank rescues in fall 2008."[232] The alternative was writedowns and lengthy court proceedings. "A bankruptcy judge could invalidate (as a 'voidable preference') the transfer of collateral or money from

---

[230] Gillian Tett, "Global Insight: Still bristling over AIG haircut," *Financial Times*, January 14, 2010.

[231] Gretchen Morgenson, "A.I.G.'s Payouts to Companies Draw Criticism," *The New York Times*, March 18, 2009.

[232] Gretchen Morgenson, "Court Casts a New Light on a Bailout."

AIG to Goldman if the transfer took place within 90 days of the filing of the bankruptcy petition."[233]

The last thing Wall Street firms wanted was to drive AIG bankrupt. A financial corpse would yield up much less than 100 cents on the dollar. The banks wanted to be paid in full, without the delay that bankruptcy proceedings entail. Chapter 11 of the U.S bankruptcy code includes a "cram down" provision that allows the courts to confirm a bankruptcy plan over the objection of some creditors, preventing a few recalcitrant parties from holding up the settlement. The mere threat of bankruptcy thus gives distressed debtors enormous leverage. "Even first year law students in Contracts 101 learn that there are numerous exceptions to the 'sanctity of contracts,'" one pension fund advisor noted; "contracts are legally abrogated every day – a big part of our court system is given over to litigating disputes over the enforceability of various commercial contract provisions."[234] But instead of using this threat of bankruptcy when the government interceded on behalf of Goldman and other counterparties, "Tim Geithner, [Obama economic advisor] Austan Goolsbee, and Larry Summers lamely express[ed] fake anger to the media" about how much they hated to bail out AIG but felt obliged to defend the banks on the grounds of the pretended sanctity of contracts.

The threat of deferring payment for years as tedious lawsuits ran their course could have saved AIG as much as half the ultimate $182 billion it was stuck with. This prospect would have encouraged its counterparties to acquiesce quickly for a smaller payment, as typically is done in such cases. By contrast, the Congressional Oversight Panel points out: "the government chose not to exploit its negotiating leverage with respect to the counterparties. ... once the government made clear that it was committed to the wholesale rescue of AIG ... it lost the significant leverage it might have had over the thousands of AIG creditors." Indeed, the Panel concluded,

> even after the Federal Reserve and Treasury had decided that a public rescue was the only choice, they still could have pursued options other than paying every creditor and every counterparty at 100 cents on the dollar. Arrangements in which different creditors accept varying degrees of loss are common in bankruptcy proceedings or other negotiations when a distressed company is involved, and in this case the government failed to use its significant negotiating leverage to extract such compromises.

---

[233] Darren Lenard Hutchinson, "Tangled Webs: Goldman Sachs, AIG and the Feds," *Dissenting Justice*, March 21, 2009. http://dissentingjustice.blogspot.com/2009/03/tangled-webs-goldman-sachs-aig-and-feds.html
[234] Leo Kolivakis, "What Do Pensions Have in Common with AIG?" *Pension Plan Pulse*, March 15, 2009.

To have allowed AIG act in its own interest would have brought down the edifice of fictitious finance capital valuations, revealing the junk mortgage fraud. So AIG had to be stopped from defending itself and setting a legal precedent for writing down junk mortgage derivatives vis-à-vis Wall Street's financial behemoths. At one point in the trial, Greenberg's lawyer,

> Mr. Boies zeroed in on the idea of whether some banks that were "insolvent" were given more lenient loan terms than A.I.G. (The plaintiffs argue that A.I.G. at the time was solvent, but suffering from a liquidity crisis; the government disagrees.) Using one of Mr. Geithner's unpublished book interviews, he raised the subject of Citigroup and Bank of America, two banks that received bailouts in the crisis. "Certainly Citi and B. of A. were insolvent," Mr. Geithner had said during the book interview. The two men then engaged in a lengthy back-and-forth over the definition of "insolvent."[235]

In the ordinary course of business, the well-established rules of bankruptcy would have led AIG's counterparties to write down their claims. Instead, "rescuing" AIG transformed Wall Street's risky derivative wagers into government-guaranteed obligations. It was as if the high-risk trade in default insurance derivatives deserved the same backstop as FDIC-insured savings deposits and checking accounts.

The scare tactic was that the alternative was "chaos." On the systemic level this meant simply that some gamblers could not collect from what had been organized as a rigged game. Geithner explained to President Obama that "chaos" meant asking Goldman and other banks to take haircuts on the killings they had made, and even further, not paying Wall Street speculators their expected bonuses and salaries in full!

Covert maneuvering and influence peddling by Wall Street over the Fed and Treasury

When pressed by Congress and the financial media, the Federal Reserve and Treasury resisted identifying the recipients of the bailout money for months, citing confidentiality agreements. "The Panel notes that Goldman has declined to supply the Panel with the identities of its own counterparties or any documentation with respect to those relationships" or "its own hedges on AIG." The fact that Goldman and the Fed fought so hard to keep matters secret suggests that they knew quite well that Goldman was not being honest

---

[235] Aaron M. Kessler, "A.I.G. Trial Puts Geithner, and His Book, on Hot Seat," *The New York Times*, October 8, 2014.

in claiming that it had fully hedged its AIG exposure and thus would be unaffected by AIG bankruptcy.[236]

However, Bloomberg finally extracted the details of the deal by filing a Freedom of Information Act request. The documents it obtained revealed that "the banks that bought the swaps from AIG are mostly the same firms that underwrote the CDOs in the first place. ... In some cases, banks also owned mortgage lenders, and they should be challenged to explain whether they gained any insider knowledge about the quality of the loans bundled into the CDOs."[237] As one observer put matters: "This is tantamount to building a house, planting a bomb in it, selling it to an unsuspecting buyer, and buying $20 billion worth of life insurance on the homeowner – who you know is going to die!"[238]

To get paid quickly on its own terms, Goldman went to Tim Geithner, President of the New York Federal Reserve. Nicknamed "the bail-outer in chief" by Sheila Bair, Geithner selected Morgan Stanley as legal advisor to the New York Fed to come up with a solution that would "restore normalcy," that is, save Goldman from loss, just as the TARP bailout was saving Citigroup.

The way in which the Fed intervened in the AIG-Goldman squabble stood in sharp contrast to how it had strong-armed Wall Street banks to bail out Long-Term Credit Management in 1998. This was the principle of "shared sacrifice" that J. P. Morgan had organized in the wake of the 1907 crash. But the Congressional Oversight Panel pointed out that a decade of political maneuvering since 1998 had enabled Wall Street to commandeer the reins of U.S. regulatory agencies, the Federal Reserve and Treasury, which compelled

---

[236] A *Wall Street Journal* editorial discussed the secrecy that Geithner pressed to conceal future deals between the Fed, Treasury and the Wall Street sponsors of their administrators: "Under the House regulatory reform, Mr. Geithner would chair a new Financial Services Oversight Council. The council could declare virtually any company in America a systemic risk, making them eligible for intervention on the taxpayer's dime. The law firm Davis Polk reports that since this council is not an agency, it will not be subject to the Administrative Procedure Act, the Freedom of Information Act or the Sunshine Act, among other laws intended to allow citizens to scrutinize government." ("The Geithner AIG Story," *Wall Street Journal* editorial, January 13, 2010.) The names and facts ended up being revealed, but it reflects the power that Wall Street has obtained over the economy at large that neither Congress nor the law courts did anything about the misbehavior, rip-offs and falsehoods that were uncovered.

[237] Richard Teitelbaum, "Secret AIG Document Shows Goldman Sachs Minted Most Toxic CDOs," *Bloomberg*, February 23, 2010.

[238] Porter Stansberry, "This Is One of the Biggest Wall Street Frauds Ever...," *Information Clearing House*, February 26, 2010. http://www.informationclearinghouse.info/article 24873.htm.

the government to pay when the 2008 bubble burst. "By providing a complete bailout that called for no shared sacrifice among AIG and its creditors," the Congressional Oversight Panel concluded, "FRBNY and Treasury fundamentally changed the rules of America's financial marketplace" with regard to how the world's largest banks, government policy and whether or how economies cope with their bad-debt overhead:

> ... by bailing out AIG and its counterparties, the federal government signaled that the entire derivatives market – which had been explicitly and completely deregulated by Congress through the Commodities Futures Modernization Act – would now benefit from the same government safety net provided to fully regulated financial products. In essence, the government distorted the marketplace by transforming highly risky derivative bets into fully guaranteed transactions, with the American taxpayer standing as guarantor.

Still, the Panel pointed out: "Until the afternoon of September 16, 2008, it was at least possible for the government to suggest that it would let AIG fail, as a means to demand concessions from AIG's counterparties; this would have been a credible threat given that the government had just let Lehman fail." Instead, Geithner was able to intervene thanks to a little-known clause in the Federal Reserve Act giving it authority to exercise "incidental powers as shall be necessary to carry on the business of banking within the limitations prescribed by this Act." As CDS spreads on AIG widened in November, the New York Fed set up a special set of funds, called Maiden Lane (a street near the New York Fed) to buy the mortgage-backed securities held by AIG's counterparties at "100 cents on the dollar, effectively canceling out the CDS contracts. This was miles above what those assets could have fetched in the market at that time, if they could have been sold at all."[239]

This purchase paid off the gamblers, and stopped further AIG liability. Soon the price of these securities recovered, so AIG would not have ended up having to pay anywhere near as much to its counterparties as the Fed paid!

Geithner's web of deception

Geithner claimed that as head of the New York Fed through 2008 he had no choice except to pay AIG's counterparties in full, because one bank was French. Hence, he pretended, he had to grant the U.S. banks *all* their winnings on the toxic waste bets they had insured with AIG. His excuse was that French law did not permit writedowns for its banks! Indeed, he said, it would be downright "criminal" for a French bank do to what, in reality, banks all around

---

[239] "AIG and Systemic Risk," *Wall Street Journal* editorial, Nov. 20, 2009.

the world have been doing for many decades: "taking a haircut" on what they are owed. This is what the Brady bond writedowns of Latin American debts were all about in the 1980s. It is what Donald Trump has demanded of his banks often enough, and what companies under pressure normally do.

The reason for Geithner's French charade became apparent when it turned out that a chunk of the $11 billion paid to Société Générale "was subsequently transferred to Goldman under a deal the two banks had struck" when Goldman had packaged the junk mortgages selected by John Paulson. Paying Société Générale was really a way to pay Goldman.

The press was full of reports of how unyielding the French were on insisting on no writedown – until SIGTARP Neil Barofsky issued his report describing how outrageous was the claim that U.S. law did not permit discrimination among claimants. Geithner's position was that if the Federal Reserve had to pay the French bank Société Générale in full, it also would have had to pay Goldman Sachs and other U.S. financial casinos in full. But Geithner pretended that his Federal Reserve Bank of New York had no choice but to avoid paying any bank less than 100%, because its own rules prevented it from discriminating and paying the French more than Goldman.

All this soon was shown to be a lie, denied by the French. Barofsky accused Geithner of telling the public that the French government had "forcibly" rejected any concessions from it banks. To find out for himself, he reports:

> I arranged for a Saturday afternoon call with the French regulator. … she emphasized that she had not 'slammed the door' on negotiations and had been more than ready to engage in them with the Fed so long as they were at a high level and universal. But she told us that the Fed officials had never seriously pursued that option, commenting that she had been surprised when the Fed officials had never called back. When I asked her about the Fed's assertion that it would be illegal under French law to agree to a discount, she said that the French government could have waived that restriction. … 'But with no negotiations, no waiver.'"[240]

News leaked out that UBS (Union Bank of Switzerland) had quickly agreed to a 2 percent haircut, which would have amounted to $280 million for starters. Geithner failed to report this offer, presumably telling UBS to sit tight while he insisted that the Treasury pay all the banks in full. His subordinate, the New York Fed general counsel, Thomas Baxter,

> confirmed that the Fed staff had consulted with Geithner about UBS's offer and that, instead of telling them to negotiate further, Geithner had given the order to effectively pay the banks full price for the bonds. We were stunned. Rather than pounce on UBS's

---

[240] Neil Barofsky, *Bailout: An Inside Account of How Washington Abandoned Main Street While Rescuing Wall Street* (New York: Free Press, 2012), pp. 186–87.

apparent willingness to negotiate and use that as leverage with the others, he had simply folded the tent.[241]

Describing the stonewalling he received about all this, Barofsky writes that Geithner (who by this time had moved up to Treasury) served Goldman and other banks by undercutting "any chance of getting relief for the taxpayer by deciding that no once concession would be accepted unless all of the banks agreed to the exact same percentage reductions."[242] Geithner emerged from this episode as something of a partner in crime for giving in so quickly when Goldman and other banksters reached for the moon. "I've always wondered why none of A.I.G.'s counterparties didn't have to take any haircuts," remarked Sheila Bair upon leaving the FDIC. "There's no reason in the world why those swap counterparties couldn't have taken a 10 percent haircut. There could have at least been a little pain for them. They didn't even engage in conversation about that. You know, Wall Street barely missed a beat with their bonuses."[243]

The bonus kerfuffle distracts attention from where the bailout money went

It is an indication of the extent to which the banking system and high finance had degenerated into grabitization that Geithner whined that it would signal the "end of capitalism" not to keep paying bonuses and salaries to the bankers whose behavior had caused the crash. In his 2015 memoir *Believer: My Forty Years in Politics*, President Obama's campaign advisor David Axelrod reports that he

> was "livid" when he found out that Geithner and Summers "had quietly lobbied" against an amendment to the stimulus that would have restricted the payment of bonuses at firms that received bailout funds. Those bonuses had become a huge political sore point for the administration, but the finance guys argued that retroactive steps to claw back the money would have violated existing contracts. "This would be the end of capitalism as we know it" Geithner told Axelrod …[244]

Law professor Bill Black explains how this one-sided idea of "breaking contracts" favored Wall Street against the economy and its long-term viability.

---

[241] *Ibid.*, p. 187.
[242] *Ibid.*, p. 184.
[243] Sheila Bair, interview with Joe Nocera, *The New York Times*, July 10, 2011.
[244] Sam Stein, "David Axelrod Describes The No Good, Very Bad Minefield Of Obama's Early Presidency," *Huffington Post*, February 10, 2015. http://www.huffingtonpost.com/2015/02/10/david-axelrod-obama_n_6649688.html.

"Preventing banks that received bailouts from paying future bonuses is not 'clawing back' bonuses. Clawing back bonuses means recovering bonuses that were improperly paid based on false accounting statements that massively overstated bank income. Neither of the practices I have described would have 'violated existing contracts.'"[245]

Even before Axelrod's revelation, the matter had come to a head regarding AIG's bonuses to the company's financial wreckers. On March 17, 2009, precisely half a year after the bailout, AIG announced that it would pay $165 million in "retention awards," its euphemism for bonuses, to 400 employees at its London office. Total bonuses were said to possibly reach $450 million for the financial unit, and $1.2 billion for the entire company over the next two years.

Although the $165 million in bonuses amounted to only 0.1% of AIG's $182 billion bailout, it afforded an opportunity to distract attention from the much larger giveaways to Wall Street bankers. Having voted for the AIG bailout as a senator, President Obama now tried to publicly distance himself: "I've asked Secretary Geithner to use that leverage and pursue every legal avenue to block these bonuses and make the American taxpayers whole." Larry Summers chimed in: "There are a lot of terrible things that have happened in the last 18 months, but what's happened at A.I.G. is the most outrageous."[246] As the *Wall Street Journal* editorialized over these crocodile tears:

> The Washington crowd wants to focus on bonuses because it aims public anger on private actors, not the political class. … Since September 16, AIG has sent $120 billion in cash, collateral and other payouts to banks, municipal governments and other derivative counterparties around the world. … It's not capitalism, in which risk-takers suffer the consequences of bad decisions.[247]

Only the top-ranking "Too Big To Fail" banks were saved from the debt leveraging that plagued the rest of the economy. AIG's counterparties were liberated from losses, but homeowners suffered defaults, while cities and states faced abandonments and plunging tax revenues. Employees lost their jobs, normal investors lost, and "taxpayers" were stuck with the obligation to pay the Wall Street giants.

---

[245] Bill Black, "Geithner: 'The End of Capitalism as We Know It,'" *New Economic Perspectives*, February 10, 2015. This is the blog of the UMKC economics department.

[246] Edmund L. Andrews and Peter Baker, "Bonus Money at Troubled A.I.G. Draws Heavy Criticism," *The New York Times*, March 15, 2009.

[247] "The Real AIG Outrage," *Wall Street Journal* editorial, March 17, 2009. The Congressional Oversight Panel criticized the New York Federal Reserve for failing to "tell Treasury about the retention program for more than three months." This secrecy had become the norm. Apparently the New York Fed learned of the AIGFP retention bonus plans in November 2008, but did not see fit to tell Treasury about them until the end of February 2009.

President Obama capped the hypocrisy by asking Treasury Secretary Geithner to prepare an accounting charade to give the impression that the government actually made money on the deal. This contrived exercise served to distract attention from the fact that the Federal Reserve's Maiden Lane entity had paid 100% of the face value of CDOs that were selling on the open market at only half the price. Geithner's public relations calculation did not take into account such overpayments, tax giveaways, subsidies and below-normal interest rates that financial analysts normally use to evaluate gains and losses.

These multiple forms of giveaway broke more than a century's tradition for how governments are supposed to handle crises, prompting the Congressional Oversight Panel to conclude: "The government's actions in rescuing AIG continue to have a poisonous effect on the marketplace." They reflected how the financial "marketplace" – Wall Street – had captured government regulatory agencies, disabled Congressional oversight and neutered the law courts in order to make sure that no bank manager or CEO involved in the financial crisis would ever be jailed, fired, or even have his salary and bonuses clawed back.

Geithner will appear repeatedly in the next few chapters, flying to Europe as well as around the United States to make sure that his Wall Street constituency would be paid at the economy's expense. Reviewing how his memoir *Stress Test* (2014) sought to whitewash his behavior by depicting himself as "a firefighter, constantly on call to extinguish a fresh blaze," *Financial Times* columnist John Kay found "many things wrong with this analogy. ... the stuff [Geithner] used to douse the fires is not cold water but a stream of liberal credit – precisely what set the blaze alight in the first place. Better, perhaps, to limit access to matches and petrol, and to construct firebreaks. Perhaps the problem is one for the police as well as the fire service. Handcuffs might be as useful as the fire hose."[248]

The obvious question that government regulators sought to prevent the public from asking was why not nationalize the reckless banks whose entire net worth was less than the government's $25 billion TARP loan? Citigroup and Bank of America (and very nearly Goldman and other investment banks) were insolvent without the government giveaways. Taking over ownership and oper-

---

[248] John Kay, "Why banking crises happen in America but not in Canada," *Financial Times*, June 4, 2014. Matt Stoller ("The Con-Artist Wing of the Democratic Party," 2014) concludes: "After reading this book [*Stress Test*] and documenting lie after lie after lie, I'm convinced that there's more here than just a self-serving corrupt official. There's an entire culture, of figures at Treasury, the Federal Reserve, in the entire Democratic Party elite structure, and in the world of journalism, a culture in which Geithner is seen as some sort of role model."

ating them as a public financial option would have enabled the government to fire the officers responsible for the bad (often crooked) loans, and recoup what they had paid themselves in salaries and bonuses on the deception that their management was making money, not losing it. After all, bank managers of such institutions did not provide productive management but just the opposite: They acted in a predatory way that poisoned the financial system with "toxic waste."

The government's failure to take ownership gave managers, stockholders and bondholders a free lunch. Why did the government only move against AIG – and even then, not to stop rewarding its London financial managers, but to pay those of Goldman and other Wall Street institutions to preserve and subsidize the behavior that had caused the crisis? A *New York Times* editorial summed up the inequity at work regarding the corruption and insider dealing that emerged from Greenberg's lawsuit over the seizure of AIG to pay better-connected bankers:

> Mr. Greenberg rests his claim partly on the fact that the government imposed tougher terms on A.I.G. than on bailed-out banks. The government, for example, took a controlling equity stake in A.I.G., largely wiping out shareholders. In contrast, it left shareholders at bailed-out banks intact, even at arguably insolvent institutions like Bank of America and Citigroup. The injustice in that disparate treatment, however, is not that A.I.G was treated too harshly, but that the banks got off too easy. If the government had taken control of, say, Bank of America, taxpayers would have shared directly in its recovery. Instead, the subsequent gains flowed to shareholders who, but for the bailouts, would have been ruined.
>
> The government also took control over how the A.I.G. bailout money was spent. The bank bailouts, in contrast, had virtually no strings attached. That harmed the public because there was no way for the government to force the banks to increase lending and help homeowners, even though officials had said that the bailouts would foster lending and foreclosure relief.
>
> It's certainly true that the government deserves criticism for how it spent the A.I.G. bailout money: It funneled the money to the banks to make them whole on deals they had done with A.I.G., instead of requiring them to absorb some of the losses. But again, the real victim of the overly generous treatment of the banks is the American public.[249]

Fortunes were made by betting on the *inability* of debtors to pay – and being able to collect via government bailouts to favored insiders. This money could have been created just as readily to save homeowners from default. But it was given to the banks, while letting them foreclose on mortgages gone bad at the very outset. The economy has not recovered – except for the economy of the One Percent.

The next few chapters will trace how this bad-debt dynamic is unfolding from the United States to the Eurozone.

---

[249] "The Real Bailout Victims," *New York Times* editorial, October 24, 2014.

17

Wall Street Takes Control and Blocks Debt Writedowns

> The president [Obama] chose his team, and when there was only so much time and so much money to go around, the president's team chose Wall Street.
>
> Elizabeth Warren, *A Fighting Chance* (2014)

Voters in modern democracies tend to support politicians who draw the most beautiful pictures of how a fair and prosperous economy would operate. The more clearly a candidate can vocalize popular desires for upward mobility, lower living costs and deterrence of fraud and greed, the more likely they are to be elected. As the quip attributed to George Burns, Groucho Marx and others puts it: "The secret of life is sincerity and fair dealing. If you can fake that, you've got it made."

What voters wanted in the U.S. 2008 presidential election was a change away from multi-billion dollar gifts to Wall Street and the Cheney-Bush foreign military adventures. Barack Obama presented himself as the "hope and change" candidate. In an atmosphere shaped largely by public anger at the bailouts, he and other Democrats spoke of writing down mortgages for underwater homeowners, rolling back bank salaries and bonuses, and re-empowering the regulatory agencies that the Reagan, Bush and Clinton administrations had gutted. Congress had not written any of this into its TARP legislation or pressured government agencies to limit how banks could spend the giveaways they received. The hope was that this would change with a strong voter mandate that gave Democrats control of the House of Representatives and Senate as well as the presidency. The political path was open to enact far-reaching reforms.

Obama quickly slammed the door shut. Although having run on a populist platform, his role was to deliver his Democratic Party's liberal constituency of urban labor, racial and ethnic minorities, environmentalists and anti-war advocates to his campaign contributors. Over the past half-century the Democratic Party's strategy has been to create a menu of promises in two columns. Column A reflects the hopes and changes that voters want. That is the platform on which the Democrats ran. Column B represent what the party's major contributors and lobbyists want. Obama won the election by verbalizing the hopes of the 99 Percent, but did in practice what his campaign backers from the One Percent wanted. His language was populist, his policies oligarchic and aimed to prevent change.

Adept at applying this about-face with grace and a smile, Obama named former investment banker Rahm Emanuel his chief of staff to stifle the party's left wing, and appointed Clinton's old Rubinomics gang to key policy positions, headed by Larry Summers as chief economic advisor, and Geithner at Treasury to block bank regulation or debt writedowns. Instead of responding to public aspirations to appoint regulators of Wall Street, the top administrative bureaucracy was drawn largely from Goldman Sachs and Citigroup, excluding anybody as truly regulatory as the Bush administration's Sheila Bair or Neil Barofsky.

Post-2008 economic policy became that of the campaign contributors who comprised the Wall Street financed Democratic Leadership Council under Clinton. The continuity runs from the Clinton to Obama administrations via the economic policy of Summers and Jack Lew, another Rubin colleague. At the Justice Department, Eric Holder and Lanny Breuer blocked prosecution of bankers and pulled funding from FBI or Securities and Exchange Commission investigators of financial and corporate fraud.

Obama's naming of a Wall Street-approved cabinet showed his intention to block the reforms that most voters backed and expected, headed by debt relief. What voters got after 2008 was a financialized "deep state" concentrating more wealth in Wall Street's hands; no follow-through on Obama's airy talk of raising the minimum wage; and a drive to reduce the federal budget deficit at the expense of Social Security and other New Deal economic programs instead of public spending to fuel recovery.

Assigning financial policy to Geithner to block debt relief

Obama left economic policy to the Treasury, assigning Secretary Geithner the pro-bank role that Rubin had executed under Bill Clinton. Geithner already had served Wall Street as President of the New York Federal Reserve, whose website describes its "core mission" as being in part to "supervise and regulate financial institutions in the Second District" centered in New York City. Geithner promised his Congressional questioners at his March 2009 confirmation hearings that he had refused to perform his designated task: "First of all, I've never been a regulator ... I'm not a regulator."[250]

---

[250] L. Randall Wray, "Fire Geithner Now!" *Huffington Post*, January 8, 2010.

What then *was* his job? Sheila Bair and Neil Barofsky have described his actions to circumvent public regulations, first at the New York Federal Reserve and then as Treasury Secretary, lying outrageously to defend Citigroup. Citigroup's chairman Robert Rubin had sponsored Geithner to head the New York Fed, and had been grooming him to become Citigroup's CEO as George W. Bush's administration was ending. But rumor has it that Geithner was asked to defer his "descent from heaven" into Wall Street's high salary world in order to become Treasury Secretary and protect the banks (especially Citigroup) from what were feared to be Congressional pressures to regulate it more in the public interest.

Geithner quickly set to work crafting an even more bank-friendly policy than his predecessor Paulson had done. Under Geithner's direction bailout funding was made unconditional rather than subject to regulatory tightening. No firing of management, or even a cutback in salaries and bonuses. No cleanup in shady mortgage practices. (The MERS (Mortgage Electronic Registration Systems) scandal unfolded with zero government protection of homeowners against false bank documentation of just who owned the mortgages and how much was owed.)

Just how remarkable a feat this subversion of regulatory cleanup was is reflected in the fact that by April 2009, TARP Inspector General Barofsky had "opened twenty criminal fraud investigations into the $700 billion program" and its "cash for trash" dumping of junk mortgages on the Fed and Treasury. An early report "sharply criticized the government for failing to hold financial institutions accountable" for the money they were given.

> Charging that the plan carries "significant fraud risks", the inspector general's report pointed out that almost all of the risk in this new trillion-dollar plan is being borne by the taxpayers. The so-called private investors would be able to put up money they borrowed from the Fed through "nonrecourse" loans, meaning if the toxic assets purchased prove too toxic and the scheme failed, the private investors could just walk away without repaying the Fed for those loans. ... the government is purchasing the most suspect of the banks' mortgage packages.[251]

Geithner's undercutting of TARP showed that despite protests from Congress and the public, Wall Street could still get away with theft. Refusing to enforce reforms, Geithner became bolder as he saw his actions backed by President Obama, Chief of Staff Emanuel and Democratic congressional leaders. Former IMF economist Simon Johnson observed that troubled banks usually "are 'cleaned up' as a condition of official assistance, either by being forced to

---

[251] Robert Sheer, "Thievery under the TARP," *Truthdig*, April 22, 2009.

make management changes or being forced to deal with their bad assets. (This was the approach favored by Ms. Bair when she was at the F.D.I.C. ... The idea that there was no alternative to Mr. Geithner's approach simply does not hold water.)"[252]

Obama's false promise to write down bad mortgages

Nowhere was Geithner's unconditional support for the banks more blatant than in his neutering of President Obama's promise to reduce the debts of underwater homeowners in the Home Affordable Mortgage Program (HAMP). When $50 billion in TARP funds were committed in 2009 to help homeowners through HAMP, Obama announced his intent "to help up to 4 million struggling families stay in their homes through sustainable mortgage modifications. Hundreds of billions more were still available and could have been used by the White House and the Treasury Department to help support a massive reduction in mortgage debt."[253] In fact, as Barofsky reports in his book *Bailout*, "the conflicts of interest baked into the program would render it ineffective unless principal reduction was made mandatory."

Geithner pretended that "the losses that the banks might suffer on their first and second mortgages could push them into insolvency, requiring yet another round of TARP bailouts." Instead, he insisted that lenders be compensated for their losses on "liars' loans." Supported by Geithner, the banks banded together against underwater homeowners. "The message was clear," Barofsky concludes: "No way, no how would Treasury require principal reduction, even when Treasury's analysis indicated it would be in the best interest of the owner, investor or guarantor of the mortgage." President Obama permitted Geithner and the Treasury to block the HAMP, derailing hopes for a housing recovery by leaving "it to the largely bank-owned mortgage servicers (and to Fannie and Freddie) to determine if such relief would be implemented."[254] The effect was to leave the economy debt-ridden rather than writing down mortgages.

A conflict of interest between banks and homeowners was inherent in the HAMP program. In addition to their first mortgage, many homeowners had taken out "equity loans" as a second, subordinated mortgage – that is, second in line to be paid in case of default. Often the same bank held both mortgages.

---

[252] Simon Johnson, "The Legacy of Timothy Geithner," *The New York Times*, January 17, 2013.
[253] Neil Barofsky, "Tim Geithner's principal hypocrisy," Reuters op.ed., August 6, 2012. http://blogs.reuters.com/great-debate/2012/08/06/tim-geithner's-principal-hypocrisy/
[254] Barofsky, *ibid*.

Because first mortgages are the first in line to be repaid, "secondary" creditors bear the loss if a debtor defaults – which is why these second mortgages almost always bear a higher interest rate.

Banks used government subsidies to write down first mortgages (for which the government reimbursed them!) so that they could enable homeowners to continue paying their equity loans or other second mortgages in full. The banks thus were able to collect on liars' loans that were not subject to government reimbursement, thanks to the fact that "the initial plan didn't require the banks to write down second liens they may have held – like home equity lines – from borrowers whose original loans were modified."[255]

To dilute public support for writing down underwater mortgages, bankers and Geithner mounted a propaganda campaign to pit debtors against each other. Their divide-and-conquer ploy was to characterize homeowners with negative equity – but who still had enough income to afford to pay for their mortgages – as free riders. It would have paid for such individuals to walk away and buy a similar home at a lower price, leaving the banks holding the bad mortgage. But bank lobbyists and the Treasury tried to goad the homeowners into staying current on their payments, even when their mortgage debts were more than the home was worth. Warning about the "moral hazard" of "irresponsible" mortgage debtors getting a free ride, banks incited "responsible borrowers" to resent debtors who were offered relief for mortgages larger than the market price would cover.[256]

Bair accused Geithner of using the "moral hazard" argument in a one-sided way to buttress this double standard. "Saying that he didn't want to reward the behavior of those who knowingly got in over their heads," he had "no such concern for the mega-banks." Ultimately at issue, she concluded, was "whether our financial system should be based on a paradigm of bailouts or on one of accountability."[257]

Geithner's opposition to debt writedowns shows that instead of seeking to create a viable financial balance, the Treasury promoted a one-sided financial grab by Wall Street, leaving the economy in a debt trap. Matters got much worse when banks saw that the Geithner-Obama program enabled them to make much more money by foreclosing (and running up fees and penalties) than by writing down debts.

---

[255] Gretchen Morgenson, "Banks, at Least, Had a Friend in Geithner," *The New York Times*, February 3, 2013.

[256] Barofsky, *Bailout*, p. 197.

[257] Sheila Bair, "Why I recommend Tim Geithner's book," *Fortune*, May 19, 2014: http://finance.fortune.cnn.com/2014/05/19/sheila-bair-tim-geithner/

What sophisticated real estate investors do when in negative equity

The decline in real estate prices confronted heavily mortgaged homeowners with a choice. The "economic" option was to walk away from their property. This is called "jingle mail," for the sound made by putting the keys to the house in an envelope and mailing or handing them back to the bank, returning the collateral pledged to back the loan. Owners who walk away from underwater property lose whatever they have put into their home, but at least free themselves from having to pay much more than it is worth. It pays to make a new start with a smaller debt – or simply to rent.

The ethic of walking away from underwater real estate deals is practiced more cynically by the wealthy. Wall Street investors call this "strategic default." But mortgage bankers urge less affluent homeowners to take an "uneconomic" view of debt in terms of a personal ethic of responsibility, a moral obligation to pay debts.

While manipulating the moral bias of homeowners to stay put and keep paying the banks for loans in excess of the home's still-falling market price, the Mortgage Banking Association was walking away from its own underwater headquarters. It had bought the 10-story glass building in Washington DC in 2007 with a $75 million mortgage. "Like millions of American households," the *Wall Street Journal* noted, the association "found itself stuck with real estate whose market value has plunged far below the amount it owed its lenders."[258]

The story is one of hilarious hypocrisy. Having put down only 5% of the purchase price, the trade group decided to strategically default on its mortgage when the property lost $34 million (45%) in the declining market. The association rented offices five blocks away, announcing "that continued ownership of the building, which was financed with $75 million of variable-rate debt, would be 'economically imprudent.'" It ended up being sold for just $41.3 million. The Association's CEO John Courson refused to confirm just how much money it saved by walking away from the property, but he urged homeowners to "keep paying their loans even if that no longer seemed to be in their economic interest," because "defaults hurt neighborhoods by lowering property values." "What about the message they will send to their family and their kids and their friends?" he asked."[259]

---

[258] James R. Hagerty, "Mortgage Bankers Association Sells Headquarters at Big Loss," *Wall Street Journal*, February. 7, 2010.

[259] Available at "Mortgage Bankers Association Strategic Default," October 11, 2010, http://realestateinsidernews.com/financing-2/mortgage-bankers-association-strategic-default/.

Evidently corporate "personhood" is not subject to the ethic urged on homeowners not to walk away from underwater property but to forego their "economic" choice. The idea was for debtors to do as banks say, not as they do.

The path not taken: Debt revision for underwater homeowners

Bair described how Geithner blocked the FDIC from taking over bad banks, keeping them under Treasury protection by crying havoc that a public takeover would crash the economy and ignite a depression. This drowned out the ability of public ownership to cope with what actually has pushed the economy into depression: keeping the debt overhead on the books, shifting toxic waste onto the government's balance sheet, and setting the groundwork to slash Social Security, health care and other social spending. "Instead of ending bailouts," Geithner recruited administrators from the Fed who shared Chairman Greenspan's anti-regulatory views. Their deregulatory "blueprint for reform" gave him unilateral control to block real reform.[260]

For his part, Geithner criticized his nemesis Senator Elizabeth Warren for allegedly not understanding the nature of "fairness," claiming that "the central paradox of financial crises is that what feels just and fair is the opposite of what's required for a just and fair outcome."[261] He meant that what Wall Street claims to be fair is just the opposite of what the economy needs to recover. In his mind, what his Wall Street clientele "required" was a free hand in predatory lending and rent extraction – "wealth creation" *rentier* style. Warren "was worried about the right things," he said, "but she was better at impugning our choices – as well as our integrity and our competence – than identifying any feasible alternatives." Geithner's job as Treasury Secretary was to ensure that There Is No Alternative. He was backed by President Obama, who in 2015 echoed Geithner's condescending attack on Warren when she criticized the Trans-Pacific Partnership proposed dismantling of public regulation and tax policy.

Geithner's claim in his self-serving memoir *Stress Test*, that he did not simply serve the large banks in the way he sought to resolve the debt problem elicited a torrent of rebukes from officials who had dealt with him. Glenn Hub-

---

[260] Bair, *Bull By the Horns*, pp. 187-90.

[261] Quoted initially by Felix Salmon, "Bailouts: Geithner vs. Barofsky," Reuters, November 7, 2011, citing a remark by Geithner setting out to th G20 meetings in Europe, http://blogs.reuters.com/felix-salmon/2011/11/07/bailouts-geithner-vs-barofsky, repeated verbatim in *Stress Test* criticizing Senator Warren. See Suzy Khimm, "Timothy Geithner vs. Elizabeth Warren in new book 'Stress Test,'" msnbc, May 14, 2014, http://www.msnbc.com/msnbc/timothy-geithner-new-book-stress-test-elizabeth-warren.

bard, former chairman of the Council of Economic Advisers in George W. Bush's administration, for instance, had joined with Columbia University professor and housing market expert Christopher Mayer to propose a plan for the incoming Obama Administration late in 2008. Their proposal was to offer "millions of Americans the ability to refinance their mortgages into lower rate loans," by directing "the giant government-controlled mortgage guarantors Fannie Mae and Freddie Mac to refinance the mortgages on their books into lower-interest-rate loans." The idea was to save Fannie and Freddie from having to write them off as bad loans, while reducing mortgages to affordable market levels. This would have freed more homeowner income to spend on the economy at large. After Geithner's book came out, Hubbard told the news media that Geithner opposed the plan in 2008 and again in 2011 when there was talk of reviving it. "Tim Geithner personally and actively opposed mortgage refinancing, constantly."[262] The *Wall Street Journal* quoted his colleague Prof. Christopher Mayer as saying that "it never seemed like Geithner and the administration were ever working that hard to help stop foreclosures," and in fact that he never even tried.

Along similar lines in spring 2009, Illinois Senator Dick Durban had sought "to change the bankruptcy code so that homeowners who were underwater could modify their mortgages during the bankruptcy process." Durban's aim was to reverse the unanimous 1993 pro-bank Supreme Court decision blocking homeowners from using bankruptcy as a vehicle to write down their mortgages. The problem, however, was that Congress almost always has given "favorable treatment" to mortgage lenders rather than to debtors. It did so in 1978, using the excuse that more security for the banks (that is, less security for borrowers) would "encourage the flow of capital into the home-lending market."[263]

When bankruptcy reform passed the House and Durbin proposed in April 2009 to amend the bankruptcy law to permit mortgage writedowns, "the financial services industry pulled out all the stops, arguing that a right of bankruptcy for a homeowner would increase the cost of home loans, undermine the sanctity of contracts and promote (of course!) moral hazard." And Obama supported the banks. Prior to the presidential election he had said that he would back a change in the bankruptcy laws "to make it easier for families to stay in their homes." But he changed his position when Geithner opposed any such change, claiming (and repeating in *Stress Test*) that it would not be effective.

---

[262] Stephen Gandel, "The bigger beef between Tim Geithner and his critics," May 14, 2014, cnn.fortune.

[263] Joe Nocera, "Bankrupt Housing Policy," *The New York Times*, May 20, 2014, citing Jennifer Taub, *Other Peoples' Houses*.

Support resurfaced for the need to write down debts – whether by bankruptcy or loan renegotiation – with the publication of *House of Debt* by University of Chicago finance professors Amir Sufi and Atif Mian. Contra Geithner, they argue:

> Letting bankruptcy judges write down mortgages and providing an ambitious mortgage refinancing plan would have reduced foreclosures. For example, Geithner could have pushed for a policy to give bankruptcy judges the ability to write down mortgage debt in a Chapter 13 bankruptcy – "mortgage cram down." He could also have put forth an ambitious plan to allow solvent underwater homeowners to refinance into lower interest rates.[264]

Geithner objected that seeking such writedowns "would have further stressed a crowded bankruptcy system." But in reality "the threat of cram down would have induced more out-of-court renegotiation of mortgages." Joe Nocera of the *New York Times* cites an e-mail from Bair pointing out that giving homeowners an opportunity to file for bankruptcy would prompt mortgage holders to renegotiate the debt to a level that could be paid. And Sufi blames the Obama Administration's "obsessive focus on saving banks [that] kept homeowners from being helped. … Obama's advisers chose early on not to expend political capital forcing banks to forgive mortgage debt." The tragedy was that "Saving the banks will not save an economy if households are left drowning in a sea of debt."

Geithner turns the Home Affordable Mortgage Program (HAMP) into a fiasco

Emphasizing that Congress intended HAMP to be an essential part of the TARP bank bailouts, Barofsky describes how Geithner derailed the program, using demagogic ploys to stall reform, with no intention of following through on the public promises being made. Geithner only wanted to bail out the banks, not the economy. "By late 2009, it was becoming apparent that … Treasury refused to hold the banks accountable for the abuses to which they subjected homeowners in the program. … less than 8 percent of the funds originally allocated in TARP for foreclosure relief has actually been spent." The Treasury had "no intention of actually fixing the program," and Geithner refused "to penalize servicers who refused to comply with the program – or for that matter, with the law."[265]

---

[264] Amir Sufi, "Housing Crisis Was Overlooked," *The New York Times*, May 20, 2014. Yves Smith provides a detailed analysis in "Larry Summers' Contradictory and Dishonest Defense of Administration's Bank-Focused Crisis Response," *Naked Capitalism*, June 9, 2014.

[265] *Bailout*, pp. 193–199.

Describing "the cynicism behind the HAMP program's execution," Barofsky writes how Geithner told him that the plan all along had been for the banks to foreclose, but to avoid throwing underwater homes onto the market all at once. To prevent property prices from collapsing – which would have slashed the value of mortgage claims that banks held on their books – the HAMP plan was simply to *delay* the process, by giving homeowners a false hope of having their mortgages written down. The most widely-cited passage of *Bailout* describes how "Geithner blurted out: 'We estimate that they can handle ten million foreclosures, over time,' referring to the banks. 'This program will help foam the runway for them,'" by "keeping the full flush of foreclosures from hitting the financial system all at the same time."[266]

Slowing the pace of foreclosures would avoid crashing the market. It also would give the largest and most troubled banks an opportunity to run up late fees and penalties against mortgaged homes. These fees were charged against the property's ultimate selling price, at the debtor's expense, while slowing the pace of distress sales and hence the decline in prices for the real estate that backed bank mortgages.

Barofsky found that the Obama administration made no attempt to deliver on its "preposterous claim" that it would modify mortgages downward. It left the debts in place while foreclosures proceeded at a pace chosen by the banks. Responding to Geithner's attacks in *Stress Test*, Barofsky let loose and called him "the guy who was the architect of a financial crisis in one aspect, from his job at the Fed. He's the one who botched the bailout in ways that have caused the untold suffering of millions of people. When someone like that comes after you, it's almost a badge of honor."[267]

Behind Geithner, of course, was Obama himself, quickly breaking his campaign promise to extend the bailouts of the banks to include rescuing underwater homeowners from the mortgage debts that remained in place as real estate prices plunged. That he cared more for Wall Street than for distressed homeowners was made clear by the Federal Reserve's move to save financial institutions holding underwater mortgage-backed securities (MBS) by buying $2 trillion of these bad debts from the banks. This money could have been used to save homeowners, and with them the neighborhoods being devastated by bank foreclosures, leaving taxes unpaid while empty houses fell into ruin.

---

[266] *Bailout*, pp. 193, 157 and 199.
[267] Quoted in Rob Garver, "Geithner's Insult a 'Badge of Honor,' Says TARP Top Cop," *The Fiscal Times*, May 19, 2014. http://www.thefiscaltimes.com/Articles/2014/05/19/Geithner-s-Insult-Badge-Honor-Says-TARP-Top-Cop .

Obama's smoothness in misleading voters

One of the first books giving an intimate look inside the Obama Administration, Ron Suskind's *Confidence Men*, reported that on March 27, just two months after taking office on January 20, 2009, the new president invited the executives of thirteen leading Wall Street institutions to the White House. After listening to their arguments for why banks had to continue paying bonuses (ostensibly to get the best talent to manage their money), Obama told them: "Be careful how you make those statements, gentlemen. The public isn't buying that." He explained that only he could provide them with the political shield needed to forestall public pressure for reform, not to mention prosecution of financial fraud. "My administration is the only thing between you and the pitchforks."[268]

One leading banker attending the meeting told Suskind: "The sense of everyone after the meeting was relief. The president had us at a moment of real vulnerability. At that point, he could have ordered us to do just about anything and we would have rolled over. But he didn't – he mostly wanted to help us out, to quell the mob." As Suskind summarizes the result, which would shape the incoming administration's policy: "Obama had them scared and ready to do almost anything he said…. An hour later, they were upbeat, ready to fly home and commence business as usual."

Obama smoothly marketed his policies defending Wall Street in his interview with Steve Kroft on CBS's "60 Minutes," broadcast on December 13, 2009. Shedding crocodile tears over the fact that bankers have not shown "a lot of shame" about their behavior and outsized remuneration, the President tried to gain sympathy by showing that he knew very well why voters "are mad at the banks. Well, let's see. You guys are drawing down $10, $20 million bonuses after America went through the worst economic year that it's gone through in – in decades, and you guys caused the problem. And we've got 10% unemployment." Voicing the feelings of most voters as if they were his own, he continued:

> I did not run for office to be helping out a bunch of you know, fat cat bankers on Wall Street. Nothing has been more frustrating to me this year than having to salvage a financial

---

[268] Ron Suskind, *Confidence Men: Wall Street, Washington, and the Education of a President* (2011), p. 234. Countering Obama's pretense to oppose high salaries and support law enforcement against fraud, Eric Zuesse points out that the statement reported by Suskind is "not on the White House website; it was leaked out, which is one of the reasons Obama hates leakers." ("Retiring White House Prosecutor Says the SEC Is Corrupt," *Counterpunch*, April 9, 2014.)

system at great expense to taxpayers that was precipitated, that was caused in part by completely irresponsible actions on Wall Street.[269]

But as Barofsky pointed out: "Rather than being scaled down in proportion to their epic failures in risk management, compensation for the top twenty-five Wall Street firms in 2010 actually broke records at $135 billion"[270] What Obama's administration did was precisely to help the "fat cat bankers on Wall Street." The ones he had invited to the White House in March were his major campaign contributors, and his heart seemed to be with them.[271] His interview shows that he knew just what he was doing when Geithner and other officials bailed out Wall Street institutions "too big to fail":

> ... there is a culture there that feels that ... it's always making good decisions, and if it's not, then it's somebody else's fault. And that has to change. And the only way to change it, obviously – because so far at least, I haven't seen a lot of shame on their part – is to make sure that we've got a regulatory system in place that prevents them from putting us in this kind of pickle again.

On March 13, 2014, however, the Inspector General of the U.S. Department of Justice (DOJ) found that

> "DOJ did not uniformly ensure that mortgage fraud was prioritized at a level commensurate with its public statements. For example, the Federal Bureau of Investigation (FBI) Criminal Investigative Division ranked mortgage fraud as the lowest criminal threat in its lowest crime category. Additionally, we found mortgage fraud to be a low priority, or not [even] listed as a priority, for the FBI Field Offices we visited." In addition, the IG reported: "Many Assistant United States Attorneys (AUSA) informed us about under-reporting and misclassification of mortgage fraud cases.[272]

Matters ended even worse than Barofsky had suspected. When the dust had settled by 2015, six years after the program's inception, a report by the government's official monitor Christy L. Romero, showed that only 887,001 borrowers had had their mortgage costs reduced. "Instead of helping some four million borrowers get loan modifications ... banks participating in the program have rejected four million borrowers' requests for help, or 72 percent

---

[269] Transcript: 60 Minutes, President Barack Obama, Part 2, http://www.cbsnews.com/8301-18560_162-5975426.html?pageNum=2

[270] Barofsky, *Bailout*, p. 217.

[271] Penny Pritzker, for whose family Obama had made hundreds of millions of dollars as a community organizer gentrifying Chicago's black slums, had introduced him to Robert Rubin a decade earlier. Upon arriving in the Senate, Obama chose as his mentor the world's master coach in sanctimonious hypocrisy, Joe Lieberman, senator from Connecticut's insurance industry.

[272] "Audit of the Department of Justice's Efforts to Address Mortgage Fraud," quoted in Eric Zuesse, "Retiring White House Prosecutor Says the SEC Is Corrupt," *Counterpunch*, April 9, 2014.

of their applications, since the process began." The program was merely voluntary, and banks managed to lose the paperwork on applications or otherwise stalled. "CitiMortgage, a unit of Citibank, had the worst record, rejecting 87 percent of borrowers applying for a loan modification. JPMorgan Chase was almost as bad, with a denial rate of 84 percent."[272a] Romero's report criticized the Treasury for not making sure that homeowners were not wrongfully rejected. While Geithner blocked the regulatory system from writing down debts, Attorney General Eric Holder blocked the Justice Department from making perpetrators pay for their excesses. Their mantra was that the economy needs bankers to resume lending so that borrowers can go deeper into debt – as if this really will create more jobs and restore prosperity. As President Obama put matters in his "60 Minutes" interview:

> ... now that the system is stable, I think it is very important for us to get a system in place that prevents us from being lassoed to folks who are making bad decisions and benefitting from it. And what's most frustrating me right now is you've got these same banks who benefitted from taxpayer assistance who are fighting tooth and nail with their lobbyists up on Wall Street or up on Capitol Hill fighting against financial regulatory reform.

But the economy still is not stable, largely because President Obama appointed deregulators precisely to "lasso [the financial system] to folks who are making bad decisions and benefitting from it." Like Margaret Thatcher in Britain, he claimed that there was no alternative to giving bankers everything they ask for.

Obama was enabled to move to the right by Wall Street loudly proclaiming that he was hurting them, not helping them. Ron Suskind explained to Jon Stewart on *Comedy Central* why President Obama kept Tim Geithner on as Treasury Secretary despite his refusal to draw up a plan to take over Citigroup as he was asked to do:

> Jon Stewart: We keep hearing that Wall Street guys hate Obama. And my sense is, "Why?" They've had it as good as anybody in this country over these past 2½ years, probably better. What's their beef, in this? (Applause)

> Ron Suskind: It's interesting. I asked the same question. I talked to a senior Wall Street guy and said, "What gives with this thing with Obama? You know, you're after him, he's anti-business. You know, god! – he couldn't have done more. He basically opened the federal purse for you guys. He saved your skin... And he says, "No no! You see, of course he's not anti-business. But when we say he's anti-business he just ends up doing *more* for us. So we're going to keep saying it."[273]

[272a] Gretchen Morgenson, "A Slack Lifeline for Drowning Homeowners," The New York Times, August 2, 2015

[273] http://thedailyshow.cc.com/videos/yvr0hw/exclusive—-ron-suskind-extended-interview-pt—2. September 20, 2011.

The road to debt peonage

Bankers' "product" is debt. They promote the cover story that lending on "easier" terms (larger loans against income and property values) will widen the market for home ownership. There is no doubt that liars' loans, fraudulent property appraisals and restrictions on debtors' access to bankruptcy relief enable more people to get the credit needed buy homes. But to the extent that the economy-wide effect of such "looser" credit terms is to bid up real estate prices, homebuyers are obliged to go even further into debt to obtain housing. Banks end up with the lion's share of real estate rental value, which is paid out as interest.

Mortgage credit becomes predatory when it is not created with safeguards to keep loans within the reasonable ability of homebuyers to pay. (The old guideline was 25% of the borrower's income.) "Easy" bank credit turns the security of homeownership into debt-ridden austerity and hence chronic financial insecurity. This is the situation into which the U.S. economy has been pushed today.

A similar proliferation of real estate debt has forced Eurozone economies into debt deflation and austerity. On both continents the cost of irresponsible lending is being borne by the borrowers (and behind them, "taxpayers"), not the lenders. Limiting the safety valves of bankruptcy and debt write-downs, there is no opportunity to bring bank loans in line with the ability to pay. What appears at first glance to be credit to enable people to buy homes thus becomes a lifetime claim on a widening swath of their earnings.

That is the banks' marketing plan: to siphon off the benefits of rising wages and salaries as debt service, preventing this income from being used to raise living standards. Without "jingle mail," banks will lend beyond the value of the collateral being pledged, intending to come after the debtor's overall income (and that of co-signers, as in the case of most student loans), and failing that, to make "taxpayers" pay for their losses. This public liability for bad bank loans is what wrecked Ireland and other Eurozone countries.

The remaining chapters of this book describe the oligarchic strategy of bankers in what has become a class war against labor and the economy, using foreign debt pressure on governments to privatize and un-tax resource rent extraction.

18

From Democracy to Oligarchy

If we cannot change economic policy through elections, then elections are irrelevant and it is useless to vote.

Georgos Katrougalos, the administrative reform minister in the new SYRIZA government in Greece.[274]

We are living today in a transition period much like that of Athens c. 330 BC when Aristotle wrote his *Politics*. Seeing inequality widen as his city-state became an empire, he described how wealthy families tend to emerge within democracies to become a financial oligarchy. Book V of *Politics* traces how these oligarchies indebt a rising proportion of the population to themselves, creating hereditary estates on which to found aristocratic dynasties.

In time, rivalries develop within the leading aristocratic families, and some decide to overthrow other elites of the old order by "taking the multitude into their camp." In the 7th century BC, populist tyrants gained power in Corinth and other wealthy Greek cities by canceling the debts, redistributing the land and driving the old ruling elites into exile. Democracy was introduced more peacefully by reformers in 6th-century Athens. Solon banned debt bondage in 594, and Kleisthenes locked in political democracy in 508. But an oligarchy emerged once again, to be followed by aristocracy, democracy, and so on in Aristotle's eternal political triangle.

Destruction of democracy by the creditors and property owners who make up the One Percent thus is not a new phenomenon. The leading Roman historians blamed the destruction of Republican liberty on the rising power of creditors overpowering democracies. Using violence to block the reforms proposed by the Gracchi brothers in 133 BC, Senate leaders initiated a century of social war that ended in debt deflation and, in due course, serfdom.

From Greece and Rome to today's world, the driving force in the transition from democracy to oligarchy has been the fight by creditors against debtors.

---

[274] Jim Yardley, "Lawmakers (Just Not Greece's) Approve a Bailout Extension," *The New York Times*, February 28, 2015.

From the United States to Europe, creditors are taking over government agencies to control public policy and the tax system to undermine debtor rights, privatize public property in their own hands, and impose the modern equivalent of debt serfdom.

Gaining this degree of control in democracies requires winning voter approval. A deceptive mask of demagogy is created to depict government as costly and inherently corrupt – as if planning by the financial sector is more efficient and not even more corrupt, and as if government is not the only power able to check FIRE sector *rentiers*. The trickle-down economics of Ayn Rand and Frederick Hayek is mobilized to persuade voters that a mixed public/private economy of checks and balances is "the road to serfdom" – so as to clear the path for a financial road to neofeudal financialization of basic infrastructure, home ownership, education, health care and retirement savings.

In this way, the controls over state power are subtly maneuvered from democratic means to the demands of the oligarchs. The state will remain in financial hands until the power of oligarchs to control government fiscal and monetary policy is checked, along with their rhetorical deception as to how economies work. In the fiscal sphere, for instance, the wealthy One Percent seek to avoid being taxed by appealing to all "taxpayers" to demand cuts, as if there is no distinction between earned and unearned income, between productive and predatory ways of gaining wealth, between gains for the 99 Percent and those of the One Percent. Bankers and elites accuse regulation and law enforcement as being incursions on personal freedom and "free enterprise," and depict financial "reform" as deregulation – the opposite of what Reform Era meant a century ago.

Financial strategists in nations subject to democratic ratification of policies face a challenge over how to get voters to elect governments that impose austerity, regressive tax policies and anti-debtor bankruptcy laws of the sort that authoritarian Third World oligarchies and military dictatorships imposed from the 1960s onward.

Financial tacticians start by limiting the sphere over which democratic choice is allowed. Control over the Executive Branch of government is shifted to central banks and Treasuries staffed by bank apparatchiks. The cover story for this regulatory capture is that central bank "independence" from partisan politics is a "hallmark of democracy" – as if making financial policy independent from oversight by elected legislators is democratic! Bankers trot out neoliberal professors to preach that only professionals drawn from the ranks of leading financial institutions (*i.e.*, to act as their lobbyists) have the expertise needed to set monetary policy. This ideology denies that there is any such thing as careers in public service to check the potentially predatory behavior of high finance. The only entrance path to regulatory agencies is held to be the revolving door between the large financial institutions and government.

Today's financial alliance with real estate and monopolies

The financial sector has not always opposed democracy. Chapter 4 has described how bankers supported democratic reform in 19th-century Britain, forming an alliance with industrial interests to extend voting rights to the population at large to roll back the landed interest. This aim of taxing and controlling *rentier* interests was a driving force of Europe's 1848 revolutions. The goal was to break the stranglehold of surviving post-feudal landlord interests that controlled governments and enacted protectionist agricultural tariffs such as Britain's Corn Laws, aiming at self-sufficiency rather than foreign trade.

To profit from the burgeoning industrial prosperity, foreign trade and its associated investment in railroads and canals, the liberal financial-industrial program sought to free markets from these legacies of feudalism. Up to the outbreak of World War I in 1914, reformers in the leading industrial nations aimed to make economies more competitive by bringing prices in line with actual necessary production costs, by minimizing the rakeoffs extracted by absentee landlords and monopolists.

Today's financial sector – and the One Percent behind it – has inverted this political program. It has joined in an alliance with real estate, natural resources and monopolies. Instead of public investment in infrastructure to lower the costs of doing business, this FIRE-sector alliance is hijacking governments to promote privatization and rent extraction. The "free market" has been redefined to mean freedom *for* the *rentier* class to create a tollbooth economy, not freedom *from* their predatory incursions to extract unearned income in today's New Enclosure Movement. Its advocates trumpet this not as class war, but as "the end of history," as if it is inevitable and There Is No Alternative.

The first incursion is made in the executive branch of government via central banks and treasuries. The strategy is to impose pro-creditor laws governing bankruptcy and foreclosure, regulation and taxation of bank activities and property. Toward this end, finance capital now operates largely through supranational financial institutions. Staffed with Geithner-like clones in today's banalities of economic evil, the IMF and World Bank, followed by the European Central Bank and European Commission, seek to impose austerity and privatization sell-offs while loading economies down with domestic and foreign debt that becomes today's main lever of control – claiming that all this will make economies richer and raise living standards.

Populist politics in the service of Wall Street

The transition phase to oligarchy retains the political trappings of "managed democracy." Throughout the world the traditional left has become so neoliberalized (one may almost say Thatcherized) that its 19th-century origins are long forgotten in favor of today's postmodern focus on social and cultural issues. Economic policy is left to seemingly objective technocrats drawn from the right wing. Tony Blair's "New Labour" Party in Britain, the French Socialist Party under François Hollande and Greece's Pasok party behind George Papandreou did not propose economic or financial alternatives to the privatization, austerity and tax shift off the FIRE sector onto labor. All saw their support plunge in the June 2014 Euro-parliament elections, when the only parties talking about economic issues were rightwing populists (with the exception of Syriza in Greece and Podemos in Spain).

Since 2008, Obama has adopted a similar strategy of ethnic and cultural identity politics, remaining silent about his economic agenda to defend Wall Street against debt writedowns, and to deregulate finance (supporting the pro-corporate Trans-Pacific Partnership and its associated Trade in Services Agreement, TISA). Obama also cemented the groundwork to balanced the budget by a neoliberal reform program of downsizing Social Security and Medicare to pave the way for their privatization.

The Thatcher-Pinochet rhetoric of "labor capitalism" and "worker ownership of the means of production" (by stock ownership managed by Wall Street) was trotted out to urge employees to "take responsibility" for their retirement by placing their pension savings in the hands of money managers. This was the goal that George W. Bush had sought but failed to achieve in 2004 when the stock market faltered. A Republican president hardly could have succeeded in privatizing Social Security over a Democratic Congress. Only a Democratic president could mute such opposition, just as in Britain only the Labour Party could have silenced left-wing opposition to out-Thatcherizing the Conservatives by privatizing the railroads and other transportation in the notoriously pro-financial Public-Private Partnerships.

The way in which Obama stacked his 2009 Federal Commission on Fiscal Responsibility and Reform revealed the policies his backers wanted to see rationalized to the public. To head the panel he appointed Clinton corporatist Erskine Bowles and former Republican Senator Alan Simpson. Bowles and Simpson defined fiscal responsibility as balancing the budget (without raising taxes on the wealthy) and "reform" as cutting back Social Security. The goal was to finally achieve Wall Street's dream of steering Social Security contributions into privatized accounts that money managers would invest to further financialize the economy, with an initial influx of funds to bid up stock market prices in a new bubble.

When Obama's Bowles-Simpson Commission urged Social Security "reform" to balance the U.S. budget, they did not have the crude excuse that European politicians used: The Euro treaty limits budget deficits to only 3% of GDP (as discussed in the next chapter). This constraint enables governments to blame the Constitution for blocking Keynesian expansion since 2009, as if austerity is a fact of nature instead of a tactic in class warfare.

The assumption that no government spending can take the form of capital investment, and that all budget deficits are simply a deadweight drain on the economy, inverts the direction in which civilization has been travelling for thousands of years. There is no accounting offset for public investment as an asset, reducing the deficit from "current" spending. It is as if only the private sector has a balance sheet with assets and productive spending on it. The irony is that account keeping and profit-and-loss statements were innovated in the temples and palaces of Mesopotamia some five thousand years ago!

European Central Bank and IMF credit is extended to governments only to give to banks, to lend to bid up real estate and asset prices and thus save themselves from losses on the over-lending that is shrinking the economy. Austerity and privatization is built into the model – and is applauded as "lowering production costs," "rationalizing labor" and "making economies competitive."

All this requires an ideological bodyguard of junk economics. Public disdain is averted by pretending that the lobbyists are "specialists" and hence their economic class war is above politics. The U.S. Presidency and foreign prime ministers now leave policy making to apparatchiks nominated by major campaign contributors. Nominal heads of state use their office as a bully pulpit to preach neoliberal economic ideology in the service of financial elites. A common tactic to sell anti-labor "reforms" (one should call them counter-reforms) is to blame the U.S. and European budget deficits on populations aging and receiving more expensive health care, and on social programs benefiting low-income families rather than on the financial minority getting richer by shifting the tax burden onto labor to cause austerity leading to falling tax revenues and deeper budget deficits. Blame is placed on the victims, not their financial victimizers.

Debt polarization likewise is depicted as a demographic problem, characterizing creditors as the elderly who have saved prudently for retirement, not the One Percent who inherit fortunes without having to save wages from their own work. The polarization of wealth thus appears to be the result of "objective" natural causes, not partisan oligarchic politics.

Indeed, as tax revenues fall in response to rising debt service and the tax burden shifts onto labor (along with higher rake-off of prices for privatized hitherto public services), financial lobbyists use fiscal deficits as an opportunity to call for auctioning off public infrastructure. Creditor leverage over public deficits (especially in foreign currency) is wielded to turn public roads into toll roads. Other public investments are financialized as similar tollbooth opportunities. These privatizations increase the cost of living and doing business, making the economy higher-cost even as it is being impoverished. That is how democracy devolves into neofeudal oligarchy.

To the financial sector, the most important privatization is that of money creation. The aim is for economies to become dependent on bank credit rather than government spending to provide the money and credit needed to grow. This dream was realized during Bill Clinton's administration, which ended the 1990s by running a budget surplus – that is, by taxing more out of the than spending into it. The money supply grew solely by expanding the economy's debt overhead, not by government money creation.

Quantitative Easing subsidizes asset-price inflation

For half a century after the 1930s, deficit spending was viewed as a way for governments to revive economies in times of slowdown. Government money creation to finance deficits was viewed as increasing output and employment. And as full employment was approached, consumer prices and wages would increase in proportion to growth in the money supply.

This tendency of government spending to raise prices encouraged bondholders and anti-labor interests to demand monetary tightness and high interest rates to keep wages from rising. Today's financial interests have made an about-face. They are all in favor of money creation by central banks as long as it is not for "Keynesian" spending on public projects that employ labor or otherwise increase the purchase of goods and services.

This money creation was not counted as part of the federal budget deficit because it was treated as a *quid pro quo* – as if the Fed were merely providing short-term liquidity in exchange for a swap of sound long-term assets. It did not confront the solvency crisis when it pumped in good official money in (over-)payment for the junk mortgage credit created by the banks.[275] But this

---

[275] A *liquidity problem* reflects merely temporary shortage of cash, *e.g.* when banks are afraid to lend more in a high-risk environment that soon blows over. The underlying revenue stream is not in doubt, only the credit available to buy a revenue-yielding asset. A *solvency crisis* occurs when loans exceed the underlying value of the collateral (and interest charges exceed the revenue) for more than a temporary period. This obviously was the case as falling property prices rendered millions of homes insolvent.

sleight-of-hand merely covered up the debt overhead problem. Providing liquidity to banks – and stopping a run by depositors – does nothing to resolve the debt burden. Without writing down debts, subsidizing the banks leaves the overhead in place to continue siphoning off so much income that more breaks will occur in the economy's chain of payments. A short-term solution of "confidence" does not solve the long-term problem that should be rattling "confidence" that an economy can truly recover without debt writedowns. The key principle in such situations is that debts that can't be paid, won't be paid. The Geithner-Obama administration pretended that the economy could carry them and pay them off, if only the banks were given enough to lend yet more money to the indebted economy. That was supposed to be what Quantitative Easing was all about.

The new Wall Street-endorsed easy credit was not "spent into the economy" by paying for public services or investment in public infrastructure. It was not given to homeowners or used for debt relief. Instead, the Federal Reserve provided credit to Wall Street banks at near-zero interest rates under Quantitative Easing (QE). The excuse was that banks would turn around and lend out this money to revive the economy. Bank lending at interest was claimed to be more efficient than government spending by bureaucrats – as if all public spending was simply a deadweight loss.

This deceptive logic has proved to be flat wrong and, in fact, a deliberate diversion from where bank credit actually goes and what it is spent on. The first financial fiction is that economies can extricate themselves from debt by borrowing yet *more* from banks – presumably to make new debt-leveraged gains from rising asset prices being inflated by this credit. So we are plunged back in the bubble economy's game plan.

The reality is that since 2008, banks have *not* lent out their bailout funds or their reserves at the Fed to "put America back to work," pumping credit into domestic investment or consumer spending on goods and services. Wall Street has used the Fed's helicopter money drops mainly to speculate in foreign currencies and interest-rate arbitrage. Banks have also have extended credit for derivatives gambles, takeover loans and other transactions in financial securities and assets. But they have pulled back their lines of credit to homebuyers and credit-card users, and to small and medium-sized businesses. Mortgage debt has been called in rather than increased, credit-card debt has been scaled back, and small and medium-sized businesses have been unable to borrow more. The only category of lending that has spiked upwards is student loans.

In contrast to the past century of economic models that treated capital investment as responsive to interest rates, the aim of today's QE to lower interest rates is not to make new tangible capital investment more profitable.

It aims first and foremost to re-inflate asset prices for the securities that banks hold and lend against. Secondarily, QEW makes debt-financed corporate take-overs and raids more profitable, as well as stock buybacks. Such debt financing is the antithesis of new capital investment and employment. By trying to pre-serve wealth in the form of creditor claims held mainly by the One Percent against the 99 Percent, the Fed's QE policy actually makes new tangible invest-ment relatively *less* remunerative than speculation. New hiring is not spurred.

Low rates do subsidize the banks, but their lending and speculation is decoupled from tangible investment in the "real" economy of production and consumption. To make matters worse, today's low risk-free interest rates tempt pension funds to gamble in a desperate effort to make the returns needed to pay pensions without requiring larger employer contributions. They are gam-bling in the Wall Street casino, which always wins against its "counterparties" and customers.

In economies plagued by debt-ridden austerity and tax favoritism for finance and rent extraction over labor and industry, low rates of interest fail to stimu-late real investment. This dynamic results in what Keynes called a Liquidity Trap, where low interest rates fail to fuel new capital investment and employ-ment. This scenario is plaguing the U.S. economy today, while Europe is engulfed even more deeply in debt deflation.

Banks oppose solving the problem of debt deflation by writing down debts to "free" more income for spending on goods and services. They advocate reducing wages and scaling back pensions to squeeze out more and more income to pay exponentially rising debt service.

Where is a viable left, and what should its program be?

In autumn 2008, voters were up in arms against the bailouts to Wall Street on terms that shifted the losses from reckless lending, financial deregulation and outright fraud onto the government and therefore "taxpayers." Yet they were powerless to deter Democratic and Republican leaders from supporting Wall Street and blocking debt writedowns. Likewise in Ireland, the government yielded to Eurozone demands that it turn reckless bank losses into heavy tax burden to weigh down the economy and drive many Irish to emigrate. Spain, Portugal and Greece were all conquered "democratically" by high finance, taking on debt to the IMF and ECB to bail out government bondholders.

Voter reaction finally erupted in Europe's May 2014 elections, which saw a stunning reaction against the ruling coalition of right and nominally left par-ties. New parties on the nationalist right and populist left emerged to redraw the electoral map.

Paul Craig Roberts noted that the major media in the United States and Europe "heavily demonized third parties, such as Nigel Farage's Independent Party (1993) in the UK and Marie Le Pen's National Front Party (1972) in France. The establishment is already at work explaining that these electoral victories along with [Virginia Tea Party] Brat's are due to their anti-immigration status." However, "the main target of Farage and Le Pen is not immigrants" but the relinquishing of authority to a European Union bureaucracy run for bankers and bondholders.[276] Nationalists were offering almost the only available protest, as the left parties were still demoralized and almost embarrassed to campaign for economic resistance to the financial takeover of Europe. In contrast to Social Democratic and labor parties a century ago, there is little political advocacy of public investment, taxing *rentiers* or even restoring more progressive taxation of income and wealth in general. The resulting political vacuum has seen only right-wing parties protest against pro-creditor regimes.

The U.S. reaction closest to that of Europe occurred in the June 2014 Virginia primary. David Brat, a hitherto unknown and barely-funded Tea Party candidate, unseated Republican Congressional leader Eric Cantor. His message was explicitly anti-Wall Street: "All the investment banks in New York and DC – those guys should have gone to jail. Instead of going to jail, they went on Eric's Rolodex."[277] Denouncing the conservative Republican Congress as much as Democrats "for being in the pocket of 'Wall Street crooks' and D.C. insiders," Brat accused "the folks who caused the financial crisis" of occupying prime positions in the Obama Administration as well as the Republican leadership.[278]

The common denominator inflaming the anti-government passions of the Tea Party in the United States and the nationalist anti-Euro parties in Europe is outrage against governments that have been hijacked by bankers to impose financial austerity and reverse classical progressive taxation. The real solution is not the Tea Party's nihilistic reaction against to government as such, but to mobilize its regulatory and tax politics (and legal system) to support economic growth and prosperity. Financial interests have secretly manufactured a faux oligarchic populism opposing taxation and regulation. Yet like Europe's nationalist parties, the Tea Party is capable of making a tactical "left run" around the traditional labor-based parties. Its success reflects the failure of traditionally left parties to put forth a sufficiently radical alternative.

---

[276] Paul Craig Roberts, "Is Dave Brat a Marked Man?" *Counterpunch*, JUNE 12, 2014.
[277] Tom Braithwaite, "Brat win delivers blow to Wall St pack," *Financial Times*, June 12, 2014.
[278] David Dayen, "Cantor's Loss a Triumph for Anti-Corporate Right-Wing Populism," *Naked Capitalism*, June 12, 2014.

Debt deflation, austerity and the crisis of democracy

Europe as well as America is now being obliged to pay down debts run up during the Bubble years that peaked in 2008. Paying mortgage debts, student loans, credit card debt, corporate debt, state, local and federal government debt transfers income – and increasingly, property – to bankers and bondholders. This debt deflation stalls economic growth by shrinking spending on goods and services, and hence on new capital investment and employment.

"When the Japanese private sector began to deleverage in the early 1990s," Wolfgang Münchau noted in his *Financial Times* column, "the government increased its debt to absorb the shock." But the Eurozone's fiscal compact imposes fiscal deflation on top of debt deflation. This will increase "the political backlash … Even if deleveraging could work economically – which is not clear – it may not work politically.[279] Voters will revolt against being subjected to debt deflation and austerity while the One Percent monopolize the gains.

The question is: how will the political resistance to the financial power grabs be manifested? Will popular frustration take the form of unfocused anti-government politics hijacked by the vested financial interests? Or, will the classical progressive reform movement re-assert itself?

The emerging financial oligarchy

Wall Street's lobbyists have drafted a Trans-Pacific Partnership and its European counterpart whose terms the Obama administration has kept secret even from Congress. What *is* known is that these treaties would block governments from regulating the financial and corporate sectors to enact environmental protection and impose cleanup charges. The object is to remove policy from democratic choice by shifting control of government to a "technocrat" bureaucracy drawn from the financial and other *rentier* sectors and run by an army of Geithner lobbyists who will tell the public that There Is No Alternative to shifting tax policy and monetary power from elected governments to the IMF and the European Central Bank, Wall Street and the City of London. Neoliberal politicians claim to feel the pain of indebted and unemployed voters, but say there is nothing they can do except to follow this advice to impose austerity and bail out the banks so that they will be able to lend more.

The rising debt service and debt-inflated housing prices in the face of falling wages were ignored until the Occupy movement explained why the economy is stalling: deteriorating consumer demand as income is earmarked

---

[279] Wolfgang Münchau, "Europe faces the horrors of its own house of debt," *Financial Times*, June 16, 2014.

for debt service. It should not be surprising that an economy 70 percent dependent on consumer spending stalls when creditors, monopolists and property owners extract tribute from indebted borrowers, renters, students and users of public infrastructure services. In effect, these groups are paying reparations for losing the financial and neo-class war that they didn't even realize was being waged.

So we are brought back to the fact that in biological nature parasites produce an enzyme that sedates the host's perception that it is being taken over by the free luncher. In today's financialized economies the enzyme consists of junk economics. The popular media distract attention from how it has been possible for the Federal Reserve to create what is now more than $4 trillion in Quantitative Easing without spurring price and wage inflation. Morally, why have the banks' large uninsured depositors, bondholders and gambling "counterparties" been bailed out in a period of debt deflation for the rest of the economy? Why did the Fed not create this credit to pay *off* the debts? Why were the debts left in place, leading to foreclosures that destroyed entire neighborhoods while the largest banks were rescued to resume their extravagant bonuses and dividend payouts?

Selling out voters to campaign contributors promoting pro-One Percent policies has led both major U.S. political parties to be distrusted by large swaths of the electorate. In view of how the Occupy Wall Street demonstrations won worldwide emulation by catalyzing awareness of how big money has corrupted our government and our economy, it seems remarkable that no Democratic or other would-be left coalition has sought to mobilize the widespread rejection of today's pro-bank policy. Advocacy of truly socialist policies might stun the beltway class with its popularity, as Syriza has done in Greece (described in Chapter 24 below).

The Tea Party (and libertarians with roots in the anarchist tradition) fail to realize that only a government strong enough to tax and regulate Wall Street can check today's financial and *rentier* power grab. Attacking "big government" without distinguishing between Big Oligarchy and a Progressive Era mixed economy – what used to be called socialism – dilutes efforts to regulate and tax wealth, and ends up being manipulated to support the vested interests, Koch Brothers-style.

Why hasn't a Syriza-type third party arisen in the United States? Why do labor unions, racial and ethnic minorities and taxpayers shy away from creating an alternative to the Democratic Party whose Wall Street "Rubinomics" wing has seizedcontrol? Why is no interest group focusing on financial reform to a degree that environmental protection, racial equality or even gay rights have done?

From the United States to Europe, the leading traditional parties are supporting yet more privatization, financialization and rent seeking. This aban-
donment of what used to be the Progressive Era's Great Awakening has
enabled the financial oligarchy to undercut democratic politics, the courts, the
tax system and even the law. Yet no party has mobilized the righteous indignation that Occupy Wall Street liberated by expressing what most people felt:
that the alternative to the One Percent monopolizing wealth is debt writedowns
and financial reform to create a public banking option.

Part III

Austerity as a Privatization Grab

19

Europe's Self-Imposed Austerity

If there is a second meltdown, it probably will not come from some new panic over the sudden discovery of toxic assets. It will come from a political revolt against the retrenchment, austerity, and social destruction to which the crisis has led. That revolt probably will not originate in the United States. But it might come in Spain, Portugal, Ireland, Italy – or Greece. Especially from Greece. And it would not be a minute too soon.

James K. Galbraith, "The first great financial crisis has not ended,"
The International Economy, Fall 2013, p. 25.

Fiscal austerity was written into the eurozone's[280] 1993 Maastricht criteria: A condition for governments adopting the euro currency was to limit budget deficits to only 3 percent of GDP, and overall government debt to 60 percent of GDP. This blocks the now 28-member eurozone governments from reviving employment by public spending programs.

Even more deflationary are the euro's monetary constraints. In contrast to the U.S. Federal Reserve's ability to create new money, the European Central Bank (ECB) was not set up to monetize government spending. Article 123 of the Lisbon Treaty (effective since December 2009) prevents it from lending directly to governments. The ECB only buys bonds from banks and other holders, not directly from governments.

Leaving governments without a vehicle for their own money creation has plunged the eurozone into much deeper unemployment and debt deflation than the United States has suffered. Yet the "hard money" constraint seems so technical that instead of denouncing it for crucifying the continent on a cross of privatized bank credit, Europe's major "socialist" parties – from Tony Blair's New Labour in England to George Papandreou's Pasok in Greece – have been neoliberalized and are leading the fight to impose monetary austerity and privatization. Scaling back public spending and privatizing infrastructure is neoliberalism's alternative to classical social democracy.

---

[280] The eurozone consists of users of the euro, which is simply a currency like the dollar, not to be confused with the European Union. The eurozone and euro therefore are lower case, not proper nouns, reflecting also the continent's low self-esteem.

Privatizing money creation and basic infrastructure is a revolutionary reversal of government's traditional role. Creating money was long assumed to be a public function, indeed a key criterion of qualifying as a nation-state. For thousands of years money was a creation of palaces, temples and other public institutions. But bank lobbyists and anti-government ideologues designed the eurozone in a way that deprives governments of a central bank able to do what the Bank of England and the U.S. Federal Reserve were created to do: monetize deficit spending. The task of providing the economy's rising need for money and credit is left to bankers and bondholders.

Privatizing credit and debt creation leads to debt deflation while at the same time adding financial carrying charges to the cost of living and doing business. Combined with fiscal deflation (limiting the size of government deficits and shifting taxes regressively off wealth onto consumers), this squeezes economies. This straitjacket is euphemized as the Stability and Growth Pact, an Orwellian label for imposing instability and stagnation. It is part of the EU Fiscal Compact that went into effect on January 1, 2013.

The Pact centralizes the power to oversee national budgets in the hands of the European Commission – the European Union's executive body. There is no provision to write down mortgages or other personal and business debts. Payment to bondholders (but not pension debts to labor) is enforced even when this pushes economies into depression and bankruptcy. Uninsured depositors, bondholders and counterparties are to be paid in full, with interest, even in reckless banks (until Russian and other depositors in Cyprus banks were singled out to take a "bail-in" hit in 2013).

Like the U.S. Treasury and Fed, the EC and ECB are controlled by the banking sector, whose war against government's role in the economy is aimed most of all against labor. Europe's "troika" – the ECB, European Commission (EC) and the International Monetary Fund (IMF) – deems double-digit unemployment, rising emigration and distress sales of public property to be a price worth paying to dismantle government's ability to create money, tax wealth and invest capital in public infrastructure. These neoliberal constraints are neoliberalism's alternative to classical social democracy, depicted as milestones on civilization's road to The End of History.

Seeking to break labor union power (especially in the public sector) and depress wage levels, financial planners pretend that economies can work their way out of debt by "internal devaluation": slashing wages and public spending, ostensibly to make economies "more competitive" and help their exports. Rising unemployment and emigration are held to redistribute labor "where it is needed," that is, needed to prevent wages from rising in more rapidly growing economies.

What ends up being exported is the most employable and skilled labor. Capital flees as well. Two of the major victims, Latvia and Ireland, are applauded as success stories along this road to debt serfdom, as if their tax shift onto labor and falling wages are a not an economic death grip but pave the way for a future takeoff. The terms "reform," "streamlining" and "greater competitive efficiency" are favorite neoliberal euphemisms for turning the EU Constitution into a straitjacket to block recovery.

All this is a far step from classical free markets. The political economy of industrial capitalism aimed to replace post-feudal monopolies, absentee land-lordship and banking with public ownership, or at least to fully tax rent extraction. Today's post-classical view is that all government spending and taxes are inefficient and inflationary. There is no recognition that providing public services at cost or freely will lower prices.

Another fiscal element of this financial war is to applaud privatization sell-offs are as being more efficient, despite the rising prices that economies must pay for essential services financed by interest-bearing debt. Prices for infra-structure services rise for privatized monopolies, which are allowed to incor-porate the takeover-interest charges into their rate base (while treating them as tax-deductible). These policies raise the cost of living and squeeze household budgets even as wage levels fall.

The effect has been to leave Latvia and Ireland (as well as Greece) in an economic dead zone. These countries are being forced to relinquish control over government monetary policy and to relinquish public taxation or mini-mization of the economic rent from land, natural resources and infrastructure monopolies, while tax revenue falls and labor has had to emigrate to find work in the creditor nations.

Forcing taxpayers to pay for policies dictated by unelected financial bureaucrats

Political theorists define a state as having three paramount powers: to create money, levy taxes and declare war. By depriving member governments of the ability to create their own money, the eurozone's Lisbon and Maastricht treaties block countries – and the eurozone itself – from monetizing their fiscal deficits.

The Eurozone is thus repeating the creditor-oriented policy that led to debt deflation after Europe's Napoleonic Wars ended in 1815, and after America's Civil War ended in 1865. First Britain and then the United States rolled back the price of gold (and hence of commodities and labor) by running budget surpluses to suck money and income out of the economy. It is the same defla-tionary ideology that led Germany to try to pay unpayably high reparations to the Allies, who in turn imposed austerity on themselves by trying to pay their arms debts to the United States after World War I.

Such austerity is the creditor's idea of a well-run economy. Prices and wages fall, increasing the difficulty of paying back debts taken on at the higher "old" prices. Unemployment suppresses wages, leading to defaults that transfer property to creditors. When bankers depict this debt and price deflation as "stability," they simply mean increasing their power over labor and industry.

What is remarkable is that today's debt deflation is occurring without a war having taken place. This time the most problematic debts are private, owed by homebuyers and businesses. Public debts stem increasingly from tax cuts on property and wealth – and in Ireland, from taking bad bank debts onto the public balance sheet.

Ireland's real estate bubble ("economic miracle")

The ECB's prime directive mirrors that of the U.S. Treasury under Paulson and Geithner since 2008: Governments are to take full liability for paying uninsured bank depositors and bondholders, even when high interest rates are paid by banks engaging in reckless lending and insider dealing. Next to Iceland's three notorious banks that collapsed in 2008 (Landsbanki with its Icesave affiliate, Glitner and Kaupthing), the two most reckless European banks were the Anglo Irish Bank and the Royal Bank of Scotland. All these banks attracted mainly foreign "hot money" unconcerned with risk.

ECB President Jean-Claude Trichet visited Ireland's central bank in May 2004 and praised its "Celtic Tiger" takeoff (1994-2007): "The process of transformation that Ireland began over four decades ago has become a model for the millions of new citizens of the European Union."[281] Ireland's "economic miracle" (the financial sector's euphemism for a bubble) combined a race to the fiscal bottom with an absence of bank regulation. The country's low 12.5% corporate income tax attracted high-profit U.S. firms such as Google, Facebook, Twitter and Yahoo to make Ireland their global headquarters to avoid worldwide taxes.

Irish banks increased their borrowing from foreign depositors and bondholders from €15 billion in 2004 to €110 billion in 2008. The vast inflow was squandered to fuel a real estate bubble that inflated property prices fivefold by 2007. A remarkably high 87 percent of Irish families bought homes on credit – leaving few people to buy the new luxurious mansions being built by developers

[281] Philip Pilkington, "Are the Irish People to Blame for Reckless Borrowing?" *Naked Capitalism*, Feb. 2, 2012.

without much concern for actually finding buyers. Most of the bank loans had no foundation in realistic market valuations.

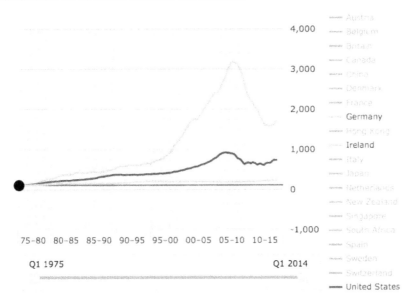

Figure 8: House prices, Ireland, Germany, United States (Source: Nicholas Shaxson, "Did Ireland's 12.5 Percent Corporate Tax Rate Create the Celtic Tiger?," Naked Capitalism, March 12, 2015).

By far the most heedless loans were made by Anglo Irish Bank. By no stretch of the imagination were Anglo Irish's madcap lending practices "systemic."[282] It was not a regular bank serving the overall economy, but a financial operation advertising for large wholesale deposits (mainly from non-Irish investors) and lending them to large borrowers, especially to the bank's owners to buy its stock, bidding up its price much as Iceland's banks had done. This self-financing is an age-old fraud scheme,[283] and most countries ban it.

---

[282] Michael Lewis, "When Irish Eyes Are Crying," Vanity Fair, March 2011, points out: "Anglo Irish Bank had only six branches in Ireland, no A.T.M.'s, and no organic relationship with Irish business except the property developers. It lent money to people to buy land and build: that's practically all it did. It did this mainly with money it had borrowed from foreigners. It was not, by nature, systemic. It became so only when its losses were made everyone's."

[283] For a description of how banks boost their share prices by covertly financing the bidding up of their stock, see Friðrik Már Baldursson, "Gambling for Resurrection in Iceland," Naked Capitalism, January 7, 2014, originally posted at VoxEU: "In writing l'Argent (1891), Emile Zola consulted records of the 1882 fall of Union Générale, whose CEO Paul Bontoux had done just that. It was illegal even then, and he was tried and convicted. Zola's fictional character Aristide Saccard followed the same path."

But like Iceland and other countries whose "light touch" permitted bad banks to end up crashing the economy, Ireland had no real bank regulators. It relied on the advice of its central bank. And the advice of central bankers is the same everywhere: Don't interfere with lending, and make sure that all creditors get paid in full, even speculators.

That is how financial "free markets" preserve "confidence." It ends up meaning bailouts.

Bad lending and fraud crash the banks

The property bubble burst when new deposit inflows – and hence, bank lending – stopped in 2008. Seeing housing prices begin to plunge, large depositors started to withdraw their funds from Irish banks. Interest rates rose sharply as bondholders anticipated that the government might leave bad debts to be settled between reckless banks and risk-taking speculators. That would have been the most logical thing to do, after all.

The bank run prompted the ECB to make the same misrepresentation to Ireland that the U.S. Treasury was making at home. It insisted that the problem was only one of temporary *illiquidity*, as if banks loans were sound and fully backed by the value of collateral. The real problem was *insolvency* from junk mortgages and insider deals to bank owners. The collateral ended up being mainly empty or half-built houses.

Crooked bankers understate their losses, and international financial institutions, such as the ECB, back their overly optimistic promises that the problem is minimal, easily handled and only temporary. This is the financial sector's chronic cloud of illusion – a failure to distinguish between a liquidity problem and underlying insolvency. Blind to this distinction, Ireland's government took the ECB's advice to deter a run on the banks by providing an unlimited guarantee to uninsured large depositors and bondholders that it would stand behind the banks and pay the full high-risk high-interest rates promised.

Most of these large depositors were foreign, mainly from Britain. They played the extractive role that British landlords had played in the 19th century. Ireland had a long tradition of fighting landlords, from the Catholic Association of the 1820s to the Land League of the 1880s, and Sinn Féin that won independence from England in 1922. But its political leaders surrendered to European credit lords without a fight.

Like Iceland's banks, those of Ireland were far too big to rescue without bankrupting the country. Ireland's six largest banks claimed that their overall losses were merely €4 billion. Anglo Irish Bank's officers upped their early estimate, but still lied when they asserted that they had only lost €7 billion. The government became an accomplice (soon punished by voters) by accepting this pretense and yielding to ECB advice to take full liability for paying large depositors and bondholders. On January 20, 2009, Ireland took Anglo Irish onto its balance sheet as public liability. The bank's officers were fired, but they just laughed when the government asked them to please forego the lucrative golden parachutes they gave themselves on their way out.

There was no Irish deposit insurance agency to bail out large depositors, and indeed no legal obligation to do so. Ireland could have let its banks default, wiping out the deposits or loans invested in bad loans. But as the extent of bad bank lending became more obvious and defaults seemed likely by November 2010, the ECB and IMF arranged a €100 billion loan to the Irish government, claiming that this was necessary to avoid financial "contagion" throughout the eurozone.

Geithner nudges Ireland's 2010 capitulation to the ECB

According to the now classic accounting of Dublin economics professor Morgan Kelly, Tim Geithner played an intrusive role in pressuring Ireland to capitulate to the ECB:

> The IMF, which believes that lenders should pay for their stupidity before it has to reach into its pocket, presented the Irish with a plan to haircut €30 billion of unguaranteed bonds by two-thirds on average. [Finance minister Brian] Lenihan was overjoyed, according to a source who was there, telling the IMF team: "You are Ireland's salvation."
>
> The deal was torpedoed from an unexpected direction. At a conference call with the G7 finance ministers, the haircut was vetoed by US treasury secretary Timothy Geithner who … believes that bankers take priority over taxpayers. The only one to speak up for the Irish was UK chancellor George Osborne, but Geithner, as always, got his way. An instructive, if painful, lesson in the extent of US soft power, and in who our friends really are.
>
> … the ECB walked away with everything it wanted. The IMF were scathing of the Irish performance, with one staffer describing the eagerness of some Irish negotiators to side with the ECB as displaying strong elements of Stockholm Syndrome.[284]

---

[284] Morgan Kelly, "Ireland's future depends on breaking free from bailout," *Irish Times*, May 7, 2011. http://www.irishtimes.com/newspaper/opinion/2011/0507/1224296372123.html.

We now know more. "An examination of the disclosed calendar of US Treasury Secretary Tim Geithner by the research institute Bruegel revealed that … between January 2010 and June 2012, 58 out of 168 calls of Geithner to European officials went to the president of the ECB (Pisany-Ferry 2012)." Pisani-Ferry, "Tim Geithner and Europe's phone number," 2012, November 4, Bruegel, http://www.bruegel.org/nc/blog/detail/article/934-tim-geithner-and-europes-phone-number/ accessed 24th November 2012, quoted in Norbert Haring, "How central bankers and textbooks distort the nature of banking and central banking," *Real-World Economics Review* #62 (March 25, 2013).

A senior U.S. official issued a weasel-worded protest pretending that it was impossible for an American to dictate European bank policy. "The official pointed out the ECB and the European Commission (EC) did not want to impose haircuts on bondholders who loaned money to Irish banks. 'The ECB and EC were both dead opposed and they are decisive. The US is not a decision maker on European issues.'"[285] In other words, all central bankers are willing to crucify economies on a cross of debt. They don't need U.S. urging.

Ireland's central bank governor Patrick Honohan duly conveyed the ECB's policy to Lenihan. The pliable finance minister filed to recognize that debts taken on by governments are different from what banks owe uninsured depositors and private bondholders. Government borrowings from official international institutions such as the ECB or IMF are almost impossible to write down. Once Ireland capitulated to the ECB, it was too late to write down the bad bank debts, because depositors and bondholders already had taken their money and run.

Dublin professor Kelley (cited above) argued that Ireland should not have maintained its September 2008 bank "guarantee long after it had become clear that the bank losses were insupportable." [286] The government should have seen that it had been misled and that the ECB was not giving advice reflecting the national interest, but defending its constituency – bankers. Bondholders and uninsured depositors should have been given shares in the bad banks, instead of borrowing from official financial institutions to cover depositor withdrawals.

Instead, paying off these risk-taking creditors created a lost decade of Irish growth. The government issued €31 billion of promissory notes to the European bank authorities that advanced the funds to wind down Anglo Irish. "When interest charges are included the total cost to the exchequer is estimated at €47 billion" over ten years. For the six main Irish banks, "Dublin faces a bill of at least €63 billion."[287] The sum rose to $85 billion in dollar terms by the start of 2014. "To put it in perspective, the European Union has just agreed to create a fund of $75 billion to deal with all future banking crises in its member states."[288] Ireland had agreed to pay more than all the rest of Europe put together for all of the continent's bad bank loans!

---

[285] Michael Brennen, "US rejects claims it 'torpedoed' write-off," *Independent*, May 9, 2011, http://www.independent.ie/irish-news/us-rejects-claims-it-torpedoed-writeoff-26730671.html

[286] Kelly, "Ireland's future depends on breaking free from bailout."

[287] David Gardner, "Voters likely to say No without debt relief," *Financial Times*, March 1, 2012.

[288] Fintan O'Toole, "Ireland's Rebound Is European Blarney," *The New York Times*, January 10, 2014. He adds: "Particularly galling to most Irish people is that there is now an almost

Under the former "Bagehot rule," bad banks were supposed to be left to fail. Their stockholders and large uninsured depositors would have been stuck with a loss, and bondholders would have been paid in bank stock rather than cash. But what Sheila Bair observed regarding the U.S. bailout ("It's all about the bondholders") was repeated in Ireland. To save everyone from taking any loss, the government agreed to take full liability, even for asset-backed securities and subordinated debt.

Anglo Irish's failure would not have injured Ireland's economy. But by the time the public guarantee expired in 2010, private creditors had run off with the money. Their place was taken by EU financial authorities. Even the *Financial Times* editorialized that this heavy official borrowing was a great mistake: "By taking on the liabilities of the banking system in full, Irish taxpayers have rescued foreign creditors, who should have taken a hit for the crash. When euro-zone leaders decide about Ireland's bank debt, they should not use the behaviour of a few reckless bankers as an excuse to punish an entire country."[289]

The government transferred all the losses from earlier debt leveraging onto taxpayers. The national debt nearly doubled, from 64 percent of GDP in 2009 to 125 percent by 2013. All of Ireland's GDP growth was earmarked to pay the ECB for the loans that enabled foreign bank creditors to receive high-risk interest without having to suffer any loss, as if putting the interest of speculators first is perfectly natural.

No referendum asked voters what they wanted, but their choice became clear in January 2011, two months after the capitulation. Fianna Fáil and its Green Party allies were voted out overwhelmingly and replaced by a Fine Gael/Labour coalition led by Enda Kenny. But the new government maintained its commitment to pay the European Union's "rescue package," turning Ireland into what a *Financial Times* editorial characterized as "Europe's indentured slave."

> Dublin's European partners ... want Irish taxpayers to throw more money into holes dug by private banks. As part of the rescue, Dublin must run down a pension fund built up when Berlin and Paris were violating the Maastricht rules. ... so long as senior bondholders are seen as sacrosanct, fire sales of assets carry a risk of even greater losses

---

casual admission that [this No Bondholder Left Behind policy] was a pretty crazy idea. Olli Rehn, the European Union's economic affairs commissioner and one of the chief architects of Irish strategy since the crash, now says, 'In retrospect, I think it is quite easy to spot some mistakes like the blanket guarantee for banks.' This admission, though, does not imply any change of policy. 'But that is now water under the bridge,' he went on to say."

[289] "Inside the bubble," *Financial Times* editorial, June 26, 2013.

to be billed to taxpayers. Enda Kenny, Fine Gael's leader and presumptive taoiseach, claims he will renegotiate the deal. The likely outcome is a face-saving but useless compromise: in return for a lower interest rate, Mr Kenny will stand by his predecessors' suicidal conflation of bank and sovereign debt.[290]

That is indeed what happened. Ireland voted with a 60 percent majority in May 2012 to accept the fiscal pact, without any relief for the harsh loan terms accepted by the previous regime. That prompted nearly 10 percent of the population to vote with their feet and leave – almost 400,000 out of 4.5 million since 2007, mostly the best educated youth, emulating their counterparts in neoliberalized Latvia and Greece.

David Begg, head of the Irish Congress of Trade Unions, claimed: "The troika has done more damage to Ireland than Britain ever did in 800 years." Jamie Smyth noted in the *Financial Times*: "One in five of the 942,440 outstanding mortgage accounts has either fallen into arrears of more than 90 days or has been restructured because of a borrower's inability to pay. About half of the 101,652 restructured mortgages, in which homeowners or buy-to-let investors are offered interest-only deals, have slipped back into arrears."[291]

The ECB and other creditors applauded Ireland's willingness to impose austerity to pay for the debts that it naively had believed were making it rich in the years leading up to 2008. A video has gone viral on the web of a troika delegation meeting with Irish officials in Dublin early in 2012, in which ECB representative Klaus Masuch tried to curry popular support by telling reporters about how well Ireland was coping. His sanctimonious narrative prompted journalist Vincent Browne to stand up and ask about

> the fact that the ECB forced our government to guarantee private bankers' debt that our public finances could ill-afford? Debts that the Irish people never consented to through their elected representatives? … your Central Bank forced our government to bail out private bankers so that non-Irish banks to which the money was ultimately owed would not need to be bailed out by Frankfurt, Berlin or Paris?
>
> … Why did Europe's central bank, our central bank, force a small nation to take on private debts without their consent? [292]

Ireland's new president Michael Higgens, who assumed office in November 2001, complained that his country was praised "as the eurozone's model

---

[290] "Ireland's winter of discontent," *Financial Times* editorial, March 1, 2011.
[291] Jamie Smyth, "Ireland: Bleak houses," *Financial Times*, April 30, 2013.
[292] Mr. Masuch's response was to gather his papers and walk out of the room. To see the video, google "Vincent Browne versus ECB official." See especially http://yanisvaroufakis.eu/2013/10/25/the-dirty-war-for-europes-integrity-and-soul-europe-inaugural-public-lecture-uws-state-library-of-new/.

bailout patient" simply because "we are pragmatists" instead of seeking a confrontational stance against drastic budget cuts. "It would have been of immense benefit naturally to growth, employment creation and investment if the ... commitment of separating banking debt from sovereign debt had in fact been implemented."[293] But this hand wringing was as far as he went.

The IMF issued a scathing report in January 2015 blaming Ireland for taking neoliberal ECB advice and borrowing from it and the IMF. Despite IMF compliance and partnership in the loan, the report faulted the Irish government:

> The failure to "bail in" unsecured creditors to a bank rescue that cost Irish taxpayers €64 bn and bankrupted the country was based on the view that doing so would have serious adverse "spillover" effects in other eurozone countries, even though such risks were "not obvious". Moreover, the level at which Irish bank bonds were trading at the time implied that holders of senior unsecured bank bonds were expecting to take a haircut on their bond holdings, according to the fund.
>
> The IMF's observations, in a report published today that is effectively its verdict on its role in the €67 bn Irish bailout, are likely to reignite arguments in Ireland about the cost and consequences of the bank rescue, the most catastrophic financial event in recent Irish history. ...
>
> The IMF said that as a result of the failure to impose losses on bank creditors, "many in Ireland question why Irish taxpayers should be the ones covering the cost of addressing such euro area-wide concerns. A bail-in or other solution that would have 'mutualised' these costs would likely have resulted in more equitable burden sharing."[294]

Nonetheless, the IMF report concluded, Ireland's bailout was unnecessary to prevent "contagion." It was part of the "cry havoc" strategy that bankers deployed from the United States to Europe: "the IMF appears unconvinced by arguments that imposing the haircut would have spread contagion across the eurozone. Even if spillover risks were important, 'steps could have been taken to ringfence these through appropriate policy responses in the affected markets.'"

By 2014, Ireland's level of investment fell to 9 percent of GDP, comparable to Guinea-Bissau, Yemen and Somalia, all beset by strife and civil war. Housing prices fell to half their 2007 level. But Irish families remained liable for the full mortgage debt they borrowed. That dynamic is the root cause of the country's debt deflation, unemployment and emigration. "Some 165,000 Irish people between the ages of 15 and 24 have emigrated in the past five years, while the

---

[293] Jamie Smyth, "Irish president warns of EU upheaval," *Financial Times*, May 2, 2013.
[294] Vincent Boland, "IMF criticises Irish failure to impose 'bail in'," *Financial Times*, January 30, 2015.

proportion of the population aged between 15 and 29 fell from 23.1 per cent in 2009 to 18 per cent [in 2014]. ... an estimated 1m 'active Irish passport holders' were living abroad. That is more than a fifth of the Irish population, which stood at 4.6m in April 2014."[295]

Ireland is making marginal progress toward alleviating personal suffering from bankruptcy by shortening the period of bankruptcy punishment from twelve to just three years, and urging banks to write down mortgage debts to reflect actual market prices. But there is nothing like America's "jingle mail" practice in which homeowners can walk away and free themselves from debt, leaving the bank holding properties on which it has over-lent. Irish debtors are liable to pay mortgages that often are twice what their home is worth in today's still-crumbling market. Without much prospect of earning their way out of debt, they find themselves obliged to emigrate.

Without recognizing that the government was recklessly advised from the start and therefore making an about-face regarding the debts to the ECB and IMF, all that Ireland can do is take marginal and token steps within its financial straitjacket. Britain has no such "pragmatic" shyness. On January 14, 2014, Conservative Chancellor of the Exchequer John Osborne told a conference: "The biggest economic risk facing Europe doesn't come from those who want reform and renegotiation – it comes from a failure to reform and renegotiate. It is the status quo which condemns the people of Europe to an ongoing economic crisis and continuing decline."[296]

The next day, Nigel Farage, leader of the UK Independence Party, announced that Europe's Parliamentary elections in May 2014 "are really going to be ... a battle of national democracy versus EU State bureaucracy. ... Up until now everybody has thought ... the development of the European Union ... was inevitable. That myth of inevitability will be shattered by the European elections this year."[297] And so it was, with rising counter-pressure in 2015 by populist anti-creditor parties.

---

[295] Vincent Boland, "Ireland pleads with emigrants to come home," *Financial Times*, March 4, 2015. The report adds: "A study by academics at University College Cork in 2013 found that Ireland had experienced 'significantly higher levels of emigration per capita' as a result of the financial crash than other countries affected by the eurozone crisis. The exodus was explained by the fact that nearly two-thirds of the emigrants had third-level qualifications — often in the information technology and health sectors, skills coveted by other countries."

[296] Nicholas Watt, "Reform EU or Britain quits – George Osborne lays down ultimatum," *The Guardian*, January 14 2014.

Membership in the eurozone has become synonymous with financial dominance, debt deflation, and government responsibility for bailing out banks, their uninsured depositors and bondholders – all in the context of "light touch" deregulation permitting fraud to flourish, with its costs being shifted onto taxpayers.

The missing alternative is debt writedowns. The virtue of a debt writedown policy, permitting mortgage debtors to walk away and leave their banks holding the empty property bag, is that it obliges banks to be prudent not to over-lend (at least, that was the theory before banks began to securitize bad mortgages and sell them to naïve buyers).

Ireland provides a prime example of what happens when debts are not written down:

> one-in-six mortgage borrowers are in default on their loans. However, two-thirds of those loans have never been restructured. … what is still missing, in many quarters, is … recognition by bureaucrats and bankers that failure is an inevitable part of the market system, and that it sometimes pays to wipe the slate clean rather than endlessly sweep problems under the carpet.
>
> Letting borrowers run away from bad loans may not be healthy; but it is even less healthy to leave a chunk of the population trapped in the virtual prison of debt that can never be repaid.[298]

Instead of coming to this recognition, Ireland became one of the harshest critics of Greece's attempt in 2015 to avoid succumbing to "the Irish disease." Criticizing SYRIZA's bold stance, Ireland's leaders in effect said what must have been on their minds: "My God, what have we done? Even the IMF is criticizing us for going along with Europe and bailing out the banks and imposing austerity. If SYRIZA wins and reverses austerity in Greece, then our sacrifice of our economy and the poverty we've imposed has been needless and we didn't have to do it."

---

[297] Nigel Farage, "Big Banks, Big Business and Big Bureaucrats Run the EU," January 15, 2014, http://www.ukipmeps.org/articles_779_Farage-A-Battle-of-National-Democracy-vs-EU-State-Bureaucracy.html

[298] Gillian Tett, "Jingles that sound the beginning of recovery," *Financial Times*, October 24, 2014.

20

The Financial Conquest of Latvia: From the Soviet Orbit to Neoliberal Austerity

> The European debt crisis is not a conflict among nations ... The financial crisis in Europe, like all financial crises, is ultimately a struggle about how the costs of the adjustment will be allocated, either to workers and middle class savers or to bankers, owners of real and financial assets, and the business elite.
>
> Michael Pettis, "Syriza and the French Indemnity of 1871–73"[299]

The "Baltic Tiger miracle" has been as disastrous as that of Ireland. On January 1, 2014, Latvia's government accepted the eurozone's ideology of fiscal and financial austerity, despite opinion polls showing a majority of voters opposed to joining. While Greece and other countries were debating whether these "conditionalities" would drive them out of the eurozone (and Icelanders lost interest in joining it), Latvia became its 18th member. As Europe's most extreme neoliberalized economy, its experience provides an object lesson for the dynamics of debt deflation, public spending cutbacks and refusal to tax land rent or monopoly rent, which pro-bank writers applaud as a success story. It certainly has been a success story for Swedish and other bankers.

Post-Soviet economies were free of public debt, business debt, real estate and personal debt or other bank loans when they obtained their political independence in 1991. Their residential and commercial real estate, transportation facilities and highly educated population could have provided the foundation for a competitive low-cost modern economy. Every family could have been given its home at a nominal price. Prime real estate and infrastructure monopolies were turned over to insiders on such terms. But by the time most families started to buy home ownership, prices were soaring.[300]

---

[299] February 4, 2015, http://blog.mpettis.com/2015/02/syriza-and-the-french-indemnity-of-1871-73/.

[300] People were given "renter's rights" for nearly free housing, although with limited resale potential. Eventually, people were able to use government vouchers to buy property. Prices soared as banks provided credit.

The debt-free situation with low housing costs and a broad array of public services did not last long. Latvia imposed Europe's heaviest taxes on labor and industry, and the lightest on real estate and finance. Its miniscule property taxes left almost the entire rental income available to be capitalized into bank loans, and property prices spiked to among the highest levels in Europe.

Like other post-Soviet economies, Latvians wanted to achieve the prosperity they saw in Western Europe. If Latvia actually had followed the policies that built up the industrial nations, the state would have taxed wealth and income progressively to invest in public infrastructure. Instead, Latvia's "miracle" assumed largely predatory forms of rent-seeking and insider privatizations. Accepting U.S. and Swedish advice to impose the world's most lopsided set of neoliberal tax and financial policies, Latvia levied the world's heaviest taxes on labor. Employers must pay a flat 25 percent flat tax on wages plus a 24 percent social-service tax, while wage earners pay another 11 percent tax. These three taxes add up to nearly a 60 percent flat tax before personal deductions. In addition to making labor high-cost and hence less competitive, consumers must pay a high value-added sales tax of 21 percent (raised sharply from 7 percent after the 2008 crisis). No Western economy taxes wages and consumption so steeply.

Latvia's heavy taxation of labor finds its counterpart in a mere 10 percent tax on dividends, interest and other returns to wealth, and the lowest property tax rate of any industrial economy (as described below). This fiscal policy retards employment while subsidizing the real estate bubble that is the chief feature of Latvia's "Baltic miracle."

From the time the Baltics achieved their independence from the Soviet Union, they opened their economies to foreign bank affiliates, mainly from Scandinavia. Latvia's few domestic banks were created by insiders to handle their own operations, and increasingly to receive government deposits, which they lent to themselves or to business associates to buy up the assets being privatized.[301] When the largest bank, Parex (with 17 percent of Latvian deposits)

---

[301] The major domestic Latvian bank was Parex, owned by Valery Kargin and Viktor Krasovitsky. Starting a travel agency, they used it as an opportunity to get the Soviet Union's first foreign exchange license – a temporary monopoly that enabled them to make enough money to found Parex in 1992. It crashed (largely from its bad real estate loans) and was nationalized on November 8, 2008. Latvia borrowed from the EU and IMF to take over all its liabilities, just as Ireland did with its bankrupt banks. See Robert Anderson, "Latvia nationalizes Parex Bank," *Financial Times*, December 4, 2008, and *BloombergBusiness Week Magazine*, July 6, 2003. http://www.businessweek.com/stories/2003-07-06/valery-kargin-viktor-krasovitsky.

became insolvent in November 2008, the government took it over to avoid seeing its own deposits wiped out, and to stop a bank run to Swedish banks.

Foreign bank branches financed the real estate boom, whose interest charges became a financial tax burdening the nation's labor and industry. As occurred in Ireland, leaving the debts in place when the bubble burst drove an estimated ten percent of the population to emigrate. Yet voters have kept re-electing governments committed to austerity.

The explanation is to be found in the trauma associated with Russian domination during and after World War II. Stalin arrested, killed or drove into exile an estimated 50,000 Latvian professionals in the 1940s.[302] Bringing in Russian workers created a legacy of resentment that made the Baltics turn toward Europe after the Soviet Union broke up. Revival of nationalism enabled neoliberal politicians to play the ethnic card, pointing to the fact that the major critics of austerity are parties supported by the Harmony Center coalition, backed largely by the one-third of the population that is Russian-speaking.

Those who advocate taxing real estate and financial wealth, or even supporting public spending, protecting consumers and other economic regulation are accused of threatening a return to Communism. A black-and-white contrast is drawn: either Soviet-style socialism, or neoliberal ideology denying that there is any such thing as a viable mixed economy.

Latvia's alternative to Soviet-style bureaucracy was a far cry from classical democracy utilizing its endowments to achieve an American- or European-style success. It fell subject to a smash-and-grab privatization of the Soviet-era assets created prior to 1991. Instead of undertaking the social spending and infrastructure investment found in successful Western economies, the "Baltic miracle" featured a privatized oligarchy, dependence on foreign banks, and wage austerity.

A similar failure is Krajbanka, which originated as Latvia's Postal Savings Bank dating back to 1924. It was bought by Lithuanian and Russian businessmen, accused of massive fraud by the time the Latvian government took it over in 2011.

[302] The first deportations were in 1941 (from 12 to 15 thousand), peaking in 1949 (around 40 thousand). See Latvian Ministry of Foreign Affairs, http://www.mfa.gov.lv/en/policy/history/briefing-papers/briefing-paper4/. I provide a background in "Stockholm Syndrome in the Baltics: Latvia's neoliberal war against labor and industry," in Jeffrey Sommers and Charles Woolfson, eds., *The Contradictions of Austerity: The Socio-Economic Costs of the Neoliberal Baltic Model* (Routledge 2014), pp. 44-63, and "How Neoliberals Bankrupted 'New Europe': Latvia in the Global Credit Crisis" (with Jeffrey Sommers), in Martijn Konings, ed., *The Great Credit Crash* (Verso: London and New York, 2010):244-63.

Latvia's FIRE-sector bubble

In the absence of a Federal Reserve-style central bank to finance its post-Soviet transition, Latvia relied mainly on Scandinavian banks. Supplemented by flight capital from Russia, this foreign credit inflated the Baltic real estate bubble. Foreign banks found a fertile ground in Latvia's tax policy that left almost all economic rent tax-free. Early property taxes were a fraction of 1 percent, at unrealistically low land appraisals.[303] Even as land prices soared, Latvia left property almost tax-free (finally enacting a modest real estate tax schedule in 2013).

The other loan market was for the public assets being privatized, mainly former public monopolies. Sweden became the major source of loans to the Baltics. Its banks allocated credit where they found the most money could be made – for speculation and real estate. Almost no effort was made to restructure industry and agriculture to generate the foreign exchange to import capital and consumer goods not produced at home. No longer having Soviet markets to supply after the old USSR production linkages were uprooted, industrial enterprises were dismantled for their land value, scrapped or gentrified into real estate developments.

Foreign borrowing enabled Latvia to finance its import-dependency and trade deficits until 2008. Families borrowed from foreign bank branches to buy apartments or build homes, taking out loans denominated in euros or other foreign currency. The resulting real estate bubble "solved" Latvia's balance-of-payments problem of how to pay for deepening foreign dependency.

This reliance on foreign banks was common for the post-Soviet countries, mainly to buy housing that was escalating in price. But it proved to be a Ponzi scheme based on borrowing more and more money. Little lending was used to put in place means to earn the foreign currency needed to pay back the debts.

Latvian tax policy was as much to blame as financial policy. Instead of taxing the land's soaring site value, Latvia left it free to be pledged to bankers to keep the real estate bubbles expanding. The country did not even have land-value map when it gained its independence. The Soviet Union did not charge rent, so Latvia's property tax agency had only the 1917 real estate assessment records to go on – some three-quarters of a century out of date.

Even today (2015) Latvia has no land assessment map, and its property tax structure is the most inequitable in Europe, contributing to the country's polarized Gini coefficient for wealth and income distribution. Its low property tax

---

[303] Residential property is now (2015) taxed at 0.2%, 0.4% or 0.6% depending on its value. Commercial property is taxed at 1.5%.

is largely responsible for the heavy debt burden on real estate, because whatever the tax collector relinquishes is available to be paid to banks as debt service. The combination of heavy taxes on employment, little tax on property and a flood of foreign bank credit to inflate real estate prices was the essence of the Baltic Miracle. It was applauded as if debt-financed real estate were a sign of prosperity, not an overhead imposing heavy housing and financial charges paid to foreign banks.

Until 2015, Latvians were paid wages in domestic lats, but owed their mortgages in euros, with some sterling, Swiss franc and dollar loans. Letting foreign bank branches make loans almost entirely in foreign currency violates a prime directive of sound financial policy: *To avoid currency risk, do not take on debts denominated in a foreign currency.* A weakening balance of payments leads to a declining exchange rate, raising the domestic-currency cost of paying these debts.

Soon after the crash of September 2008, foreign banks stopped the mortgage lending that was Latvia's main source of financing its trade deficit. Flight capital from Russia into Latvian banks also abated as oil prices fell back. To prevent the Latvian lat from depreciating, the government sharply cut back spending. The resulting austerity program was given a neologism, "internal devaluation," meaning lower wages by running a budget surplus to drain spending power out of the economy.

The austerity program prompted ten thousand Latvians to turn out in protest on a freezing and dark January 13, 2009. By March, Latvia was suffering the world's steepest one-year plunge in house prices (which had peaked in April 2007).[304] Despite having emerged debt-free in 1991, Latvia had become Europe's most debt-strapped country, without using this credit to modernize its industry or agriculture.

To prevent a run on the currency, Joaquin Almunia of the European Commission presented a letter to Latvia's Prime Minister and Finance Minister on January 26, 2009, spelling out the terms on which the ECB and IMB would lend Latvia money to support its exchange rate. The letter directed Latvia to use the credit exclusively to pay its debts to Western bank affiliates and "for targeted capital infusions or appropriate short-term liquidity support [for banks]. However, financial assistance is not meant to be used to originate new loans to businesses and households," that is, not to help Latvia develop export capacity to earn its way out of debt:

---

[304] Nina Kolyako, "Knight Frank: Latvia registers most rapid reduction in house prices in Q1," *The Baltic Course*, May 26, 2009. http://www.baltic-course.com/eng/real_estate/?doc=14159.

> Worryingly, we have witnessed some recent evidence in Latvian public debate of calls for
> part of the financial assistance to be used *inter alia* for promoting export industries or to
> stimulate the economy through increased spending at large. It is important actively to
> stem these misperceptions.[305]

Eurozone and IMF credit thus was provided only to support foreign banks. Supporting the exchange rate enabled investors and kleptocrats to move their funds out of the economy for more foreign funds than if the lat depreciated.

Many Latvian officials had a personal interest in avoiding devaluation of the lat. Most that I have met had heavy foreign-currency mortgages. Central bank head Ilmars Rimsevics was said to owe euro debts that would have left him underwater on his several mortgages if Latvia had devalued following the 2008 crash (even though his salary was higher than that of Ben Bernanke at the Federal Reserve, despite the fact that Latvia's GDP is only about half that of today's collapsed Detroit area).

Commissioner Almunia's "conditionality" left Latvia in the position of a nation defeated in war and having to pay reparations, in this case to meet Swedish demands that banks must be paid in full, on time and without a haircut before money could be spent to revive the economy. Latvia's government succumbed to a literal Stockholm syndrome, defending the Swedish financial interests that were reducing its economy to debt bondage.

This debt deflation hardly is what Latvia expected when it turned to the West for assistance. The neoliberal advice it received was simply to privatize its assets with an anti-labor flat tax such as no EU nation imposes on its own population. U.S. and European-trained advisors turned a blind eye to the fact that the post-Soviet economies were paying for imports simply by borrowing against the property with which they emerged at independence. The core EU nations stood by for two decades watching insider dealings that their own prosecutors never would have permitted at home.

Saving Latvia's banks, not the economy

By the spring of 2010, Latvia's real estate prices had plunged by 70 percent and the government was aiming to reduce public-sector wages by 30 percent, hoping that private-sector wages would follow suit. On May 25, I headed a foreign advisory delegation with Jeffrey Sommers that met with the Financial and Capital Market Commission. Our discussion focused on how the banks were coping with the real estate crisis. The Commission's chairperson, Irena Krumane, explained that her agency's role was simply to see that the banks

---

[305] Joaquin Almunia, "letter B-1049 Brussels." 26 Jan. 2009. 1 May 2009. http://www.fm.gov.lv/faili/bildes/preses_relizes/dok/Almunia_letter-ENG.pdf.

remain solvent by making sure that their loans were secured by adequate collateral, without regard for the economy-wide cost.

Krumane told us that despite her regulatory agency's warning about the real estate bubble, Latvia's mortgage debt was twice as high as would have been the case if bank regulators had moved as fast as Estonia and Lithuania. The problem was regulatory capture. Commercial banks were her agency's source of funding. Swedish banks in particular – the largest lenders in Latvia – blocked tighter regulatory standards. Wanting to make the largest loans possible, they opposed attempts to confirm their income or loan quality. So the Latvian authorities saw their role simply as being to make sure that the banks could get repaid for their loans and remain solvent, regardless of how reckless their lending was.

It was indeed reckless. In June 2006 my colleague Jeffrey Sommers had asked the head of the real estate division for one of the top Swedish banks in Latvia why it was continuing to lend to an inflated property market. "We know it will crash," Sommers was told, "but everyone's annual bonus depends on making more money, and we can't stop now." The financial dancing thus continued, just as it did in the United States and other countries.

The bank regulators told us that it would be "central planning" to set higher capital adequacy and reserve requirements against mortgage loans. The reason European Union rules give little regulatory power to governments is precisely to prevent such allegedly "arbitrary" intrusions into ostensibly free markets – the kind of regulation that is done quite normally in the United States and Britain. By preventing Latvia from requiring higher reserves for mortgages than for loans to industry and commerce, neoliberal ideology blocks regulators from stopping the real estate bubble, even if they might want to do so.

One of the reasons for our visit was the absence of an up-to-date land register to assess property. The regulators coped with this problem by shifting the backing for bank loans away from actual property values to focus on the borrowers' income – getting not only the borrowers themselves, but as many members of their family as possible to co-sign the loan as sureties, whose income the banks could garnish in case of default. This saved the banks but devastated families when housing prices in Riga plunged 68 percent from their 2007 peak, pushing 54 percent of Latvian real estate into negative equity.[306]

---

[306] Ott Ummelas, "More than Half Swedbank Mortgages in Latvia Exceed Collateral," Bloomberg, July 24, 2009, http://www.bloomberg.com/apps/news?pid=20601095&sid=ayclk5 MrouBU. By comparison, some 37 percent of Lithuanian real estate was in negative equity, as prices in its capital, Vilnius, were down 28 percent.) Prices in Tallinn, Estonia's capital, had fallen by 53 percent, pushing a reported 24 percent of homes into negative equity.

This approach was the opposite of the American "jingle mail" permitting borrowers to walk away from underwater mortgages. Latvian banks had no responsibility to relate loans to the property's value. When defaults spread as real estate prices fell deeper into negative equity, banks went after the family members who had co-signed mortgage loans. The regulators told us that they could not direct banks to write off part of their loans, because that would be the equivalent of nationalization! Their only recourse was to ask that banks voluntarily reconfigure the loans – which, of course, the banks showed little interest in doing. So the officials charged with regulation merely sat back while banks siphoned off Latvian income and paid it to their head offices in Sweden and other credit capitals.

Any thought of steering finance to promote lending to industry or commerce – or to avert a real estate bubble by taxing real estate site rents – was rejected as interference with "the market," a euphemism for letting banks do whatever they want. This inability to regulate banks in the public interest effectively places them in the role of central planners. The economy-wide effect of such financialization was that many homeowners had to earmark 30 to 40 percent of their income to pay banks. If they lost their job, or if "internal devaluation" reduced their wages, the banks got to take whatever their co-signors earned.

Neoliberal debt deflation, emigration and financial tribute

This predicament left homeowners in negative equity with the classic neoliberal "free market" choice: pay up, or free themselves from debt by emigrating. Some 10 percent of Latvia's population has left since 2000, and roughly 14 percent of the working-age population, with emigration accelerating after the 2008 crash. In 2013 a full 10 percent of "Latvian" live births were reported to have occurred in Britain! As in other countries subjected to austerity, Latvian emigration is concentrated in the most highly educated and employable population: 25 to 35 years old. Latvians joke about collapse by 2030, by which time the last person to leave the airport is asked to please turn off the lights.

Emigration entails a loss of the capital that has been invested in rearing, educating and training labor that is forced to migrate to find work. What is now driving European labor to emigrate is harsh debt policy. One is reminded of Adam Smith's discussion of how fugitives from the Italian town of Lucca brought silk manufacturing techniques to Venice in 1310. He blamed Italy's oppressive political autocracy.[307] But instead of blaming Europe's most trau-

---

[307] Adam Smith, *Wealth of Nations*, Book III, ch. iii (Cannan ed., 6th ed., London: 1961), Vol. I, p. 429. I discuss this passage and related emigration and trade theory in *Trade, Development and Foreign Debt*, p. 22.

matic "internal devaluation" for these New Exiles, many Latvians accept the applause from neoliberals celebrating their country as a success story. It has been made the poster child for the kind austerity imposed on Greece, Spain and Italy.

Neither Ireland's nor Latvia's economic problems and emigration stem from the government spending that neoliberals blame. The problem was irresponsible and unregulated commercial banking, reinforced by the idea that economies can get rich by borrowing abroad to inflate real estate prices at home. Real estate's rental value was transferred to foreign bankers in the form of interest charges, with reckless banks being bailed out at taxpayer expense. It was a travesty of "free markets" to lower wages and domestic spending by enough to pay loans extended at far above market levels. The effect of this neoliberal policy can only be debt deflation, depression and more emigration.

Bank-oriented planning blocked Latvia from creating a public bank to finance its post-Soviet transition. The population's checking and savings deposits – and even those of public agencies – had nowhere to be placed except in private banks. The moral of Latvia's and Ireland's economic plunge is thus the opposite of what neoliberals depict. Banking should be a public utility. Otherwise, its lending preferences will thwart industrial growth, employment and living standards. Credit will be created mainly to buy or take over existing properties, infrastructure and companies, bidding up their cost to make basic needs more expensive rather than competitive.

Commissioner Almunia's letter to Latvia's leaders reflects the ECB's guideline of printing money only to buy government bonds long since issued, to prop up their price so that bondholders can sell them with minimal loss. That is what ECB President Mario Draghi meant when he pledged in summer 2012 to "do whatever it takes" to save bond prices from falling as a result of rising interest rates. The EU does little to aid the "real" economy, but only offers help in sacrificing labor and industry to benefit creditors.

The Aftermath: Banks blame victimized borrowers, not themselves

Most economists depicted the dismantling of Soviet-era industry and the former public sector as "creative destruction," a necessary transition toward Western-style market economies. This was achieved by giving public infrastructure to political insiders in a "grabitization" exercise. The result was a much steeper concentration of wealth than characterizes Western nations. Yet looking simply at GDP growth, neoliberals claimed that until 2008 the Baltics and Central Europe were on a path to catch up with the West.

By 2008 it became apparent that the post-Soviet economies had not really *grown* as much as they had been financialized and indebted. *Forbes* economist Mark Adomanis calculated in 2014 that if convergence of these economies with those of the West

> continues at its 2008–13 pace (about 0.37% per annum) it would take the new EU members over a hundred years to match the core countries'□average level of income. ... to the extent that Central Europe's most rapid and sustained burst of convergence coincided with a credit bubble that is highly unlikely to be repeated, it seems more likely than not that the region's convergence will be slower in the future than it was in the past.[308]

The means of self-support have not been put in place. A deepening trade deficit has been financed by foreign borrowing, which now poses a chronic balance-of-payments drain of debt service. No longer having a real estate bubble to bring in enough foreign exchange to finance the trade deficit, all that these countries have to export is their people. Instead of making economies more competitive, austerity drives those who can emigrate to leave in search of work. As Adomanis concluded: "To the extent that Europe's future will be one of tight money and tight budgets, that suggests that Central Europe will be in for a rough ride."

Instead of performing a productive function, banks created debts by operating an economy-wide Ponzi scheme, obtaining high short-term returns based on valuations of property whose prices could be supported only by further lending on increasingly "easy" debt-pyramid terms. This inflated the price of housing, the economy's largest cost category. Earmarking income to pay higher debt service was largely responsible for shrinking domestic market demand and employment opportunities.

Bank opposition to writing down mortgages to market levels

What should be done to cope with the debt burden left over from such bubbles? To what extent should the banks and bondholders who provided the money for such schemes (at high returns, presumably reflecting the degree of risk) be obliged to absorb the losses? Stated the other way around, to what extent should Latvian debtors be allowed to walk away from property whose mortgage exceeds the market price?

These questions were raised in Latvia's Saeima (Parliament) in January 2014 when the left-leaning Harmony Centre alliance proposed an amendment to the nation's Real Estate Tax Law to approve the "jingle mail" principle. The

---

[308] Mark Adomanis, "Central Europe's Convergence With The West Has Slowed Dramatically," Forbes.com, January 24, 2014.

amendment was passed in its first reading. (Parliament rules call for three read-ings.) But despite being Latvia's largest party (it won 28 percent of the vote in the 2011 parliamentary election), the fact that Harmony Centre's support came mainly from Russian-speakers enabled neoliberal parties to accuse its proposal of being "pro-Russian" and hence anti-Western. These parties united to exclude Harmony Centre members from office.[309]

Bank lobbyists threatened to sharply raise interest rates and increase the required down payment for new homebuyers to 50 per cent or more (com-pared to the usual 10 percent) to compensate them for the increased risk if the "jingle mail" option was legalized. What banks objected to was the idea that they are supposed to allocate the economy's savings and credit by realistically determining how much borrowers can afford to pay. Mortgage loans are sup-posed to be secured by basing them on the realistic rental value of the property. The jingle-mail safety valve keeps banks responsible for competent credit analysis. Banks that fail to do this *should* bear the loss.

Preparing for the Saeima's third (final) reading of the Insolvency Law in June 2014, banks advocated a "small print" change: The mortgage debtor's obligations would be deleted "only in cases when, during the insolvency process the home is sold," not when the debtor actually stops paying. This would en-able banks to prolong the interim and extract payments from debtors and co-signers for as long as possible.

The bank lobby prodded the Economy Ministry to send a letter to the Saeima on July 3, 2014, asking that the "jingle mail" draft law (called Aban-doned Keys in Latvia) be withdrawn from the plenary meeting's agenda by a majority of votes. Since the draft had been scheduled for consideration, the only ploy was to stall by prolonging the term for proposals. When it came up again, on September 25, Igor Pimenov of the Harmony Centre coalition said:

> This [Abandoned Keys] provision means much more than a step towards borrowers in trouble. It is the legal framework, which changes dramatically the rules of conduct in the real estate market … It provides a reference that banks and other creditors should be sufficiently responsible and lend proportionately, [so that] the bank will no longer lend credit that exceeds the value of the collateral.[310]

---

[309] The situation is politically complex. While there is a progressive faction within Harmony Center working toward reforms on behalf of consumers, the party contains enough revan-chist elements to enable neoliberal banking interests to maneuver ethnic Latvians to oppose reforms by playing the nationalist card.

[310] Igor Pimenov, personal communication translating his Saeima speech and the arguments cited above.

Bank lobbyists used an Orwellian rhetorical twist, urging "more freedom" for loan-takers to accept harsh bank terms. Banks would tell borrowers that a loan would be available to buy a property only if they waive their rights to the "Abandoned Keys" clause.

The bankers' slogan of "free choice" thus threatens a *loss* of economic freedom for homebuyers obliged to overpay and over-borrow for housing. The effect is to invert the classic banking principle that if loans are made on a realistic basis, property on which debtors default can be sold at a market price that will cover what the bank is owed.

The logic for leaving banks in private hands assumes bankers are realistic in their credit allocation. The events of 2008 shattered this myth. As debts proliferate without limit, the ECB and EU Commission pressure governments to reimburse creditors in full. "Taxpayers" are to make up the losses too large to be borne by mortgage debtors' ability to pay, until the economy grinds to a halt as debt deflation pushes it into bankruptcy.

A return to classical bank policy would deem loans fraudulent and annul debts when creditors do not lend with any reasonable calculation of how the debt can be paid in the normal course of economic life. Loans made without such a calculation should be considered predatory. The natural check on such behavior is to permit mortgage debtors to walk away from their homes, free of the debts attached to them, letting title revert to the banks that over-lent.

Across Europe – except in the post-Soviet economies where neoliberalism is presented as the lone alternative to Soviet-era planning – popular support is rising to reject a eurozone run in the interests of banks and foreign creditors. A 2013 Eurobarometer survey reported that only 31 percent of European citizens trusted the European Union, down from 57 percent on the eve of the 2008 crisis. Support for the euro "has dropped sharply to 56% in Spain, 53% in Italy, 50% in Portugal and just 44% in Cyprus. Even in France, support stands at just 63%."[311] By the May 2014 elections nationalist anti-bank opposition had risen even steeper, led by Marine Le Pen's Front National in France, Geert Wilders' anti-immigration and anti-Islamic Party for Freedom in Holland, Nigel Farage's U.K. Independence Party, and north Italian separatists supporting Pepe Grillo's Five Star Movement.

Bankers are seeking to capture government and make financial policy immune from democratic choice. What promised to be a progressive social democratic Europe half a century ago is turning into a power grab by financial

---

[311] Simon Nixon, "'More Europe' Pitch Gets Harder to Sell," *Wall Street Journal*, January 6, 2014.

predators. The EU has confronted Greece, Cyprus and other indebted economies with an option of suffering debt deflation or leaving the eurozone. Since Greece's Syriza coalition took the electoral lead in opposing the financial and fiscal austerity, the creditor response has been to dare Greece to withdraw – and to suffer a transitional financial chaos if it tries to save itself from being crushed by unemployment, bankruptcy and emigration.

21

Creation of the Troika: Its Pro-Bank, Anti-Labor Agenda

The idea that the euro has "failed" is dangerously naive. The euro is doing exactly what its progenitor – and the wealthy 1%-ers who adopted it – predicted and planned for it to do. ... Removing a government's control over currency would prevent nasty little elected officials from using Keynesian monetary and fiscal juice to pull a nation out of recession. "It puts monetary policy out of the reach of politicians," [Robert] Mundell explained]. "Without fiscal policy, the only way nations can keep jobs is by the competitive reduction of rules on business." ... Hence, currency union is class war by other means.

Greg Palast, "Robert Mundell, evil genius of the euro."[312]

Unlike the bank-fueled real estate bubbles of Ireland, Latvia and Spain, Greece's problems stem from government debt. Tax evasion was widespread under the alternating conservative and socialist governments that replaced the 1967–74 military dictatorship. Both parties under-taxed the country's tycoons (and wealth in general), and used public employment as political patronage. Budget deficits rapidly increased the public debt.

Under the Maastricht Treaty a precondition for adopting the euro in 2001 was that public debt could not exceed 60 percent of GDP. To meet this condition, Bank of Greece head Lucas Papademos conspired with Goldman Sachs to create Enron-style "off balance sheet" window dressing to conceal the real deficit and debt levels. Papademos sold government debt to the investment bank, promising to buy it back at a much higher price incorporating a higher interest rate. To mask the charade as an interest-rate derivative swap, he recorded the sale as "revenue," reducing the reported debt but committing

---

[312] *The Guardian,* June 26, 2012. Having taught at the University of Chicago during its "peak-Pinochet years," 1965–72, Mundell won the Nobel Economics Prize in 1999 for his theory of "optimum currency areas." They were to be entirely private-sector entities, excluding public money creation and taxation.

the government to pay back Goldman Sachs out of future revenue until 2019.[313]

The stratagem came to light eight years later, soon after the Socialist Party (Pasok) won Greece's national elections in October 2009 behind George Papandreou. His father Andreas had founded the party in 1974, and George had led it since 2004. He had been elected president of the Socialist International in January 2006, and was unanimously re-elected in 2012. So his tenure as Prime Minister showed how far "socialism" has moved from what the word meant a century ago. Papandreou's party bowed to the demands laid down by Europe's bankers and bondholders to impose austerity.

In December 2009 the finance ministry revealed that Greece's 2008 budget deficit was $12\frac{1}{2}$ percent of GDP, twice the earlier reported amount and over four times larger than the eurozone's official 3 percent limit. Investors began selling off Greek bonds, worrying that government could not pay. Falling bond prices reflected the high risk premium, appealing mainly to speculators. By March and April 2010 the "big three" accounting firms – Moody's, S&P and Fitch – lowered Greek bonds to "junk" status.[314]

Fear began to spread that writing down Greek debt might open the floodgates for the rest of Europe, as had occurred in Latin America a half-century earlier. Bonds of Spain and Portugal were sold off in the early months of 2010. With no visible means to pay, these three economies were beginning to look as toxic as the American and Irish junk mortgage markets had become.

The IMF loses credibility by joining the "troika" to bail out bondholders

Fearing "contagion" – the prospect of a debt writedown spreading across the eurozone in the debt-strapped PIIGS (Portugal, Ireland, Italy, Greece and Spain) – the European Central Bank (ECB) and European Commission (EC) were concerned single-mindedly with saving bondholders from taking a loss.

[313] Louise Story, Landon Thomas Jr. and Nelson D. Schwartz, "Wall St. Helped to Mask Debt Fueling Europe's Crisis," *The New York Times*, February 13, 2010. When its predatory policy became known, Goldman sold the deal to the National Bank of Greece in order to assuage the public outcry. For further details see Nicholas Dunbar and Elisa Martinuzzi, "Goldman Secret Greece Loan Shows Two Sinners as Client Unravels," Bloomberg, March 6, 2012. Papademos had joined the neoliberal Trilateral Commission in 1998, and was European Chairman of at the time he was appointed Prime Minister of Greece to act on behalf of creditors in the 2011 financial emergency (see Chapter 22 below).
[314] G. Tichy, "Credit rating agencies: part of the solution or part of the problem," *Intereconomics*, Vol. 46 (2011), No. 5, pp. 232–262.

They insisted that Greek taxpayers be liable for the earlier government fraud. The ECB made it clear that it would help Greece only on the condition that it pay bondholders in full. This attracted vulture funds: speculators hoping to make fortunes by buying bonds selling at low prices as investors shied away from risk. They gambled that the ECB and IMF might arm-twist the Greek government to pay more than financial markets and ratings agencies believed was realistic.

As the IMF's annual meeting in Washington approached in April 2010, Greek officials urged its staff economists to concur with the ratings agencies and markets, and urge the ECB to moderate its hardline position and write down the debt.

For the IMF, Greece's dilemma seemed a godsend, offering a chance to recover its position as an "honest broker" assessing public debt-paying capacity. It had lost credibility in 2001 by participating in a bailout of Argentina that went bad almost immediately. By 2006-07 the Great Moderation was peaking, leaving the IMF with no major customers. Debtor governments recognized that the IMF's knee-jerk austerity "medicine" threatened to bleed their economies and make them even *less* able to pay bondholders.

To be accepted by the eurozone's financial agencies, the IMF agreed to a Faustian bargain. The European Commission was staffed by pro-austerity bank ideologues, and the ECB was run by hardline monetarist Jean-Claude Trichet. He did not want Fund involvement except as window dressing to endorse his demands for payment in full.

Before heading the ECB, Trichet was chairman of the Paris Club, created in 1956 to take a hard line with the Argentine government on behalf of creditors. At the ECB he continued the Paris Club's default position: insisting that public-sector debtors or guarantors can and must pay whatever is owed. This involves not admitting that any limit exists as to how much can be paid, because recognition of a limit would lead to the conclusion that bondholders must take a "haircut" for having lent too much. Fearing that IMF analysts might take this position (as they indeed did), the European Commission negotiated an austerity program before the IMF could get involved.

The ECB and EC excuse for refusing to take a loss on their bailout loans is that to do so would violate the EU rule that no country's taxpayers should support another country. (The ECB refuses to think about creating tax-free electronic money for this purpose.) This makes the European Union different from a true political union such as the United States. It is "every country for itself." It is as if each state in the United States had to be self-sustaining, with no tax revenue raised in any given state (say, New York) to be spent in other states.

On paper, the IMF's articles of agreement seemed to qualify it to play a reasonable mediating role. It had learned from its 2001 Argentine debacle that it should stop lending to debtor governments without concern for their ability' to pay. In 2003 the IMF executive board established "ability to pay" criteria that debtor countries had to satisfy in order to borrow beyond the normal limit (200 percent of their IMF quota). These conditions included: "A rigorous and systematic analysis ... that there is a high probability that debt will remain sustainable; Good prospects of regaining access to private capital markets; and ... a reasonably strong prospect of success."[315]

The aim was to avoid financing bailouts that soon would collapse. That seemed good in principle, but the IMF's political leaders overrode its staff and board members who came to the same conclusion as ratings agencies and the bond market: there was no foreseeable way in which Greece's debt burden could be paid out of economic growth and tax revenue. Given that its debt was *not* sustainable, there was little hope of borrowing more in private markets. Investors saw no politically palatable means of paying off the debt. The market in Greek government bonds was limited to vulture funds and the Franklin Templeton Fund (with some $7 billion as of 2015). So IMF acquiescence to ECB and EC ideology and politics was doomed to fail.

The government's budget deficit had widened to 13.6 percent of GDP in 2009. By April 2010 it became obvious that private credit would be forthcoming only at steeply rising interest rates. From Washington, Obama and Geithner urged a bailout on behalf of Wall Street, "given US banks' $3.6 trillion exposure to European banks."[316] And regardless of what IMF staff economists thought, the Fund's leaders owe their jobs to Washington and Brussels. In practice this means to Wall Street, Frankfurt and the Paris Bourse.

The troika's austerity conditions for bailing out Greek bondholders

Washington and Brussels had three inexorable demands. First and most basic, bondholders should be paid in full. To achieve this aim, the IMF, ECB and EC formed a troika to lend governments enough money to give bondholders

---

[315] For details of how these IMF criteria were overridden by Strauss-Kahn and other senior leadership for the 2010 Greek loan see Susan Schadler, *Unsustainable Debt and the Political Economy of Lending: Constraining the IMF's Role in Sovereign Debt Crises*, CIGI Papers #19, October 2013. Schadler was deputy director of the IMF's European Department from 1999 to 2007, and earlier had worked for the U.S. Treasury. The following discussion relies heavily on her whistle-blowing report.

[316] Blustein, *Laid Low, The IMF, the Euro Zone and the First Rescue of Greece*, CIGI Paper No. 61, April 7, 2015, p. 14. https://www.cigionline.org/sites/default/files/cigi_paper_no.61 web.pdf .

time to dump their holdings. The implicit threat was "pay up or we'll render you financial outcasts."

The troika's second demand was that debtor countries "reform" labor markets by breaking union power and rolling back workplace reforms put in place over the past century. The pretense was that this would make labor more "competitive," that is, less expensive to hire.

> Laws protecting workers from firing would be revised, as would policies that gave advantages to unions in wage bargaining. Professions and trades that for decades had enjoyed restrictions from competition – law, auditing, pharmacy, engineering, architecture and road haulage – would be opened up. ... Bloated state enterprises, such as the national railway and other public transportation companies, would be streamlined.[317]

The third troika demand was that when countries could not pay bondholders out of current income and tax revenue, they had to start selling their public domain to private investors – without imposing limits on how much the new buyers could charge as they set up tollbooths on roads and for water, electricity and other basic services. This ultimate result of bailout "stabilization" loans has been repeated so often that it must be considered to be the real aim of IMF, ECB and EC policy.

The IMF's head Dominique Strauss-Kahn planned to run for the French presidency and did not want to antagonize French voters or its banks, which were the major holders of Greek bonds (variously reported to range from €31 to €60 billion, compared to €23 to €35 billion for German banks). In May 2010, French President Nicolas Sarkozy rounded up what would become a multi-year €110 billion loan pledge from European governments to pay bondholders.[318]

IMF staff economists reviewing the ECB austerity program for Greece found it "unrealistically harsh," and believed that a debt writedown was necessary.

> If Greece, like Argentina, had an unsustainable debt, a big IMF loan could be granted only on condition that the debt was restructured – so said the No More Argentinas rule. Imposing a haircut promptly would ensure that the burden of loss would fall on the private creditors who had lent money to Greece in the first place. Giving Athens a big international rescue loan, with no haircut, would shift the burden to taxpayers.

---

[317] Blustein, *Laid Low*, p. 9.

[318] See Carlo Bastaten, "Saving Europe: How National Politics Nearly Destroyed the Euro (Brookings, 2012, ch. 13, cited in Blustein, (*Laid Low*, p. 11), and Olivier Besancenot and Pierre-François Grond, "The Greek People are the Victims of an Extortion Racket," *Le Monde*, May 14, 2010, translated, http://www.informationclearinghouse.info/article 25488.htm (May 19, 2010). In November 2011 at Cannes, Merkel and Sarkozy met ahead of the G-20 meeting to put more pressure on Greece.

But Strauss-Kahn evidently feared that supporting this position would lead ECB and EC officials to reject IMF participation. The price of acceptance by these two eurozone institutions was to not interfere with their demands. The above-quoted autopsy of the IMF's surrender turning it into a junior partner concludes that a debt writedown

> simply was not tolerable to Europe's senior-most lenders, the most implacable of whom was the ECB's Trichet. The issue arose at an ECB meeting in the spring of 2010, when Jürgen Stark, a member of the six-person executive board, argued that Greece's debt was unsustainable, and that therefore the solution should include losses for private creditors.

The ECB president "blew up," according to one attendee. "Trichet said, 'We are an economic and monetary union, and there must be no debt restructuring!' this person recalled. 'He was shouting.'"[319]

So on May 9 the IMF capitulated, joining the ECB and EC to form the troika, and funded over a quarter of its €30 billion three-year stand-by arrangement with Greece. This was by far the largest loan the IMF had ever made. Although its usual rules limited a country's annual borrowing to 200 percent of its quota, the Greek loan was 3,200 percent![320] This "saved" Greece from defaulting on a large amortization payment falling due.

Shares of French banks, which had invested heavily in Greek bonds, jumped by 24 percent. Yields on Greek government bonds receded from the nearly 17 percent level anticipating default to "only" 15.7 percent. But instead of reviving the economy, the new borrowing helped finance over €60 billion capital flight from Greek banks to Switzerland and other banking centers. This drain forced banks to stop lending, starving domestic business to the point of leaving exporters unable to obtain credit to ship goods to buyers. The ensuing Greek austerity led to nearly 30 percent unemployment and a deeper economic collapse than had occurred in the Great Depression of the 1930s.

Susan Schadler, a former deputy director of the IMF's European Department, cites two political pressures responsible for "jerry-rigging" its debt sustainability analysis (DSA): "Europe's refusal either to accept restructuring or to provide more funding on easier terms; and the IMF's eagerness to be involved, even if the program did not chart a path to debt sustainability and renewed market access."[321]

---

[319] Blustein, *Laid Low: The IMF, the Euro Zone and the First Rescue of Greece*, CIGI Paper No. 61, April 7, 2015, pp. 10f. https://www.cigionline.org/sites/default/files/cigi_paper_no.61web.pdf.

[320] Schadler, *Unsustainable Debt*, p. 8. The previous record breaker was Korea, at 1,900 percent of quota in 1997.

[321] Schadler, *Unsustainable Debt*, p. 10.

Greece was told to emulate Latvia! It was instructed to starve the economy by cutting government outlays by 7 percent over the next two years, while raising tax revenues by 4 percent. These conditions were based on forecasts fudged to give an illusion of viability. "For example, exports of Greek goods and services were assumed to increase by 65 percent over six years."

IMF directors saw that bailing out Greece's bondholders would cause economic disaster. Rene Weber, Switzerland's IMF representative, found the bailout assumptions "overly benign. Even a small negative deviation from the baseline growth projections would make the debt level unsustainable over the longer term." (The program collapsed in just two years.) The Indian director Arvind Virmani warned "that the planned fiscal tightening would be a 'mammoth burden [that] could trigger a deflationary spiral of falling prices, falling employment, and falling fiscal revenues that could eventually undermine the program itself,' so a default or restructuring might be 'inevitable.'"[322] But having registered their doubts, the directors did not interfere with Strauss-Kahn going ahead with a loan that forced Greece into depression by taking over debts owed to private bondholders without the write-down that financial markets had expected.

The "Systemic Risk" loophole to neutralize IMF opposition to bailout loans

To enable lending to proceed when the IMF's sustainability criteria were not met, its bureaucrats designed the "systemic risk waiver." It was a model of circular reasoning that might well be taught to philosophy students. "Severe debt crises all carry the risks of systemic spillovers,"[323] notes Schadler. The global financial system was deemed to be endangered if a debt payment was missed or a haircut imposed on bondholders, because "confidence" was threatened. Any haircut for bondholders might cause panic and "contagion." So it doesn't matter *what* IMF economists say regarding debt sustainability. The IMF is committed to preserving "confidence" at all costs – confidence that the troika will lend governments enough to pay their bondholders and speculators in full (but not pension funds). The systemic risk waiver means that no bondholder

---

[322] Blustein, *Laid Low*, p. 15. The Brazilian representative Paulo Nogueira Batista "used the term 'Panglossian' to describe the staff's projection of a V-shaped recovery." In Germany, former Bundesbank president Karl Otto Pohl also urged a writedown privately held debt.

[323] Schadler adds (*Unsustainable Debt*, pp. 13-14): "In introducing the systemic risk waiver, the IMF effectively ducked an assessment of [the loan's economic] cost ... in the heat of the moment, when Fund involvement was seen as essential to avoid a disorderly default."

should lose. Labor and taxpayers must pay for the losses from risky loans, or else there will be "contagion."

When global bankers wring their hands about the financial system melting down, what they really mean is that the top One Percent may lose some of the astounding amount of wealth they have accumulated since the Bubble years. To save the One Percent from loss, IMF, ECB and EC policy insists that the economy and its 99 Percent must shrink. "Lending arrangements with Ireland approved in December 2010 (2,322 percent of quota) and with Portugal approved in February 2011 (2,306 percent of quota) used the systemic risk waiver on debt sustainability," Schadler complained. "For Ireland, Fund staff pursued a restructuring option that would have reduced doubts about debt sustainability – a writedown of bank debt held by senior creditors – but failed to prevail within the troika."

The claim that debt writedowns for bondholders would create systemic financial breakdown by destroying "confidence" is a public relations myth. Crafted by bondholder lobbyists as part of their Cry Havoc strategy, it is kindred to Geithner's pretense that the ATMs would have run out of cash and people could not have got access to their bank accounts if no bailout occurred.

Evidence that this is simply a scare tactic was provided in March 2012 when Greek bonds finally were written down 60 to 75 percent. There was no contagion. Looking back on the fateful April 2010 decision, Schadler concludes: "Contagion – including to Spain and Italy – would have been brought forward, but few argued that it would have been worse than it turned out to be."[324]

In a similar vein, Blustein reflects that "that the IMF "should have been on the opposite side of the negotiating table from the ECB, rather than on the same side."[325] But Strauss-Kahn looked to his own political reputation in France and agreed to get the IMF accepted into the troika by joining the ECB's pro-bondholder policy. Since March 2012 it has continued to use the Systemic Risk waiver for debt restructurings, because its "staff have not found a high probability of debt sustainability. Yet the high level of funding continues. Is there any justification beyond political expediency?"[326]

---

[324] Schadler, *Unsustainable Debt*, p. 12.
[325] Blustein, *Laid Low*, p. 16. He concludes: "suppose Strauss-Kahn had quietly told the IMF's Troika partners that very soon thereafter, the Fund would insist on a restructuring. ... He might have said that while Europe was free to do as it pleased with its own money, the IMF's loan would be contingent on a restructuring taking place later in 2010, so that Greece would obtain the relief it needed in a timely fashion and taxpayers would not end up assuming losses that banks ought to incur."
[326] Schadler, *Unsustainable Debt*, p. 12.

The events of 2011 showed that "confidence" meant whistling in the dark and refraining from measuring the debtor's realistic ability to pay. This suspension of disbelief was politically necessary because once it is recognized that debts *can't* be paid out of tax revenues and austerity, basic moral principles call for debts to be nullified. No debtor nation should be obliged to commit economic suicide, dismantle its public domain and force 5, 10 or 20 percent of its population to emigrate, as did "success story" Latvia, duly followed by Greece. At issue is what interest should take priority: creditor demands, or the economic growth and employment of sovereign nations.

The upshot

By March 2011, Greek bonds were again being dumped at heavy discounts, and savings were fleeing the economy. But instead of raising business taxes or cracking down on the notorious evasion by the tycoons who dominated both leading political parties, the politicians froze pensions, increased the sales tax (VAT) that consumers had to pay, and announced a schedule of privatization sell-offs.

Large numbers of Greeks refused to pay the higher access charges set for road tolls or other public services. The police refrained from enforcing collection, and public-sector labor unions called a two-day nationwide strike, which soon expanded into an anti-austerity "I won't pay" movement similar to Occupy Wall Street and Spain's Revolt of the Indignant.

Breaking from the ECB's hard line, German Finance Minister Wolfgang Schäuble proposed a seven-year debt moratorium, and insisted on a haircut for bondholders as a condition for further aid to Greece. He also asked for IMF participation to play a moderating role.[327] His reality check panicked the market, as did many prominent economists who saw the illogic in creditor demands. Martin Wolf explained the impossibility of Greece paying off the bailout loan on the terms being offered:

> Assume that interest rates on Greek long-term debt were 6 per cent, instead of today's 16 per cent. Assume, too, that nominal GDP grows at 4 per cent. ... even to stabilise debt, the government must run a primary surplus (before interest payments) of 3.2 per cent of GDP. If Greek debt is to fall to the Maastricht treaty limit of 60 per cent of GDP by 2040, the country would need a primary surplus of 6 per cent of GDP. Every year, then, the

---

[327] Patrick McGroarty and Brian Blackstone, "Rift Over Greece Deepens in Europe," *Wall Street Journal*, June 11, 2011.

Greek people would need to be cajoled and coerced into paying far more in taxes than they receive in government spending.[328]

The *Wall Street Journal* also saw the mathematical impossibility of Greece being able to pay its debts, given the high interest rates and discounts on Greek government bonds recognizing the inevitability of default. "Germany would like banks to roll over their Greek debt. But Greece cannot possibly pay 17% interest rates for 10 years. So if banks roll over debt at market rates, Greece's eventual default is ensured." The newspaper reported that (as of June 17, 2011) default insurance "cost $182 per year to insure $1,000 five-year Greek debt, implying a 63% probability of total loss in five years."[329]

Focusing on the short run, EU creditors argued that to refuse their bailout conditions would prompt even more capital flight. Banks would collapse and anarchy ensue. Luxembourg's Prime Minister Jean-Claude Juncker threatened that if Greece did not knuckle under to European finance ministers, the EU would block IMF release of its scheduled June contribution to the loan package. On June 1, Moody's lowered Greece's credit rating to junk (Caa1, down from the already low B1), estimating a 50/50 likelihood of default. Standard and Poor's followed suit.

On May 25, a mass demonstration in Athens' Syntagma Square erected tents for a long occupation. As negotiations with the troika escalated, Conservative leader Antonis Samaras said on May 27: "We don't agree with a policy that kills the economy and destroys society. ... There is only one way out for Greece, the renegotiation of the [EU/IMF] bailout deal." He rejected Papandreou's €110bn ($155bn) bailout package "on the grounds that the belt-tight-

---

[328] Martin Wolf, "The eurozone's journey to defaults," *Financial Times*, May 11, 2011.Four years later he wrote: "In 2010, it became clear the money would not be repaid. Rather than agree to the write-off that was needed, governments (and the International Monetary Fund) decided to bail out the private creditors by refinancing Greece. Thus, began the game of 'extend and pretend'. Stupid lenders lose money. That has always been the case. It is still the case today. ... What is open is whether the Greeks will devote the next few decades to repaying a mountain of loans that should never have been made." ("Mythology that blocks progress in Greece," *Financial Times*, April 22, 2015.) The debt burden doubled from 2010 to 2015.

[329] John H. Cochrane and Anil Kashyap, "Europe's Greek Stress Test," *Wall Street Journal*, June 17, 2011. The ECB began to buy Greek government bonds on the open market in May 2010. A year later, by June 2011, it had purchased over €80 billion worth, "replacing private funding that has run away ... All the private bondholders will soon have cashed in their debt, and only the ECB, IMF, governments and government-guaranteed banks are left. ... If Greece defaults and Greek banks fail, the ECB is stuck with junk collateral. This explains why ECB President Jean Claude Trichet insists that there must be 'no credit event, no selective default.'"

ening agreed in return … is choking the life out of the economy."[330] On Sunday, June 5, more than 70,000 Greeks gathered outside parliament to protest EU demands for €50 billion of state assets to be sold and cutbacks public sector employment. The growing Syntagma Square camp raised banners: "Take back the new measures" and "Greece is not for sale."[331]

EU officials demanded "that domestic politics should not get in the way of a reinvigorated recovery programme,"[332] their euphemism for deeper austerity and non-recovery. Protests grew more violent, but Parliament passed a second austerity bill on June 29, capped in July by a pension "reform" cutting back promised retirement income and raising the retirement age for women to qualify for pensions from 60 to the 65-year level at which men qualified.

Talk of Greece leaving the euro weakened the currency's exchange rate as investors sold Eurobonds for dollars and even sterling. By July, a new package called for a 50 percent reduction in the face value of most remaining privately held debt. The new salvation was held to be privatization. The government drew up a timetable for sales to reach €15 billion by 2013. One *Financial Times* columnist called this "a political provocation and an act of economic vandalism," anticipating what indeed happened: "Under the scheme now likely to be agreed, any shortfall in privatisation receipts would therefore open a finance gap. The creditor countries would then almost certainly ask Greece to plug the gap through even more austerity. Such a strategy is financially reckless and politically irresponsible."[333] Unionized employees of the Public Power utility moved to stave off privatization (and the inevitable wave of downsizing) by threatening to strike, prompting Papandreou to promise that the government would retain 51 percent control.[334]

Creditors hoped to reverse social democratic values by using debt leverage. Without it, Greece would not be forced to (1) reduce employment and wage via public spending cutbacks and anti-labor reforms, (2) privatize its public utilities, and (3) oblige the Socialist/Conservative tandem to relinquish control of economic policy to troika apparatchiks. "The restructuring of domestic law

---

[330] Reuters, "Greece PM fails to win austerity reform backing," *Financial Times*, May 28, 2011.

[331] Karin Hope, "Thousands protest against Greek austerity," *Financial Times*, June 6, 2011.

[332] Kerin Hope, "Rift widens on Greek reform plan," *Financial Times*, June 7, 2011.

[333] Wolfgang Münchau, "Maybe Greek MPs would be right to say No," *Financial Times*, June 27, 2011.

[334] Kerin Hope and Peter Spiegel, "Greece in line of fire over inability to hit targets," *Financial Times*, May 10, 2011.

debt was completed in March 2012 and of foreign law debt two months later."[335] By yearend over 60 percent of Greek debt was shifted into official hands. Bondholders had won, having cashed in their holdings without having to suffer a writedown. Greek taxpayers paid.

Former IMF officials held out hope of rectifying matters. As the risk of a new Greek default loomed in mid-April 2015, Ashoka Mody, former Deputy Director in the IMF's Research and European Departments, urged: "Instead of demanding repayment and further austerity, the IMF should recognize its responsibility for the country's predicament and forgive much of the debt." But this is prevented as long as the IMF adheres to the "fateful mistake" it made in 2010. "Instead of allowing Greece to default on its insurmountable debts to private creditors, they chose to lend it the money to pay in full."[336]

Former IMF officer Schadler points out that when that organization's staff saw in 2010 that Greece's debt was unsustainable, they "reportedly made it clear that the strategy chosen would involve significant losses and that European official creditors must bear their entirety." Mody agrees: "To reassert its independence and redeem its lost credibility, it should write off a big chunk of Greece's debt and force its wealthy shareholders to bear the losses."

The collapse of Inter-Ally debts and German reparations in the 1920s showed that "debts that can't be paid, won't be." What blocks this awareness among neoliberal economists is their fantasy is that all debts can be paid by squeezing out a large enough fiscal surplus. Neoliberals are incorrigible in preferring to indulge their pro-creditor and anti-labor sentiments in the face of the reality that fiscal austerity shrinks the economy and hence the ability to produce a surplus to pay creditors.

---

[335] Schadler, *Unsustainable Debt*, p. 9.
[336] Ashoka Mody, "The IMF's Big Greek Mistake," Bruegel blog, April 21, 2015. http://www.bruegel.org/nc/blog/detail/article/1615-the-imfs-big-greek-mistake/.

22

High Finance Turns Democracy to "Junk"

It is not possible to demand that the new Greek government follows the course of the previous one – which, we must not forget, failed miserably. ... otherwise, elections would need to be abolished in those countries that are in [an Austerity Program]. ... In other words, this means the complete abolition of democracy in Europe, the end of every pretext of democracy, and the beginning of disintegration and of an unacceptable division of United Europe. This means the beginning of the creation of a technocratic monstrosity that will lead to a Europe entirely alien to its founding principles.

Prime Minister Alexis Tsipras, "Europe at crossroads," *Le Monde*, May 31, 2015.

High finance and democracy do not go well together. Irish voters rejected the Lisbon Treaty, and Icelandic voters responded with a resounding "No" in a referendum over whether to accept Gordon Brown's financial conditions. So Europe's central bankers were understandably fearful of giving Greeks a chance to vote against the bailout terms. A "No" vote would have posed at least a moral and hence perhaps even a legal ground to reject payment of government debts taken on in the face of strong popular rejection.

Post-1980 politics from Greece to Ireland, Spain, Portugal and Italy led parties calling themselves socialist and democratic (as well as Democrats in the United States) to put the interest of banks and bondholders above those of labor and deliver their constituencies to the financial class. Scaling back pensions and social spending while privatizing infrastructure monopolies reverses what socialism traditionally meant.

The turnabout was strongest among Tony Blair's "New Labour," and by the Greek Pasok socialists joining with the Conservative Party to impose austerity. In 2010 they agreed with German Chancellor Angela Merkel not to permit voter "interference" with the conditions laid down by the troika for bailing out French, German and U.S. banks at Greek taxpayer expense. Pasok initially proposed to put the Eurozone's austerity program to a public referendum, but Merkel insisted that this be cancelled when it became clear that Greek voters opposed the program's austerity conditions.

The inevitable political reaction to troika demands for austerity was pressure to reassert control over Greece's national budget and protect its resources.

Seeing a policy gap that seemed unbridgeable, the press coined a new word: Grexit, for Greek exit from the euro.

By ratifying the bailout's austerity conditions without giving voters a say, Prime Minister Papandreou and his Pasok party leaders destroyed themselves politically. Surrendering to a Baltic-type "internal devaluation" policy, they claimed that There Was No Alternative to lowering wage levels and employment. "Papandreou himself has admitted we had no say in the economic measures thrust upon us," said one leftist in 2010 as the government was cutting back public spending. "They were decided by the EU and IMF. We are now under foreign supervision and that raises questions about our economic, military and political independence."[337]

Just as was feared, the troika's loan terms made Greece's debt problems worse by stifling the economy. Capital flight increased, forcing Greek banks to reduce their credit lines to businesses, depriving them of the credit they needed to function and export. The ensuing downward spiral widened austerity rather than reducing Greece's budget deficit – the same result that austerity policies had been producing for half a century! Greece became a cruel experiment much like Latvia to test how far a population can be impoverished before protesting and saying, "Stop. There *must* be an alternative."

Budget deficits of Greece's size obviously could not continue. But creditors rarely urge restoring balance by taxing the wealthy or having a central bank create the money for domestic spending (unless it is to give to financial institutions). They insisted that Greece balance its budget by selling public land, tourist sites, islands, ports, water and sewer facilities, and Aegean gas exploration rights.

Selling assets is different from taxing *rentiers* and other well to do players. Asset sales do not *reduce* deficits; they merely *finance* them. They reflect the failure to tax wealth or create central bank money. The two leading Greek parties were unwilling to tax the elites or reverse the rampant corruption patronage. Such a failure indeed leaves no alternative but for the indebted economy to be carved up by its creditors.

"Democracy is Junk"

Papandreou had long advocated holding referendums on national policy. On June 12, 2008, prior to his election as Prime Minister, he had urged Greece to emulate Ireland and hold a referendum on whether to sign Europe's neoliberal Lisbon Treaty. After the Greek government passed the austerity bill surrendering to the troika's bailout terms on October 20, 2011, he announced

---

[337] Helena Smith, "The Greek spirit of resistance turns its guns on the IMF," *The Observer*, May 9, 2010.

his intention to hold a "consensus" referendum on whether or not to accept the program. The Greek cabinet gave unanimous support on October 31, and a Parliamentary vote was scheduled for November 4.

Papandreou met with Merkel and Sarkozy in Cannes on November 1, just before the G-20 meetings were to open two days later. Opinion polls showed that two-thirds of Greeks rejected the conditions attached to the bailout, but wanted to stay in the eurozone. Demonstrations spread throughout Greece advocating a "No" vote. So the Germans and French tried to frame the issue in a narrow way designed to get a "Yes" answer: Did voters want to be part of Europe?

The aim was to avoid asking the really important question: Did Greek voters want to impose a decade of depression on themselves, cut public services, impose anti-union labor "reforms," and sell off the Athenian water supply, its port, their beautiful islands and their gas rights in the Aegean to Germans and other creditors?

Papandreou probably expected that the threat to hold a referendum would strengthen his hand in preparation the G-20 meetings and persuade the ECB to loosen its bailout terms. But Sarkozy and Merkel told him that the troika would not release the €8 billion being held until it was clear that *all* the leading Greek parties gave assurances that they would pay according to the terms being laid down. The first bond payment was due in seven weeks, on December 19. Merkel was reported to have "said the aid tranche could only be disbursed once Greece has met all the conditions and there was a positive outcome of the Greek referendum."[338] Finance Minister Schäuble cast the issue as follows: "If Greece accepts the burden and efforts required by the aid programmes, if it wants to stay within the euro zone, then we will support it."[339]

Returning to Athens, Papandreou reversed his advocacy of a referendum. "This is not a question of only a programme," he announced, reframing the issue along Merkel-Sarkozy lines. "This is a question of whether we want to remain in the eurozone." Setting his sights on a parliamentary vote, Papandreou told his Pasok colleagues "that there was no need for a referendum after the conservative opposition promised to support the terms of a €130bn bailout from the European Union, European Central Bank and International Monetary Fund. ... 'if we have consensus, then we don't need a refe-

---

[338] Peter Spiegel, Hugh Carnegy and Chris Giles, "EU suspends €8bn in Greek aid," *Financial Times*, November 3, 2011.

[339] "Debt crisis: Greek PM wins cabinet support for EU bailout referendum," *The Telegraph*, November 2, 2011.

rendum.'"[340] Conservative leader Antonis Samaras chimed in to promise that he "would do everything in his power to stop the referendum."[341]

These bipartisan statements calmed markets. Bond yields receded, stock prices rose and so did the euro's exchange rate against the dollar. But the machinations to cancel the debt referendum prompted an editorial in Germany's major newspaper, the *Frankfurter Allgemeine Zeitung* by Frank Schirrmacher, "Democracy is junk": "He who submits a vital issue to a referendum is a public menace to Europe. This has been the message from the markets – and ... from the politicians too."[342]

At stake was whether Greek politicians would cede economic planning to the EU bureaucracy. Germans had coined a word, *ordoliberalism*, to describe technocratic enforcement of "stability" administered from the top down.

Geithner intervenes in Euro-Greek negotiations on behalf of U.S. bank gambles

The explosion of global credit took the form of debts that far exceeded the ability to be paid. Bondholders, banks and wealthy investors would lose from a Greek default, especially the major French and German banks. So would the U.S. Too Big To Fail banks that treated the Greek crisis as a financial sporting event, writing credit default swaps betting that Europe would lend Greece the money to pay. In October 2010, Treasury Secretary Geithner had insisted that the Europeans not write down Greece's debts, fearing that Ireland, Portugal, Spain and Italy might demand similar treatment. In addition to threatening bank solvency throughout Europe, Wall Street had written so many credit-default swaps that the U.S. financial system might crash. Geithner threatened that this would bring down the European economy as well if the ECB did not insist on extracting payment in full.[343]

---

[340] Tony Barber, Kerin Hope, Peter Spiegel and David Oakley, "Greek PM scraps referendum plan," *Financial Times*, November 3, 2011.

[341] Costas Paris and Alkman Granitsas, "Papandreou Faces Open Revolt in Party," *Wall Street Journal*, November 1, 2011, and Rachel Donadio, "Greek Leader Survives Vote, Bolstering Deal on Europe Debt," *The New York Times*, November 5, 2011.

[342] http://www.presseurop.eu/en/content/article/1128541-democracy-has-junk-status, PressEurope, November 2, 2011.

[343] Earlier, on July 25, the Treasury reported that Geithner had met with Greek Finance Minister Evangelos Venizelos in Washington and "underscored the need for continued and full implementation of the program" by holding to a hard line. See Ian Talley and Alkman Granitsas, "Geithner Lauds Greek 'Progress' on Economy," *Wall Street Journal*, July 26, 2011.

When the G-20 meetings began on November 3, 2011 at Cannes, President Obama urged the European leaders to put more money into the European Financial Stability Fund so that it could lend Greece enough to save it from defaulting – and incidentally permit U.S. investment banks and speculators to win the bets they had made on Greek bonds.

Matters focused on a technical issue: Would a majority agreement among bondholders to write down Greek debt constitute a default? Standard & Poor's had cut Greece's credit rating by two notches in May 2011, on the assumption that even a "voluntary" writedown or extension of debt maturities on its 2010 bailout loans "would likely constitute a distressed exchange," that is, a "selective default."[344] That meant that Wall Street and other banks that had written default insurance would be liable to pay the bondholders. This is what led President Obama to lobby Europe not to forgive Greek loans, but extend *new* credit to enable Greece pay the bondholders and enable U.S. financial bookies to avoid having to pay off.

At the Boeckler Foundation's annual economic meeting in Berlin (and also in meetings in Frankfurt) in early November, I heard bankers and other attendees express shock at how U.S. national policy was nakedly lobbying for Wall Street campaign contributors. One politician told me that President Obama had demonstrated to Europe that no matter who was president of the United States, no matter how high hopes might have seemed for a progressive solution, Europe could not depend on U.S. leadership.

The To protect U.S. banks that took AIG-type gambles by writing default insurance for bondholders of Greek debt, the ECB suggested euphemizing default as a "voluntary renegotiation," asking banks and other bondholders to voluntarily write down the debt. But German politicians insisted that bondholders take a loss, especially in view of the steep interest rates that recent buyers of Greek bonds were receiving. Interest is supposed to compensate for risk, after all – but vulture investors were hoping for payment in full.

The G-20 meetings ended in disarray, unsure of how far Greece could be pushed.

Greek politicians rule against voters

Greece's coalition government feared that supporting austerity would drive voters into the arms of the newly formed anti-bailout Syriza coalition. "A leading Pasok lawmaker quit the party, narrowing Papandreou's slim majority

---

[344] Richard Milne, Tracy Alloway and Ralph Atkins, "S&P moves to cut Greek credit rating," *Financial Times*, May 10, 2011.

to 152 of 300 seats, and several others called for a government of national
unity followed by a snap election, which the opposition also demanded."
However, Papandreou warned: "Elections at this moment not only equal
disaster but could not take place in the best interest of the people." He
proposed: "There is one solution: To support the (EU bailout) deal with a
multiparty approach, without elections, with a strong government."[345] Needing
151 votes to accept the eurozone's terms, Papandreou won the vote of
confidence narrowly on November 4, 153 to 145, and then yielded to pressure
from New Democracy and LAOS, and resigned halfway through his scheduled
four-year term.

Greece's third-largest party was Aleka Paparriga's Communists (with 21
seats). Along with Alexis Tsipras's Syriza (9 seats), they opposed the austerity
measures and called for elections. Seeing that Pasok had lost its constituency,
the New Democrats supported their call, as did the Conservatives.[346]

It took four days of bargaining between Papandreou's divided Pasok,
Antonis Samaris's New Democracy conservatives and the hard-right Popular
Orthodox Party (known as LAOS) to agree on how to avoid being blamed for
accepting the ECB's austerity program. They announced jointly on November
5, 2011, that There Was No Alternative but to form a non-partisan "caretaker
government" to implement the €130 billion ($177 billion) bailout plan agreed
to at the October 27 Brussels summit. Samaris said that in view of ECB insistence that Greece show "a clear mandate" accepting the bailout terms, an
immediate new election was needed to secure a €8 billion loan tranche in mid-
December and avoid default.

On November 11, Papandreou he turned over the post of prime minister
to his economic advisor, Lucas Papademos – the same man who had spent his
last two years at Greece's central bank, 2001-02, arranging the notorious
Goldman Sachs debt swap that had concealed the government's actual position
for Greece's transition from the drachma to the euro. His success helped elevate
him to the post of Vice President of the ECB from 2002-2010, so his appointment to head the coalition government was obviously to administer Greek submission to the bailout's conditions.

Praised in the financial press as a "non-political personality with a strong
economic background"[347] (meaning pro-financial and anti-labor), Papademos

---

[345] Leo Kolivakis, http://pensionpulse.blogspot.com/2011/11/end-of-greek-crisis.html
[346] Kerin Hope, "Talks for new Greek government to begin," *Financial Times*, November 5,
       2011.
[347] Kerin Hope and Alex Barker, "Greece to form coalition government," *Financial Times*,
       November 7, 2011.

warned parliament that rejecting the eurozone's bailout terms would be a cat-astrophe, and urged it to give him a mandate for austerity. He won a vote of confidence on November 16 to negotiate the terms that Greece would have to follow to obtain the loans to bail out its bondholders.

A furor erupted when the *Financial Times* published a 10-page EU-IMF list of "prior actions" that Greece would be required to take. The terms started with a "right to work" law opening up "closed" unionized professions in edu-cation, construction and public companies scheduled to be privatized so as to make them more attractive to prospective buyers. Greece also was told to cut 150,000 more government jobs over the next three years, especially in health care and pensions. The already low €750 monthly minimum wage would have to be reduced, and the annual two-month salary bonus for private sector wor-kers eliminated.

Reminiscent of foreign creditors taking control of Latin American customs houses in the 19th century, Germany called for tax revenue to be put into a special fund giving priority to holders of the new bailout bonds. "Athens would only be allowed to spend on the normal functioning of its government after servicing its debt."[348] A eurozone budget commissioner would be empowered to oversee the Greek Parliament and veto spending that might divert tax re-venue away from bondholders. To cap matters, the IMF and ECB would with-hold future bailout tranches if Greece procrastinated on privatizing key assets.

To give the impression that this was being negotiated with some *quid pro quo*, the ECB offered to relinquish the price gains it had made when it bought €40 billion in Greek government bonds at steep discounts from their face value of about €55 billion. By reducing the risk of nonpayment, the ECB had ended up with a windfall (as had many speculators). To alleviate some of the debt burden, the ECB would lend Greece money to purchase and retire the bonds at the low price the ECB had paid. This saved Greece about €15 billion. But it was merely a drop in the bucket compared to the devastation the Greek eco-nomy would soon be made to suffer after Parliament passed the economy-wide austerity plan on February 12-13, 2012, despite public protests.

The problem, of course, is that the neoliberal economists who created the ECB had tied its hands deliberately to prevent the bank from lending *to* govern-ments. It was set up only to extract revenue *from* governments – the opposite of a "real" central bank.[349]

---

[348] Peter Spiegel and Kerin Hope, "Call for EU to control Greek budget," *Financial Times*, January 27, 2012.

[349] Kerin Hope, Peter Spiegel and Ralph Atkins, "Greek leaders ready to back austerity deal," *Financial Times*, February 9, 2012. The ECB transferred its €40 billion in Greek bonds to

Privatizing assets when IMF forecasts of austerity's success fail to materialize

When the myth that austerity will create a budget surplus fails, bankers promote the follow-up myth that the only way to pay bondholders is a mass forfeiture of assets. The ECB and EU Commission accordingly demanded privatizations to finance Greece's budget deficit. "Greece is for sale – cheap – and Germany is buying," reported the *Wall Street Journal*. "German companies are hunting for bargains in Greece as the debt-stricken government moves to sell state-owned assets to stabilize the country's finances."**350**

The paper published an op-ed suggesting that Greek bonds be "backed by real Greek assets," on which bondholders could foreclose directly if the government missed a payment. "I'm convinced that the only way out of Europe's financial crisis is for Germany to essentially own Greece," suggested hedge fund manager Andy Kessler.

> In this case, you would convert Greek debt, denominated in euros, into long-term German bonds backed partially by the good faith of the German government but also backed by Greek assets—you know, utilities, railroads, tollways, airports, cellphone services, tourism, Ouzo factories and maybe even the islands of Santorini and Mykonos. If (some say when) the Greeks default, the Germans or new bondholders end up with the assets, much like in a home foreclosure…. The new owners would then go in and rationalize each business and fire whom they must to make each enterprise profitable, in private versus public hands. This is an old trick of U.S. manufacturers, sell an old factory to someone else and have new, unknown owners fire the workers.**351**

Deutsche Telekom announced its intention to pay €400 million (about $590 million) to raise its stake in Hellenic Telecommunications to 40 percent (an additional 10 percent over what it already held), promising to cut labor costs. A European Commission report provided a list of state-owned enterprises slated for privatization, including "Energy – Public gas utilities (DEPA & DESFA), Hellenic Petroleum (HELPE); Water – Thessaloniki Water (EYATH), Athens Water (EYDAP); Transport – Athens Airport (AIA), Regional airports,

---

an intermediary (the European Financial Stability Facility) at the low market price it had paid for them. "Mr Draghi said the bank could not accept losses on its Greek holdings because this would amount to the central bank directly financing the Greek government. Such 'monetary financing' is illegal under European Union treaties. However, 'If the ECB distributes profits to some of its member countries … that's not monetary financing,' he said."

350 Christopher Lawton and Laura Stevens, "Deutsche Telekom, Others Look to Grab State-Owned Assets at Fire-Sale Prices," *Wall Street Journal*, June 7, 2011.

351 Andy Kessler, "The 'Brady Bond' Solution for Greek Debt," *Wall Street Journal*, June 29, 2011.

Railways (Trainose); Postal Services – Hellenic Post (ELTA); Arms Manufacturing – Hellenic Defense Systems (EAS). There will also be concessions to manage public assets awarded to private sector companies including Hellenic motorways, the state lottery, regional airports, and large regional ports."[352]

Europe's war against debtor countries was turning into class war, which always ends up being waged on the political battlefield. One financial analyst noted that the money raised for putting up islands and public buildings, ports and the water system for sale "will barely put a dint in Greece's now-unpayable public debt."[353] Creditors simply hoped to take as much as they could, in the absence of public protests to stop the selloffs.

That is why bankers resort to anti-democratic methods in opposing any political power independent of creditor interests. The aim is to centralize financial policy in the hands of "technocrats" drawn from the banking sector – not only Lucas Papademos in Greece, but also Mario Monti in Italy almost simultaneously (as described in the next chapter). The fear is that democratically elected officials will act "irresponsibly," that is, in the interests of the economy at large rather than catering to the demands of banks and bondholders.

The IMF's role in Greece's bondholder bailout prompts a German constitutional crisis

Opposition to a true central bank to monetize public budget deficits is based on the fantasy that this would cause hyperinflation, such as the Weimar Republic suffered in the early 1920s. The reality is that nearly all hyperinflations result from paying foreign debt. The highly political effect of a "hard money" policy blocking central banks from financing budget deficits is to leave credit and money creation for private bankers.

Lacking central banks to monetize public spending, eurozone governments must borrow from bankers and bond investors. Neither the ECB nor the IMF lend to fund domestic budget deficits. The IMF lends mainly to support exchange rates. But Greece's public debt did not pose a devaluation problem, because it was denominated in euros. This limitation prompted Germany to

---

[352] European Commission, *The Second Economic Adjustment Programme for Greece First Review-December 2012*, page 33–35 http://ec.europa.eu/economy_finance/publications/occasional_paper/2012/pdf/ocp123_en.pdf, cited in Joseph Zucune *et al.*, *Privatising Europe: Using the Crisis to Entrench Neoliberalism.* http://www.tni.org/sites/www.tni.org/files/download/privatising_europe.pdf, pp. 9f. Full report at *UNDESA, World Economic Situation and Prospects 2012.*

[353] Don Quijones, "Death By A Thousand Cuts: The Silent Assassination Of European Democracy," *Naked Capitalism,* January 7, 2014 (originally posted at Testosterone Pit).

accuse the IMF and ECB of illegally overstepping their original purpose, citing the IMF's Articles of Agreement:

> A member state may obtain IMF credits only on the condition that it has "a need to make the purchase because of its balance of payments or its reserve position or developments in its reserves." Greece, Ireland, and Portugal are certainly not short of foreign exchange reserves ... The IMF is lending because of budgetary problems, and that is not what it is supposed to do. The Deutsche Bundesbank made this point very clear in its monthly report of March 2010: "Any financial contribution by the IMF to solve problems that do not imply a need for foreign currency – such as the direct financing of budget deficits – would be incompatible with its monetary mandate."[354]

The ECB also aims at saving the banks, which requires bailing out the governments whose bonds they hold. A Greek default would plunge the country's largest banks (the major domestic holders of Greek bonds) into negative equity. But Germany's constitutional *Verfassungsgericht* court has rejected fiscal union and a common Europe-wide budget to be financed by the ECB acting as a true central bank creating money for public spending. The constitutional problem *concerns how to allocate among Eurozone members the cost of funding governments and, behind them, banks and other bondholders.*

If the ECB does not simply create money like the Federal Reserve does, *some* country's government ("taxpayers") must bear the cost. Germany is unwilling to subsidize other eurozone countries. That is why former Bundesbank head Karl Otto Pöhl told *Der Spiegel* that "against all its vows, and against an explicit ban within its own constitution, the ECB has become involved in financing states," despite the fact that the EU Treaty "explicitly states that no country is liable for the debts of any other."[355]

This is not the social democratic authority that European reformers dreamed of after World War II. It is antithetical to a United Europe empowered to set a common budget, a uniform tax code and financial regulations applying to all member countries. Lacking political and fiscal union, all that is left is a free trade and immigration zone whose financial policy is dictated by creditors, mainly German.

---

[354] Roland Vaubel, "Europe's Bailout Politics," *The International Economy*, Spring 2011, p. 40.

[355] "Former Central Bank Head Karl Otto Pöhl Bailout Plan Is All About 'Rescuing Banks and Rich Greeks,'" *Der Spiegel*, May 18, 2010. Purchases of bonds of governments "under financial stress" (conditional on their "good" behavior) are made via the ECB's Outright Monetary Transactions program. It has not been put into legislation as a result of German constitutional objections, but its proposed use has deterred speculative raids. See Wolfgang Münchau, "Mario the Magician," *The International Economy*, Spring 2014, pp. 12–14.

Seeing economic planning shifted into the hands of proconsuls empowered to overrule parliaments to channel tax policy to bail out bankers and bond-holders instead of promoting growth and employment, Greek voters rejected the Conservatives along with the "socialist" Pasok in 2014. Both had fatally accepted the EU "conditionalities." Greek voters finally got over their fear of confronting European bankers, electing the Syriza coalition in January 2015 to carry out its pledge to reject the bailout's demands for debt servitude and privatization.

23

High Finance Installs Technocrats as Proconsuls

> ... Europe's elites are behaving today as if they understand neither the nature of the crisis that they are presiding over, nor its implications for the future of European civilisation. Atavistically, they are choosing to plunder the diminishing stocks of the weak and the dispossessed in order to plug the gaping holes of the financial sector, refusing to come to terms with the unsustainability of the task.... things could get worse in perpetuity, without ever getting better.
>
> Yanis Varoufakis, "How I Became an Erratic Marxist,"
> *The Guardian*, February 18, 2015.

When former finance minister Evangelos Venizelos became Pasok's leader after Papandreou stepped down in 2011, one of his first actions was to declare an amnesty for the tax evaders responsible for much of the budget deficit. As finance minister he already had shepherded through a tax law in 2011 reducing the property tax by 60 percent "for properties larger than 2,000 square meters – about 21,000 square feet ... Mr. Venizelos thus carved out a big exemption for the only people who could afford to pay the tax: the rich."[356] The evidence was visible in the mansions and swimming pools. This was Pasok's travesty of "socialism."

Hope for a Europe-wide reform had been a great attraction of European unification. Many Greeks felt that perhaps the crisis would be worth it if the foreign technicians would come and help enforce an honest tax system to clean up the corrupt insider dealing. But Venizelos managed to "lose" the Lagarde List given to him in 2010 naming "roughly 2,000 Greek citizens with Swiss bank accounts," including "officials with offshore companies, friends and relatives of government ministers, bankers, publishers and those involved in the black market." French prosecutor Eva Joly (whom Iceland's government had retained to clean up its corrupt banks) pointed out: "We know there are 120 billion belonging to the Greeks in Switzerland. This is money that of course is exempted from taxation. If you tax the 120 billion by 40 percent, you'll find

---

[356] Kostas Vaxevanis, "Greece's Rotten Oligarchy," *The New York Times* op-ed, January 7, 2013.

48 billion."[357] That would have sufficed to pay Greece's foreign debt. But nothing was done, except to arrest Mr. Vaxevanis who published the list, charging him with invasion of privacy!

Instead of helping Greece sequester these funds and stem tax evasion, ECB and EC negotiators demanded that Parliamentary leaders pledge not to interfere with capital flight ("free movement of capital"), and to make labor ("taxpayers") pay the national debt.

The Austerity Program of February–March 2012

Matters came to a head on February 9, 2012. The three coalition party leaders agreed to cut public sector jobs, lower the minimum wage by 22 percent, amputate pensions by 15 percent, permit new owners to fire employees at will, and reduce 2012 budgetary spending by €325 million.[358] The excuse was that these "growth-enhancing structural reforms" would promote employment. The actual result was to increase unemployment to 21 percent of the labor force, and nearly 50 percent for new entrants 15 to 24 years old.

On February 12, Parliament passed the austerity package by a vote of 199 to 74. Tens of thousands of protesters demonstrated in Syntagma Square chanting "thieves, thieves." Five banks and many other buildings were burned and shops on major streets were looted, prompting four thousand riot police to fire tear gas into the crowd.[359]

LAOS, the coalition's third party, withdrew its 16 legislators from the government prior to the vote, hoping to gain support in the coming elections against Pasok and the Conservatives. LAOS expelled the two members who voted for the bailout, while the two coalition parties expelled 43 deputies who did *not* vote for the bill. Six cabinet ministers and undersecretaries resigned in protest. "Tonight we're deciding our destiny for the next decade," Pasok leader Venizelos announced. He expedited parliamentary rules to "restrict debate on the new measures to a single 10-hour session … 'so that … day the financial and banking markets have got the message …'"[360]

---

[357] http://e24.no/makro-og-politikk/eva-joly-slakter-kriseavtalen/20117622. A bankruptcy: Eva Joly believes that Greece must be treated as a liquidation.

[358] Joshua Chaffin and Alex Barker, Ralph Atkins and Kerin Hope, "Eurozone dismisses Greek budget deal," *Financial Times*, February 10, 2012.

[359] Alkman Granitsas, Matina Stevis and Nektaria Stamouli, "Greece Passes Sweeping Cuts," *Wall Street Journal*, February 13, 2012.

[360] Kerin Hope and James Wilson, "Greece passes vote as violence erupts," *Financial Times*, February 13, 2012 (print edition).

Papandreou's endorsement of austerity did not deter the world's Social Democratic and Labour parties from unanimously electing him for a second term as head of the Socialist International that year. But the fears of Pasok defectors proved right. Trying to pay the troika has plunged the country into a deeper depression than that of the 1930s. Pasok received only 13 percent of the vote in the May election, drifting down to 12 percent in the June runoff (down from its former 44 percent). In 2015 it won only 4.7 percent, seventh and last among the recognized parties.

Fearing that Greece might not commit the economic suicide its politicians promised to impose, ECB negotiators made the surrender ironclad: The February 20 deal listed "24 'prior actions' that Greece must complete by the end of the month, before aid is released."[361] To prevent the election scheduled for April 2012 from reversing the agreement that they had reached with the leading politicians, EU negotiators insisted that all parties commit themselves again to support the deal. They also demanded faster privatizations. Pasok and New Democracy signed the pledge to obey the bailout terms regardless of the election results. This prompted the columnist Wolfgang Münchau to show righteous indignation akin to Schirrmacher's "Democracy is Junk" protest:

> When Wolfgang Schäuble proposed that Greece should postpone its elections as a condition for further help, I knew that the game would soon be up. We are at the point where success is no longer compatible with democracy. The German finance minister wants to prevent a "wrong" democratic choice. Similar to this is the suggestion to let the elections go ahead, but to have a grand coalition irrespective of the outcome. ... clearly the most extreme proposal is to suspend the elections and keep the technical government of Lucas Papademos in place for much longer.[362]

Most economic journalists saw what the demonstrators realized: Austerity would drive the economy deeper into debt and make the budget deficit worse. "Wow, this is what debt slavery looks like on a national level," wrote Yves Smith, editor of the economic blog *Naked Capitalism*. "Greece looks on its way to be under the boot of bankers just as formerly free small Southern farmers were turned into 'debtcroppers' after the US Civil War."[363]

---

[361] Peter Spiegel, Gerrit Wiesmann and Matt Steinglass, "Athens faces tough bail-out terms," *Financial Times*, February 17, 2012.

[362] Wolfgang Münchau, "Greece must default if it wants democracy," *Financial Times*, February 20, 2012. See also Costas Lapavitsas, "Why it is in Greece's best interest to leave the euro," *Financial Times*, May 24, 2012.

[363] Yves Smith, "Will Greeks Defy Rape and Pillage By Bankers?" *Naked Capitalism*, May 30, 2011. She adds: "This debt servitude eventually led to rebellion in the form of the populist movement."

The euro's design for turning democracy into financial oligarchy

Greece's economic problem and that of other southern eurozone members stems from the way in which the euro was created in 1999, without a real central bank or European-wide tax policy. The original ideal of European Union was to end the continent's long history of military conflict. That has been achieved (save for Serbia and Ukraine). But the essence of any state consists of three powers: to issue its own money, to levy taxes and to declare war. A real United States of Europe would have a real central bank to monetize budget deficits, spending the money into the economy in the same way that the U.S. and other governments do. Lack of a public money-creating institution means that budget deficits must be financed by bondholders, and new credit creation by bankers. That means rising debt, whose carrying charges lead to austerity and force recourse to the IMF and ECB acting on behalf of high finance.

That is where Europe got off on the wrong track when it created the euro in 1999. Governments cannot create money or levy economy-wide taxes without a parliament empowered to tax one state to spend in others. Europe was not yet ready for such a union. Instead of empowering a parliament to levy continent-wide taxes and spend them where most needed, the EU constitution states that no country's citizens can be taxed to benefit others. Germany and the northern European countries are not obliged to finance Portugal, Ireland, Italy, Greece or Spain. It is as if the United States could not tax New York and other prosperous eastern states to develop the West and South, but required each state to finance its own growth out of its own tax revenue or bond issues.

The eurozone limited its central bank to creating money only to lend to commercial banks. This meant starting the eurozone with a financial system controlled by banks and bondholders. Privatizing the privilege of money creation traditionally held by the state, the EU blocks financing budget deficits by public money creation. A real central bank could create its own money as an alternative to taxation, as the U.S. Federal Reserve and Bank of England do. But no such eurozone institution exists, thanks to banks lobbying that only they should create money and credit.

A "non-political" central bank is an oxymoron. The putative "father of the euro," economist Robert Mundell is reported to have explained to one of his University of Chicago students, Greg Palast: "the euro is the way in which congresses and parliaments can be stripped of all power over monetary and fiscal policy. Bothersome democracy is removed from the economic system."[364]

---

[364] Greg Palast, "Trojan Hearse: Greek Elections and the Euro Leper Colony," *Truthdig*, January 29, 2015. http://www.truthdig.com/report/item/trojan_hearse_greek_elections_

This ideology threatens to turn democracies into oligarchies by locking in a bank-run economy. Viewing government money creation as inherently inflationary, it insists that credit should be kept tightly under commercial bank control.

Mundell's idea of fighting inflation was to un-tax the wealthy, on the pretense that they will invest their income productively as job creators, not destroyers. Also, Mundell, the ECB and IMF aim at reducing the power of labor unions so as to minimize wages – as if this does not also shrink the domestic markets, leading to deeper budget deficits.

The euro and the ECB were designed in a way that blocks government money creation for any purpose other than to support the banks and bondholders. Their monetary and fiscal straitjacket obliges the eurozone economies to rely on bank creation of credit and debt. The financial sector takes over the role of economic planner, putting its technicians in charge of monetary and fiscal policy without democratic voice or referendums over debt and tax policies.

Blocking governments from financing public deficits by central bank money creation obliges them to borrow from bondholders. Interest payments absorb a rising proportion of public budgets, leading to bondholder demands to cut back pensions, Social Security, medical care and other social programs. This ideology of fiscal austerity is the essence of today's *rentier* war to create financialized New Europe.

So here is the conundrum: Monetary union was supposed to be a first step toward political union. But its pro-bank bias threatens to break up the EU by forcing Greece and other debt-strapped economies to withdraw. No sovereign nation can be obliged to suffer debt deflation, fiscal deflation and a steady drain of its population through emigration, shortening life spans and declining health standards such as have plagued Greece under the troika's austerity demands.

This is the context that has led Syriza Finance Minister Yanis Varoufakis to explain that his aim is not merely to save Greece from impoverishment, but to save Europe by reviving the idea that governments should promote labor and industry, not *rentiers*. It means public control over banking and credit, tax and regulatory policy. Instead, the EU's administrative power has been used to block public spending, impose fiscal and financial austerity and support financial oligarchy. Historian Perry Anderson describes how different this is from what was promised when the European Economic Community was created in 1957:

---

and_the_euro_leper_colony_20150129/ taxation. (I suspect that Palast is paraphrasing the last sentence to delve into what really is meant.)

Referendums are regularly overturned, if they cross the will of rulers. Voters whose views are scorned by elites shun the assembly that nominally represents them, turnout falling with each successive election. Bureaucrats who have never been elected police the budgets of national parliaments dispossessed even of spending powers. ... parties lose members; voters lose belief that they count, as political choices narrow and promises of difference on the hustings dwindle or vanish in office.[365]

Financial vultures redefine "human rights"

Seeing an opportunity to make a killing on steeply discounted Greek bonds as the country's financial position weakened early in 2012, vulture funds mounted a radical legal challenge when Greece proposed a law forcing private-sector bondholders to take losses. Their lawyers claimed that if "investors receive less than they are owed, that could be viewed as a property rights violation – and in Europe, property rights are human rights."[366] Demanding payment of full face value for bonds bought at a fraction of that amount, they prepared to sue Greece in the European Court of Human Rights.

The aim was to redefine human rights to mean the right of creditors to expropriate public assets and reduce debtor-country populations to bondage. Public spending to provide jobs at a living wage was to take second place to creditor rights to seize government assets and tie them up in courts for years in lawsuits.

To counter bondholder claims "in the Court of Human Rights that their property rights had been violated," Greece obtained eurozone support to impose settlement terms "on all investors by writing collective-action clauses [CAC's] into the contracts of its old bonds." The aim was to prompt the 10 to 15 percent of bondholders who were holdouts to "exchange their old bonds for new bonds – preferring the new discounted bonds to their old ones, which may become worthless."[367] But bondholders ganged up to promote their "right" to block any international forum empowered to bring debts in line with the ability to pay, thereby violating "property rights" to seize the property of debtors.

---

[365] Perry Anderson, "The Italian Disaster," *London Review of Books*, May 22, 2014.
[366] Landon Thomas Jr., "Hedge Funds May Sue Greece if It Tries to Force Loss," *The New York Times*, January 19, 2012.
[367] Landon Thomas Jr., "Greek Debt Talks Again Seem to Be on the Verge of a Deal," *The New York Times*, January 29, 2012.

What Greece lost by the bailout

On February 21, 2012, the IMF and ECB agreed to provide Greece's government with a €130 billion ($171 billion) line of credit, in time to meet €14 billion of payments falling due on March 20. They pressed for investor agreement to reduce the nominal debt (which bond markets already had written down to one-fifth of its face value) to a "sustainable" 120 percent of GDP by 2020. The face value of Greek bonds was cut in half and swapped for new bonds yielding a lower interest rate, but reflecting more creditor-oriented terms.

Earlier bonds had been issued under Greek rules. As a sovereign nation it could have changed their terms. That is what makes a nation sovereign. If Greece had left the eurozone and replaced the euro with drachmas, it could have re-denominated its bonds in depreciated currency, or written down debts to only a fraction of their face value, reflecting the steep market discounts at the time. To block these options, bondholders insisted on replacing the old bonds with ones issued under London rules specifying that if Greece left the eurozone, its bonds would still be owed in the euros in which they were issued. Drachma payments thus would rise in proportion to the degree of currency depreciation. Greece also capitulated to German demands that it earmark tax revenue in a segregated account to pay bondholders.

When Greece received the €130 billion bailout on March 13 (with €28 billion coming from the IMF), markets priced the new bonds at only over a quarter of their face value to yield 13.57% (nearly for times the 3.65% coupon), a distress level that indicated expectation that Greece ultimately would have to default. Venizelos told reporters "that the holdouts were 'naïve' in thinking they would be paid in full."[368] But the International Swaps and Derivatives Association (ISDA) did not declare a formal default, because "no bondholder had actually suffered a haircut."[369] More than 85 percent of bondholders agreed to the swap. Despite being the largest sovereign bailout in history, the Greek refinancing made hardly a ripple in financial markets.

Most investors had long since sold out, and recent buyers did quite well. But some 5.3 percent of bondholders elected not to participate in the refinancing, trying to force the government to make the swap compulsory by

---

[368] Charles Forelle, "Greece Defaults, and Tries to Move On," *Wall Street Journal*, March 10, 2012.

[369] Agustino Fonteveccia, "ISDA Says Greece in Default, CDS Will Trigger," *Forbes*, March 9, 2012, http://www.forbes.com/sites/afontevecchia/2012/03/09/on-greece-defaults-and-the-future-of-derivatives/

obliging agreement by an 85 percent majority of bondholders. This ploy enabled holdouts to collect on credit default swaps (CDS). According to ISDA's credit derivatives definitions, CDS can be triggered if a debt restructuring is agreed between "a governmental authority and a sufficient number of holders of such obligation to bind all holders," making it mandatory.[370] Getting the ISDA to classify the bond swap as a "credit event" enabled holdouts to collect default insurance from their counterparties. "The auction's outcome meant that sellers of the $3.2 billion in outstanding swaps will pay $2.5 billion in compensation to buyers."[371]

The amount was small relative to the overall debt swap, because the price of default insurance was so steep that investment banks writing the CDS did not have to take much of a loss. The main losers were the Greek banks and pension funds that had bought the bonds at early prices. The Greek government and its taxpayers ended up in a similar position to that of Ireland, owing debts to the IMF and ECB, to which it is much harder to cancel or renegotiate debts than is the case with private bondholders.

The aftermath

A general election was held on May 6, 2012. It was the first opportunity voters had to throw out the governing Pasok party. But both leading parties had agreed to adhere to the loan's conditions regardless of the election results. Warning voters that rejecting the bailout would mean leaving the eurozone enabled New Democracy to narrowly beat Syriza's newly formed anti-austerity coalition, 19 percent to 17 percent.

A runoff was scheduled for Sunday, June 17. New Democracy again won narrowly with 29.7 percent, over Syriza's 26.9 percent, by frightening voters that if Greece rejected the austerity conditions, it would have to leave the eurozone. The party's leader, Antonis Samaras, formed the usual coalition government with Pasok. Having pledged not to reduce the minimum wage by 22 percent, Samaras made an about-face and wrote a letter to the EU leaders affirming that his government was "fully committed" to enforcing the program,

---

[370] Katy Burne, "ISDA: Greek Debt Restructuring Triggers CDS Payouts," *Wall Street Journal*, March 9, 2012. According to the ISDA's definitions: "The listed events are: reduction in the rate of interest or amount of principal payable (which would include a 'haircut'); deferral of payment of interest or principal (which would include an extension of maturity of an outstanding obligation); subordination of the obligation; and change in the currency of payment to a currency that is not legal tender in a G7 country or a AAA-rated OECD country."

[371] Charles Forelle and Katy Burne, "Insurance Pays Off in Greece," *Wall Street Journal*, March 19, 2012.

"its targets, its objectives and all its key policies" as agreed with ECB negotiators in February.

Almost immediately, on June 21, the Democratic Left (DIMAR, which an exodus of anti-austerity Pasok politicians had joined on March 22) withdrew from the coalition, leaving the government with a razor-thin majority of 153 out of 300. That was enough to approve new austerity measures on July 17, laying off thousands of workers and cutting wages in the public sector.

Privatizations lagged, largely because the EU bureaucracy yielded to U.S. pressure against Russia. The gas agency Depa was supposed to account for half the stipulated €2.6 billion of Greek asset sales in 2013. Negotiations seemed to be bearing fruit with Gazprom, in which Russia's government owns a controlling 50.1 percent share. But EU officials opposed the purchase, fearing "Moscow's already tight grip on the European market," and warned Gazprom "not to proceed with an offer."[372] Privatization was to be only for U.S. and European buyers. The Greek economy was subjected to even more austerity, because the bailout deal with Europe specified that: "Any slippage in meeting the privatization revenue targets must be 50% covered by additional spending cuts."[373]

Greece's economic collapse continued unabated. Its debt rose to 175 percent of GDP by spring 2014, so that paying interest to bondholders absorbed 6.5 percent of GDP (the 3.75% interest coupon x 1.75). Unemployment rose to 27 percent, and over 50 percent for young job seekers. Despite wages declining by about a third, the government announced plans to lay off 15,000 public-sector workers and shift another 10,000 to other jobs to drive them down further. Future Syriza Finance Minister Varoufakis described the troika's approach as being "to 'extend and pretend' by having the eurozone's surplus nations pile huge new loans on the insolvent deficit states on condition that the latter agreed to reduce their national incomes."[374] This led to yet more debt, requiring yet more privatizations to pay it off.

---

[372] Kerin Hope, "Greece suffers Gazprom blow," *Financial Times*, June 22, 2013: "Gazprom, the only prospective bidder, was expected to offer about €800m for a controlling stake in Depa after months of negotiations with the Greek government on the terms of sale ... Gazprom is already Greece's main supplier of natural gas, which is delivered through a pipeline from Bulgaria under a renewable bilateral agreement running through 2016."

[373] Alkman Granitsas and Nektaria Stamouli, "Setback for Greek Privatization Plans," *Wall Street Journal*, June 11, 2013. The EU wanted to diversify its gas supplies by "supporting prospective pipelines that circumvent Russian territory—such as the Nabucco West and Trans-Adriatic Pipeline—that would carry Azeri gas to Europe via routes through the Balkans. The TAP pipeline in particular crosses Greek territory and there were concerns that Gazprom's presence in Greece could somehow impede that deal."

[374] Yanis Varoufakis, "Europe in 25 years – my 'futuristic' piece in Europe's World," October 4, 2013. http://yanisvaroufakis.eu/2013/10/02/europe-in-25-years-my-futuristic-piece-in-europes-world

Voters reject Socialist-Conservative austerity

Voters in Greece's May 2014 local elections started to turn toward Syriza, which pledged to reject this austerity" policy. The next month Greece's highest court ruled that the wage cuts imposed two years earlier, in February 2012 "on police officers, firefighters and military personnel under a sweeping austerity plan were unconstitutional. ... Pending cases are questioning whether wage cuts imposed by the troika violated the Constitution."[375] This ruling led to legal claims against the government for up to €300 million in restitution for cleaning workers, police officers, university professors and other professions. "The mounting pile of judgments has now become a serious obstacle to the austerity drive of Prime Minister Antonis Samaras, with the International Monetary Fund warning this week that the 'adverse court rulings' threaten to undo the country's reforms ... Besides potentially having to reverse many of its public-sector layoffs, Greece could be obliged to scramble for one billion euros, about $1.35 billion, in back pay."[376]

But the damage was done. The EU had broken the Greek economy. Property taxes had increased sevenfold, and Eurostat reported that unemployment reached 27.8 percent by winter 2013, and over 59 percent for youth. Consumer spending was down 7 percent, while U.S. hedge funds were buying strapped Greek banks to take over the financial system.

Deepening discontent forced a new parliamentary election on January 25, 2015. European Commissioner Jean-Claude Juncker demonized Syriza's logic as "extreme" and warned Greek voters not to support the "wrong outcome."[377] But resentment against the traditional parties enabled Syriza to win over 36 percent of the votes, for 149 seats in the 300-member parliament. Greek law awards 50 extra seats to the winning party, so this was only two seats short of a majority, which Syriza achieved by working with another opponent of euro-zone austerity, the nationalist ANEL party.

---

[375] Liz Alderman, "Greece Has a Surplus, but Maybe Not for Long," *The New York Times*, February 6, 2014.

[376] Niki Kitsantonis, "Greece Wars With Courts Over Ways to Slash Budget," *The New York Times*, June 13, 2014.

[377] Varoufakis accused this intrusive intervention into the Greek election as revealing "a deep-seated contempt for democracy and a colonial attitude that makes a mockery of the notion of a Union that respects the sovereignty of its member-states." yanisvaroufakis.eu/2014/12/15/interviewed-by-thomas-fazi-for-oneuro-greece-the-eurozone-and-the-prospects-of-a-syriza-government/. Posted on December 15, 2014 by yanisv, from EUnews. He adds: "The European Commission is supposed to be answerable to the citizens of member-states. The citizens of member-states are not answerable to the Commission and, by definition, the Commission can have no view on what is a 'correct' and what is a 'wrong' electoral outcome."

In his post-election victory address, Syriza leader Alexis Tsipras claimed that Greece was not obliged to enact the austerity measures or pay the troika the roughly $270 billion that former politicians had promised. "The Troika is dead," he announced, and threw down the gauntlet by appointing Varoufakis finance minister. Claiming that his financial program aimed to save not only Greece but all Europe from neoliberals, Varoufakis described the troika's visiting oversight teams as "clueless political personnel, in denial of the systemic nature of the crisis, is pursuing policies akin to carpet-bombing the economy of proud European nations in order to save them."[378]

The *Financial Times* was supportive of Greece's need to make a fresh start than were many "socialist" parties. An editorial noted that Mr. Varoufakis may

be right to query the technical expertise of the troika. The IMF has already admitted to having been too optimistic about Greek growth. More debt should have been restructured. ...

But what matters more to the reform of the economy is the continuing dominance of an oligarchic class. This includes a banking sector with over 40 per cent of loans non-performing, according to the IMF, which drags on industry. A vigorous recovery may require a thorough banking recapitalisation that converts debt into equity and replaces management. Under the troika's tutelage, very little was done to confront the oligarchs, or to tackle endemic tax avoidance.[379]

Isolating Greece to deter emulation ("contagion") of debt write-downs

To financial interests, austerity's proven failure to revive growth doesn't matter. Their aim is extractive, and they are determined that Syriza not provide a viable alternative. When Varoufakis asked one European Commissioner in 2012 why he insisted on raising taxes when the troika's own models showed that this would worsen the downturn, he was told that austerity was "the only way of demonstrating to Italy our resolve to be tough on their people if they fail to tighten their budget."[380]

---

[378] Yanis Varoufakis, "How I Became an Erratic Marxist," *the Guardian*, February 18, 2015. See also http://www.zerohedge.com/news/2015-02-06/yanis-varoufakis-sums-europe-one-sentence.

[379] "Athens plots a daring escape from the troika," *Financial Times* editorial, February 3, 2015.

[380] Yanis Varoufakis, "EU centralisation-without-representation: a reply to Frances Coppola, Simon Wren-Lewis and Niall Ferguson," *Open Democracy*, October 6, 2014. https://www.opendemocracy.net/can-europe-make-it/yanis-varoufakis/eu-centralisationwithoutrepresentation-reply-to-frances-coppola-.

Realism is the greatest challenge to neoliberal austerity, and pro-austerity regimes in Spain, Ireland and Portugal fear that Syriza's success would spread a more realistic body of economics. Regimes holding power in these countries demanded a hard line to make Greece an object lesson to deter emulators such as Podemos in Spain, which mobilized a "Revolt of the Indignant" movement, and Italian parties vied to replace the ruling coalitions in which both "left" and "right" politicians supported neoliberal policies. Speaking to his party members on February 28, Tsipras said: "Spain and Portugal formed 'an axis of powers' which had attempted to scupper Greece's recent debt negotiations with the rest of the EU. 'Their plan was, and is, to bring down our government and to bring it to an unconditional defeat before our work begins to bear fruit,' he said, suggesting that Spain, in particular, feared the rise of its own anti-austerity left."[381]

Leaving the euro threatens an interim of anarchy, but so do EU demands for austerity and privatization. The problem isn't simply that the troika wants Greece to balance its budget. Europe's finance ministers want Greece to do so in a way that imposes austerity to lower wages, not by taxing the rich. Varoufakis has decried the fact that the formerly left-wing parties have let themselves be co-opted to limit democratic politics to innocuous social "lifestyle" choices that do not threaten financial interests, while accepting austerity leading to perpetual fiscal emergency and debt serfdom. "The great objective behind 19th-century liberalism," he wrote, "was, as Marx never tired of pointing out, to separate the economic sphere from the political sphere and to confine politics to the latter while leaving the economic sphere to capital."[382]

The financial sector's strategy is to distract voters from understanding how the buildup of debt claims shrinks the economy's ability to pay. Without knowledge of the alternative tax and financial policies available, *rentier* interests will be able to maintain control over tax policy and central bank money creation. Their great fear is democratic control by the 99 Percent acting in its own interest to legislate debt write-downs, progressive taxation and a reversal of privatization sell-offs – in other words, to understand that there *is* an alternative.

---

[381] Guy Hedgecoe, "Political fault line widens between Greece and Iberia's anti-Athens axis," *The Irish Times*, March 5, 2015. The article adds: "'The only reason Passos Coelho is less vocal [than Rajoy] in criticising Syriza is that in Portugal there is no Podemos,' says António Costa Pinto, of Lisbon University's Institute of Social Science."

[382] Yanis Varoufakis, "How I Became an Erratic Marxist," *The Guardian*, February 18, 2015.

24

The Troika's Road to Debt Serfdom

...what's so pernicious about the morality of debt: the way that financial imperatives constantly try to reduce us all, despite ourselves, to the equivalent of pillagers, eyeing the world simply for what can be turned into money – and then tell us that it's only those who are willing to see the world as pillagers who deserve access to the resources required to pursue anything in life other than money.

David Graeber, *Debt: The First 5,000 Years*

The IMF's Articles of Agreement forbid it to make loans to countries that clearly cannot pay. There is no realistic model by which Greece can pay back the loans from the IMF and European Central Bank. As discussed in Chapter 22, IMF staff economists sought in 2012 to break from the ECB and EU Commission. Noting "the depth of anger amongst IMF officials against Germany, Frankfurt and Brussels," that is, against being tied to the ECB's pro-bondholder lobbying, Varoufakis reported that in February 2013 one IMF economist "put it to me in no uncertain terms, 'the Europeans forced us into a program for Greece that sullied the IMF's image.'"[383]

Former Mexican finance minister Guillermo Ortiz warned that the IMF was in danger of losing "its credibility and independence" by indulging in the same "illusory debt arithmetic" that has been causing economic disaster for half a century if it endorsed the even more austerity-prone ECB. Austerity worsens budget deficits and raises the ratio of public debt to GDP, he explained, making it

> highly improbable that the measures announced last week will cut Greece's debt-servicing cost by a sufficient amount to meet the new target of 124 per cent debt-to-GDP by 2020, as the recession is likely to deepen. ...
>
> During the Latin American "lost decade" ... the region's debt profile deteriorated continually as the fund failed to address the issue of insolvency and treated the problem as one of illiquidity. Every year the IMF would project gross domestic product to rise and

---

[383] Yanis Varoufakis, "The IMF's Anger – and what it means for the Eurozone's crashing Periphery," June 6, 2013. http://yanisvaroufakis.eu/2013/06/06/the-imfs-anger-and-what-it-means-for-the-eurozones-crashing-periphery/.

debt-to-GDP ratios to fall, sustaining the illusion that these countries were not fundamentally insolvent. Every year the opposite occurred.[384]

The *Wall Street Journal* revealed a 50-page internal IMF document acknowledging that in making its $47 billion loan to Greece – the largest in its history – the IMF had "badly underestimated the damage that its prescriptions of austerity would do to Greece's economy." Blaming pressure from eurozone countries protecting their own "banks [that] held too much Greek government debt," the IMF document admitted that

> Greece's debt level remained undented, but it was now owed to the IMF and euro-zone taxpayers instead of banks and hedge funds. The IMF also said its own analysis of the future development of debt was wrong 'by a large margin.' … The IMF had originally projected Greece would lose 5.5% of its economic output between 2009 and 2012. The country has lost 17% in real gross domestic output instead. The plan predicted a 15% unemployment rate in 2012. It was 25%.[385]

The IMF's own published review of Greece acknowledged "the finding that the SBA-supported program had made overly optimistic assumptions, including about growth …[386] *Financial Times* columnist Wolfgang Münchau described this document as "an outcry against the eurozone consensus" that austerity would promote growth.[387] But instead of blaming the neoliberal model for the Greek disaster, the IMF tepidly wrote: "some considered that to be the case only with the benefit of hindsight." This was the excuse that U.S. and British bankers used in claiming that nobody could have seen the financial crash coming.

Recognition of austerity's destructive consequences erupted at the IMF's annual meeting in Washington in October 2013. One official called its Debt Sustainability Analysis "'a joke,' a [European] commission official described it 'a fairy tale to put children to sleep' and a Greek finance ministry official said it was 'scientifically ridiculous.'"[388] Staff members accused the IMF of violating its rules by making bad loans "to states unable to repay their debts,"

---

[384] Guillermo Ortiz, "Lessons from Latin America's debt crisis for Greece," *Financial Times*, December 6, 2012.

[385] Matina Stevis, "IMF Admits Mistakes on Greece Bailout," *Wall Street Journal*, June 5, 2013.

[386] IMF Executive Board Concludes 2013 Article IV Consultation, Completes Third Review of the Extended Fund Facility (EFF), and Discusses Ex Post Evaluation of 2010 Stand-By Arrangement (SBA) with Greece, Public Information Notice (PIN) No. 13/64, June 5, 2013: https://www.imf.org/external/np/sec/pn/2013/pn1364.htm.

[387] Wolfgang Münchau, "Hail the outbreak of honesty about Greece's bailout," *Financial Times*, June 10, 2013.

[388] Matina Stevis, "IMF and Europe Part Ways Over Bailouts," *Wall Street Journal*, October 12, 2013.

simply to pay bankers and bondholders. Antonio Borges, a former European director at the IMF, told the *Wall Street Journal* reporter the preceding June: "The divorce between Europe and the IMF is real."[389]

Nonetheless, it remained questionable whether the IMF would change its policies. Incoming IMF head Christine Lagarde, Varoufakis wrote, was "adopting a pattern first displayed by her predecessor: Disagree with Europe's analysis and policies but, at the crucial moment, back down and legitimise these policies through complicity."[390] Lagarde indeed showed how incorrigible the IMF was by saying that it would do the same thing again, even with hindsight![391]

The ECB and BIS demand austerity, not central bank financing

IMF and EU austerity philosophy has been tunnel-visioned in acting as if that the way to spur economic growth is to un-employ labor, lower its wages, scale back pensions and health care, and sell off monopolies to rent-seeking predators. The effect is to shrink economies, not help them recover. The austerity programs that used to be imposed mainly on Third World countries are now being applied to Europe to squeeze out tribute. As W. C. Fields replied in *My Little Chickadee* when asked if the card game was a fair game of chance: "Not the way I play it, no."

By earmarking tax proceeds to pay creditors instead of revive the economy, the ECB seemed to violate the Lisbon Treaty's Article 127 (clause 5) obliging it to contribute to "the stability of the financial system." Austerity creates unemployment, instability and even less ability to pay. Evidently "stability" is just a euphemism for keeping bond prices high, as if the sky will fall if bondholders

---

[389] Matina Stevis, "Greeks Left Out Of Top-Level Bailout Meeting," *Wall Street Journal*, February 1, 2014, reported that by February 2014 the IMF seemed recalcitrant to go along with the ECB's rip-off of Greece. "Concerns are growing because €11 billion of Greek government bonds mature in May. The IMF hasn't disbursed any aid to Greece since July and is €3.8 billion behind in scheduled aid payments. The IMF insists on having a clear view of the country's finances 12 months ahead, and this condition hasn't been met."

[390] "The IMF's Anger …" June 6, 2013.

[391] A letter from Peter Doyle in Washington DC to the *Financial Times*, February 5, 2015, "IMF has not admitted to any forecasting error," notes: "Christine Lagarde, the IMF's managing director, and Poul Thomsen, leader of the IMF team that produced those extraordinarily wayward forecasts and the policies based on them (and since elevated to IMF department director for Europe), both said in response to the ex-post review of IMF work on Greece that in the same circumstances they would do the same again. There has been no admission of error by the IMF."

take a loss. And instead of "internal devaluation" (lowering wages by increasing unemployment) making economies more competitive by reducing production costs, financialization siphons off wage income and hence shrinks markets. This lowers profits, deterring companies from investing and expanding, and this economic shrinkage worsens the government's budget deficit.

Ponzi Austerity

Before taking over as finance minister to extricate Greece from its debt trap, Varoufakis defined the problem as Ponzi Austerity. Neoliberalized governments lower domestic income by enough to pay the European Central Bank, IMF and bondholders. But imposing austerity shrinks the economy, making it even harder to produce a surplus to pay. "Ponzi austerity schemes, just like Ponzi growth schemes, necessitate a constant influx of new capital to support the illusion that bankruptcy has been averted."[392]

The troika's "extend and pretend" policy gave an illusion of viability by lending debtor countries enough to pay exponentially growing debts to bond-holders:

> The ECB allowed the Greek government to issue worthless IOUs (or, more precisely, short-term treasury bills), that no private investor would touch, and pass them on to the insolvent Greek banks. The insolvent Greek banks then handed over these IOUs to the European System of Central Banks ... as collateral in exchange for loans that the banks then gave back to the Greek government so that Athens could repay ... the ECB. If this sounds like a Ponzi scheme it is because it is the mother of all Ponzi schemes. A merry go around of Ponzi Austerity which, interestingly, left both the insolvent banks and the insolvent Greek state a little more... insolvent while, all along, the population was sinking into deeper and deeper despair.

"Ponzi growth" based on steadily increasing credit must end in a crash. Athens finally will have to "default on the bonds that the ECB owned," Varoufakis concluded. "But this was something that Frankfurt and Berlin considered unacceptable. The Greek state could default against Greek and non-Greek citizens, pension funds, banks even, but its debts to the ECB were sacrosanct."

Pretending that exponentially rising debts can be paid by imposing deepening austerity is leading to clashes in Spain and Italy over whether to be ruled by constitutional democracy or by central planning by foreign creditors who define what is "best" for indebted economies simply by what is best for them-

---

[392] Yanis Varoufakis: Ponzi Austerity – A Definition and an Example," November 9, 2013. http://yanisvaroufakis.eu/2013/11/08/ponzi-austerity-a-definition-and-an-example/. See also http://yanisvaroufakis.eu/2013/10/25/the-dirty-war-for-europes-integrity-and-soul-europe-inaugural-public-lecture-uws-state-library-of-new/.

selves. They are unwilling to relinquish tax and regulatory power or money creation to democratic control, fearing that this may lead to debt write-downs, taxation of *rentier* wealth and reversals of privatization.

Ideally, a fair and equitable society would regulate debt in line with the ability to be paid without pushing economies into depression. But when shrinking markets deepen fiscal deficits, creditors demand that governments balance their budgets by selling public monopolies. Once the land, water and mineral rights are privatized, along with transportation, communications, lotteries and other monopolies, the next aim is to block governments from regulating their prices or taxing financial and *rentier* wealth.

The neo-*rentier* objective is threefold: to reduce economies to debt dependency, to transfer public utilities into creditor hands, and then to create a rent-extracting tollbooth economy. The financial objective is to block governments from writing down debts when bankers and bondholders over-lend. Taken together, these policies create a one-sided freedom for *rentiers* to create a travesty of the classical "Adam Smith" view of free markets. It is a freedom to reduce the indebted majority to a state of deepening dependency, and to gain wealth by stripping public assets built up over the centuries.

Fictitious economic models as tactics of deception

In place of classical political economy, today's foundation myth is that all income and wealth is earned productively – as if there were no economic rent (unearned income) as a legacy of feudalism's *rentier* privileges, and no inherited wealth or insider giveaways. Yet these have been the shaping forces of history. That is why they were the focal point of classical political economy – to free society from such privileges and bias.

A society's analytic concepts determine the kind of reality it creates. That is why parasites start by taking control of their host's brain. Neoliberal enzymes aim to sedate the industrial host into believing that the financial sector is part of the real economy, not external to it and extractive. That is the first myth. Modern national income and GDP accounting formats treat tollbooth systems and other rent seeking as "output." Bankers claim to obtain their salaries and bonuses by "creating wealth" (adding to GDP). But they demand to be rescued by taxpayer bailouts (or new central bank money creation) when the bubble that they finance bursts, dispelling the economic fictions they have created. The "service" that bankers claim to provide – managing the economy's money in ways that increase prosperity – turns out to be a neo-*rentier* economy based on unearned wealth and income.

A second myth is that all debts can be paid without deranging social values and polarizing economies by transferring property to creditors. This fiction is maintained by denying the tendency for debts to grow exponentially beyond the ability to be paid out of current income. An illusion is fostered that paying creditors by selling off public infrastructure will add to productivity and efficiency. The reality is rent seeking. A parallel financial myth is that corporate raiders "create wealth" by pump-and-dump tactics of stock buybacks and higher dividend payouts instead of long-term investment.

Financial lobbyists use these myths to numb popular awareness that today's overgrowth of debts can be paid only by imposing widespread poverty. As a cover story for their asset grabs, creditor elites cloak themselves in a libertarian denunciation of governments as being reckless by running budget deficits and central banks for monetizing public spending into the economy. Public investment, regulatory checks and progressive taxation are accused of being deadweight overhead.

By ignoring the degree to which banks lend to inflate prices for real estate, stocks and bonds, this ideology aims to persuade voters to let *rentiers* dismantle progressive government and reverse centuries of democratic reform. High finance seeks to appoint its representatives to run the central bank, Treasury and key regulatory agencies instead of elected administrators governing in the economy's long-term interest.

The Bank for International Settlements (BIS) insists that debts must be paid

The path of least resistance to a financial oligarchy is to create global authorities to override governments. The IMF and World Bank have performed this function since World War II, imposing austerity and privatization on debtors. The past decade has seen the ECB and EU Commission take a similar hard line. On November 12, 2011, the day after the EU pressured Greece to replace Prime Minister Papandreou with bank economist Papademos, it brought similar force to bear on Italy to replace Prime Minister Silvio Berlusconi with Mario Monti, a Goldman Sachs advisor since 2005 and then European Chairman of the neoliberal Trilateral Commission.

Like Papademos, Monti served bondholders by implementing austerity, raising taxes on labor and consumers (but not on finance and real estate) and scaling back pensions. On January 20, 2012, he introduced labor "reforms" making it easier for companies to fire employees, and abolished fixed charges for numerous professions from taxi drivers to doctors and lawyers. When voters were given a chance to reject his policies a year later, in February 2013, his

Civic Choice coalition came in a distant fourth. So it hardly is surprising that the financial sector opposes democratic choice.

The Bank for International Settlements (BIS) was created in 1929 to help resolve the breakdown stemming from Germany's high reparations debt. The Bank was empowered to limit the payment of hard-currency reparations to what Germany could earn.[393] The fact that the BIS was accommodating to Germany in the Nazi period led many Allied politicians to advocate dissolving the Bank in 1945.

Instead, it became a central bank for central banks. Reflecting the capture of such banks by commercial bankers, it now insists that debtor economies must be run on behalf of creditors, even at the cost of imposing prolonged depression – the condition *from* which it helped save Germany in the early years of its operation.

As a meeting place for central bankers, the BIS oversees the Basel Agreements that set global capital adequacy requirements for banks to back their deposits and loans. This gives it a crucial role in coordinating global creditor strategy. The June 2014 annual BIS report proposed to use the post-2008 debt overhang as an opportunity impose anti-labor reforms and cut back government spending to pay bondholders and banks.

Debt stagnation, or merely a business cycle downturn?

The starting point of the 2014 BIS report is the main theme of the present book: We are not in a typical cyclical downturn, but have reached the culmination of a long buildup of cycles. Each recovery since 1945 has added more debt, increasing carrying charges that divert spending away from current goods and services (debt deflation, as Chapter 8 has discussed). The debt overhead is preventing recovery. We are in a "balance-sheet recession" resulting from the buildup of debt attached to real estate and other assets.[394]

---

[393] I review the analysis of the ability to pay In *Trade, Development and Foreign Debt* [1992, new ed. 2010]. *Super-Imperialism:* [1972, new ed. 2002] discusses the politics of inter-government debts since World War I.

[394] Richard Koo of Japan's Nomura Research Institute popularized the term in *Balance Sheet Recession* (2003), to explain Japan's debt deflation after its real estate and stock market bubble burst in 1990. While the Japanese were obliged to pay off the heavy mortgage debts they had taken on, their government sharply increased taxes on consumers. Adding fiscal deflation to debt deflation caused real estate prices to crash for every kind of property, each quarter for more than a decade. The Bank of Japan lowered the interest rate, but commercial banks lent abroad in the "carry trade" rather than for domestic investment and employment in the stagnant economy. Too polite to characterize the debt buildup as having been a bubble, the BIS notes Koo but does not discuss Minsky.

Most business cycle theory focuses on the rise and leveling off of wages, prices and interest rates, with recessions leading "automatically" to recovery. But a balance sheet recession forces people to save in the form of paying down debts. Just as the debt buildup has spanned a long series of business cycles, debt deflation lasts much longer than typical business downturns. Instead of being automatically self-correcting, recovery will be slow because debtors are obliged to pay debts by cutting back their other spending. That is the essence of debt deflation. It is like paying reparations.

"The road ahead may be a long one," the BIS warns. High debt ratios for businesses, households and governments will take a long time to work off, implying a "painful deleveraging and extended periods of feeble growth," making global economic recovery "much slower ... compared with standard business cycle recessions." [395]

But instead of urging that the debt overhead be written down to enable economies to resume growing, the BIS insists that economies sacrifice themselves on the altar of past debts run up to banks and bondholders. "Real" growth – in the form of new capital investment, public spending and rising living standards – is to be crowded out by having to pay creditors. "More emphasis on [balance sheet] repair [that is, "saving" by paying down debt] and reform implies relatively less on expansionary demand management." Reducing consumer demand and public spending is necessary to leave more income available to pay bondholders. This "balance sheet repair" means plunging economies into a depression.

To make matters worse, the BIS hopes to use the financial crisis as an opportunity to force labor "reforms" – breaking labor unions and kindred policies to lower wages, scaling back pensions, and cutting back public spending.[396] This is the opposite of what the Reform Era meant a century ago. Neoliberals have hijacked the term to mean "de-reform." It is the same destructive austerity that has discredited the IMF's programs. Already in 1982, Raul Prebisch, founding Secretary General (1964-69) of the United Nations Conference on Trade and Development (UNCTAD), described how creditors demanded that Latin America run its economies on behalf of foreign bondholders: "in the name of economic freedom they would justify sacrificing political freedom," imposing privatization and distorting Latin American political as well as eco-

---

[395] Bank for International Settlements, 84th Annual Report, 1 April 2013–31 March 2014 (Basel, June 29, 2014), p. 45. http://www.bis.org/publ/arpdf/ar2014e.pdf?utm_source= Credit+Writedowns&utm_campaign=df4d581eb1-.

[396] The BIS report suggests that the desired policies should include deregulating protected sectors, such as services, improving labour market flexibility, raising participation rates and trimming public sector bloat" (p. 15).

nomic development to support client oligarchies. "You praise political freedom and individual rights. But don't you realize that in these lands of the periphery, your preaching can only bear fruit through the suppression of freedom and the violation of those rights?"[397]

A similar complaint might be lodged against the eurozone's imposition of austerity in the face of voter opposition. Martin Wolf was one of the first to warn against the retrograde BIS remedy and, by implication, the EU austerity policy it echoes:

> [T]he notion that the best way to handle a crisis triggered by overleveraged balance sheets is to withdraw support for demand and even embrace outright deflation seems grotesque. The result, inevitably, would be even faster rises in real indebtedness and so yet bigger waves of bankruptcy that would lead to weaker economies and so to further increases in indebtedness. [The BIS] demands fiscal retrenchment. ... the BIS wants to see monetary stimulus withdrawn, too ... It plays down both risks and costs of deflation, despite the huge overhang of debt that it also stresses.[398]

The BIS thus has made quite an about-face from its origins. Although it was created to free Germany from impossibly high creditor demands, its 2014 report fails to recognize that fiscal austerity and debt deflation worsen the debt problem by shrinking the economy, it opposes deficit spending.

Chapter IV of the BIS report does recognize debt writedowns as a last alternative. "Scenario analysis suggests that a debt trap is not just a remote possibility for some countries," it warns.

> In some cases, unsustainable debt burdens have to be tackled directly, for instance through writedowns. Admittedly, this means that somebody has to bear the ensuing losses, but experience shows that such an approach may be less painful than the alternatives. For example, the Nordic countries addressed their high and unsustainable debt levels after the banking crises of the early 1990s by forcing banks to recognise losses and deal decisively with bad assets, including through disposals. ... This provided a solid basis for recovery, which came relatively quickly.

Focusing on household debt, the BIS blames banks for reckless over-lending in an atmosphere of easier credit (encouraged by central bankers) and urges banks to restructure or even write down underwater mortgages. But there is little recognition of the widspread damage caused by debt deflation as the banks' "product." Central banks never discuss publicly the extent to which ng debts, arrears and penalties simply be forgiven.

---

[397] Raul Prebisch, "Monetarism, Open Market Policies and the Ideological Crisis, *Cepal Review* **17**, August 1982 (quoted in Kari Polanyi Levitt, *From the Great Transformation to the Great Financialization* (2013), p. 230.
[398] Martin Wolf, "Bad advice from Basel's Jeremiah," *Financial Times*, July 2, 2014.

When polluters cause environmental damage – or contractors of badly constructed buildings cause accidents – the remedy is to pay restitution. If IMF and ECB directives have caused economic shrinkage and losses, what compensation is appropriate?

ECB austerity demands

Eurozone austerity philosophy was made most blatant in a 2011 *Financial Times* interview with ECB board member Lorenzo Bini Smaghi. He seems to be Europe's version of Tim Geithner. To him, the problem is not creditor demands, but pressures to *reject* them. Reflecting his University of Chicago indoctrination, Bini Smagclaims that there is only one solution: adopting anti-labor and anti-consumer "structural reforms and fiscal adjustment measures included in the programme."[399] When asked about how default or restructuring would solve Greece's problems, he replied that a debt writedown "would push Greece into a major economic and social depression," not save it *from* depression! "In the euro area debts have to be repaid ... That has to be the principle of a market based economy." The reality, of course, is that debt deflation destroys the economy.

The interviewer pointed out that "Otmar Issing, your former colleague, says Greece is insolvent and it 'will not be physically possible' for it to repay its debts. Is he right?" No, replied the Italian banker: "It is a fairy tale." A debt writedown would cause Greek banks holding Greek bonds to fail, leaving the country without a means of payment for checking and savings accounts. The economy therefore needs to be sacrificed to prevent banks from taking big losses – so that it will *not* collapse. This exercise in circular reasoning refuses to recognize that if the bonds *are* paid, this will shrink the economy, making more debts go bad.

Criticizing Bini Smaghi's arrogant attack on Greek voters for "being 'irrational' in rejecting austerity," Paul Krugman wrote that he "exemplifies the European elite in this crisis: moralizing, sententious, always wrong yet always convinced that the other side of the argument is ignorant and unwashed."[400]

---

[399] Ralph Atkins, "Transcript: Lorenzo Bini Smaghi," *Financial Times*, May 30, 2011. After leaving the ECB in 2011, Bini Smaghi enjoyed his "descent from heaven" to reap his secular reward as a non-executive director of Morgan Stanley International and Harvard University faculty member.

[400] Paul Krugman, "Mysterious Arrogance," *The New York Times*, May 18, 2012. He adds: "Few people have been as consistently wrong in insisting that the initial Greek plan was feasible, that no debt restructuring was necessary or desirable"

IMF and ECB economists try to save face by claiming that their underestimate of the destruction wrought by their demands for austerity was the result of innocent optimism. Yet the same misunderstanding – that countries can pay *any* magnitude of debt, given sufficient budget surpluses, wage cuts and stripping of public assets –has been repeated decade after decade.

Greek voters are not so naïve. When they finally got a chance to go to the polls, they showed that they recognized quite clearly that austerity does not restore stability. It is financial warfare against labor, social spending and public ownership.

European banks block creation of a real central bank

Bini Smaghi noted in his above-mentioned interview that after defaulting in the early 1980s, "the Latin American countries still had a central bank that could print money to pay for civil servants' wages, pensions." But he claimed that funding government budget deficits was a step toward hyperinflation, by which he seems to mean rising wages. "So they got out [of the crisis] through inflation, depreciation and so forth." The reality was that currency depreciation resulted from having to pay debt service, to which Bini Smaghi seems blind.

EU rules block governments from monetizing public spending, he explained, in order to force economies to rely on "responsible" commercial bank credit in contrast to public money creation. "In Greece you would not have a central bank that could finance the government, and it would have to partly shut down some of its operations, like the health system."

This is precisely the fatal flaw in the euro's design: the lack of a central bank to finance public spending. Varoufakis has described the eurozone "as a perverse economy in that it has a Central Bank without a state to direct it, and states without a Central Bank to back them up."[401] The problem is political. Creating a real central bank – perhaps by establishing a Greek Treasury to perform central bank functions – would infuriate European high finance.

Lacking a central bank of their own obliges national governments to rely on bondholders, who extend credit only on extractive terms that tend to be adverse to long-term national prosperity. The choice is thus whether to submit to debt-ridden austerity, or to stop paying creditors and endure the transition period of withdrawal from the euro's straitjacket.

---

[401] Yanis Varoufakis, "Monetising the... ECB," http://yanisvaroufakis.eu/2013/05/20/monetising-the-ecb-the-latest-insult-to-be-added-on-greeces-multiplying-injuries/, May 21, 2013.

There is no international tribunal to bring sovereign debts in line with the
ability to pay, or to adjudicate who should absorb the losses from government
debt refinancing or defaults. As the next chapter describes, such a venue would
define a body of legal principles recognizing the unfairness of bondholders or
vulture funds buying defaulted bonds on the cheap and threatening to disrupt
national financial systems and cause chaos so as to grab their assets if their
demands for payment in full are not met.

25

U.S. Courts Block Debt Writedowns

Default is not an Argentine problem, restructuring is not an Argentine problem, it is a world problem, it is a problem of global capitalism, of the system in which we live.

Axel Kicillof, Argentine Minister of the Economy[402]

The seemingly obvious response when a nation's foreign debt grows too large to pay – that is, to pay without having to impose a downward spiral of austerity – is to write it down. Shying from endorsing this in 2001, the IMF lost face (as noted earlier)[403] by refinancing Argentina unpayably high debts that went into default almost immediately. In 2005, and again in 2010, President Néstor Kirchner confronted bondholders with a take-it-or-leave-it offer: They either could accede to steep writedowns or not get anything at all.

By 2005 the market for these Argentine bonds consisted mainly of speculators who had bought them at heavy discounts reflecting the risk of default. It was obvious that the IMF would not again step in to help bondholders. Sovereign bond markets were becoming limited to speculators. Most evidently came out well enough that 76 percent (holding $76.5 billion) agreed to the deal. But the restructuring failed, and a new unilateral bond swap was offered in 2010. This time a remarkably high 92.4 percent of bondholders agreed.

However, a small group of vulture funds saw a chance to make a killing. Paul Singer's Elliott Management affiliate in the Cayman Islands had been buying heavily discounted Argentine bonds since the 2001 crisis. By 2013 he had spent about $49 million for bonds with a face value of perhaps $250 million. Singer sued in New York federal court, demanding (and winning) payment at their full face value, plus accrued interest and expenses that amounted

---

402 Quoted in "Argentina Dances With Default," *Wall Street Journal* editorial, July 28, 2014.
403 For the IMF's official mea culpa of its neoliberal response to Argentina's crisis and its erroneous forecasts, see *Lessons from the Crisis in Argentina*, http://www.imf.org/external/np/pdr/lessons/100803.pdf. Para #58: "serious consideration should already have been given to an involuntary debt restructuring, with reduction in the present value of the debt, accompanied by an exit from the currency board arrangement."

to $832 million. Other such funds had bought even more bonds, and waited for the outcome of Singer's lawsuit to claim similar windfall gains.

At that time there were few Collective Action Clauses (CACs) binding minority bondholders to the will of the majority. Also, most international bonds were still issued in U.S. dollars, requiring payments to go through the U.S. banking system at some point. To keep control in American hands, U.S. diplomacy has opposed any international court to mediate between debtor countries and bondholders, and has refused to submit to arbitration by the International Court of Justice in The Hague. This leaves no rules or global arbiter to assess how much creditors should lose when loans go bad.

Singer's lawsuit against Argentina ended up in the hands of Second Circuit Judge Thomas Griesa. During 2014-15 he handed down a series of judgments that have thrown the legal framework for the world's sovereign government debt into disarray. Griesa ruled that none of the 92.4 percent of bondholders who had agreed to Argentina's refinancing could get paid a single dollar until Singer's fund was paid in full, with cumulative back interest, legal costs and an array of damages. Argentina appealed Griesa's one-sided ruling to the U.S. Supreme Court, which upheld its terms, and Singer began to attach property of the Argentine government throughout the world.

The cost of this judgment was so large that Argentina would be bankrupted if it complied. Griesa's set of "nuclear" rulings applied not only to Argentine debt paid to U.S. holders but also to foreign holders. In effect, he ruled that *no* writedowns are legal. No government's debt can be written down if *any* holder disagrees, regardless of how voluntarily they may be negotiated or how reasonable they may be. This made it legally unworkable for governments and their major bondholders to negotiate debt write-downs.

Argentina's sovereign debt crisis

As a serial defaulter, Argentina has long been in the center of sovereign debt crises. Back in 1890, its default nearly brought down Baring Brothers, the English merchant banking house. Yet by 1953, Juan Peron had paid off Argentina's entire foreign debt as part of his nationalist economic program. (Already in 1946, had refrained from joining the IMF, viewing it as an arm of financial imperialism.) After Peron overthrow in 1955, Argentina returned to international financial markets, but its debt remained tolerable – until its 1976-83 military dictatorship, when foreign borrowing soared from $8 to $48 billion.

Matters grew more desperate after 1989. Carlos Menem's "Washington Consensus" regime gained access to international financing by agreeing to back every peso with matching dollar reserves, with full convertibility from

1991 to 2002. Argentina did not issue a single peso of its own currency without buying an equal value of U.S. Treasury bonds to back it up. This created a "one-to-one" peso/dollar ratio, mainly with borrowed or "privatization-derived" dollars that sat idle in the central bank as monetary reserves.[404]

By 2001 the "one-to-one" link to the dollar broke down, aggravated by low agricultural export prices. Trade dependency and capital flight deepened as industry and food production was subjected to austerity, ending in riots that brought down the government. The country's sovereign debt soared to $82 billion during the regime's last four years of neoliberal rule, 1998-2002, now remembered today as Argentina's Great Depression or, better yet, as its Great Neoliberal Depression.

The ensuing sovereign debt default was the world's largest at the time. It also was the most legally convoluted. To minimize investor risk – and hence the interest rate to be paid – Argentina's military junta had agreed to settle any payment disputes under the laws of New York, designating the Bank of New York Mellon as its paying agent. This concession has led to today's legal turmoil setting precedents that threaten to explode the global system governing creditor claims against sovereign governments for bonds denominated in dollars or that involve payment via U.S. banks. Argentina's debt negotiations are subject to New York State rulings by a judge who has enabled vulture funds to block Argentina and the majority of its bondholders from implementing the settlement they reached to scale down the debt.

There were attempts to prevent this anarchic situation. The 2001-02 Argentine crisis led the IMF's First Deputy Managing Director, Anne Krueger, to propose a sovereign debt restructuring mechanism (SDRM).[405] But the United States blocked such an institution. Permitting a judicial power to estimate limits on a government's ability to pay would have let debt leverage pass out of the hands of U.S. diplomats and investors.

Argentina's debt write-downs of 2005 and 2010, and the holdouts

Argentina's economy began to recover after 2002 as booming commodity prices helped improve the trade balance. This enabled the new Judicialist (Peronista) president, Nestor Kirchner (2003-07), to open negotiations to settle the debts his predecessors had run up. In early 2005 bondholders agreed (reluctantly, to be sure) to exchange $63 billion (over three-quarters) of

---

[404] For the historical background see Paul Blustein, *And the Money Kept Rolling in (And Out): Wall Street, The IMF, and the Bankrupting of Argentina* (New York: Public Affairs, 2005).

[405] Anne O. Krueger, *A New Approach to Sovereign Debt Restructuring* (IMF, 2002).

defaulted Argentine bonds for new ones, worth just over a quarter of the original face value.[406]

Bonds with almost $19 billion in face value were not exchanged. In 2010, after another five years of negotiation, Argentina made a new agreement with holders of over 92 percent of its bonds (headed by Italian and Spanish funds). To persuade remaining minority holders to accept the new and final terms, it passed a Padlock Law stipulating that holdouts would lose their right to be paid anything at all if they did not accept the scaled down new bonds in exchange for the old ones. After 2010 these bonds were sold at a fraction of their face value as most creditors considered them unpayable.

Today's problem lies with the vulture funds that bought these old pre-2002 Argentine bonds at distress prices when repudiation looked probable. These funds are called vultures because they feed on "dead" bonds in default. Complaining that "these hedge funds who have bought the bonds at 20-30 cents to a dollar ... now want to be repaid in full citing contractual obligations, "Argentine Minister of Economics Axel Kiciloff has pointed out that Singer's fund had bought the bonds "with the sole purpose of obtaining a favourable judgment to make an exorbitant profit."[407]

In addition to demanding 100% of the bonds' full face value, Singer asked for twelve years of accrued interest (compounded), punitive damages, and reimbursement for the legal expenses incurred in his approximately 900 attempts to embargo and seize Argentine assets in any countries that would recognize his claim. His ploy had worked before. In 2008, British Courts had awarded his fund full face-value principal and interest arrears on Congo debt. The ruling enabled him to seize the proceeds of Congo oil sold to Marc Rich's Swiss trading company Glencore International.[408]

---

[406] J. F. Hornbeck, "Argentina's Defaulted Sovereign Debt: Dealing with the Holdouts," Congressional Research Service, February 6, 2013. http://fas.org/sgp/crs/row/R41029.pdf: "On January 14, 2005, Argentina opened the bond exchange hoping to reach a final settlement on the $81.8 billion face value of debt plus $20.8 billion of past due interest (PDI). The default was unprecedented for its size ($102.6 billion), lengthy resolution (over three years), low recovery rate (27%–30% on a net present value basis), and large residual holdout (24% of creditors). ... $18.6 billion of bonds were not tendered and remained in dispute along with accrued interest, $6.3 billion of Paris Club arrears, and $9.5 billion of IMF debt."

[407] Axel Kicilof, "Vulture funds are showing their true colours," letter to *Financial Times*, July 10, 2014.

[408] Greg Palast has spent many years describing Singer's strategy of buying distressed debt, *e.g.* in *Vultures' Picnic: In Pursuit of Petroleum Pigs, Power Pirates and High-Finance Carnivores* (New York: 2011). Singer was the second-largest donor to the American Enterprise Insti-

Pressured by Jubilee 2000 to rein in such practices, Britain's Debt Relief (Developing Countries) Act 2010, capped the amount that creditors could demand from what the IMF classify as Highly Indebted Poor Countries (HIPC). The act was directed largely against Singer's activities.[409] Under present English law, "bondholders have no rights to file suits. Only the bond's trustee can do that, and the trustee can be compelled to act only if a large number of bondholders demand it."[410] U.S. law has no such protection.

Singer's strategy was to cause enough nuisance that Argentina's government would satisfy him on better terms than it had settled with the majority of bondholders. Moving to grab Argentine assets on October 2, 2012, Singer's lawyers asked Ghana to impound Argentina's naval training ship *Libertad*, docked in the nation's busiest commercial harbor. Argentina claimed diplomatic immunity for its vessel, and on December 15 the UN International Tribunal for the Law of the Sea ruled that Ghana had to release it.[411] But in the meantime, Second Circuit court Judge Griesa awarded Singer's fund a court victory that gave a novel interpretation to international debt law.

Judge Griesa's rogue court rules for the vultures

On November 22, 2012, Griesa directed the Bank of New York Mellon, Argentina's designated paying agent, to stop disbursing Argentina's payments to the 92.4 percent of bondholders that had reached settlement on its pre-2002 debts. No payment to these bondholders could be made, Griesa ruled, until Argentina paid Singer's fund in full under the terms of the old bonds that he had bought at junk prices. This created a crisis vastly larger than the $1.3 billion awarded to Singer.

> If Argentina does comply with the ruling, Moody's Investors Service said on Monday that it could set a legal precedent for other holdouts who together claim nearly $12 billion in unpaid debts. If Argentina does not fully meet its payments in December, however, the exchange bondholders could demand immediate payment on the entire $20 billion they

---

tute in 2008 (giving $2.3 million), and a major fundraise for Milt Romney in his 2012 presidential run. He also is a large funder of AIPAC ($1.5 million in 2010-11), topped by $3.6 million to the anti-Iran lobby, the Foundation for Defense of Democracies (FDD), a pioneer in designing economic sanctions. See Eli Clifton and Ali Gharib, "The Iranophobia Lobby Machine," *The Nation*, August 4/11, 2014, pp. 21-24.

[409] For details see http://www.whitecase.com/alerts-09072010-2/#.U8kmPRaHsgc. British law does not include Argentina in its list of the 40 HIPCs.

[410] Floyd Norris, "Not Crying for Argentina," *The New York Times*, August 30, 2013.

[411] Jude Webber and Xan Rice, "UN tells Ghana to release Argentine ship," *Financial Times*, December 15, 2012. Belgian and German courts also refused to distrain Argentine bank accounts.

are owed. And if this happens, "the injunction will have turned a relatively minor default into a cataclysmic default that will further unsettle the already fragile global economy," the exchange bondholders warned.[412]

Former Argentine central bank governor Mario Blejer accused the holdouts of seeking to profiteer on bonds they had bought at prices that implied a high risk of default: "if investors are willing to accept higher risks in order to cash in on the additional spread," he argued,

> they cannot renege on the potential cost when the risk of default becomes a reality. Default, in this context, is … a legitimate, if unfortunate, part of the game. It is not consistent to benefit from a risk-taking premium and insist on full payment in all circumstances. The legal protection extended to bondholders by Judge Griesa goes against the very nature of risk-taking. If all holdouts are eventually paid in full, the entire price-setting mechanism in sovereign bond markets is rendered inconsistent.[413]

Former Economy Minister Hernan Lorenzino likened the ruling to the United States sending in the Fifth Fleet – "judicial (or legal) colonialism."[414] "No one in his right mind would accept a restructuring deal," he pointed out, "if holdouts with a good attorney could wait and collect 100%."[415] It was one thing for bondholders to settle for a writedown that reflected a lower but realistic ability to pay, but quite different when they knew that those who refused to be reasonable would end up winning much more.

Lorenzino promised to appeal the verdict up to the U.S. Supreme Court, where it was expected to end up because of the implications for U.S. foreign relations. These decisions are supposed to be subject to the Executive Branch, and hence to the Attorney General and State Department over and above the domestic bankruptcy law that formed the narrow basis for Judge Griesa's ruling.

The State Department joined the U.S. Treasury in filing a brief with the Appeals Court warning that upholding Griesa's decision "could damage the status of New York as a chief world financial center and cause 'a detrimental

---

[412] ASSOCIATED PRESS, "Judge Orders Argentina to Pay Holdout Investors," *The New York Times*, November 23, 2012. http://www.nytimes.com/2012/11/23/business/global/us-judge-orders-argentina-to-pay-holdout-bondholders.html?ref=business&_r=0.

[413] Mario Blejer, "Argentina shows that default can be indispensable," *Financial Times*, November 26, 2012.

[414] Robin Wigglesworth and Jude Webber, "Argentina angered at hedge fund court win," *Financial Times*, November 23, 2012. They add: "In a similar case in 2004, the New York Federal Reserve argued that the vulture funds' methods represented "terrorism of payments and settlement systems."

[415] Ken Parks and David Luhnow, "U.S. Orders Argentina to Pay All Creditors," *Wall Street Journal*, November 22, 2012. A similar point is maid by David Martinez, "America's judges are jeopardising international finance," *Financial Times*, op ed, March 8, 2013.

effect on the systemic role of the U.S. dollar' by encouraging countries to denominate their debt in other currencies and put them outside the jurisdiction of United States courts."[416] The IMF likewise warned of the "systemic implications" if higher courts upheld the decision. Ruling in favor of the holdouts would block governments from adopting Collective Action Clauses even when the vast majority of bondholders recognize the need to do so, and thus could "risk undermining the sovereign debt restructuring process."[417]

The U.S. Court of Appeals brushed aside such concerns in March 2013, refusing to re-hear the vulture fund judgment with a full panel. This left standing the hedge fund's argument that despite having bought the bonds on the secondary market at discount ranging from 65 up to a more likely 85 percent, it never agreed to take less than 100% of their face value. It wanted legal rulings to erase the risk that markets had assigned.

Judge Griesa reiterated that the Bank of New York Mellon would be in contempt of court if it paid the post-2010 bondholders without paying Singer's funds $1.3 billion in principal plus full back interest on the original pre-2001 bonds. This made default likely, even for Argentine bonds denominated in euros, because the bonds had designated the same bank as paying agent, regardless of the currency being paid. Bond prices quickly fell below 55 percent of face value, and the price of default insurance rose by 35 percent.[418]

The legal technicalities at issue (the devil is in the details)

Argentina had thought that its Padlock Law had established the majority Collective Action principle, but what also was needed was legislation from the creditor nations. The *Financial Times* expressed the hope that the U.S. Congress might write a law similar to what Britain had passed in 2010, stipulating that "any company suing one of the 40 heavily indebted poor countries in UK courts for debt payments could only get as much as if they had taken part in HIPC debt relief."[419] Already in 2005 the Bank of England's Financial Markets Law Committee judged it incorrect to use *pari passu* clauses to block payments to creditors simply because others were not paid.

---

[416] Floyd Norris, "Not Crying for Argentina but Fearful of a Ruling," *The New York Times*, August 30, 2013.

[417] Aldo Caliari and José Antonio Ocampo, "Argentina's bondholders deserve their day in court," *Financial Times*, July 10, 2013.

[418] Bob Van Voris & Katia Porzecanski, "Argentina Loses Bid for Full-Court Rehearing on Bonds," Bloomberg, Mar 26, 2013. http://www.bloomberg.com/news/2013-03-26/argentina-loses-bid-for-full-court-rehearing-on-bonds.html.

[419] Letter From Mr Tim Jones. *Financial Times*, June 23, 2014, citing the paper's June 18, 2014 editorial "Ending Argentina's lengthy bond battle."

Courts often write down debts for private-sector debtors, invalidate claims
or block collection by creditors for various reasons. "The IMF has tallied more
than 600 sovereign restructurings in 95 countries between 1950 □and
2010."[420] But Judge Griesa denied such intervention in the case of Argentina.
At issue is the *pari passu* rule that all creditors must be treated without ranking
or favoring one group over another.

The only modification for debt relief since 2003 has been greater use of
Collective Action Clauses to force recalcitrant speculators to adhere to what a
large majority of creditors agree to. Greece's 2012 debt refinancing, for
instance, included a CAC stipulating that if over 85 percent of bondholders
agreed to new terms, their decision would bind all remaining bondholders.
This bound all parties to an agreement by the majority. Such clauses protected
major creditors as well as debtor countries from vulture funds hoping to make
a killing by buying bonds that financial markets priced as having little chance
of being paid off at par value. To prevent holdouts from interfering with bond
refinancing, the European Union now requires all sovereign debt with more
than a one-year maturity to be issued with such clauses. However, CACs do
not apply to bonds issued before such clauses were adopted.[421]

Judge Griesa ruled that without such a CAC clause, any creditor that
refuses a debt writedown can hold out for 100% of the bond's face value. This
would be the case even when bonds have been bought at only pennies on the
dollar after over 90 percent of holders agree to settle for a lesser amount based
on the realities of what the debtor country can pay.

The usual interpretation of what at the *pari passu* concept of "equitable
treatment" means in practice, as Tim Samples (a professor of business law at
the University of Georgia) explains, is Argentina's view "that what the 92.4
percent supermajority of bondholders received should be the same principle
that the vulture funds should get." But Griesa's "idiosyncratic" interpretation
"is that if Singer's fund is paid 100% of the face value of the original bonds,
all other holders of the replacement bonds also need to be paid as if their earlier bondholdings were worth 100 cents on the dollar, not the 20 percent or so
at which the market had priced them."[422] In this view, the vultures determine

---

[420] Robin Wigglesworth and Jude Webber, "An Unforgiven debt," *Financial Times*, November
      28, 2012.
[421] Even such clauses have serious shortcomings. See the discussion by Samples and Stiglitz
      below.
[422] Tim Samples, "Rogue Trends in Sovereign Debt: Argentina, Vulture Funds, and Pari
      Passu Under New York Law," [2014], *Northwestern Journal of International Law and Busi-
      ness*, p. 34. http://ssrn.com/abstract=2403342. Finding "rogue courts or rogue precedent
      in sovereign debt" to be as important as rogue debtors and "rogue creditors, the infamous

what the majority gets, not vice versa. All parties would have a right to the bond's full original terms, even if a majority agrees to settle for less. So a majority cannot commit other bondholders to a writedown.

This definition of *pari passu* would block governments from settling with a majority as long as there are holdouts. "The holdout group will receive far better terms than the vast majority of creditors," spelled out economist Joseph Stiglitz, because "any future creditor of any future bond issuance will not receive payment before the holdouts of any previous restructuring."[423] Judge Griesa ruled as if none of this really should matter when bonds are issued with CAC clauses. But sovereign bonds issued prior to the Greek 2012 issue lack such a clause. This leaves them vulnerable to blockage by vulture funds that refuse to comply with majority debt settlements, throwing such settlements into limbo.

Calling the ruling in favor of Singer "extortion backed by the US judiciary," *Financial Times* columnist Martin Wolf noted that despite "the ease with which US corporations can walk away from their creditors is breathtaking," no such leeway or adjustment exists when it comes to nations and their governments.[424] The intent is to subordinate government power to Wall Street and London bankers.

Judge Griesa's "rogue" ruling was a radical rewrite of international law to mean that there can be no renegotiation to write down dollarized debts that may be made subject to New York Second Circuit court ruling that all holdouts must be paid full value of else they can seize the assets of debtor countries – unless a CAC is already in place to override the *pari passu* principle for each and every bond. This means that the 93 percent of Argentina's bondholders

---

'vultures' of sovereign debt," Samples points out that Griesa's reading "represents a drastic change in a sovereign's options in the face of default— namely the ability to prioritize payments, long considered a privilege of sovereign borrowers." Anna Gelpern, "Argentina Lost! Elliott Won! Pari Passu Rules! (... or Why I Love Being a Law Professor ...)," *Sovereign Debt*, October 26, 2012 (re-posted on *Naked Capitalism*, Oct. 28, 2012) points out that in principle, Singer could go after Argentina's subscription to the IMF and World Bank! The ongoing discussion by Gelpern and other law professors is available at http://www.creditslips.org/creditslips/sovereign-debt/.

[423] Stiglitz, Supreme Court of the United States, REPUBLIC OF ARGENTINA, Petitioner, v. NML CAPITAL LTD., ET AL., Respondents. On Petition for Writ of Certiorari to the United States Court of Appeals for the Second Circuit BRIEF OF JOSEPH STIGLITZ AS AMICUS CURIAE IN SUPPORT OF PETITIONER. March 24, 2014. http://www.creditslips.org/files/stiglitz_brief-1.pdf, pp. 5f. Also at http://www.bancroftpllc.com/wp-content/uploads/2014/03/2014-03-24-Stiglitz-Amicus-Brief.pdf

[424] Martin Wolf, "Defend Argentina from the vultures," *Financial Times*, June 25, 2014. See also Robin Wigglesworth and Alan Beattie, "Bankruptcy regime for countries urged amid Argentina debt battle," *Financial Times*, January 7, 2013.

who agreed to the swap cannot be paid without paying Singer's fund full face value, 100 cents on the dollar – plus accrued compound interest, penalties and legal expenses.

The Supreme Court refuses to hear an appeal of Griesa's decision

Having failed in their appeal to the full Second District federal court – whose judges found no reason to reject Judge Griesa's logic – Argentina's next step was the U.S. Supreme Court in what the *Financial Times* called the ongoing "trial of the century."[425] It looked like a replay of Florida's "stolen" 2000 election, with David Boies (who had represented Al Gore) acting for Argentina while Ted Olson, George W. Bush's solicitor general, represented Singer's NML Capital. The Treasury, IMF, World Bank and French government filed *amicus* briefs supporting Argentina's position. But in June 2014 the Supreme Court refused to review Griesa's decision, viewing the legal issue simply as one of local contract law, as if it had no bearing on international relations.

U.S. bankruptcy law is based on how to divide up the assets of business ventures or families gone broke. Creditors are given "discovery" rights to find out what assets are available to be seized. Most such proceedings are localized, while life goes on as normal for the overall economy. Seizing foreign government assets is a much higher order of magnitude, but Supreme Court Justice Antonin Scalia saw matters in the same trivial light as Judge Griesa, treating sovereign economies like ordinary debtors, whose forfeiture of property would have only a marginal economic effect: "if a case was filed in New York against a 'deadbeat property owner,' and the debtor was ordered to pay up, why couldn't the creditor demand to know if there was property in Florida to go after?' Of course, keeping the two steps separate, Scalia said, the creditor would then have to ask the Florida courts to 'attach" that property; but why not let the creditor find out about it?"[426]

The problem with this reading, Justice Ruth Bader Ginsberg pointed out, was that the right to undertake discovery of all the assets Argentina owned tacitly implied a follow-up right of seizure. In response to Olson's argument that Argentina was no different from other debtors when it came to demands for information about assets that could be taken to satisfy debts, she protested that "this is a sovereign. It is immune except as to commercial activity in the

---

[425] Wigglesworth and Webber, "An Unforgiven Debt," *Financial Times*, November 28, 2012.

[426] Lyle Denniston, Argument analysis: The problem when a pitfall opens, SCOTUSblog (Apr. 21, 2014), http://www.scotusblog.com/2014/04/argument-analysis-the-problem-when-a-pitfall-opens/

United States." Argentina's New York lawyer Jonathan L. Blackman pointed out that inasmuch as Argentina is immune from having to forfeit its military arsenal, embassies and other national assets, there was no reason to permit creditors to ask for such an inventory.[427]

Leaving Judge Griesa's ruling in place to govern Argentine debt, the Supreme Court affirmed that Argentina had to provide Singer's vulture fund with a list of all the assets it possessed, anywhere in the world, military and civilian alike, even where they were protected from seizure by sovereign immunity as was the *Libertad* ship. The vulture funds were to be allowed to try again and again – billing all legal expenses to indebted Argentina![428] On July 16, 2014, Singer's public relations arm ran full-page ads in the *Financial Times*, *Wall Street Journal* and *New York Times* concluding with the words: "Argentina, Default Is Your Choice." The ad claimed that by paying his funds, Argentina's economy would gain "as much as $70 billion in lower interest costs over the next ten years." The meaning was clear enough: Singer's funds would create enough nuisances to force Argentina to pay a high risk premium in global capital markets if it did not surrender.

This is not like simply closing down a restaurant to pay its suppliers and other creditors. Upholding Griesa's ruling threatened to drive foreign countries in general away from borrowing in dollars. Non-U.S. bondholders sought to strike down Griesa's ruling on the ground "that the euro bonds are governed by English law, and payments on those bonds are made outside of the US through foreign entities, therefore a US court does not have jurisdiction to impede those payments."[429] The IMF protested that: "We are concerned about possible broader systemic implications."[430] Floyd Norris accused the Supreme Court of turning "the world of sovereign debt restructuring on its head. In so

---

[427] "Recognizing that other countries have much more limited discovery than is available in the United States, Justice Ginsburg argued that "[a] court in the United States has no warrant to indulge the assumption that, outside our country, the sky may be the limit for attaching a foreign sovereign's property in order to execute a U.S. judgment against the foreign sovereign. No other justice joined her dissent." http://www.law360.com/articles/550797/district-courts-now-have-broad-discovery-discretion.

[428] Jorge Vilches, "The Trial of the Century?" *Counterpunch*, July 23, 2014: "That means letting vulture funds know exactly where Argentina has property that can be embargoed, so that they don't waste time, money and energies finding that out."

[429] Vivianne Rodrigues and John Paul Rathbone, "Unpaid investors in Argentine bonds seek to quash NY ruling," *Financial Times*, July 4, 2014.

[430] Ian Talley, "IMF Issues Warning on Argentina Debt Defeat," *Wall Street Journal*, June 17, 2014.

doing, the court most likely damaged the status of New York as the world's financial capital."[431]

Blocking Argentina's ability to pay via U.S. banks

To show good faith toward its legitimate bondholders, Argentina defied Judge Griesa's order by depositing $539 million in the Bank of New York Mellon to pay the interest due on June 30, 2014, plus $183 million to pay non-dollar bondholders.[432] The judge directed the Bank to return the money, "calling the transfer an 'explosive action' that disrupted potential settlement talks with holders of defaulted debt."[433] He also insisted that Argentina send representatives to New York to negotiate with Singer's fund.[434]

But it was obvious that there was no solution to negotiate. Argentina's Rights Upon Future Offer (RUFO) rule stipulated that the parties who accepted the writedown would share in any new settlement made with the holdouts down through 2014.[435] If it paid Singer's vulture fund 100 cents on the dollar, it would have to pay all the former bondholders retroactively on the same terms. The immediate cost would be $15 billion, amounting to $120 billion over the years to come, far beyond any reasonable scale.

As shaped by Judge Griesa, the Court of Appeals and the U.S. Supreme Court, current U.S. law forms a financial vise to prevent countries from escaping from debt deflation, *rentier* serfdom and seizure of their assets by cred-

---

[431] Floyd Norris, "Ruling on Argentina Gives Investors an Upper Hand," *The New York Times*, June 20, 2014.

[432] Peter Eavis, "Action by Argentina Seems to Defy Judge's Order on Bond Payments," *The New York Times*, June 27, 2014, and Ed Stocker and Vivianne Rodrigues, "Argentina deposits $832m to pay bonds," *Financial Times*, June 26, 2014.

[433] Bob Van Voris and Katia Porzecanski, "Ruling Risks New Argentine Default as Monday Deadline Approaches," *Bloomberg*, June 27, 2014. Judge Griesa also "denied a request by holders of euro-denominated exchange bonds, who argued that his orders shouldn't apply to those securities as their payments are made entirely outside of the U.S. The judge replied that his orders apply to payments made by Argentina, which agreed to U.S. jurisdiction when it issued the original bonds."

[434] Special Master mediator Daniel Pollack's $12,000 daily fee would amount to $250,000 for 22 days. http://www.infobae.com/2014/07/15/1580783-la-argentina-debera-depositar-us125-mil-pagar-los-honorarios-del-mediador.

[435] Anna Gelpern, "Argentina: The RUFO Crazy," *Credit Slips*, July 23, 2014, describes RUFO as "a promise by Argentina to the restructured bondholders that, should it give holdouts more favorable terms, the restructured bondholders would get the same. So if NML and friends get 100 cents plus exorbitant past-due interest on the defaulted 1994 bonds, the restructured bondholders get to claim the same for themselves. The ever-un-dramatic Argentine press has done the math, and came up with a $500 billion bill."

itors. Griesa's ruling threatens that without restructuring onerous foreign debts, entire economies will be driven into depression, unemployment and emigration of young labor, capped by pressures for insider privatizations.

Creating an alternative legal framework for debt writedowns

Avoiding such financial warfare requires a global arbiter to override the "trial of the century's" precedent. Griesa's rulings prevent governments in general from scaling back dollar-denominated debts that lack the post-2012 Collective Action Clauses binding minority holders to decisions by a specified majority or, under British law, a trustee representing the majority. At issue is whether a few holdouts can impose anarchy on the international economy by blocking the legality of debt writedowns negotiated as an alternative to outright default or repudiation.

In summer 2014 over four hundred banks, bond investors and debtor countries worked via the International Capital Market Association to limit the ability of vulture funds and other holdouts to block settlements and compromises by using Collective Action Clauses on new bond issues. These CACs define the terms for future default rulings, binding all investors to decisions agreed by a 75 percent majority. The clauses would apply to all of a debtor country's bonds, so as to prevent holdouts from buying a majority of a single issue and then trying to throw the entire spectrum of the country's bonds into courts (as is presently the case). Judge Griesa's ruling would be rendered obsolete by defining the *pari passu* clause to mean "equal treatment but not equal payments for bondholders."[436]

The global debt overhead has grown so large that the financial war fought over creditor-debtor relations has come to overshadow the class warfare between labor and its employers. In a passionate, even tearful speech on August 19, 2014, President Christina Kirchner (who succeeded her husband after he died in office in 2007) escalated Argentina's debt crisis into an issue of global principle:

> When it comes to the sovereignty of our country and the conviction that we can no longer be extorted and that we can't become burdened with debt again, we are emerging as Argentines. … If I signed what they're trying to make me sign, the bomb wouldn't explode now but rather there would surely be applause, marvelous headlines in the papers. But we would enter into the infernal cycle of debt which we've been subject to for so long.[437]

---

[436] Elaine Moore, "New rules agreed for sovereign defaults," *Financial Times*, August 29, 2014.
[437] Charlie Devereux, Camila Russo and Katia Porzecanski, "Argentina's Bonds Decline on Plan to Offer Local-Law Swap," *Bloomberg*, August 20, 2014. http://www.bloomberg.com/news/2014-08-19/argentina-to-pay-bondholders-in-local-account-to-skirt-ruling.html.

The practical effect of Judge Griesa's rulings has been to make global sovereign debt settlements impossible to implement if they involve U.S. dollar payments or U.S. courts. This blocks any negotiated writedowns of sovereign debt – any writedown at all. Any hedge fund or other creditor, no matter how small their bondholding, can demand full face value for any bond that has been renegotiated, even if the large majority of holders agree to a swap designed to bring debts within a government's ability to pay.

Matters came to a head on June 5, 2015. As Argentina had warned, Griesa extended his ruling beyond just Singer's funds, to include the approximately five hundred other holdouts and vulture funds that did not accept the terms of the 2005 and 2010 restructurings.[438] Argentine economic writer Jorge Vilches points out that Kenneth Dart's EM Ltd. owns $595 million worth of defaulted Argentine bonds (more than Singer's $503 million in his NML Capital). "In addition to Dart, there are approximately $2.4 billion worth of bonds out there that are governed by New York law and in the hands of other holdout investors." Starting to pay these holdouts 100% on the dollar for their old bonds would leave Argentina "right back where it started."[439]

Dubbed "me too" bondholders, they were awarded $5.4 billion beyond Griesa's original ruling to pay Singer $1.6 billion. Economy Minister Axel Kicillof accused the funds of using Singer's claims as a cat's paw to establish legal grounds for the rest to pile on – a trap they had planned all along:

> The "vulture" funds tried to show that the amount to pay was small compared to the foreign currency reserves so to make the country pay before other creditors would show up. The opposition economists fell into the trap, asking us to pay the holdouts. ... As Griesa now acknowledges for all creditors of Argentina the same terms as the 'vulture' funds, we will be asked to pay between US$15 billion and US$17 billion. That's a lot of money considering that our foreign currency reserves are US$34 billion.

The creditors' ultimate aim, Kiciloff accused, was to carve up Argentina by forcing privatization sell-offs. "If Argentina takes new debt to pay them, international agencies would make the government implement adjustments

---

[438] Herald staff with DyN, "Kicillof: Griesa's ruling proves we were right," *Buenos Aires Herald*, June 8, 2015. http://www.buenosairesherald.com/article/191128/kicillof-griesa's-ruling-proves-we-were-right. "A total 120 petitions from 526 plaintiffs have been filed before Griesa, who had set March 2 as a deadline for those claims. Most of them were filed by NML, Aurelius, Blue Angel, Lightwater, Blue Castle, Old Castle, Capital Ventures and EM — all major holdout funds which also represent smaller organizations."

[439] Jorge Vilches, "Real Hurt, Real People: Argentina's "Me-Toos" Make Sure No Vultures Left Behind," *Counterpunch*, June 11, 2015. Dart renounced his American citizenship in favor of the Cayman Islands and, in 1994, of Belize.

and privatize state companies." That has become the financial aim since the Thatcher-Reagan era: in a modern Enclosure movement privatizing the public domain of debtor countries.

Instead of financing capital investment to earn profits by producing more, the new financial strategy is to pry away rent-extraction opportunities – and to turn rent extraction into interest. The major such opportunities are currently public enterprises.

This financialization strategy confronts countries with the need to create an alternative to being crucified on the cross of existing debts. The tangible economy of labor and production should take priority over creditor demands. This principle needs to be built into a body of international law to enable sovereign governments to override foreign debt claims in the public interest.

26

Financial Austerity Or a Clean Slate?

Blaming the wolf would not help the sheep much. The sheep must learn not to fall into the clutches of the wolf.

        Mahatma Gandhi (quoted in D. G. Teldulkar, *Mahatma, Vol. 5: 1938-40*, p. 16).

Over and above Judge Griesa's ruling blocking debt writedowns, the "Western" financial system has become hostage to U.S. geopolitics. A $9 billion U.S. fine against France's Banc Paribas for dealing with Iran was followed by trade and financial sanctions against Russia. The increasingly aggressive use of such economic warfare to support American diplomacy provided a note of urgency for Russia and China, along with Brazil, India and South Africa (and Shanghai Cooperation Organization observer-state Iran) to create a monetary system immune from such pressures.

Thus it came about that on July 15–16, 2014, the same days that Paul Singer's full-page newspaper ads warning Argentina about higher interest creditor-nation charges if it did not surrender to his demands were published, the BRICS were meeting in Brazil to announce their $50 billion New Development Bank and a $100 billion clearing facility. Argentine Economics Minister Kiciloff headed a committee to work with BRICS officials to propose a global financial court such as U.S. diplomats had blocked within the IMF.

Held in the context of deepening military confrontation in Ukraine by the United States and its NATO satellites against Russia, the BRICS initiative aimed to transact trade and investment in their own currencies as well as the dollar, and hence, of U.S. banks. Avoiding financial dependency insulates economies from U.S. economic sanctions that have shown themselves to be more powerful than direct military attack in forcing countries to follow U.S. pro-creditor, anti-labor austerity, asset stripping and rent seeking.

Public media in the West denigrated the BRICS meeting by asking what Russia, China, India, Brazil and South Africa have in common. The answer is that they all are confronted with the threat of U.S., Eurozone and IMF sanctions against countries that do not submit to creditor demands for privatization selloffs and tax shifts onto labor instead of finance and rent seeking. Debtor countries are expected to conduct their foreign trade, investment and borrowing in dollars mediated by the U.S. banking system, U.S. courts, the U.S. Treasury and State Department.

This dollarized system has led the BRICS and other countries to create their own alternative in order to free themselves from U.S. sanctions and creditor-oriented rulings. Initiating an alternative to neoliberal *rentier* policy, the prospective BRICS bank and currency clearing house promises not to demand austerity and kindred anti-labor policies, or impose the Trans-Pacific Partnership (TPP) and Trade in Services Agreement (TISA) prohibitions against governments regulating finance and business, taxing or fining them for the damages and social costs ("externalities") they cause.

At issue is whether governments or banks will direct economies. Letting economies be centrally planned by mega-banks will favor extractive claims for debt service, to be paid by privatizing public assets, foreclosing on debtors and raiding companies with takeover credit and "activist" asset stripping. The new conflict is thus between a financialized *rentier* austerity and a revival of a classical mixed economy steering markets in the long-term public interest – what used to be called socialism.

Financialization is the major dynamic polarizing today's economies. Its aim is to appropriate the means of production and rent-extracting privileges for a creditor class to load labor, industry, agriculture and governments down with debt. Employment, wages and capital investment cannot recover as long as the resulting debt overhead is left in place.

Debt leveraging is a major reason why the United States and Britain have lost their industrial advantage. Debt-inflated costs for housing, education and other basic needs have priced their labor out of markets abroad and at home. Germany's ability to resist a domestic real estate bubble has been a key to its success as an industrial exporter. Yet its banks and political leaders demand financialization abroad. It is a classic case of "Do as I say, not as I do." Eurozone financial institutions have sought to impose Latvia's "model" austerity on Ireland, Spain and Portugal – and most of all, on Greece, which is being made an object lesson of how creditor powers will treat countries that try to extricate themselves from debt, unemployment, privatization, emigration and demographic collapse.

Neoliberal financialization is not how to create a viable economy. Academic theories must be mistrusted if they do not explain why financial and industrial objectives are diverging, not converging. FIRE sector lobbyists have censored economic theory so as to misrepresent Adam Smith and the anti-*rentier* spirit of classical economists who believed that a free market required public regulation to keep predatory finance and rent seeking in check, and to keep basic infastructure in the public domain.

Only by such intellectual clear-cutting to wipe out history could so much of the public come to believe what no generation ever before has believed: that the financial and related rent-extracting sectors are an intrinsic part of the "real" economy of production and consumption, not external to it and predatory on it, and that they can get money fastest by borrowing to buy assets being inflated by bank credit.

Early attempts to align banking interests with those of industry have given way to a world in which the largest corporations are managed with financial strategy in mind. Today's post-modern economic theory depicts Quantitative Easing – more borrowing – as a solution to today's debt-strapped budgets. Wall Street's public relations handouts promise that "activist shareholders" can make home buyers rich and pay pensions by stock buybacks and kindred financial engineering even without the economy really growing – simply by capital gains, raising stock prices by using earnings to buy back their own equity, while downsizing operations and scaling back research and development.

While most people – and certainly most economists and the mass media – view these asset-price gains as creating real wealth and prosperity, creditors insist that governments can pay *any* magnitude of debt, given sufficient reduction of wages, social benefits, pensions and privatization sell-offs. That axiom is the cover story for the IMF and ECB to bail out bondholders – leaving "taxpayers" in debtor countries to suffer *ad infinitum*.

I call this ideology post-modern because it rejects the Progressive Era's program of taxing *rentier* wealth and subsidizing public investment in basic infrastructure with a view toward lowering the cost of living and doing business. In a word, the "modern" economy a century ago was supposed to be socialist. Today's economy is moving in the opposite direction: toward a financialized neofeudalism and rent seeking, by spreading the politically soporific impression that There Is No Alternative.

How finance has rolled back the modern era toward neofeudalism

Instead of restructuring economies with a clean slate to resume progress, the financial class is using today's debt crisis to vest itself as the new elite to rule the remainder of the 21st century. To consolidate their position, financiers are sponsoring a property grab – privatization – and waging a war to reduce labor and industry to debt peonage by blocking government's ability to protect society against predatory credit and rent extraction.

This neo-*rentier* economy is reversing the direction of evolution that classical political economy hoped to establish. Instead of supporting industrial capital formation in an alliance against rent-extracting landlords as in the early 19th century, the financial sector has moved into a symbiosis with rent-seeking monopolies, infrastructure and natural resource privatizers. Money and credit are created to buy these assets, not to finance new industrial capital investment and employment.

In the initial wave of asset-price inflation, debt is used to bid up prices for real estate and other assets. This financialization involves carrying charges (interest, financial management fees and salaries, legal and lobbying expenses) that turn into debt deflation, leading to austerity and unemployment. Investment and employment slows, debts go bad and foreclosure time arrives.

Financial managers find it easier to carve out rent-extracting opportunities than to make profits by investing in more means of production. In the political sphere, they lobby to untax this economic rent, shifting the tax burden off of themselves. The resulting budget deficits lead to cutbacks in infrastructure spending on bridges and roads, other basic needs, underfunding pension plans, and finally by property sell-offs and privatizations.

This predatory financial dynamic stifles industrial potential, raising the specter of lapsing back into ancient usury. Much like creditors in ancient Rome, today's financial power seeks to replace democracy with oligarchy. We are seeing a resurgence of "primitive accumulation" by exponentially accruing debt dependency, foreclosure and privatization, whose effects threaten to be as devastating as the brutal military conquests of past epochs that reduced populations to serfdom.

It doesn't have to be this way

There are many alternatives to today's debt-ridden austerity. Heading the list are debt writedowns and a tax shift off labor and industry onto *rentier* income and inherited fortunes. Today's tax subsidy for debt financing should be replaced by removing the tax-deductibility of interest. And credit creation should be steered to expand the real economy, not merely to inflate asset prices.

A more realistic statistical accounting format would show how the economic surplus is invested or dissipated. This in turn requires an alternative body of theory and analysis to distinguish real wealth from overhead. That was the task of classical political economy. For two centuries it refined the concepts needed to explain why most of the buildup of wealth owned or owed to the One Percent has taken the form of claims for land rent, natural resource rent and monopoly rent, capped by financial *rentier* charges. These were the forms of revenue that classical economists hoped to collect by levying progressive taxes on land and natural resources, and by regulating natural monopolies by taking them into the public domain.

Instead, our tax system favors rent extraction and financial short-termism, enabling bondholders, bankers, stock market raiders and "activists" to eat into the economy's industrial bone while inflating access prices rise for privatized infrastructure. The aim is to transfer ownership of the vast capital expenditure sunk in the hitherto public domain – from roads to education, ports, power systems medical care and communications – to buyers on credit, with the revenue going to bankers, bondholders and stockholders. Labor is cornered onto a virtual reservation, driven into debt by being obliged to buy essential goods and services and obtain housing and an education at the proverbial Company Store.

It doesn't have to be this way. As Chapter 7 has shown, banking was on its way to becoming a public utility in the years leading up to World War I. If this trend had continued, much of today's world would receive credit cards, use deposit banking services and get loans provided at cost or at subsidized rates instead of burdened with interest charges, predatory fees and penalties. Most important, a public banking option would have been less likely to extend credit for the asset stripping and rent-seeking that characterize today's post-modern financial system.

The logic for annulling odious debts – but only those owed to Russia

The most imaginative recent rationales for annulling sovereign debts have been thought up not by Argentina, Greece or Ireland, but by U.S. strategists seeking to enable Ukraine to avoid paying the bonds it has issued or debts run up for gas imported from Russia. In the wake of the New Cold War confrontation in mid-2014 after Crimea voted heavily in a popular referendum to be re-absorbed by Russia, the Peterson Institute for International Economics floated a proposal by former Treasury official Anna Gelpern to deprive Russia of a means for enforcing its loan to Ukraine. "A single measure can free up $3 billion for Ukraine," she proposed. Britain's Parliament could pass a law declaring the $3 billion bond negotiated by Russia's sovereign wealth fund to be "foreign aid," not a real commercial loan contract worthy of legal enforcement.[440]

This would be a thunderclap shaking international debt markets. Its principle would be logically applicable to U.S. claims "foreign aid," which includes

---

[440] Anna Gelpern, "Debt Sanctions Can Help Ukraine and Fill a Gap in the International Financial System," Peterson Institute for International Economics, Policy Brief PB14–20, August 2014. http://www.piie.com/publications/pb/pb14-20.pdf.

loans to pay back American bankers and other creditors, as well as World Bank "aid" loans. The bonds held by Russia's sovereign wealth fund were denominated in euros under strict "London" rules. Furthermore, the fund required at least an AA rating for bond investments. Ukraine's B+ rating was below this level, so Russia acted in a prudent way to add financial protection by making the bonds payable on demand if Ukraine's overall debt rose above a fairly modest 60 percent of its GDP. Unlike general-purpose foreign aid, the terms of this loan gives Russia "power to trigger a cascade of defaults under Ukraine's other bonds and a large block of votes in any future bond restructuring," Gelpern noted.

As recently as 2013, Ukraine's public debt amounted to just over 40 percent of the nation's GDP – some $73 billion, seemingly manageable until the February Maidan coup led to civil war against the Eastern Russian-speaking region. Waging war is expensive, and Ukraine's hryvnia currency ruptured. A quarter of its exports come from eastern Ukraine, sold mainly to Russia (including military hardware). Kiev sought to end this trade, and spent a year bombing Donbas and Luhansk cities and industry, turning off the electricity to its coalmines, and driving an estimated one million of the region's civilians to flee into Russia. Ukraine's exchange rate plunged steadily, raising its debt/GDP ratio far above the 60 percent threshold. That gave Russia the option to make the debt payable immediately, triggering the cross-default clauses it had inserted into the euro-bonds contracted with Ukraine.

Gelpern's paper accused Russia of seeking to keep Ukraine "on a short leash," as if this is not precisely what the IMF and most financial investors do. However, "governments do not normally sue one another to collect their debts in national courts." If this should occur, the *pari passu* rule prevents some debts from being annulled selectively. That is the problem Gelpern has been describing in the Credit Slips blog with regard to Argentina's debt negotiations.

Gelpern therefore raises another possibility – that Ukraine may claim that its debt to Russia is "odious," addressing the situation where "an evil ruler signs contracts that burden future generations long after the ruler is deposed."[441]

---

[441] Gelpern traces the idea back to 17th-century international law, citing Robert Howse, *The Concept of Odious Debt in Public International Law*, UNCTAD Discussion Paper 185 (July 2007), available at http://unctad.org/en/docs/osgdp20074_en.pdf, and Seema Jayachandran and Michael Kemer, "Odious Debt," *American Economic Review* **96** (2006):82–92, as well as other sources. "In bankruptcy, when creditors cause harm to the debtor, try to gain unfair advantage over other creditors, or misrepresent the nature of their claims, judges can deny their claims, take away their votes, or send them to the back of the debt collection line." Argentinean officials had suggested using this principle to negate *their* debts.

"Repudiating all debts incurred under Yanukovich would discourage lending to corrupt leaders," she concludes.

The double standard here is that instead of labeling Ukraine's long series of kleptocrats and their corrupt governments "odious," she singles out only Yanukovich's tenure, as if his predecessors and successors were not equally venal. An even greater danger in declaring Ukraine's debt odious is that it may backfire on the United States, given its own long support for military dictatorships, corrupt client states and kleptocracies. U.S. backing for Chile's military dictatorship following General Pinochet's 1973 coup led to Operation Condor that installed Argentina's military dictatorship that ran up that country's foreign debt. Would a successful Ukrainian claim that its debt was odious open the legal floodgates for broad Latin American and Third World debt annulments?

Ukraine's sale of bonds to Russia's sovereign debt fund, as well as its contracts for gas purchases were negotiated by a democratically elected government, at low concessionary rates that subsidized industrial and household consumption. If this debt is deemed odious, what of the EU's insistence that Greece remove its Parliamentary leader Papandreou in 2011 to prevent a public referendum from taking place regarding the ECB loan? Loans made in the face of evident public opposition may be deemed to have been imposed without proper democratic consent.

Gelpern acknowledges that invoking the odious debt principle "is fraught with legal, political and market risks, all of which would play into Russia's hands." Fraught indeed! "The United Kingdom can refuse to enforce English-law contracts for the money Russia lent," thereby taking "away creditor remedies for default on this debt." But it also would end the City of London's rule of financial law, making it a US/NATO satellite.

A kindred legalistic stratagem to hurt Russia would be for Britain's Parliament to pass a sanctions law invalidating "the Yanukovich bonds." This would reduce Russia's "ability to profit from selling the debt on the market" and deny Russia legal rights to grab Ukrainian assets. "Debt contracts are routinely invalidated by the courts, rewritten in bankruptcy, and blocked by traditional sanctions," Gelpern observes. But if this can be done, why cannot the U.S. Congress pass a similar rule annulling vulture claims against Argentina and other debt-strapped Third World countries?

Gelpern's paper concludes by suggesting a universal principle: contracts "used to advance military and political objectives … should lose their claim to court enforcement." This opens quite a can of worms in view of the fact that "[t]he United Kingdom and the United States have both used military force

in the past to collect debts and influence weaker countries. Is it legitimate for
them to punish Russia for doing the same?" Are not the vast majority of inter-
governmental debts either military or political in character? On this logic, in
fact, shouldn't *all* inter-governmental debts be wiped out?

IMF support for Ukraine reflects its policy of backing regimes friendly to
U.S. investors. In April 2014 it approved a $17 billion loan program for
Ukraine. Normal IMF practice is to lend an amount only up to twice a
country's quota in one year, but it lent Ukraine's new junta eight times its
quota! Almost immediately, Ukrainian President Petro Poroshenko announced
new warfare against the eastern region to try and re-conquer Crimea. In June
2015 he announced that the €7 billion debt service falling due would be spent
instead on more military attacks on Ukraine's eastern provinces. The IMF loan
thus comes near to funding economic warfare.

International law, national sovereignty and real human rights

Should loans be deemed to be extortionate when they require austerity and
privatization selloffs? Such demands suggest that a radical change in legal and
financial structure is required far beyond Ukraine. As Argentine writers were
quick to point out:

> When Argentina suffered a massive default in 2001, the global press, including *Time* and
> *The New York Times*, went so far as to propose that Patagonia be ceded from the country
> as a defaulted debt payment mechanism. *The New York Times* article followed one
> published in the Buenos Aires financial newspaper *El Cronista Comercial* called "Debt for
> Territory," which described a proposal by a US consultant to then-president Eduardo
> Duhalde for swapping public debt for government land.[442]

Some Argentineans claim that the reckless loans made to the military dictatorship and the neoliberal Menem regime that drove the country needlessly into
debt were Odious Debts.[443] If such loans are made in the face of evident public

---

[442] Ellen Brown, "Colonization by Bankruptcy," *Counterpunch*, August 26, 2014, citing Adrian
       Salbuchi "Sovereign Debt for Territory: A New Global Elite Swap Strategy," *RT*, August
       12, 2014, http://rt.com/op-edge/179772-sovereign-debt-for-territory/

[443] The Odious Debt doctrine was formulated by Alexander Sack in 1927, but the United
       States used the principle to cancel Cuba's debt (run up by Spain's regime) in 1898, and
       Iraq's debt in 2003. For a broad survey Michael Kreme and Seema Jayachandran,
       "Odious Debt," *Finance and Development*, June 2002 (Vol. 30,No. 2), and http://www.
       jubileeusa.org/truth-about-debt/dont-owe-wont-pay/the-concept-of-odious-debt.html:
       "Odious debt is an established legal principle. Legally, debt is to be considered odious if
       the government used the money for personal purposes or to oppress the people." See also
       Ellen Brown, "Cry for Argentina: Fiscal Mismanagement, Odious Debt, or Pillage," *Truth-
       out*, August 14, 2014.

opposition, should they be deemed to have been imposed without proper democratic consent?

What is needed is a fair court to decide what is payable and what is not. As matters now stand, banks and bondholders seek to appoint their nominees as judges – the likes of Thomas Griesa treating sovereign debt as if there is no difference between a national economy and a family restaurant going out of business. It would take a different kind of public entity than currently exists to judge how far to impose austerity and transfer property to creditors to settle debts beyond the ability of governments to pay out of current revenue and, in the case of foreign-currency debts, out of balance-of-payments receipts.

In the face of concerted financial attempts to establish global neofeudalism, the world needs a declaration of sovereign human rights and political rights of nations. The principle of self-determination has long been written into international law, but the provision does not include self-determination from creditors taking over governments and appropriating their public domain to extract economic rent.

Failure to establish such a body of law will enable creditors to wage a divide-and-conquer strategy to break up one country after another, seize the public domain, impose interest charges as tribute, and shift political control to technocrats appointed to act on behalf of the world's financial centers.

IMF, ECB and BIS policy is marketed with a false view of how economies work – junk economics aimed at convincing populations that There Is No Alternative to austerity, impoverishment, unemployment and emigration under the rulership of an emerging Oligarchy of the One Percent.

The financial conflagration – some scenarios

While governments seek to avoid being subjected to debt serfdom by writing off their debts, bankers and bondholders are strategizing about how to preserve their financial claims when the day arrives that the debts must fall into default or be written down when austerity-ridden economies are unable to pay, except by borrowing more. Creditors hope to use such conditions as leverage to turn debtors into financial colonies.

The first response is an attempt to insure the uninsurable. Realistic bondholders will see that the game is up and debtors cannot earn enough to pay the compounded interest and arrears that have mounted up, especially as economies succumb to debt deflation, austerity, unemployment and emigration. Farsighted financial institutions will take out default insurance from the likes of AIG and monoline insurers, and negotiate credit default swaps with whomever they can find as counterparties. This is how John Paulson made a fortune, betting that the junk mortgage market would collapse and "going short" with his Goldman Sachs derivatives – making AIG and other insurers pay. If a crash could be fully insured, investors would collect "as if" the economy could continue unimpeded in the face of debt deflation path.

But who could afford to pay them? The amount needed to pay far exceeds the reserves of banks and insurance companies. They would have to have set aside reserves equal in magnitude to the entire exponential debt buildup – by being invested in the debts that are among those being burned in the great financial conflagration. So either these counterparties holding CDS will go bankrupt when the time arrives that the debts can't be paid, or governments will print the money or tax populations to reimburse the One Percent for losses on their investments gone bad.

Managers of these insurance companies and banks may sell increasingly risky debt-guarantee policies at rising prices. As the Ponzi-like accumulation of debt approaches its climax, their profits will rise and enable them to pay themselves higher salaries and bonuses. Then, when defaults wipe out the debts, insurers will say that there are not enough reserves to pay the CDS, or annuities and pensions for that matter, and will fold up business. But managers of companies writing these CDS will have enjoyed enough Bubble years to be able to emulate Rome's patricians and convert their takings into landed estates, gated communities or farms onto which they can withdraw.

If the stock markets crash and deprive pension funds and other investors of the financialized savings on which retirees had depended, while the One Percent seek to make up their losses from labor and the government, blaming overly generous pensions to the 99 Percent. The reality, of course, is that corporate managers and local governments have under-funded them with overly utopian financialization forecasts. Also blamed will be central banks for spending money to revive employment and GNP. But in reality, austerity crashes markets because central banks *refuse* to do this.

The crash may become prolonged where governments lack the political ability to write off debts owed to the One Percent. There is no technological or inherent economic reason for this financial Ragnarök to become the fate of North America and Europe. But it is the choice that is being promoted by the financial sector's lobbyists, pet academics and public media that fail to admit how debt deflation destroys the economy's ability to grow.

Coda: Absence of an international court to adjudicate sovereign debts

Existing bankruptcy law from New York State to the London and Paris clubs is designed to carve up assets of money-losing family restaurants, other business and personal bankruptcies, not with sovereign debt restructuring such as have thrown world financial markets into turmoil since summer 2014. That is what has made Argentina so important a battleground to create a legal alternative to the hard creditor rules adjudicated in creditor-nation courts or the IMF.

U.S. resistance to a new global court outside of its control has maintained a vacuum filled by default by local U.S. law. By letting holdouts demand full payment even when a majority of creditors agree to a write-down, the effect is to block any negotiated writedowns of sovereign debt. This pro-creditor default policy leaves no court or body of economic theory to determine the ability to pay or assess the consequences of debt repayment.

Leaving Argentina's debt resolution in the hands of local New York bankruptcy courts has spurred attempts to create an alternative global financial system to the dollar area and its satellite eurozone. The BRICS have been driven together into a critical economic mass to defend their sovereignty and policy independence. A quantum leap occurred in July 2014. Russia and its BRICS partners (China, Brazil, India and South Africa) took the lead toward creating an alternative financial system, starting with a $50 billion BRICS bank and a $100 billion intra-BRICS financial clearing system as an alternative to the IMF and World Bank.

The aim of these countries, along with Argentina and Iran, is to insulate themselves from neoliberal economic policy, debt coercion, forced privatization selloffs and asset seizures. Under today's conditions this will entail debt writedowns, backed by a body of theory to analyze an economy's ability to pay domestic and foreign-currency creditors.

27
Finance As Warfare

To simple people it is indubitable that the nearest cause of the enslavement of one class of men by another is money. They know that it is possible to cause more trouble with a rouble than with a club; it is only political economy that does not want to know it.

Leo Tolstoy, *What Shall We Do Then?* (1886)[444]

The financial sector has the same objective as military conquest: to gain control of land and basic infrastructure, and collect tribute. To update von Clausewitz, finance has become war by other means. What formerly took blood and arms is now obtained by debt leverage. Direct ownership is not necessary. If a country's economic surplus can be taken financially, it is not necessary to conquer or even to own its land, natural resources and infrastructure. Debt leverage saves the cost of having to mount an invasion and suffer casualties. Who needs an expensive occupation against unwilling hosts when you can obtain assets willingly by financial means – as long as debt-strapped nations permit bankers and bondholders to dictate their laws and control their planning and politics?

The creditor's objective is to obtain wealth by indebting populations and even governments, and forcing them to pay by relinquishing their property or its income. Such financial conquest is less overtly brutal than warfare waged with guns and missiles, but its demographic effect is just as lethal. For debt-strapped Greece and Latvia, creditor-imposed austerity has caused falling marriage rates, family formation and birth rates, shortening life spans, and rising suicide rates and emigration.

War as the catalyst for national debts

The first recorded example of compound interest calculating the tribute owed to the Sumerian city of Lagash by neighboring Umma after a fight over their buffer territory in the 25th century BC. Inscribed on the Stele of the Vultures,

---

[444] *Complete Works of Leo Tolstoy*, ed. Leo Wiener, Vol. XVIII [London: 1904], p. 124.

the astronomically high levy led to prolonged future conflict, not unlike the reparations imposed by the Allies on Germany after World War I.

From antiquity down through medieval Europe, wars were viewed as profitable propositions yielding loot and tribute. Historians find a military origin of coined money in Greece, in the form of booty being melted down and divided among the officers and troops, with a tithe donated to the city-temple. Mesopotamian, classical Greek and Roman temples were adorned with the spoils of war, monetizing their bullion in war emergencies to pay mercenaries. The word "money" derives from Rome's Temple of Juno Moneta, where the city minted its first silver and gold coins during the Punic wars with Carthage. It was said that the honking of the Juno temple's geese warned Rome's commander of the impending attack by the Gauls in 390 BC. Hence, Juno's epithet Moneta, from Latin *monera*, "to warn" (also the root of "monster," an omen).

"Money, endless money, is the sinews of war," wrote Cicero in his *Philippics* (43 BC). Not only money, but credit, too. Venice financed the Crusade against Constantinople in 1204 for a quarter of the loot, which it and other Italians monetized and lent to secular kings to wage their own wars of conquest. This influx of silver and gold from the looting of Constantinople catalyzed the financial sector's rise to power. After 1492 the looting of the New World provided silver and gold to finance the expansion of commerce – and also the increasingly expensive imperial rivalries to carve out new conquests.

Financializing the costs of war led to public debts and the modern bond market. Rulers borrowed to buy cannons and build navies, pay troops, hire mercenaries and support allies. Indeed, warfare became financialized long before industry or real estate. And as in any financialized sector, creditors usually ended up with the winnings. Governments issued interest-bearing *bonds*, a word that originally meant physical shackles on bondservants, a fitting analogy for the position in which governments found themselves. They typically paid off these war debts by selling land, mines and creating public monopolies to exchange for bonds they had issued.

War debts as the mother of royal monopolies

The Church's banking orders – the Knights Templar and Hospitallers – lent to kings and nobles at the top of the social pyramid, first to embark on the Crusades and then to wage wars backed by the papacy. Being uniquely free from religious censure against gain-seeking – along with the high status of their borrowers – permitted an end-run around Church doctrine condemning the charging of interest. It was only a short step to legitimize commercial credit, on the ground that trade helped unify nations as part of divine order giving each region its own particular role to play in global harmony.

Playing the role that the temples of Athena and Juno Moneta had done in antiquity, bankers financed military conquest. Unlike the case in antiquity, owing royal debts to private bankers (often foreign) instead of to public temples led to a proliferation of taxes to pay their interest charges. Rulers sought to pay down the principal by creating Crown trading monopolies and selling them for payment in royal war bonds.

The new owners tended to be foreign. The Dutch became major investors in England's Crown monopolies (including the Bank of England, formed in 1694) as high finance became the mother of monopolies: the East and West Indies Companies in Holland, England and France after about 1600, and the South Sea and Mississippi Companies in the 1710s. Remitting their dividends and interest abroad caused a balance-of-payments drain whose monetary effect was like paying tribute to military victors.

The traditional objective of warfare – conquest of the land and natural monopolies to siphon off their rent – has become the prime objective of today's high finance. The strategy is more peaceful, but retains a tributary character. Debt leverage forced Britain and France in the 17th and 18th centuries, the Ottoman Empire in the 19th century, Latin American and African governments the 20th century, to sell off assets to buyers eager to turn public services into opportunities for rent extraction.

Since 2008 a similar strategy of asset grabbing has been used against Portugal, Ireland, Italy, Greece and Spain. The idea is to enable privatizers to turn industrial economies into tollbooth opportunities. The idea in today's New Enclosure Movement is to privatize what used to be called the Commons. Russians call this grabitization – privatization of public enterprises and natural resources by insiders and their backers.

Novelists and historians have been more willing than economists to recognize this dynamic. Honoré de Balzac quipped in *Le Père Goriot* that behind every family fortune is a great theft, long forgotten or indeed "never been found out, because it was properly executed." But not all such origins are forgotten. A century ago Gustavus Myers' *History of the Great American Fortunes* uncovered how many family fortunes were taken from the public domain by colonial land grants, bribery and insider dealing – and how such fortunes quickly take a financial form.

Having gained enough control over government policy to privatize public assets, the financial sector provides credit to buy the right to install tollbooths on hitherto public roads, railroads, airlines and other transport infrastructure, phone and communications systems. The aim is to extract monopoly rent instead of providing basic services freely or at subsidized rates. Financialization means using this rent extraction for debt service.

Avoiding war's financial cost leads to classical liberalism

Until the world went off gold in 1971, waging war and paying interest to foreign bondholders required payment in bullion. Gaining monetary bullion by running a trade surplus required competitive pricing of industrial exports. This meant minimizing the cost of labor and its living expenses. Imperial economies that spent vast sums on wars and colonial rivalries raised money by taxing cities and consumers to pay interest on their war debts.

In Book V of *The Wealth of Nations*, Adam Smith describes how each new war loan in England was given a specific dedicated excise tax to pay its interest. By the time of the Seven Years War between the French and British in America (1754-63), such war making and taxing was raising labor's cost of living and hence the basic wage, as did the creation and sale of monopolies. High taxes and prices deterred the development of industry, limiting the ability to wage war. That was the basic conundrum that inspired Britain to transition to "free trade imperialism."

The perception that military fighting had become a losing proposition economically led early liberals such as Smith to oppose royal wars, colonization and the taxes levied to pay their costs. The cost of imperial overhead was more than most empires were worth. Smith urged Britain to give the American colonies their independence so as to free it from having to bear the cost of their defense. His contemporary Josiah Tucker described the colonies as "a millstone around the neck of England." It was cheaper to give them political liberty, using credit and investment as more efficient modes of exploitation.

A rising element of cost in the modern world reflects the pricing of infrastructure services. Public investment traditionally has sought to minimize such costs. But banking viewed great infrastructure projects such as railroads and canal building (capped by the Panama and Suez Canals) as major opportunities to profiteer at the economy's expense. Underwriting fees and speculative gains have been as important as interest extraction, while fraud and kleptocracy always have been rife. That is how America's railroad barons, monopolists and trust builders became the nation's power elite a century ago, and how post-Soviet oligarchs seized public assets after the neoliberal 1991 "reforms." This is what makes financialization antithetical to classical economy's value and price theory.

Financial avoidance of public taxes and duties

Now that land ownership has been democratized – on credit – a majority of most populations (two-thirds in the United States, and over four-fifths in Scandinavia) no longer pay rent to landlords. Instead, homeowners and commercial property investors pay most of the rental value to bankers as mortgage interest. In the United States, bankers obtain about two-thirds of real estate cash flow, largely by reducing property taxes. The more the financial sector can reduce the government's tax take, the more rent is available for new buyers to pay interest to banks for loans to buy property. This explains why the financial sector backs anti-tax "Tea Party" protests.

It is much the same in industry. Financial analysts pore over corporate balance sheets to measure the cash flow over and above the direct cost of production and doing business. This measure is called *ebitda*: earnings before interest, taxes, depreciation and amortization. Owners and their creditors aim to make as much of this income tax exempt – and they achieve this largely by making interest a tax-deductible expense.

Creditors always have sought to break free of tax liability. Lower property taxes leave more rent available to pay bankers, and making interest payments tax-deductible leaves more corporate cash flow available to be paid to bondholders than to stockowners receiving dividends. Banks now receive most of the rental value of land as mortgage interest, at the expense of the tax collector, while bondholders obtain a rising share of corporate profits (or more accurately, of overall ebitda – earnings before interest, taxes, depreciation and amortization) also at the tax collector's expense.

All this lowering of taxes on finance and real estate widens government budget deficits. If bankers can also block governments from creating public money to finance these deficits, the shortfall must be met by borrowing from private bankers – or else, taxes may be raised on labor and industry. And in due course as public debts grow too large to be paid out of shrinking tax revenue, creditors demand that governments balance their budgets by privatizing public assets and enterprises. The effect is to turn the public domain into a vast set of rent-extracting opportunities for banks to finance.

This is the kind of resource grab the IMF and World Bank imposed on Third World debtors for many decades. It is how Carlos Slim obtained Mexico's telephone monopoly to impose exorbitant charges on business and the population at large. It can be seen most recently in the demands by the European Union, European Central Bank and IMF to force Greece and Cyprus to pay their foreign debts by selling whatever land, oil and gas rights, ports and infrastructure remain in their public domain. What is privatized will become an opportunity to extract monopoly "tollbooth" rents.

This financialization and rent extraction is quite different from what classical economists defined as "profit" made by investing in plant and equipment and employing labor to produce goods and services. The financial sector makes its gains by its privilege of credit creation to obtain interest, fees, and commissions, paid largely out of land rent and monopoly rent. All these forms of revenue are external charges on top of production costs.

The role of debt in the war against labor

As labor's wages rose above subsistence levels a century ago, economic futurists depicted a post-industrial leisure economy. Left out of account was that the passport to middle-class status involved democratizing property ownership and education on credit, driving labor into debt to buy housing and, more recently, to get an education.

Financial exploitation of labor also occurs when corporate raiders buy out stockholders with high-interest "junk" bonds as their weapon of choice. The effect is to turn industry into a vehicle for bankers to load down with debt. Corporate raiders may pay their creditors by seizing or downgrading employee pension funds from defined benefit plans (in which workers know how much they will receive when they retire) to "defined contribution plans." In the latter, employees only know how much is to be paid in each month, not what will be left for them after financial managers take their cut.[445] (It's a big cut.) Pension maneuvering becomes a tactic in class warfare when companies threaten to declare bankruptcy if employees do not renegotiate their pension rights, wage levels and working conditions downward.

The rule of the financial jungle is that big fish eat little fish. Companies use Employee Stock Ownership Plans (ESOPs) to buy up their own stock, enabling managers to cash out their stock options at a higher price. A rule of thumb has long been that about half the ESOPs are wiped out in corporate bankruptcies.[446] After Sam Zell's leveraged buyout of the *Chicago Tribune*, the newspaper's employees were left holding an empty ESOP.

Federal Reserve Chairman Alan Greenspan described the role of rising personal and mortgage debt in today's evolving class warfare. Under normal conditions unemployment at the relatively low 1997 rate (about 5.4 percent, the same as in the boom years 1967 and 1979) would have led to rising wage levels as employers competed to hire more workers. However, Greenspan

---

[445] In 1979, 28 percent of American workers were beneficiaries of defined benefit programs that guaranteed them an income from the day they retired until the day they died. That number is now only 3 percent.

[446] Peter Drucker, *The Unseen Revolution: How Pension Fund Socialism Came to America* (New York: 1976), p. 36: The ESOPS promoted by Louis Kelso and others "would make the workers 'owners' but, for half or more of them, in bankrupt companies or declining industries, thus depriving them of the pension they need."

explained to the U.S. Senate, a high rate of unemployment no longer was needed to hold down wages. All that was needed was job insecurity:

> As I see it, heightened job insecurity explains a significant part of the restraint on compensation and the consequent muted price inflation.
>
> Surveys of workers have highlighted this extraordinary state of affairs. In 1991, at the bottom of the recession, a survey of workers at large firms indicated that 25 percent feared being laid off. In 1996, despite the sharply lower unemployment rate and the demonstrably tighter labor market … 46 percent were fearful of a job layoff.[447]

Despite the increase in labor productivity from fewer strikes and more intensive working conditions), U.S. wages were failing to rise. A major reason, Chairman Greenspan pointed out, was that workers were afraid to go on strike or even to complain about working conditions for fear of losing their paychecks, defaulting on their mortgage and falling behind on their monthly credit card bills and seeing their interest rates explode as their credit ratings declined. In July 1997 testimony he said that a major factor contributing to the "extraordinary" U.S. economic performance was "a heightened sense of job insecurity and, as a consequence, subdued wage gains."[448] Bob Woodward reported that Greenspan called this the "traumatized worker" effect as attrition spread the same volume of work among fewer employees, squeezing out higher "productivity."

Median U.S. household income rose by a mere 15 percent during 2001–06 while mortgage credit inflated the cost of housing by 74 percent. Heavy mortgage debt and other housing and living costs have made workers feel one paycheck away from homelessness. As employees became debt ridden, widespread home ownership became a euphemism for a cowed labor force. Austerity's squeeze on labor is tightened rents and consumer debt rise, along with shifts to part-time or lower-wage jobs and outright unemployment.

Financial appropriation of labor's disposable personal income

The classical idea of a post-industrial leisure economy was to free nations from rent and interest overhead to bring prices in line with necessary direct costs of production, with governments subsidizing basic services out of progressive taxes or new money creation. By contrast, today's financialized version of "free

---

447   Statement by Alan Greenspan, Chairman, Board of Governors of the Federal Reserve System, before the Committee on Banking, Housing, and Urban Affairs, U.S. Senate, February 26, 1997 - Statements to the Congress. A Transcript also was published in the April 1997 *Federal Reserve Bulletin*.

448   Testimony of Chairman Alan Greenspan before the Committee on Banking, Housing, and Urban Affairs, U.S. Senate July 22, 1997: "The Federal Reserve's semiannual monetary policy," http://www.federalreserve.gov/boarddocs/hh/1997/july/testimony.htm.

markets" obliges families to spend their life working mainly to pay banks for the credit needed to survive in today's world.

Saddling students and homebuyers with debt has turned their hopes and ambition into a road to insolvency. People can choose *which* bank to borrow from, *which* home to buy with a 30-year working-life mortgage, and *which* college to take out an education loan to attend. But whatever their choice, they are subjected to a financialized version of the Company Store, a deregulated and predatory economy. Something must give way when earnings are unable to cover the stipulated debt service. If banks do not write down their loans, foreclosure time arrives and assets will be forfeited.

Next to home ownership, education is the path to the middle class. Student loans are now the second largest category of personal debt (over $1.3 trillion as of 2015, exceeding the volume of credit-card debt). Carrying charges on this debt absorb over 25 percent of the income for many graduates from lower-income families.

The 2005 U.S. bankruptcy code, written largely by bank and credit-card lobbyists, makes it harder to write off personal debts in general, and nearly impossible for student loans to be cleared. The effect is to turn many graduates into indentured servants, obliged to spend much of their working lives paying off the debt taken on to obtain a degree – or even for failure to complete their studies, most notoriously at for-profit crypto-colleges funded by government guaranteed student debt. The easiest way for many graduates to make ends meet is to live at home with their parents. Inability to save enough for a home of their own slows the rate of marriages and family formation.

By imposing an access fee on the entry point into the middle class job market, privatizing and financializing the educational system raises the cost of living and. This reverses the policy long followed by the United States, Germany and other successful nations that made their economies more competitive by providing education and other basic services freely or at subsidized rates. Creating a need for loans at the educational choke point turns universities into vehicles for banks to earn government-guaranteed interest.

Much as interest charges on home mortgages end up giving banks a larger sum than the sales price received by the sellers, student loan payments often give the bank as much interest income over time as the college or trade school has received as tuition. Consumer credit, home mortgage and education loans thus treat the labor force much as feudal landlords treated the land and its occupants: as a source of tribute.

From finance capitalism to neofeudalism

Hiding behind an Orwellian rhetoric that inverts the classical idea of a free market, financial planners are leading the world down the autocratic path that Spain and France took five hundred years ago. Without contributing to production, *rentier* income is overwhelmingly responsible for the wealthiest One Percent obtaining 73 percent of U.S. income growth since the 2008 crash, while the 99 Percent have seen their net worth decline. Yet in contrast to classical economics, Piketty's much-applauded neoliberal attempt to explain today's economic polarization does not single out finance and rent-seeking, so his remedy does not include focusing tax collection on *rentier* income or de-privatizing infrastructure monopolies by restoring a mixed public/private economy.[449]

The drive to widen political democracy was expected to avoid this fate. Voters were expected to elect politicians who would put in place fiscal and regulatory checks against *rentiers*, so that industrial capitalism could use its economic surplus to expand markets and, in the process, raise living standards. The idea of asset-price inflation as a financial strategy, extending credit in ways decoupled from helping economies grow, was nowhere on the intellectual horizon. Thorstein Veblen was almost alone in explaining how Wall Street's financial engineering was undercutting industrial capital formation.

Paying bankers and bondholders at the "real" economy's expense is antithetical to industrial capitalism. The financial business plan is to turn economies into a set of rent traps, carving out privileges whose purchase and sale is financed by banks and bondholders. Instead of lowering the cost of basic services to make economies more competitive, the effect is to load them down with debt to extract interest, fees and *rentier* overhead. This destructive policy inflates the economy's cost structure by building in higher user fees for the privatized monopolies and a rising flow of debt service to bankers, while imposing debt and rent deflation on the core economy.

Replacing government as our epoch's central planners, the aim of Wall Street, the City of London, Frankfurt and other financial centers is to draw into their own hands all the economy's net income, followed by the assets that produce it. It is easier to make money by financial manipulation and debt-leveraged bubbles than by the hard work of designing new products, organ-

---

[449] I elaborate this point in "Piketty vs. the classical economic reformers," in Edward Fullbrook and Jamie Morgan, eds., *Piketty's* Capital in the Twenty-First Century (World Economics Association Books, 2014), pp. 189–202.

izing production facilities, hiring and training labor and a marketing and sales force. That is why the shift of economic and social planning into the hands of financial managers has undercut the U.S. and British economies as industrial exporters.

Financializing the income streams from tollbooth privileges is not about earning profits by tangible productive capital investment. It is about appropriating the public domain on credit. This financial mode of expropriation reverses the happy assumption that the momentum of historical progress will, by itself, ensure the primacy of legal systems regulating property and creditor/debtor relationships in the economy's broad long-term interest. The consequence of real estate, corporate control, monopoly rights and access to education and other basic needs being bought increasingly on credit is to turn nominal ownership into mere stewardship on behalf of the banks and bondholders. This locking of populations into paying financial tribute is now portrayed as a moral and legal right.

The *rentier* rake-off of revenue is not a necessary cost of production. It makes economies less competitive. Instead of the industrial capitalism envisioned by classical reformers who hoped to free the economy from rent-extracting elites, this *rentier* mode of exploitation is a regression to feudal-type privileges for elites to charge extortionate prices for basic needs. It is what Hyman Minsky called "money manager capitalism," allocating savings and credit to serve the One Percent in extractive ways, pushing a widening swath of the population into austerity and negative equity.

Today's bankers and bondholders are expropriating property owners in ways not anticipated a century ago, when elites worried that socialism might play this role. At that time the financial sector appeared to be the strongest buttress of the security of property, if only because collateral needs to be secure in order to be pledged for a loan. But foreclosure-wielding creditors always have threatened to expropriate indebted owners.

The greatest threat to broad income distribution, economic efficiency and higher living standards thus turns out not to be finance capitalism, not socialism. Families have been pushed, prodded and seduced onto the debt treadmill to pay a rising tribute for what they imagine is to be their economic independence in owning a home. Bank mortgages accounted for 60 percent of the overall value of U.S. housing by 2012. As market prices fell while debts remained in place after 2008, the share of homes actually owned by American homeowners plunged below 40 percent. The price is long-term debt servitude, along with the cost of getting an education these days.

The financial cover story to reverse classical tax and economic reforms

Under classical political economy and socialism (at least of the type expressed after Europe's 1848 revolutions), governments were to receiving the rental income of land and natural resources. Instead, today's financial sector is privatizing these rents for itself and its clients. In conjunction with this rent extraction, the essence of debt serfdom is to siphon off disposable personal income by obliging homebuyers, students and consumers to pay all their net earnings above subsistence as interest. For most homebuyers, market equilibrium prices are set at the point where debt service absorbs the full site-rental price. This phenomenon reflects the degree to which the core policy aim of classical economic doctrine has been reversed and, if the financial sector has its way, consigned to oblivion.

A similar predatory financial dynamic has taken over industry. As Chapter 8 has described, creditors finance corporate raiders who pay out profits as interest and cut back capital investment so as to use earnings simply for stock buybacks and quick dividend payouts to raise its price. Financial short-termism is thus the opposite of industrial forward planning and tangible capital formation.

Bankers depict their extraction of debt service as a necessary cost of production, as if the economy would not work without their service of allocating resources to decide who best should receive credit. In reality, banks push debt onto anyone with property to collateralize or earning power to sequester. Their business plan is to maximize financial claims *on* the means of production, up to the limit at which interest absorbs the total disposable income – leaving debtors to perform the economy's actual work.

Pro-creditor ideology depicts loans and credit as enriching borrowers along with lenders in a fair bargain that produces gains for everyone. Borrowers acquiesce in the financialization of real estate as long as they believe that buying homes (or academic degrees) on credit may enrich them. They are willing to submit to austerity if they believe it is a necessary interlude to resume economic progress. The reality is that it sinks them deeper into debt, while widening government budget deficits and leading to demands by the One Percent to cut back social services, starting with pensions and Social Security.

Pro-creditor deceptions require censoring the economic history of how financial dynamics actually have evolved, because the lessons are clear enough over the millennia. Little lending has funded new means of production. That is the financial tragedy of our time: Neither the banking system nor the stock market is funding tangible capital formation to increase production, employment and living standards. Instead, exponentially rising debt service creates a chain reaction that weighs down the economy until it collapses into an inert leaden state.

Meanwhile, the One Percent endow business schools and "think tanks" to convince the public that there is no such thing as unearned income and wealth. The demographic effect of blurring this concept can be seen in statistics of rising suicide rates, shortening life spans and falling birth rates, and emigration.

A blind spot to these corrosive effects of financial practice is what makes post-classical *rentier* ideology "value-free." Making money from privatization, asset-price inflation (the Bubble Economy) and corporate looting is euphemized as "wealth creation." Banks create credit to bid up prices of existing real estate, stocks and bonds, while the stock market serves as a vehicle for corporate raiding and leveraged buyouts to replace equity with high-interest bonds. Instead of alleviating debt pressures, the financial system raises dependency on further credit to carry the debt burden.

The destructive character of financial conquest

The owl of wisdom only flies at night. Only after a major collapse is it easier to see the wrongheaded turns that have been taken. Debt-leveraged buyouts have not financed new capital investment, but have bled companies to pay bondholders and activist shareholders. But until Warren Buffet characterized Wall Street's derivatives as weapons of mass financial destruction, most economists failed to recognize the destructive power of debt creation and how the One Percent lend out their savings to indebt the 99 Percent. The effect is much like the physicist J. Robert Oppenheimer's 1965 description of the atom bomb's Trinity Explosion, when he recalled the *Bhagavad Gita*'s words of Vishnu: "I am become death, destroyer of worlds."

From F. Scott Fitzgerald's *The Great Gatsby* to Tom Wolfe's *Bonfire of the Vanities*, novelists have symbolized the very rich as irresponsible auto drivers killing innocent pedestrians. "They were careless people, Tom and Daisy," wrote Fitzgerald; "they smashed up things and creatures and then retreated back into their money or their vast carelessness or whatever it was that kept them together, and let other people clean up the mess they had made."

That is what makes the rich different. The collateral damage from their attacks is as irresponsible as it is devastating. They are insensitive to how their actions impact the life of others. Posing as "job creators," *rentiers* claim to be proxies acting like shepherds as a virtual government. Their wealth is supposed to trickle down, somehow, as if by helping themselves financially, they also will help economies grow. So today's creditors call financialization "wealth creators," whom Goldman Sachs describes as "doing God's work."

Just as the drivers in *Gatsby* and *Bonfire* responsible for crashes left others to bear the blame, so the One Percent seeks to shift responsibility onto the financial victims ("the madness of crowds"). Governments are blamed for running deficits, despite the fact that they result mainly from tax favoritism to the *rentiers*. Having used FICA paycheck withholding as a ploy to cut progressive tax rates on themselves since the 1980s, the One Percent blame the indebted population for living longer and creating a "retirement problem" by collecting the Social Security and pensions.

This is financial warfare – and not all wars end with the victory of the most progressive parties. The end of history is not necessarily utopia. The financial mode of conquest against labor and industry is as devastating today as in the Roman Republic's Social War that marked its transition to Empire in the 1st century BC. It was the dynamics of debt above all that turned the empire into a wasteland, reducing the population to debt bondage and outright slavery.

Livy, Plutarch and other Roman historians placed the blame for their epoch's collapse on creditors. Tacitus reports the words of the Celtic chieftain Calgacus, c. 83 AD, rousing his troops by describing the empire they were to fight against:

> Robbers of the world, having by their universal plunder exhausted the land ... If the enemy is rich, they are rapacious; if he is poor, they lust for dominion; neither the east nor the west has been able to satisfy them. ... To robbery, slaughter, plunder, they give the lying name of empire. They make a wasteland and call it peace.[450]

The peace brought by Rome turned out to be a world reverting to subsistence production on the land as cities became deserted. Rome became the model of what happens to economies that do not annul their debts but polarize between creditors and debtors. Its history – and hence, antiquity – ended in a convulsion of depopulation and a Dark Age.

Commanded by a creditor oligarchy, Rome's imperial conquest was belligerent, with an oppressive anti-labor spirit that Tacitus explained elsewhere (*Agricola* 32): "It belongs to human nature to hate those you have injured." The financial sector's awareness of how rapaciously it obtains its wealth makes it fear and hence hate its victims.

---

[450] *Agricola* 30: *Auferre, trucidare, rapere, falsis nominibus imperium; atque, ubi solitudinem faciunt, pacem appellant.* Translation based on the Loeb Classical Library edition. The chieftain's sentiment can be contrasted to the Orwellian motto "peace given to the world" frequently inscribed on Roman medals, so Tacitus may have been using sarcasm and irony.

So we are brought back to the basic theme of this book: Contrary to expectations when the Industrial Revolution was gaining momentum, finance is stifling industrial potential, raising the specter of lapsing back into the ancient usury dynamic with exponentially accruing debt dependency. Much like creditors in ancient Rome, today's financial power seeks to replace democracy with oligarchy. We are seeing a resurgence of "primitive accumulation" by debt creation, foreclosure and privatization.

The oligarchic strategy is to politicize this financial drive. Here as usual, novelists are ahead of the economics textbooks. As Mario Puzo summarized matters in his movie scenario for *The Godfather*, Part III (1990):

> Vincent Mancini: Don Lucchesi, you are a man of finance and politics. These things I don't understand.
> Don Lucchesi: You understand guns?
> Vincent Mancini: Yes.
> Don Lucchesi: Finance is a gun. Politics is knowing when to pull the trigger.

The ECB, EU commission and the IMF held the financial gun to Greece's head in June 2015, and pulled the political trigger to pressure Greece to a "regime change" by threatening the Greek Prime Minister Tsipras with financial crisis if he did not adhere to the program negotiated by the pro-austerity Pasok and Conservative coalition he had recently been elected to replace.[451] The weapon perhaps is better characterized as a financial noose, drawn tighter each day.

---

[451] Claire Jones, "ECB tries to avoid having any blood on its hands," *Financial Times*, June 24, 2015.

28

Is the Mode of Parasitism Over-shadowing the Mode of Production?

In an era of finance, finance mostly finances finance.

Jan Toporowski, *Why the World Economy Needs a Financial Crash and Other Critical Essays on Finance and Financial Economics* (London: 2010), p. xl.

Nearly all economic writings published in the late 19th and early 20th century defined wealth in terms of the means of production: factories, plant and machinery, technology and public investment in infrastructure and education. Seeing the Industrial Revolution's soaring rise in productivity stemming from the use of energy – from water power to steam power to internal combustion engines and electrification – economists anticipated a leisure economy.

Today's deepening austerity, unemployment and emigration is not a failure of this technological potential; nor is it the kind of overproduction crisis that early critics of industrial capitalism warned about: wage labor being paid too little to buy the goods it produces. Employers exploiting wage labor are always a problem, of course. But today's overwhelming economic problem is predatory finance, to a degree that few expected a century ago, with the notable exception of Thorstein Veblen.[452]

Thomas Piketty's *Capital in the 21st Century* has quantified what nearly everyone knew intuitively: The One Percent have doubled their share of wealth over the past generation. Less attention has been paid to *how* they amassed this wealth. It has not been by investing in capital goods and hiring labor in the way textbooks describe industrial capitalists as doing. Most fortunes are

---

[452] Marx discussed the "all-devouring" dynamic of compound interest, but expected capitalism to avoid it as banking became industrialized and productive. Since Lenin and Rudolf Hilferding wrote about finance capitalism in the World War I period, the political left has focused more on labor issues than on finance and rent.

made by rent seeking and debt pyramiding, financializing real estate and corporate industry, and creating or privatizing monopolies.[453]

The most pressing political struggle of our time is how to cope with financial centers in control of central banks and governments, plunging economies deeper into austerity, leaving the industrial economy by the wayside. "Banks no longer 'lend' to the non-bank business sector," writes UMKC professor Jan Kregel. "If at all they primarily lend to themselves, *i.e.* to other financial institutions."[454]

The taproots feeding this financial power are real estate rent, natural resource rent and monopoly rent, which are capitalized into interest-bearing debt and debt-leveraged "capital" gains. This financialization based on rent extraction has transformed the character of wealth. Instead of investing in plant and equipment to hire more labor to produce more output, money is made financially, while the economy shrinks.

Already in the 19th century, economists across the political spectrum, from Marx to Henry George, described financial claims as "fictitious capital." Frederick Soddy, the great English chemist and polymath, called financial claims "virtual wealth." But few expected creditor claims in the form of bonds, stocks and bank loans on the "liabilities" side of the balance sheet, to become dominant over the asset side – the material means of production. That would be like a shadow taking over a body. But that is what has occurred.

There was no thought that free-lunch rent would be capitalized into interest-bearing bank loans to become the basis for most bank credit and debt creation. Rent was expected either to be taxed away (if rent-yielding land rent and natural resource rent was left in private hands) or rent-yielding assets would be nationalized and socialized

Financialization of economic rent is mainly responsible for polarizing today's economies, and then shrinking them by debt deflation. Today's financial mode of "wealth creation" by arbitrage, derivative gambles and credit pyramiding – capped by foreclosure and privatization – is overpowering the industrial mode of production, making fortunes on a much vaster scale than profits created by industrial capital. These fortunes are made at the economy's expense. In alliance with other rent-extracting sectors, finance acts from above

---

[453] I elaborate this point in "Piketty vs. the classical economic reformers," in Edward Fullbrook and Jamie Morgan, eds., *Piketty's* Capital *in the Twenty-First Century* (World Economics Association Books, 2014), pp. 189-202.

[454] Jan Kregel, "Is this the Minsky Moment for reform of financial regulation?" in Sebastian Dullien, Eckhard Hein, Achim Truger and Till van Treeck, *The World Economy in Crisis – the Return of Keynesianism?* (Marburg 2010), p. 225.

the industrial economy to indebt it and then rake off debt service, while inflating access prices to housing, education and infrastructure services.

So much of the wage earner's paycheck must be diverted to pay debt service and rent extraction that the domestic market for goods dries up. Instead of the promised leisure economy, the world is entering a financialized Age of Austerity. Labor may be paid more and more, but its rising wages are stripped to pay the Finance, Insurance and Real Estate (FIRE) sector.

Unproductive fortune building, free lunches and their apologists

No one likes freeloaders. Children of the rich are especially prone to worry about being unproductive. "Inheritors of wealth," a psychologist on the Wells Fargo wealth team observes, "'feel they don't deserve money and have shame and guilt. They feel isolated and closeted.' Even the language we use to describe such people is mocking ... 'There are so many negative words attached to inheritors: trust-fund baby, silver spoon, spoiled brat – there's no positive associations.'"[455]

In contrast to this negative but realistic self-image, lobbyists for *rentiers* provide their clients with a productive mask. For banks, the trick is to convince borrowers that debt leveraging will help borrowers obtain wealth – and to accept their losses when their dreams turn into a living nightmare, blaming themselves instead of the system. The public relations aim is to numb popular awareness of the fact that running into debt historically has meant losing the homestead and the public Commons of entire nations. Claiming that there is no free lunch, they depict the One Percent as productive helpers in a symbiosis for mutual gain. Indoctrinating his Harvard students to defend the One Percent who get rich in banking and finance, America's leading textbook writer Greg Mankiw attributes their wealth to their "service" of allocating society's resources:

> Those who work in banking, venture capital and other financial firms are in charge of allocating the economy's investment resources. They decide, in a decentralized and competitive way, which companies and industries will shrink and which will grow. It makes sense that a nation would allocate many of its most talented and thus highly compensated individuals to the task.

Bankers appear as prudent lenders guiding credit to what is most productive. "Right, right," comments one blogger: "These are the clowns who allocated a shit-ton of capital to building whole counties full of homes with styrofoam

---

[455] Dr. Jamie Traeger-Muney, quoted by Emma Jacobs, "Shrinks with cash on the couch," *Financial Times*, January 10, 2014.

pediments during the last housing bubble, which culminated in the largest
upward transfer of wealth in world history."[456] But despite the fact that
financial institutions have proven to be a disaster in the way they have allocated
savings and credit mainly to indebt the rest of the economy, it has been a
calamity for the 99 Percent, not for themselves. Their maneuverings have made
them rich.

Most fortunes grow simply by inertia, accruing interest and rent charges
"in the recipient's sleep," to paraphrase John Stuart Mill's description of landlords. The winning strategy is to extend credit to indebt the rest of society. The
debt overhead that makes most of the money for the One Percent is paid for
by the 99 Percent, leaving less and less for investment or living standards. So
today's main political issue is how to save economies from the financial sector's
alliance with rent extractors – and the *rentiers'* coordinated attack on the government's power to tax wealth or allocate resources. To protect their wealth,
the super-rich depict their takings as adding to productivity, and fight against
democracy, land reform, progressive taxation, socialism, and strong government as potential threats to their takings. Their weapons are deception, force
and bribery, backed by control of the courts.

Modes of production vs. modes of appropriation

The financial crisis now plaguing Western economies is age-old. Throughout
history the greatest fortunes have been obtained by lending and foreclosing,
above all by privatizing the Commons (the public domain) by indebting
governments to force sell-offs, or simply via insider dealings and fraud. It would
be a travesty of language to say that the resulting privatization rents, financial
extraction and "capital" gains are "earned."

Somebody must lose when debts grow too large to be paid. So bankers and
bondholders seek to capture the government to protect themselves from losses –
leaving pensioners, mortgage debtors and students to deal with the backwash
of debt deflation. For the public sector, debt-strapped governments from Ireland to Greece are told to obey creditor demands to scale back schooling,
health care and infrastructure maintenance, and to privatize the public
domain.

---

[456] Lambert Strether, "Stay classy, Greg: Mankiw on What the Rich Deserve, and Why They
Deserve It," *Naked Capitalism*, February 19, 2014, quoting Mankiw's *New York Times* op-
ed., "Yes, the Wealth Can Be Deserving," February 15, 2014.

Sacrificing the economy on the altar of debt

The financial system has been saved at the economy's expense. It is a measure of how predatory today's public policy has become that the huge banking conglomerates that provided credit were kept intact, but not the businesses and households whose balance sheets were being destroyed. Solving the debt problem for the 99 Percent would involve writing down the savings and other financial claims on the opposite side of the balance sheet. But the One Percent has placed its representatives in the Treasury and the Federal Reserve, and backed the election of the leading Congressional Committee figures dealing with banking.

The political problem always comes down to the question of who will bear the losses. The One Percent insist that if the personal, real estate and corporate debts of the 99 Percent are to be written down, the government will bail out creditors. The 99 Percent must pay in another way – in their capacity as tax-payers. when debtors no longer can pay funds. Making the 99 Percent poorer is thus not an accidental byproduct of the behavior of the One Percent. Bank lobbyists have put their own Tim Geithners in place precisely to act as their defenders in such situations. If they succeed in blocking bad debt debts from being written down, bankers and bondholders will kill the economy by plunging it into austerity.

When debts cannot be paid, the choice is between annulling them, or keeping them in place and letting creditors foreclose or bailing them out with public funds. Favoring creditors polarizes economies by siphoning income and transferring assets upward to creditors. This financial conquest must be blocked by resuming the fight to tax unearned income and indeed, to minimize it in the first place, by protecting basic public services (including banking) from being appropriated by rent extractors.

Today's economies will stagnate unless they are freed from *rentier* parasitism and debt creation. The financial oligarchy will bring its creditor power to bear against labor and democratic government regulation, worsening poverty and stripping the environment to pay the exponentially expanding debt overhead.

What kind of postindustrial economy will we have?

Today's most pressing economic fight is not simply between labor and employers. It is being waged by *rentier* interests against labor, industry and government together. This makes today's reform task more far-reaching than the social-democratic movement a century ago. Financial and *rentier* reforms play little role in the party platforms of today's ostensibly socialist and labor parties. From Britain to Greece and even the United States, they are leading the fight for balanced budgets and fiscal austerity at the Tony Blair, Barack Obama and Papandreou extreme. It is as if recovery depends on the super-rich getting richer, not on rescuing debt-ridden Greece and Cyprus, Ireland, Italy and Spain.

The problem that will occupy the next few generations is how to undo the financial knots into which today's economies have been tied. Clearing away the overgrowth of debt requires countering the neoliberal junk economics crafted to disable society's defense mechanisms against financialization and unearned income. There have indeed been courageous U.S. officials, such as Sheila Bair and Neil Barofsky, whose sense of fairness was offended by the giveaways to the large banks and their bondholders. Former Wall Streeters Nomi Prins and Yves Smith, the intellectual force behind the *Naked Capitalism* website, have explained the financial rip-offs at work. UMKC's Modern Monetary Theory website *New Economic Perspectives* provides a commentary on how needless today's financial austerity is, in light of the power of central banks to fund economic growth. But their voices are all but drowned out by the parroting of pro-bank austerity economics across the political spectrum.

Nobody anticipated that democratic societies would vote for policies that would support the One Percent by impoverishing themselves. Political leaders treat interest and economic rent as secondary concerns while welcoming asset-price inflation and privatization. The economic vocabulary has been corrupted to depict exploitation as wealth creation – which it is for the One Percent under the current system, but at the cost of the 99 Percent.

Latvians have repeatedly voted for neoliberals imposing Europe's most extreme austerity. Most notoriously, Ireland's politicians paid foreign bond-holders and "hot money" arbitrageurs at the cost of imposing domestic poverty. Voters finally replaced its neoliberal politicians, but the new party coalition did not repudiate the debts that were taken on.

In the United States, Britain and France, no major political party or labor organization has challenged the oligarchic principle that tax rules, financial regulations and the legal system should be run for the benefit of the FIRE sector serving the One Percent. Today's passivity by the 99 Percent in the face of a *rentier* counter-Enlightenment reflects the degree to which voters have come to accept the neoliberal financial and tax system as part of the natural environment, as if there indeed is no alternative.

What is needed is a perspective enabling people to see the reforms that would counter today's corrosive FIRE-sector mode of fortune-creation. The difficulty in promoting this understanding is that its logic and implications are radical – as they were in the 19th century, when they were sponsored by a broad range of reformers, from the "Ricardian socialists" around John Stuart Mill

urging nationalization of land rent (by outright purchase or rising land taxation) and Christian socialist ideals of communalism to Marxism, based on
nationalizing all means of production, factories as well as public infrastructure.
It seemed that the residue of feudalism was being swept away at the very least
by land taxation and anti-trust legislation, while banking was becoming industrialized.

But this has not occurred. The leading efforts to free economies from the
legacy of feudalism were defeated. After World War I the focus of value and
price theory on economic rent was replaced by a more trivialized economics
curriculum excluding the concept of unearned income and the distinction
between productive labor and overhead.

Will financialized economies self-destruct?

Warning against sacrificing the economy to subsidize the financial sector, chief
Financial Times commentator Martin Wolf writes that the key policy guide
should be: "First 'do not': do not pay too much attention to the financial sector's
self-interested bleating. ... The financial sector has put the economy into
trouble. If the government is forced to take part of the risk of putting the system
back together again, it must protect the public interests first." As a final "do
not," he urges, "do not bail out mortgage lending via government subsidies. By
now it should be evident that the British obsession with speculative home
ownership is a snare and a delusion. Let the market deflate, as it should."[457]

If creditors have their way, they will destroy the economy. Citigroup chief
economist (and former advisor to Goldman Sachs) Willem Buiter acknowledged in 2012 that: "The most likely insolvent sovereigns – Greece, Portugal,
Ireland, Cyprus and possibly Spain, Italy and Slovenia," cannot grow without
debt restructuring. He saw the risk of sovereign default highest for Ireland's
€63 billion of official debt. "Austerity fatigue in the periphery and growing
bailout fatigue in the core mean that the ECB/euro system is the only Santa
Claus capable of filling the solvency gaps of sovereigns and banks in the euro
area."[458] But German, Dutch and Finnish finance ministers opposed this.

The financial system had become reckless by joining in a *rentier* consensus
with the One Percent to oppose government powers to tax or regulate any
form of wealth – and against labor seeking to improve its working conditions,

---

[457] Martin Wolf, "How to meet the dangers facing Britain," *Financial Times*, September 17, 2008.
[458] Willem Buiter, "Only widespread debt restructuring can save the euro," *Financial Times*, October 16, 2012.

wages and pensions, even though "winning" the war against labor destroys the domestic market and hence the ability to pay debts owed to the financial sector.

It doesn't have to be this way. It is now two centuries since the Saint-Simonian proposals to subordinate credit to serve industry. Classical tax policy sought to ward off the *rentier* economy that the post-World War I century has brought about by un-taxing economic rent, privatizing basic utilities, and failing to socialize banking to prevent bank credit being lent against economic rent. Debts cannot be written down as long as people imagine that keeping them in place is necessary to prevent depression by preserving confidence in the financial system. Such "confidence" helps deepen today's malaise.

Industrial capitalism or finance capitalism?

Lenin said that capitalists would sell Communists the rope to hang them. But capitalists themselves have produced the rope in the form of predatory finance extracting interest, dividends, fees and various forms of rent from industry, real estate, households and also from governments. "Capital gains" are produced by debt pyramiding, which paves the way for debt deflation of the "real" economy.

The question is whether finance capital can survive simply by lending to speculators in search of interest, rent extraction and asset-price gains or gambles as finance capitalism mutates into casino capitalism. Of course there are many necessary functions provided by banks. But the collapse of today's financialized economies into negative equity is largely the product of a few giant Wall Street institutions, as economist Randy Wray notes: "We have 4500 honest banks. We have a half dozen huge banks that are run as control frauds. Our financial system's main problems can be found among those SDIs – systemically dangerous institutions. We will not get back our economy or our government until we close them."[459]

Fiscally, today's problem is akin to that of 16th-century Spain, whose landed aristocracy taxed labor and incipient industry in the towns while living tax-free in luxury. In 18th-century France a similar tax shift sparked the Great Revolution. That was the only way to break the *rentier* stranglehold adding to the cost of labor and its products.

---

[459] L. Randall Wray: "The Greatest Myth Propagated About The FED: Central Bank Independence (Part 3)," *Naked Capitalism*, January 12, 2014. Originally posted at UMKC's *New Economic Perspectives*.

Today's financial counter-revolution against the reform movement of the 19th and early 20th centuries has shifted taxes off the FIRE sector onto labor and industry, much as did medieval Spain. The Republican administrations of Ronald Reagan and George H. W. Bush cut income taxes on the top brackets and capital gains taxes on real estate and finance, while adding a proliferation of sales and value-added taxes and wage withholding set-asides (and quadrupling the U.S. public debt between 1981 and 1992).

Adding this regressive fiscal burden to the debt overhead has left only one way for the economy to survive without cutting back consumption levels: to borrow from banks to buy what wages and salaries no longer are sustaining. So *more* debt seems to be the only solution to today's over-indebtedness. That is the inner financial contradiction of our post-bubble economy.

Financial and debt reform will still leave labor and environmental problems

It is easy to forget how optimistic Marx and other socialists of his day were about the future of industrial capitalism. He expected the industrial mode of production to emerge victorious over all forms of parasitic *rentier* activities. Enlightened class consciousness and political democracy were expected to usher in a world of rising living standards, better working conditions and less unfair distribution of income.

Like most evolutionary economic forecasters of his day, Marx expected industrial capitalism to free itself from the "excrescences" of landlordism, monopolies and other forms of exploitation. But the banking and landlord class that were mutual enemies in Ricardo's day have joined forces since World War I. As this has occurred, Social Democratic and Labour parties abandoned the issue of land rent to the Liberals and Single Taxers (whose ranks dwindled rapidly). And despite an early 20th-century focus on finance capitalism by Rudolf Hilferding, Lenin and other Marxists, monetary and debt analysis has been left mainly to right wing bank advocates, from followers of Ludwig von Mises to Chicago-type monetarists.[460]

In the early 20th century the fight between employers and labor was expected to be *the* major tension shaping future politics. But today, Labor is fighting simply for jobs, seeing a harmony of interest with employers in place

---

[460] In Volume III of *Capital* (and Vol. III of *Theories of Surplus Value*) Marx spent more effort than any other economist of his day analyzing the *rentier* drives of finance and groundrent. This makes it all the more striking that his nominal followers today have all but ignored these "Volume III" discussions.

of the class conflict of a century ago – and imagining that finance helps industrial hiring rather than downsizing and out-sourcing it.

Housing has become more widely distributed, public pensions and health care have at least been promised, and a new world of opportunities has opened up. But the democratization of homeownership has enabled lobbyists for large commercial and rental property owners to make untaxing real estate a seemingly democratic aim. This demagogy reached its pinnacle in California's notorious Proposition 13, which froze taxes on commercial and rental properties as well as homes.

Coupled with other tax favoritism for real estate and finance, the result has been a sharply regressive tax shift enabling financial power to grow stronger than industrial power. Industry is being financialized more than finance has become industrialized. The remedy is to write down debts and reform the tax system. Our financial problem is like a parasite on a sick body. The host needs to get rid of the intruder before it can heal itself.

Downsizing finance will not, in itself, avert the threatened privatization of the post office, water systems, roads and communication, or cure the high cost of privatized medical insurance and other infrastructure. Once you remove the debt drain and *rentier* burden from industrial capitalism will still leave the familiar old class tensions between employers and their workers. This will still leave the familiar labor problems of industrial capitalism – the fight to provide fair working conditions and basic necessities to all citizens, as well as to avoid war, environmental pollution and other social strains.

However, the rise of financial power is working against all these objectives, preventing society from healing itself. As Alan Greenspan noted in the passages cited earlier, hooking "traumatized labor" on the debt treadmill is a major factor deterring workers from pressing for wage increases and better workplace conditions. Without resolving the debt overhead and providing a public option for banking services, the other problems are made much worse.

Ancient mythology asked how King Midas could survive with nothing to eat but his gold. This threatens to be a metaphor for today's finance capitalism – a dream that one can live purely off money, without means of production and living labor. To avoid this fate, the remedy must add financial reform to the 19th century's unfinished revolution to sweep away the surviving inequities of post-feudal land grabbing, seizure of the Commons and creation of monopoly privileges. These are the vestiges of the past appropriations and insider dealing that underlie rent seeking and endowed a financial system that remains grounded in neofeudal practice instead of investing in industry and human well being.

Part IV

There *Is* an Alternative

29

The Fight for the 21st Century

> If Europe wants the division and the perpetuation of servitude, we will take the plunge
> and issue a "big no." We will fight for the dignity of the people and our sovereignty.
>
> Alexis Tsipris, rejecting the eurozone's bailout terms in June 2015[461]

In 1933, as the wake of World War I's financial wreckage gave way to the Great Depression, the philosopher H. G. Wells wrote a novel about the conflict he expected to emerge by the last quarter of his century. Reminding his readers of the "perennial struggle of life against the creditor and the dead hand," he described society's "forward effort" seeking to break free of past debts and financial claims. Viewing debt as a retarding force, Wells forecast that matters would come to a head in the year 1979 when his fictional character Austin Livewright would publish *Bankruptcy Through the Ages*. "We need only refer the student to the recorded struggles in the histories of Republican Rome and Judaea between debtor and creditor; to the plebeian Secessions of the former and the year of Jubilee of the latter."[462] The year 1979 indeed turned out to be precisely when interest rates peaked at a modern-era high of 20 percent.

As an example of the parallel struggle against landowners seeking to avoid taxes, Wells cited England's Statutes of Mortmain (1279 and 1290) protecting the land from passing to the Church via bequest, foreclosure or sales made to avoid the epoch's feudal duties. Throughout history there has been a constant tension between royal or public authority, and creditors or wealthy patrons seeking to indebt the land and its population to themselves so as to replace public power with their own. But whereas the great political fight of the 19th century was to nationalize or tax land and natural resource rents, today's fight must be to socialize banking and finance, which have become the ultimate recipient and hence main defender of such rents.

---

[461] Quoted in Ambrose Evans-Pritchard, "Syriza Left demands 'Icelandic' default as Greek defiance stiffens," *The Telegraph,* June 18, 2015, quoting http://www.avgi.gr/article/5616948/al-tsipras-eimaste-etoimoi-gia-biosimi-sumfonia-i-to-megalo-oxi-.

[462] H. G. Wells, *The Shape of Things to Come* (New York 1933), p. 35. This thought was omitted from the 1936 movie *Things to Come* ostensibly based on Wells' novel, despite the fact that Wells wrote the screenplay.

The actual financial crisis of 1979 was resolved in a way that led in the opposite direction from what Wells had forecast and progressive economists recommended. Instead of debtors achieving a clean slate to wipe out the debt overhead, the incoming 1981–92 Reagan-Bush administration sponsored a wave of new credit/debt, so large that interest rates declined steadily during the 1980s.

At first, this debt creation was used to inflate property and stock markets. Whereas the Vietnam War and ensuing Carter inflation (1977-80) had bid up wages and commodity prices, the subsequent neoliberal inflation bid up asset prices, reinforced by tax cuts on real estate, capital gains and the upper income brackets. This shift to regressive taxation was the reverse of what economists and futurists had expected. Instead of economies becoming more equal, they polarized increasingly between creditors and debtors.

The Reagan-Bush budget deficits quadrupled U.S. public debt, while easier credit fueled a debt overgrowth that became precisely what Wells foresaw and warned against: a dead hand of financial claims leading to the crash of 2008 and its aftermath. Contra Wells, the world barely put up a fight to break free from this dynamic. Shifting the tax burden and the cost of bank bailouts onto labor and "taxpayers" after 2008 gave Wall Street (and its counterparts abroad) the power to hold entire nations in debt.

Restructuring the financial system is hard to do when people are engulfed in a crisis, especially when they imagine that they can recover by borrowing more – and fear that there is no alternative. The reality is that history is rife with possible remedies. These remedies almost always involve debt writedowns.

There *is* an alternative

If we were designing a perfect world we would put the economy's long-term interests above financial short-termism. We would organize banking and financial systems in a way to keep credit productive and within the ability of debtors to pay. In cases where predatory credit and debt exceeds the means to pay or threatens to impose austerity and debt deflation, it would be annulled.

The reason why the world isn't pursuing such restructuring is that creditors have gained power over governments and public opinion to persuade people that it is possible for economies to continue along the present path, and even that austerity can somehow restore balance and prosperity.

Few people would expect that as financial crises intensify and polarize economies further between creditors and debtors, governments will fail to restructure the financial system. But Hayek's hyperbole in *The Road to Serfdom* characterizes public planning, taxation and regulation as metaphoric serfdom.

This reflects the One Percent's fear and even hatred of democracy, progressive taxation, and public enterprise and social spending programs. In their place, Hayek's acolytes would set economies on the road to literal debt serfdom, a state of dependency in which access to housing and education requires taking on a lifetime of debt.

The way that history was supposed to unfold was that banking would provide credit for capital investment. Public services were to be offered at falling prices (ultimately freely) to a widening population. But instead of evolving toward such "socialism," bankers and wealthy elites found rent extraction to be their major source of gain. Calling their opposition to a government strong enough to keep them in check "libertarian," their aim is simply to replace democratic government with planning by bankers and bondholders. To call their rent extraction and debt-financed asset-price inflation "wealth creation," is to adopt the vocabulary of *rentiers*.

Ten Reforms to Restore Industrial Prosperity

1. Write down debts with a Clean Slate, or at least in keeping with the ability to pay
2. Tax economic rent to save it from being capitalized into interest payments
3. Revoke the tax deductibility of interest, to stop subsidizing debt leveraging
4. Create a public banking option
5. Fund government deficits by central banks, not by taxes to pay bondholders
6. Pay Social Security and Medicare out of the general budget
7. Keep natural monopolies in the public domain to prevent rent extraction
8. Tax capital gains at the higher rates levied on earned income
9. Deter irresponsible lending with a Fraudulent Conveyance principle
10. Revive classical value and rent theory (and its statistical categories)

1. *Write down debts that block recovery*
A convulsion of bankruptcy is the price to be paid for the financial sector's sabotage of the tax system and regulatory capture of oversight agencies. Chapter 9 has described how most observers in 2008 saw that over-lending for junk mortgages had caused a bubble (asset-price inflation), and urged that debts should be scaled back to the ability to be paid (*viz*. §9 below). Such writedowns in 2008 would have avoided the widespread foreclosures that threw ten million homes onto the market at distress prices. Banks opposed such writedowns because this would have imposed losses on themselves, their bondholders and other financial players.

The Federal Reserve created enough monetary reserves for the banks to make up for their losses, but nothing to bail out homeowners. No pressure was exerted to take "troubled" (that is, overly aggressive and predatory) banks public or prosecute their officers for the mortgage frauds and underwriting frauds that were part and parcel of the crash. The FDIC was prepared to do this with Citigroup in 2008, using the bank's surviving reserves to cover the claims of insured depositors – as distinct from stockholders, bondholders and uninsured counterparties.[463] But it was blocked by the Treasury.

In addition to creating money directly for banks to borrow as reserves (earning a "free" interest markup), the Fed sought to re-inflate the real estate market so that bank mortgages could recover their price levels. Banks refrained from foreclosing on homes in arrears largely to keep Fannie-Mae-insured loans on their books, adding late fees and penalties to their interest charges against mortgage debtors.

Bankers depict even a partial debt writedown as threatening anarchy – their euphemism for having to take a loss when the system they designed and deregulated goes bust. But the alternative to writedowns is financial breakdown and impoverishment. A Clean Slate would make a public option for banking easier to introduce. This would help banks evolve into public utilities. It also would facilitate the rent taxes that 19th-century free market reformers intended.

Trying to save appearances by keeping bad debts on the books has led to debt deflation gnawing into consumer demand and business investment. So we are left with the inconvenient truth that if financial claims are *not* annulled, the result must be an increasingly top-heavy oligarchy imposing chronic austerity, making it even harder to pay down the debt burden.

2. *Tax economic rent to save it from being capitalized into interest payments*
To help prevent such financialization from recurring after a debt writedown, it is necessary to reform tax policy by focusing it on rent extraction and "capital" gains. Otherwise, banks and financial markets will continue to create credit mainly against land rent for real estate, natural resource rent for the oil and mining sectors, and monopoly rent for infrastructure being privatized from the public domain.

Land rent heads the list because real estate remains the largest asset in nearly every economy. As Chapter 7 has described, some 80 percent of new bank credit takes the form of mortgage loans, whose main effect is to bid up

---

[463] Uninsured parties could have been given stock ownership of what remains. Steven Gjerstad and Vernon L. Smith suggest this resolution for future TBTF banks in "Bonds, Not Bailouts, for Too Big to Fail Banks," *Wall Street Journal*, August 12, 2014.

property prices. This price rise serves as poisoned bait for homebuyers (and also "activist shareholders" in the stock market) hoping to get rich by debt-leveraged "capital" gains that increase their net worth on paper.

These gains cannot be sustained if the debt creation process smothers the economy. In 2011 the U.S. housing finance agency raised its guarantee for mortgage debt service to 43 percent of family income, up from the customary 25 percent rule of thumb prior to the 1980s. Down payments were reduced in 2013 from 5 percent to just 3 percent. These looser guidelines enable families to borrow more – and housing prices rise to however much a bank will lend. But instead of elevating families into the middle class, the inflation of home prices becomes a treadmill to debt peonage. Inflating prices for rent-yielding assets creates a vested interest in expanding unproductive credit creation to prevent a collapse of asset prices leading to negative equity. This forces the economy to choose between two evils: yet more debt ("extend and pretend," inherently short-term), or the inevitable bankruptcies and forfeitures to creditors in the end.

Classical rent theory demonstrates what seems to be counter-intuitive: Raising property taxes holds *down* what banks will lend, and hence the price of housing, because *rent paid to the tax collector is not available to be capitalized into bank debt*. But the financial sector popularizes the illusion that lower property taxes will make home ownership more affordable. Bankers know that lower taxes will leave more of the property's rental value available for *new* buyers to pay interest (or existing owners to borrow against by taking out "home equity" loans). What homeowners seem to gain in property tax cuts ends up being paid in higher mortgage costs of buying homes.

Taxing land rent (and also natural resource rent and monopoly rent) has three positive effects. First, it keeps property prices low by preventing this rent from being capitalized into bank loans. Second, it frees labor and industry from taxes on wages, profits and sales, alleviating most family budgets. Third, banks will be obliged not to create as much new debt that merely becomes a cost of transferring ownership rather than contributing to real output and productivity. Taxing rent is administratively easy. The United States has over twenty thousand appraisers whose job is to assess the market value of buildings and land separately.

In the case of natural resources, oil and mining companies typically buy crude from producer countries at low prices reflecting actual production costs. Payment is made by tax-avoidance "flag of convenience" countries such as Panama or Liberia (which conveniently use the U.S. dollar), which sell the oil at a markup to refineries in the oil-consuming nations. This markup is pure resource rent, not "profit" in the classical sense. It is untaxed.

For monopolies, economic rent is revenue that cannot be explained by spending on tangible capital investment and labor. There is a long tradition of untangling the maze of fictitious cost accounting. During World War II, the U.S. Government applied this principle in its Excess Profits Tax, much as earlier regulators calculated fair-market value for railroad tariffs and other monopoly services (at least, this is what they were *supposed* to do). Investment bankers put "free lunch" rent rights at the top of their wish list of assets to be privatized, untaxed and deregulated, precisely because these are "cash cows," much like lotteries and other public revenue streams.

A debt-ridden, regressively taxed economy in which fortunes are based on rent extraction, and by financial claims *on* the nation for interest, amortization and fees, is higher-cost than an "equity" economy basing its tax system on land rent, natural resource rent and regulating monopoly pricing. If such *rentier* income is unearned and hence unfair, then so are the fortunes and hereditary estates built up from such income. Fortunately, rent takings are reversible. *A rent tax can recapture what privatizers and kleptocrats have taken.*

At issue in today's New Enclosure movement to privatize economic rent are two visions of capitalism: financial vs. industrial. A bubble economy's mode of "creating wealth" by (1) debt-leveraging and (2) taxing labor and consumers rather than economic rent has made America a high-cost economy.

To be sure, if governments collect the land rent, many existing property owners will default on their payments to the banks, or will feel obliged to walk away from their property. When banks do not receive what they had set their eyes on, many will see their reserves wiped out even more dramatically than occurred 2008. An abrupt shift to taxing rents or other revenue already pledged to banks will decimate their stockholders and bondholders. Taxing rent thus will require a public takeover of such "troubled" banks. The financial sector has forced society to make a choice: either submit to turning the economy into a *rentier*-ridden Ponzi scheme, or subordinate the banking and tax system to the aim of financing growth. That is why reform must be across-the-board, not piecemeal.

It is hard to see how economic rent can be fully taxed without a public option for banking, because the rent to be taxed already has been earmarked to pay interest. Something must give. Being taken into the public domain is the price that banks pay for over-lending to the point where interest charges often absorb the entire economic rent and crowd out the tax collector, while forcing indebted owners to default. Under these conditions, turning insolvent banks into public institutions is the easiest alternative to financial austerity and anarchy.

3. *Revoke the tax deductibility of interest*

Interest is not a cost of doing business when it is paid to transfer ownership rights to existing properties or enterprises. Debt taken on simply to buy assets is pure overhead, adding to the cost of doing business. Making interest payments on such transactions tax deductible enables the One Percent to take more from industry, real estate and commerce. This perverse incentive enables industrial firms to be raided by financial tactics to pay out more to bondholders than they can to stockholders (by paying income that otherwise would be declared as taxable profit). This encourages debt leveraging rather than equity investment, especially for leveraged buyouts that add interest charges to the cost of doing business.

Tax deductibility for interest also adds to the cost of living, to the extent that it shifts the tax burden onto wage income and consumer sales. Yet politicians end up giving tax advantages to creditors because the financial sector has become their main constituency of campaign contributors.

Just as in the case of leaving economic rent untaxed, un-taxing interest payments leaves more after-tax real estate rent and corporate cash flow "free" to be capitalized into larger loans that raise asset prices for new buyers on credit. The untaxed interest ends up being paid to bankers and bondholders. This transformation of rents and tax cuts into interest – creating "capital" gains in the process – throws Wall Street's backing behind an anti-growth tax policy whose main "product" is debt.

The convoluted rewriting and watering down of Dodd-Frank bank legislation has shown how bank lobbyists are able to stall reforms and water them down by inserting fatal loopholes. Wall Street's sway over lawmaking and courts, its capture of oversight agencies and political control over campaign financing forces economies to take radical steps to save themselves from austerity and debt peonage. And radical steps, by their nature, must be abrupt. To be effective, systemic reform must be done quickly and totally, not slowly and marginally.

4. *Create a public banking option*

Chapter 7 has shown that banking was on its way to becoming a public utility in the years leading up to World War I. A public option survives in the Post Office banks of Japan and Russia. By providing deposit and checking accounts, loans and credit cards at rates reflecting the actual cost of such services (or even at subsidized rates instead of today's interest charges, fees and penalties), a public option could free the economy from the monopoly rent now enjoyed by banks. Most important, public banking would have been unlikely to extend credit for the corporate takeovers, asset stripping and debt leveraging that characterizes today's financial system.

There are three main arguments for establishing a public bank to provide basic checking, savings and credit card services. The most obvious reason is to offer these services at minimum cost. A public option is free from exorbitant salaries and stock options, management fees and other financialization tactics, not to mention political lobbying and fines for the now chronic misbehavior of the largest banks.

A second reason for creating a public bank is the ability of Wall Street lobbyists to undermine administration of Sarbanes-Oxley, Dodd-Frank and the Volcker Too Big To Fail (TBTF) rule, and to block the appointment of Justice Department or Securities and Exchange Commission officials who actually believe in enforcing regulations. As long as both leading political parties view throwing financial criminals in jail as "the road to serfdom," the only way to prevent reckless bank exploitation is to set up public banks dedicated to providing basic "vanilla" services.

The third reason for creating a public option for banking is to separate retail banking from the "investment" banking that is becoming almost indistinguishable from casino trading in arbitrage and derivatives. The failure of existing legislation to restore Glass-Steagall's separation of these two quite different forms of banking, coupled with the inability of Congress to protect the economy from the financial sector has produced a situation where mega-banks can hold the government hostage for bailouts when the exponential growth of financial claims bursts into a repeat of the 2008 solvency crisis.

Finally, it is easier for governments to cancel debts owed to themselves than to annul those owed to private creditors. Before credit became privatized, Mesopotamian kings and Egyptian pharaohs cancelled debts owed to the palace so as to avoid widespread bondage and emigration – the fate confronting today's debt-strapped countries.

5. *Fund government deficits by central banks, not by taxes*

Money always has been a public creation. The paper money in our pocket is a form of government debt. The government created it as a kind of IOU when it paid for goods and services. That is how governments supply economies with money. The holders of such currency in turn are in the position of being creditors to the rest of the economy – and pay with this credit (which is given value by the government accepting as payment for taxes). This is the essence of Modern Monetary Theory (MMT), explained best by the followers of Hyman Minsky at the University of Missouri (Kansas City), Randy Wray and Steve Keen.

The public debt – including the money supply – would not exist if the government did not run up debts century after century, just like other countries. The deficit is what creates the economy's monetary base, which rises each year in proportion to the increase in public debt. Unlike personal debts, public debts are not expected to be repaid. To do so would extinguish the money supply. That is what happened in the late 19th century in the United States, and it imposed a serious deflation (the "cross of gold" that was crucifying debtors, who earned less and less income to pay debts taken on at higher prices).

The role of central banks is to create money electronically to spend into the economy to spur economic growth *without* entailing interest-bearing debt owed to commercial banks and bondholders. That is why financial elites oppose central bank financing of deficits. Bondholders prefer to keep governments on a taut financial leash, with central banks creating money only to bail out banks, not the economy. Bankers accuse governments of depreciating the currency and creating hyperinflation, yet over the past thirty years banks have financed the largest inflation of real estate, stock and bond prices in history. This certainly is not a more morally responsible form of inflation than government spending.

Central banks were founded to finance deficit spending. But in recent decades the financial sector has turned them into appendages of the privatized banking system. At the Federal Reserve, "Helicopter Ben" Bernanke and his successor Janet Yellen air-dropped money only over Wall Street – a net $4 trillion of electronic credit to U.S. banks since the 2008 crisis. This Quantitative Easing did not finance investment in new industrial capital, repair deteriorating bridges, roads and other infrastructure, or maintain employment. Its aim was simply to prop up bank balance sheets by supporting prices for real estate mortgages – that is, to save banks, not the economy. Re-inflating asset prices makes it more expensive for families to buy homes, reducing their purchasing power for goods and services.

Wall Street has mounted a propaganda campaign to convince voters that government budgets should be run like household budgets: in balance or even surplus. The difference is that households cannot create money. Removing the constraint of silver or gold backing for money has enabled banks to create credit without limit, except for government regulation and capital reserve requirements. Disabling public regulatory power has left credit creation to the commercial banks, which inflate asset prices on credit, adding interest charges to the economy's ownership structure. Asset-price inflation became the focus of bank lending – and seemed to justify yet more bank lending in came an economy-wide Ponzi scheme.

There is an alternative. The eurozone could have created a few €1 trillion platinum coins to finance deficit spending directly into the economy to help pull it out of austerity. It could have let the superstructure of bank derivatives collapse, wiping out financial gambles that put the banking system at risk. But bank lobbyists and right-wing ideologues have propagandized a narrow tunnel vision to prevent the United States from creating money for other reasons than to benefit Wall Street, and to prevent the European Union from having a real central bank to finance government deficits, except to help bankers and bondholders.

The pretense is that money is technocratic and requires professional (defined as suitably tunnel-visioned) anti-government ideologues. Ottawa economics professor Mario Seccareccia recently summarized how radical this anti-democratic view of money is:

Ever since the establishment of the modern nation-state in the late eighteenth and nineteenth centuries, the creation of the euro was perhaps the first significant experiment in modern times in which there was an attempt to separate money from the state, that is, to denationalize currency, as some right-wing ideologues and founders of modern neoliberalism, such as Friedrich von Hayek, had defended. ... The denationalization or "supra-nationalization" of money with the establishment that happened in the Eurozone took away from elected national governments the capacity to meaningfully manage their economies. Unless governments in the Eurozone are able to renegotiate a significant control and access money from their own central banks, the system will be continually plagued with crisis and will probably collapse in the longer term.[464]

To make matters worse, the hands of central banks in Europe and the United States are tied by the impression (sponsored by financial lobbyists) that governments should *not* run deficits but maintain surpluses that drain the economy's circular flow and oblige it to rely on commercial banks and bondholders. Instead of public credit financing economic growth, bank debt is monetized in ways that benefit creditors at the expense of their host economies.

The Citigroup and AIG bailouts were financed with a stroke of the pen. Social Security, Medicare and other social spending likewise can be financed by the central bank creating money, just as it has created money to bail out Wall Street. Even worse, FICA wage withholding pays for these programs in advance, lending this forced saving to the U.S. Treasury so that taxes can be

---

[464] Mario Seccareccia: "Greece shows the Limits of Austerity in the Eurozone. What Now?" Interview with Lynn Parramore, INET, January 30, 2015. http://www.nakedcapitalism. com/2015/01/greece-shows-limits-austerity-eurozone-now.html.

slashed further for the highest wealth brackets. The essence of Modern Monetary Theory is that governments can finance deficit spending electronically
on its own computer keyboards just as commercial banks do. The difference
between public money creation and bank credit is that the public purpose is
to promote economic growth, not asset-price inflation. National prosperity
requires spending money *into* the economy – for instance, for new capital infrastructure investment, health care and retirement pensions. Budget surpluses
would oblige such spending to be privately financed – which means much
higher prices for their services.

6. *Pay Social Security and Medicare out of the general budget*
In 1983 the Commission on Social Security Reform chaired by Alan
Greenspan recommended that instead of treating Social Security and
Medicare as public programs funded out of the overall budget, they should be
privatized into a savings program paid for mainly by the least affluent members
of society, by steadily raising the FICA payroll tax. These wage withholding
taxes are now over 15 percent (including the employer's 6.2 percent share of
Social Security levies). They do not fall on high-income earners!

This regressive tax shift away the higher income brackets functions as a
fiscal class war. It has cost wage earners hundreds of billions of dollars. The
government has raised user-fee taxes on wage earners – up to a low cut-off
point freeing earners of more than $120,000 from having to contribute. No
such user fees are imposed on banks for their $4 trillion in Federal Reserve
Quantitative Easing credit, the $800 billion TARP bailout and other subsidies.

Any politician who fails to explain that it is regressive income taxation to
subsidize the One Percent in this way – but not Social Security – can be
assumed to be in Wall Street's pocket or the proverbial "useful idiot." The
effect of self-funding social spending is to impose austerity on the 99 Percent,
"freeing" the One Percent from fiscal responsibility.

7. *Keep natural monopolies in the public domain to prevent rent extraction*
Financial lobbyists condemn public spending as deadweight, even for roads,
the post office and other basic infrastructure. They claim that privatization will
provide these services at lower prices than government can match. Yet all the
evidence points to the contrary.[465] This is largely because in today's world,
privatization involves financialization, adding charges for interest, dividends

---

[465] See for instance John Kay, "Twenty Years of Privatization," June 1, 2002, http://www.
johnkay.com/2002/06/01/twenty-years-of-privatisation.

and exorbitant salaries to managers to the break-even prices that must be charged – not to mention using profits or rents for stock buybacks to create capital gains for managers and owners.

Over and above these costs, privatizers charge as high a price as the market will bear. This margin is monopoly rent. It was to prevent this price gouging that vital infrastructure traditionally was kept in the public domain. Since antiquity, roads and transportation, canals and civic buildings have been so expensive that private ownership would have exacerbated wealth inequality and created monopolistic elites. Even medieval serfs at least had access rights to the commons to help provide for their livelihood.

Monopolies were privatized more in the United States than in Europe during the Progressive Era, so U.S. techniques of price regulation for electric utilities and railroads was more developed than elsewhere. Price gouging was analyzed as an excess of market price over carefully defined intrinsic and necessary cost-value. But Europe kept basic infrastructure in the public domain, so there was less of a regulatory tradition for the sectors privatized after 1980. And no such tradition existed when the Soviet Union's republics became independent in 1991. Their rent-extracting "grabitization" was more extreme than anywhere else in the world.

Today's New Enclosure movement is privatizing public infrastructure. These giveaways of the modern-day commons are attracting new buyers, who borrow to buy these monopoly privileges – and pay banks interest out of the prices they charge. Privatization provides banks with a loan market capitalizing rent extraction rights into bonds, stocks and bank loans. The Thatcher-Blair model for Public/Private Partnerships typifies this giveaway of public assets. (Chicago's financialization of its sidewalk parking meters is a notorious U.S. example.) This underwriting gave banks a strong motive to drive government out of the business of providing public services or of regulating and taxing rent-yielding enterprises.

Short of de-privatizing (that is, re-nationalizing) land, natural resources and monopolies to the public domain, the remedy is a rent tax, backed by a tax on excess profits and unexplained enrichment.

8. *Tax capital gains at the same progressive rates as earned income*
Some 80 percent of capital gains are in real estate, reflecting its dominant size in the economy. As in the stock and bond markets, most such gains do not reflect tangible capital investment, but result mainly from banks lending more as they loosen credit standards, *e.g.*, for junk mortgage lending in 2001-08. Real estate prices rise when central banks lower the interest rate at which profits and rents are capitalized into bank loans.

The freer the lunch, the more pressure is brought on governments to make *rentier* gains even larger, by taxing them even less. Real estate gains are not taxed if they are reinvested in new property, or if nominal ownership is located in tax havens (or when owners die). Wall Street traders enjoy a similar "loophole" that taxes their financial winnings at a low capital-gains rate.

The remedy is to tax asset-price gains at least as high as the maximum income tax rate. Otherwise, the economy will favor such gains over those from tangible investment.

9. *Deter irresponsible lending with a Fraudulent Conveyance or Odious Debt rule*
The most obvious way to deter over-lending would be to make lenders bear the cost of loans gone bad. Loans made without a reasonable analysis to ascertain that they can be repaid in the normal course of business would be deemed to have been made fraudulently.[466] Companies defending themselves against raiders in the 1980s cited the fraudulent conveyance principle to claim that the junk bonds and bank loans financing the buyouts could only be paid by carving up the company, downgrading its pension plan or closing down its long-term investment. For public debt, the guiding principle should be that bondholders should lose if the only way they can be paid is by imposing austerity, unemployment and forced emigration or sell offing the public domain. No nation should be compelled to pay creditors before meeting its own economic survival needs.

As Greece's debt negotiations were coming to a head, the Parliamentary "Debt Truth" Committee stated the problem on June 17, 2015: "People's dignity is worth more than illegal, illegitimate, odious and unsustainable debt." The demands by the Troika were found to be "aimed exclusively at shifting private debt onto the public sector."[467] The report describes how this asset stripping

[466] http://legal-dictionary.thefreedictionary.com/Fraudulent+Conveyance: "If a voluntary conveyance renders a debtor insolvent or leaves the debtor without the means of paying the debts existing at the time of the conveyance, it is fraudulent and without any legal effect, regardless of the intent of the parties." This principle is contained in Uniform Fraudulent Conveyance Act UFCA§5 and Uniform Fraudulent Transfer Act UFTA §4(a)*2)ii). Also, when "The debtor incurred or intended to incur more debt than the debtor could pay (see UFCA §6 and UFTA §4(a)."
[467] http://greekdebttruthcommission.org/wp/, http://www.parliament.gr/UserFiles/8158407a-fc31-4ff2-a8d3-433701dbe6d4/Report_web.pdf. One of the few U.S. sites to reproduce these findings was Tyler Durden, "Greek Debt Committee Just Declared All Debt To The Troika „Illegal, Illegitimate, And Odious," *Zero Hedge*, June 17, 2015. http://www.zerohedge.com/news/2015-06-17/greek-debt-committee-just-declared-all-debt-illegal-illegitimate-and-odious.

combined with demands for austerity was the legacy of the Troika's "bailout" of Greece that only helped private bondholders, not the Greek economy:

> All the evidence we present in this report shows that Greece not only does not have the ability to pay this debt, but also should not pay this debt, first and foremost because the debt emerging from the Troika's arrangements is a direct infringement on the fundamental human rights of the residents of Greece. Hence, we came to the conclusion that Greece should not pay this debt because it is illegal, illegitimate, and odious.

At issue is whether society will save indebted economies or their creditors. Bankers cry havoc at the thought of annulling debts that cannot be paid, as if the thought is unthinkable. But it is less radical than turning economies into the debt-ridden wasteland that was inflicted upon Greece. From a historical point of view, it is more radical to let debt deflation deepen austerity while banks foreclose on property than for governments to protect debtors, whose ranks constitute the vast majority of the population and businesses. Realism and maintenance of viable markets requires recognition that in the end, most debts cannot be paid.

At present we are living in a financial interregnum. If the debt buildup continues, the economy cannot avoid an exponentially deepening debt crisis as it follows an exponential Ponzi-scheme vector. Banks and bondholders will continue as long as they can, until real reforms are made and rules are set to define the conditions under which debts should be cancelled when they become disruptive on an economy-wide scale.

10. *Revive classical value and price theory, with special emphasis on debt*
As Chapter 3 has described, François Quesnay developed national income accounting to trace how much rent was taken and what landlords did with it. The subsequent value and price theory of Adam Smith and Ricardo served to isolate economic rent, enabling John Stuart Mill and other "Ricardian socialists" to demonstrate that taxing rent re-captures for society the natural resource patrimony and rising site value. This rental valuation is created not by landlord efforts but by society's overall prosperity and public investment in transportation systems, schools and other infrastructure that define "location, location and location."

The fight to recover land and natural resource rents for public use, along with making natural monopolies public, including banking, was waged in nearly every industrial nation in the decades leading up to World War I. Taxing rent aimed to lower taxes on consumers and industry, while public infrastructure lowered the prices of key economic needs. The past century has reversed matters, by privatizing the land's site value, mineral rents and basic infrastructure rents, to be paid mainly to banks as interest.

Seeking to erase memory of classical rent theory, today's financial power grab pretends that Adam Smith and his followers sought to free such rent-seeking *from* taxation and regulation, not free economies from *rentier* elites. Failure to create a more progressive tax system reflects the inability of 19th-century free market doctrine to achieve the political and lawmaking power needed to liberate economies from the vestiges of feudalism: (1) landlordism stemming from the military conquest of Europe and the regions it colonized; (2) banking in private hands with creditor-oriented laws; and (3) monopolies created by public fiat and sold to pay royal war debts or, more recently, deficits from cutting taxes on *rentiers* and the rest of the One Percent.

How to manage a debt writedown

Whereas the fight of the 19th century was to nationalize land, natural resources and monopolies, today's fight is to socialize banking and finance. By becoming the ultimate rent recipients, banks and bondholders have emerged as the major defenders of rent seeking. Having made collateralized rent-extracting privileges the basis of our credit system – mortgage debts and those of oil and privatized monopolies – banks can argue that reviving the classical program of taxing economic rents will bring down the financial system turning these rents into interest and backing the economy's savings.

These savings are highly concentrated in the hands of the One Percent, to be sure. But the symbiosis between banking, real estate and monopolies has enabled these *rentiers* to depict their interests as being those of labor and industry – if one leaves out of account the concepts of economic rent and unearned income and its fictive wealth.

The reforms cited above cannot be achieved as long as the debt overhead remains. Even with current rent extraction in place, spurring recovery requires freeing businesses and families from the debt burden. History shows how excessive rent extraction and not forgiving debts reduce economies to debt servitude and collapse. But it also reveals that there always has been a wide the range of alternatives to reverse the spread of indebtedness. If Clean Slates seem so radical as to be nearly unthinkable today, it is mainly because *rentier* ideology has suppressed awareness of most of civilization's customary proclamations spanning three thousand years, from Mesopotamia and Egypt to Athens, Sparta and Judea.

Proclaiming Clean Slates to restore economic balance – annulling the accumulation of debts when they grew beyond the ability to be paid – kept pre-Roman civilization financially stables. Mosaic Law placed this principle at the core of Jewish religion (*Leviticus* 25). Yet modern Christianity all but ignores the fact that in Jesus's first sermon (*Luke* 4) he unrolled the scroll of Isaiah and announced his mission to proclaim the Year of the Lord, as the Jubilee Year was known.

Restoring the Jubilee Year became the basis for early Christians to break away from Rabbi Hillel, whose *prosbul* clause was used by creditors to force debtors to waive their rights to a Clean Slate. Jesus's position – reflected also in the Dead Sea scrolls of the Essenes – prompted the wealthy establishment to fight so strongly against him. By this time it was too late to win the fight against Rome and its increasingly violent creditor class that ended up bequeathing a pro-creditor post-Roman law to Western civilization.

It should not be surprising that the lesson of financial history is that debts that can't be paid won't be. The great policy question of our time is *how* not to pay them: Will nations permit creditors to foreclose and take the public and private assets into their hands, holding populations in bondage? Or will they declare a clean slate and start again?

Something must give: either finance capitalism or the post-*rentier* industrial capitalism that seemed to be evolving toward socialism a century ago. Merely marginal reforms cannot save a badly warped economy. So much of the economy's land rent, natural resource rent, monopoly rent, industrial profits, personal income and central bank money creation has been attached to pay bankers and bondholders that the only means of reform is a thorough-going Clean Slate. At the end of today's dynamic of interest-bearing debt and its dysfunctional financial and tax system is an economic Dark Age and privatization of the commons.

When *rentiers* insist that There Is No Alternative, they mean that they have attached and interwoven their debt and property claims so tightly throughout the economy that any systemic alternative threatens chaos in the short run. Their aim is to limit any reforms to merely marginal scope, leaving the present financial and rent-extracting system in place.

Banks and bondholders hate classical political economy because its logical conclusion was what was called socialism (before today's "socialist" parties changed the meaning to endorse neoliberal austerity). Marx became the *bête noire* of vested *rentier* interests because he showed how the dynamics of industrial capitalism were radical in striving to subordinate the landed, financial and monopoly interests that survived from feudalism.[468] This required a strong

---

[468] It is an irony of history that his self-proclaimed followers today depict his fight primarily against industrial capitalists to the point of having dropped his discussion in Volumes II and III of *Capital* of the predicate fight against landlords and usurious bankers. This neglect is exemplified in the way that the former Soviet Union permitted neoliberals to reorganize its economies into predatory rent grabbing opportunities.

enough government to cope with the *rentier* interests and break their post-feudal stranglehold.

Instead of that future materializing, a financial counter-revolution strives to convince voters that a government strong enough to regulate and tax finance, insurance and real estate (FIRE) is the road to serfdom. That is the parasite's strategy – to numb the host's brain so that it doesn't realize that the free luncher is draining the host's growth for itself.

There are a number of ways to cut the fortunes of the One Percent back to what used to be deemed normal. Many such policies were suggested in the wake of the 2008 crisis. They involve scaling back debts to market prices in the context of the ability to pay out of current incomes. For the vast category of owner-occupied homes, for example, one way is to assess the market rental value for over-mortgaged properties and make this the monthly payment capitalized into a self-amortizing 30-year mortgage. The bank (and more to the point, its bondholders and uninsured counterparties) would absorb the loss, having over-lent against the property's value.

Another solution would be to get an honest appraisal of the property's market price and write down the debt to this level – which was supposed to be what banks lent in the first place. A third approach would be to calculate the occupant's actual income (not the "liars' loan" figure filled in by the bank's mortgage broker) and set the mortgage payment at a specified portion, *e.g.* the once-traditional 25 percent. Congress established writedowns along such lines as a condition of TARP in October 2008. But as Chapter 11 has described, incoming President Obama's choice was to leave these debts in place.

In 1931 the world economy recognized a need for a Clean Slate by declaring a moratorium on the dead hand of inter-governmental debts stemming from World War I. A similar act is needed today for today's sovereign debts in the Eurozone and indeed throughout much of the global economy. The model remains that of Germany's Economic Miracle. In 1948 the Allies enacted their Currency Reform cancelling all debts except for the wage obligations that businesses owed to their employees, plus modest personal and business savings and checking deposits up to a specified amount for basic transactions. The German economy was made essentially debt-free. That was the miracle, and what made its free market economy viable – a debt-free market.

It was politically easy for the Allies to cancel German debts because nearly all were owed to former Nazi supporters. But today's banks and bondholders hold the reins of government, their treasuries, central banks, the IMF and ECB. These creditor interests instinctively put their own gains above the aim of economic recovery, to a point that ends up being self-defeating, bringing down the whole financial superstructure.

What if the debts are not cancelled?

One way or another, today's debts will not be paid. They are too large to be paid off without further impoverishing economies and leading to further waves of default. But in the interim, until the hopelessness is recognized, a steady stream of foreclosures and privatizations will polarize economies between creditors and debtors. Sooner or later, economies will recognize that they must choose between becoming an increasingly polarized financial oligarchy or making a fresh start by clearing away the residue of over-lending and financial malstructuring.

The political problem blocking debt write-downs is that one party's debts (mainly those of the 99 Percent) are another's savings (especially those of the One Percent). It is not possible to annul debts on the liabilities side of the balance sheet without wiping out savings on the asset side. As long as "savings" (mainly by the One Percent) takes the form of debt claims on the rest of society, they will grow exponentially to hold the 99 Percent in deepening debt thrall, monopolizing the surplus – in a way that shrinks the economy.

The present course is for governments to support the financial sector, not bring debts within the ability to pay. The one-sided U.S. support for creditors since 2008 has averted a debt writedown. Early in 2013 the Fed announced that it would buy $40 billion of mortgage-backed securities each month – almost half a trillion dollars over the course of a year, while the government's housing agencies guaranteed some 90 percent of the securitized mortgage packages being written.

Financial Times columnist Gillian Tett described this government activism as a travesty of a free market. Banks stopped writing new mortgages unless the government took *all* the risk (as also is the case with student loans) by guaranteeing payment out of the public purse in the event that homeowners cannot afford to carry the debt revival. Observing that "state support like this is unprecedented anywhere in the western world," Tett cited former Treasury Secretary Paulson's warning: "Today the government is guaranteeing 90 per cent of the mortgages. If the government keeps doing this, and markets aren't allowed to work, we'll be right back where we were in 2007 and 2008."[469]

Today's government intervention is not socialism. The appropriate word is *oligarchy*. Debt protests from Iceland to Greece and Spain are rejecting bondholder demands for austerity and privatization sell-offs, voting pro-creditor regimes out of office, and demanding referendums over whether to pay financial tribute to creditors. That is why creditors are shifting their support away

---

[469] Gillian Tett, *Financial Times*, April 26, 2013.

from democracies to insist that their designated technocrat lobbyists be assigned control of economic policy.

Bondholders see rising pressure for debt writedowns as an assault on their idea of free markets. But their idea of freedom connotes debt serfdom for the population at large. Their travesty of the classical idea of rent-free markets poses the implicit question: If governments are to intervene to enforce creditor claims and bail out banks while imposing austerity, why not act instead on the side of the indebted majority? Why not choose growth rather than shrinkage ending in bankruptcy? The costs are much less, because financial recklessness would be avoided.

Unthinkable as a broad debt cancellation may seem, once we recognize that it is impossible to pay today's volume of debt (at least without tearing society apart and imposing financial neofeudalism), what remains practical is that the debts won't be paid. There ultimately is no revenue to pay. If we acknowledge this fact, then as Sherlock Holmes remarked in *The Beryl Coronet*: "It is an old maxim of mine that when you have excluded the impossible, whatever remains, however improbable, must be the truth."

The truth is that today's debt overhead can't be paid. Today's political fight concerns just *how* they won't be paid. If government debts to foreign creditors are paid by forced privatization selloffs, the former public domain and infrastructure will be turned into rent-extraction tollbooth opportunities and economies will be impoverished by *rentier* austerity.

30

Coda: The Greek Tragedy Threatens to Sink the Euro

Debt relief is not possible within the currency union. European treaties do not allow it.[470]
German Finance Minister Wolfgang Schäuble

During the six months following Syriza's electoral victory in January 2015, the troika never budged from their demand that the Greek negotiators should ignore the election results and enforce the austerity to which their predecessors had agreed. Refusing to discuss alternatives, the troika blamed the lack of progress on Prime Minister Alexis Tsipras and Finance Minister Yanis Varoufakis. What infuriated the creditors was that Syriza's calculations showed what nearly all economists recognized: austerity would leave Greece less able to pay its foreign debt.

The troika responded by intensifying its demands, turning "negotiations" into a blunt demand for surrender. As Varoufakis summed up the confrontation:

> there was point blank refusal to engage in economic arguments. … You put forward an argument that you've really worked on – to make sure it's logically coherent – and you're just faced with blank stares. … To have very powerful figures look at you in the eye and say 'You're right in what you're saying, but we're going to crush you anyway.'"[471]

Varoufakis's University of Texas colleague James Galbraith, who accompanied him to Greece, summarized the six-month standoff. The Greek team kept making concessions, but the creditors refused even to discuss a debt writedown.

---

[470] "Interview with Wolfgang Schäuble: 'There Is No German Dominance'," *Der Spiegel*, July 17, 2015. http://www.spiegel.de/international/germany/interview-with-german-finance-minister-wolfgang-schaeuble-a-1044233.html.

[471] "Yanis Varoufakis full transcript: our battle to save Greece," interview with Harry Lambert, *New Statesman*, July 13, 2015. http://www.newstatesman.com/world-affairs/2015/07/yanis-varoufakis-full-transcript-our-battle-save-greece

Their position was rigid: "when you come around and agree to what we tell you, then you're serious. Otherwise not."[472]

Economic logic was not at issue, but pure power relations. As Varoufakis summarized in his *New Statesman* interview: "austerity was never about tackling public debt," and never was intended to stabilize Greece's economy to pay back the troika. The aim was to take payment by foreclosing on the public domain, privatizing it on credit to be financed by the leading European banks. It was about replacing the democratic tradition of mixed economies, dismantling protection of labor, and turning the public investment and economic infrastructure over to rent extractors.

A revolution is not a tea party. Financial interests had no qualms about recognizing that their demand to turn Greece into a rentier tollbooth economy was indeed a revolution. They saw that what is at stake is how the remainder of the 21st century will unfold in a world adhering to the neoliberal Washington Consensus. And in this fight the troika's trump card was its ability to confront Greece with economic anarchy unless its leaders capitulated.

By late June the stalemate had thrown into question the proper relationship between creditors and sovereign states. To what extent can creditors force governments to override their laws promoting the wellbeing of their citizens? Is it fair or even legal for creditor-dictated austerity and debt deflation to cause depression, social breakdown and emigration, or should bondholders absorb losses on their over-lending?

Creditors vs. democracy

It is not the job of finance ministers to discuss such broad issues. Their job is simply to calculate how much debtors have to sell off or cut back their spending. When Greece's new negotiators refused to cut pensions or increase the budget surplus, and insisted on the need for debt writedowns, Schäuble was unyielding: "Nothing will be implemented if you dare introduce any legislation. It will be considered unilateral action inimical to the process of reaching an agreement." He ruled out any negotiation, on the ground that the terms had been "accepted by the previous government and we can't possibly

---

[472] James Galbraith, interview with Lynn Parramore, "The Greek Revolt Against Bad Economics Threatens European Elites," INET, July 9, 2015. http://ineteconomics.org/ideas-papers/blog/the-greek-revolt-against-bad-economics-threatens-european-elites. Galbraith later added that Greece "tried to get its 'partners' to recognize that economic policies that had failed to produce predicted recovery for five years should be reconsidered and changed. For this heresy, Greece was crucified, to set an example." http://www.politico.com/agenda/story/2015/07/greece-death-spiral-ahead-000152.

allow an election to change anything."[473] At that point, Varoufakis recalled, "I had to get up and say "Well perhaps we should simply not hold elections anymore for indebted countries", and there was no answer. The only interpretation I can give [of their view] is "Yes, that would be a good idea, but it would be difficult to do. So you either sign on the dotted line or you are out."

On Friday evening June 26, after five months of fruitless talks with euro-zone creditors, Prime Minister Tsipras tried to break the stalemate by taking his case to the people. He announced a referendum for Sunday, July 5, on whether to accept or reject the troika's demands for more austerity, pension cutbacks and larger budget surpluses.

Two days later, on Sunday evening, June 28, Mario Draghi upped the ante. He announced that in response to the breakdown in negotiations (that is, Syriza's refusal to surrender and its steps to slow the economic collapse), Greece's financial position had worsened so far that the European Central Bank would have to stop credit to Greek banks. This forced them to shut down on Monday and stay closed until July 7, two days after the Referendum. As matters turned out, they stayed shut until July 20.

The ECB is supposed to provide banks with liquidity and enough currency to pay depositors, not freeze the banking system. The aim was nakedly polit-ical, not only to break Greece's spirit but to make the country an object lesson alerting Spain's Podemos and anti-austerity parties in Italy and Portugal of the pain that the ECB and IMF could inflict on countries daring to ask that *their* debts be written down.

The week leading up to the referendum saw an intensifying financial crisis. Long lines formed in back of ATM machines just to obtain food money. Retirees had especially difficult problems, because pensions were paid into their bank accounts, but the banks were closed and withdrawals from ATMs were limited to only small amounts.

The conservative media blamed Syriza for failing to acquiesce in the troika's onerous terms. Urging a "yes" vote to capitulate, the conservative pop-ular press and eurozone leaders tried their best to frighten voters into viewing the referendum not as one of whether to accept the troika's take-it-or-be-crushed threat, but whether to keep the euro and remain in the European Union, for which acceptance of the euro was mandatory.

On Friday, July 3, two days before the Sunday referendum, IMF staff mem-bers released a political bombshell. Its Debt Sustainability Analysis dated the previous Friday, June 26, showed that Syriza's argument had been right all

---

[473] Varoufakis, *New Statesman* interview.

along, and that the troika negotiators had been made well aware of this: "the maturities of existing European loans will need to be extended significantly while new European financing to meet financing needs over the coming years will need to be provided on similar concessional terms." Most important, "haircuts on debt will become necessary" if austerity further weakens the economy and hence its tax returns or if privatization should still lag.[474]

These findings implied that the IMF's Articles of Agreement prohibited it from participating in the hardline terms demanded by the ECB and European Council. "Under the Fund's exceptional access criteria, debt sustainability needs to be assessed with high probability," the report concluded. Rosy forecasts of the budget surplus under austerity had to be cut back below the projected 3 percent of GDP. "However, lowering the primary surplus target even further in this lower growth environment would imply unsustainable debt dynamics. ... In such a case, a haircut would be needed, along with extended concessional financing with fixed interest rates locked at current levels." Without a "haircut" the IMF could not extend new credit. Such credit could legally be granted only if Greek debt was sustainable, but: "It is unlikely that Greece will be able to close its financing gaps from the markets on terms consistent with debt sustainability. ... Given the fragile debt dynamics, further concessions are necessary to restore debt sustainability." Vast new official lending was needed, on concessionary terms.

Tsipras and some other Syriza leaders believed that the financial war against Greece would demoralize the population and lead to a "Yes" vote to surrender to the troika's terms. For Tsipras, this at least meant that he would have done his best, blaming the right-wing media and depicting Greece as the victim of extortion and coercion. But as matters turned out, his fears were not well grounded. The troika had overplayed its hand. For most voters the response was anger, directed especially against Germany.

On Sunday, voters rejected the austerity terms that the troika had offered by 61 percent to 39 percent. Public opinion was radicalized to an extent that every reporting district in Greece voted "No" (*Oxi*). As Stathis Kouvelakis, a member of Syriza's Left Platform, pointed out: "In working-class districts you had 70 percent and above for "no," in upper-class districts you had 70 percent

---

[474] *Greece: Preliminary Draft Debt Sustainability Analysis*, IMF Country Report No. 15/165, June 26, 2015. http://www.imf.org/external/pubs/ft/scr/2015/cr15165.pdf.

[475] Sebastian Budgen & Stathis Kouvelakis, "Greece: The Struggle Continues," *The Jacobin*, July 2015. https://www.jacobinmag.com/2015/07/tsipras-varoufakis-kouvelakis-syriza-euro-debt/

and above for 'yes.' … Eighty-five percent of those from eighteen to twenty-four voted 'no.'"[475] The majority of voters showed that they were willing to take "the risk of a possible exit from the euro if that was the condition for saying 'no' to further austerity measures." Many Greeks had prepared for such an eventuality by withdrawing euro notes from the banks and even buying new autos, boats or other consumer goods they could sell if the country reverted to a depreciated drachma.

"Come Monday," Tsipras promised, "the Greek government will be at the negotiating table after the referendum with better terms for the Greek people." But the Troika upped its demands, evidently to show the futility of dragging democratic politics into the equation. The new terms called for even more extreme austerity and faster privatizations. Paul Krugman described the troika's behavior bluntly in his New York Times blog: "being a member of the eurozone means that the creditors can destroy your economy if you step out of line."[476]

The dilemma caused a crisis within Syriza's leadership. Varoufakis had headed a group developing "Plan B" to issue public euro-denominated tax anticipation notes to serve as money. He advocated that Greece should stop paying the troika and go it alone. "We should issue our own IOUs, or even at least announce that we're going to issue our own euro-denominated liquidity; we should haircut the Greek 2012 bonds that the ECB held, or announce we were going to do it; and we should take control of the Bank of Greece. This was the triptych, the three things, which I thought we should respond with if the ECB shut down our banks."[477] But Tsipras feared that there was no real choice but to submit rather than face the anarchy of being forced out of the eurozone and subjected to financial sanctions. Varoufakis was outvoted 4 to 2, and resigned.

Tsipras said the negotiations had managed to gain restructuring, but Latvia's prime minister said he would not accept any debt writedown. Finland also took a hard line, and German Chancellor Merkel confirmed that the only debt revision she and her colleagues would consider would interest-payment grace periods and longer maturities – and these only would "be discussed once there is a successful evaluation of the new Greek program." First, Greece must surrender. There was "not a single cent worth of debt relief.

---

[476] Paul Krugman, "Killing the European Project," July 12, 2015. blogs.nytimes.com/2015/07/12.

[477] See his New Statesman interview, and also Mick Krever, "Yanis Varoufakis: Greece 'made mistakes, there's no doubt'," CNN, http://edition.cnn.com/2015/07/20/world/amanpour-greece-yanis-varoufakis/index.html

Vague commitments to 'reprofile' debt – pushing repayment times backwards and lowering the interest rates – were all Angela Merkel could be persuaded to do."[478]

None of this would even be discussed until Greece accepted the "medicine" in full, no amendments. The reforms passed during January-June had to be reversed, and Greece had to collapse. Only then would debts be written down. Only *after* Greece has started to sell its banks and public domain in earnest, only *after* another 20 percent of its population has emigrated and left the economy prone and privatized would debt be written down, as there would really be nothing left to grab!

Tsipras put the troika's €86 billion take-it-or-collapse bailout conditions to Parliament, admitting in a state television interview that "although he did not believe in the deal, there was no alternative but to accept it to avoid economic chaos."[479] Opposed by many on Syriza's left but supported by the neoliberal parties, the surrender terms were passed on July 15 by a vote of 229 to 64 (with 6 abstentions). This surrendered to all the demands put forth by Schäuble, and led parliament to endorse public spending cuts of 13 billion euros, 4 billion more than the troika proposal voters had just rejected. It called for public sector wage cuts, pension cuts, a rise in value added tax to 23 per cent, and more privatizations.[480]

> *Der Spiegel*: The new program has tightened the conditions. Pensions are to be reformed, taxes increased and the labor market liberalized. Why do you think that the medicine that hasn't worked for five years will now suddenly help?
>
> *Schäuble:* The problem is that for the last five years the medicine has not been taken as prescribed. … In December, the troika made clear that Greece still hasn't tackled 15 important reforms. That must finally change.

Schäuble went so far as to hold out Latvia as a success story. "Since the 1990s, Baltic countries and countries in Central Europe have also been remarkably successful."[481] Greece was supposed to emulate their "success" – and presumably their emigration too! IMF Research Director Blanchard chimed in

---

[478] Paul Mason, "Decoding the IMF: Greek deal doomed, exit likely," July 15 2015. http://blogs.channel4.com/paul-mason-blog/greece-crisis-austerity-deal-pointless/4197
[479] Renee Maltezou and Jan Strupczewski, "IMF calls for Greece debt relief ahead of bailout vote," Reuters, July 14, 2015. http://mobile.reuters.com/article/idUSKBN0P40EO2 0150714?irpc=932.
[480] John Pilger, "The Problem of Greece is not Only a Tragedy: It is a Lie," *Counterpunch*, July 13, 2015.
[481] Schäuble, *Der Spiegel* interview, *op. cit.*

by publishing a paper insisting that the steps the IMF had taken since 2010 were correct, and that all that was needed would have been to lower Greek wages more, cut pensions more, and privatize more of the public domain to foreign rent extractors – if only Syriza had not held its obnoxious referendum![482]

The IMF's second bombshell analysis

Lagarde's backing for Germany's refusal to write down the Greek debt prompted the IMF staff to leak to Reuters on July 14, just before the Greek Parliamentary vote.[483] The internal three-page analysis had been sent to the eurozone's finance ministers on July 11, so they were fully informed when they made their unpayably high demands on Greece that the ECB's stunt to close Greek banks had made debt sustainability all but impossible, by raising "total financing need through end-2018 … to Euro 85 billion, or some Euro 25 billion above what was projected … only two weeks ago. … Greece's debt can now only be made sustainable through debt relief measures that go far beyond what Europe has been willing to consider so far." As Reuters summarized its findings: "European countries would have to give Greece a 30-year grace period on servicing all its European debt, including new loans, and a very dramatic maturity extension, or else make explicit annual fiscal transfers to the Greek budget or accept 'deep upfront haircuts' on their loans to Athens."[484]

Controverting the troika's faith in the ability of Greece "to maintain primary [budget] surpluses … of 3.5 percent of GDP" to pay its creditors, the updated IMF analysis found almost no scenario under which IMF loans could "migrate back onto the balance sheet of the private sector" at reasonable rates without a drastic writedown. Otherwise, the debt would rise to 200 percent of GDP during the next two years, requiring "additional further financing."

---

[482] Olivier Blanchard, "Greece: Past Critiques and the Path Forward," July 9, 2015: "We believed that a small primary surplus, increasing over time, was absolutely necessary to maintain debt sustainability. … Until the referendum and its potential implications for growth, we believed that, under these assumptions about the primary surplus, debt sustainability could be achieved through the rescheduling of existing debt, and long maturities for new debt." http://blog-imfdirect.imf.org/2015/07/09/greece-past-critiques-and-the-path-forward/?hootPostID=8299b6670cea64b9daad8b21e9a85fe7

[483] IMF Country Report No. 15/186: Greece: An Update of IMF Staff's Preliminary Public Debt Sustainability Analysis, July 14, 2015. https://www.imf.org/external/pubs/ft/scr/2015/cr15186.pdf.

[484] "Exclusive: Greece needs debt relief far beyond EU plans - Secret IMF report," Reuters, July 14, 2015. http://www.reuters.com/article/2015/07/14/us-eurozone-greece-imf-report-idUSKCN0PO1CB20150714?feedType=RSS&feedName=businessNews.

Greece's debt burden therefore appeared to be "unsustainable for the next several decades" and hence blocked the IMF from extending further credit or participating in new lending programs! So when Ms. Lagarde continued to reject talk of a debt haircut, it seemed not to matter *what* its staff analyzed. She seemed hopelessly compromised and the IMF lost credibility.

The problem is that the IMF's managers are subject to approval by the U.S. Treasury and must adhere to the neoliberal pretense that austerity can lead to enough budget surpluses to pay creditors. IMF research director Blanchard is known for simplistically calculating how much labor's income must be devalued to pay debts. This is the old Versailles Treaty punitive economics. The IMF is unwilling to acknowledge the error it made in its great wrong step it took in 2011, when Strauss-Kahn sided with French banks and overruled his staff's analysis that Greece's debt could not be paid. The IMF and ECB paid bondholders, bankers and speculators that never should have been bailed out, sticking Greek taxpayers (like those of Ireland) with the bad debts.

Attempting to save appearances that this debt could somehow be paid despite Greece's economy being plunged into an even deeper downturn than in the Great Depression, Lagarde defined "debt relief" in the way that Angela Merkel did: rejecting a haircut of the debt principal, proposing only to stretch out maturities, offering a grace period of no payments and a lower interest rate. Reuters reporters in effect accused the IMF of hypocrisy, quoting an "EU source [who] said euro zone finance ministers and leaders had been aware of the IMF figures when they agreed on Monday on a roadmap to a third bailout."[485] They knowingly backed a debt that could not be paid.

Many observers believed that the report would deter the IMF's Board from contributing its projected €16.4 billion to the troika's new €86 billion bailout program. Evans-Pritchard, a British journalist close to Varoufakis, wrote that the IMF report "vastly complicates the rescue deal agreed by eurozone leaders in marathon talks over the weekend since Germany insists that the bail-out cannot go ahead unless the IMF is involved." He concluded: "The underlying message of the report is that Greece is in such deep trouble that it cannot withstand further austerity cuts. This is hard to square with the latest demands by EMU creditors for pension cuts, tax rises, and fiscal tightening equal to 2pc of GDP by next year."[486]

---

[485] Renee Maltezou and Jan Strupczewski, "IMF calls for Greece debt relief ahead of bailout vote," Reuters, July 14, 2015. http://mobile.reuters.com/article/idUSKBN0P40EO201 50714?irpc=932

[486] Ambrose Evans-Pritchard, "IMF stuns Europe with call for massive Greek debt relief," *The Telegraph*, July 14, 2015. http://www.telegraph.co.uk/finance/economics/11739985/ IMF-stuns-Europe-with-call-for-massive-Greek-debt-relief.html#disqus_thread.

The *Financial Times* likewise interpreted the IMF's report to mean that it "has sent its strongest signal that it may walk away from Greece's new bailout programme, arguing that it will not be able to participate if European creditors do not offer Athens substantial debt relief," citing a senior IMF official: "We have made it very clear that before we go to the [IMF] board for authorization to release funds, we need a concrete and complete solution to the debt problem."[487] British journalist Paul Mason spelled out the dilemma: "What this means is very simple: the third bailout agreed in principle on Sunday night is doomed to fail. First because the IMF cannot sign up to it without debt relief; second because, without debt relief it will collapse the Greek economy."[488]

The third bailout uses debt leverage to force privatization in earnest

Despite the fact that Syriza was backed by IMF analysts and most of the world's economists who spoke on the topic, the eurozone's response was, in effect: "Of course there's no money. We know that. Start selling off your assets." The new bailout terms restored the €50 billion target for privatizations set in July 2011. Greek banks would be taken under foreign control to create value by foreclosing on homes whose owners had defaulted on their mortgages. (The Greek government had suspended such moves.) Then would come airports, harbors and roads, real estate, gas rights in the Aegean, and monopoly privileges that might provide rent-extracting opportunities for foreign buyers.

Instead of being a Western-style mixed economy, Greece would be entirely privatized – at giveaway prices, although the prices to be charged to users of public infrastructure would rise. "The privatisation fund was the issue that almost forced a Grexit at the marathon 17-hour, all-night summit of European leaders in Brussels earlier this month. 'It was the only thing discussed at the summit,' recalls one diplomat. At 6 am, as Greece teetered on the brink of leaving the euro, the Greek prime minister, Alexis Tsipras, was still haggling over privatisation details with his counterparts, Angela Merkel and François Hollande."[489] In a last-minute concession it was agreed that the Troika's selloff administrators would sit in Greek offices rather than in Brussels.

---

[487] Peter Spiegel and Shawn Donnan, "IMF raises doubts over its bailout role," *Financial Times*, July 15, 2015. Memo argues for huge debt relief, which the eurozone is resisting. Print version.

[488] Paul Mason, "Decoding the IMF: Greek deal doomed, exit likely," Wednesday 15 Jul 2015. http://blogs.channel4.com/paul-mason-blog/greece-crisis-austerity-deal-pointless/4197.

[489] Jennifer Rankin and Helena Smith, "The great Greece fire sale," *The Guardian*, July 24, 2015.

When *Der Spiegel* asked Finance Minister Schäuble whether this privatization and foreign control of Greek tax policy were an "attempt to turn the
country into a kind of colony," he answered: "Otherwise, the debt load is
unsustainable. And without that, it won't work." The locus of economic planning was to shift to financial centers and run on behalf of bondholders,
bankers and buyers of the privatized assets.

The Fund's June 26 Debt Sustainability Analysis had pointed out that government opposition to selling key infrastructure to rent-seeking investors limited privatization proceeds to "only about €3 billion over the last 5 years," a
full "94 percent below the target." Half the €23 billion in proceeds anticipated
for 2014–22 were supposed to come from privatizing government ownership
of Greek banks, but the crisis caused by the troika's standoff with Syriza had
increased their bad loans to a point where "it is not reasonable to assume revenues from bank sales."

The IMF staff also found that projected proceeds from selling infrastructure should be written down "in light of the government's announced intention
to add new conditions to future sales, including retention of a significant government stake and further safeguards for labor, environment, and local community benefits." The analysts suggested a realistic annual sell-off rate of only
€500 million over the next few years. This made a debt haircut necessary –
precisely what Schäuble, Merkel and Lagarde had rejected.

Varoufakis submitted an alternative proposal to Germany on June 19:

> The Greek government proposes to bundle public assets … into a central holding
> company to be separated from the government administration and to be managed as a
> private entity, under the aegis of the Greek Parliament, with the goal of maximizing the
> value of its underlying assets and creating a homegrown investment stream. The Greek
> state will be the sole shareholder, but will not guarantee its liabilities or debt.
>
> The holding company [would] "issue a fully collateralized bond on the international
> capital markets" to raise €30–40 billion ($32–43 billion), which, "taking into account the
> present value of assets," would "be invested in modernizing and restructuring the assets
> under its management."
>
> Our proposal was greeted with deafening silence.[490]

Other alternatives included taking the Greek banks public and running them
in the public interest.[491]

---

[490] Yanis Varoufakis, "Europe's Vindictive Privatization Plan for Greece," Project Syndicate
July 21, 2015 by yanisv. http://yanisvaroufakis.eu/2015/07/21/europes-vindictive-
privatization-plan-for-greece-project-syndicate/.

[491] Eric Toussaint, "Greece: Alternatives and Exiting the Eurozone," The Bullet, Socialist
Project • E-Bulletin No. 1146, July 19, 2015.

The issues at stake regarding inter-governmental debt

Given the voters' heavy July 5 rejection of demands by foreign creditors, how binding is Greece's submission? At what point does debt taken on behalf of foreign creditors under threat of financial sanctions and warfare become legally "odious"? Governments are supposed to represent the people, but Tsipras said that he capitulated at diplomatic gunpoint.

In the face of debt far in excess of the ability to pay, whose interest should come first? It is not mathematically possible to save the financial sector's over-growth of debt and also save the economy. Under current neoliberal rules, entire national economies are to be sacrificed. That is why the coming generation's political debate should focus on the degree to which creditor demands for austerity can take preference over principles of national sovereignty, democracy and economic growth.

The first premise of a reformed body of international law should be that no nation should be forced to sacrifice its growth to pay foreign creditors. The eurozone's fatal flaw was to reverse this principle. Lacking a central bank to monetize public spending, Greece's tax system was turned into "a tool in the hands of the troika" to squeeze out budget surpluses to pay creditors.[492] To deter a financial blockade on its economy, Greece was obliged to sell its public domain, impose anti-labor anti-reform policies and regressive taxes favoring finance, real estate and monopolies.

The major lever forcing fiscal deflation and leaving debtor countries in such dependency is debt owed to international institutions. Bankruptcy procedures are well established to write down business and personal debts, enabling individuals and companies to make a fresh start. Procedures also are in place for writing down sovereign debts to bankers and bondholders. But governments are unforgiving. Inter-governmental debt cannot readily be written down, no matter how destructive its terms.

The Versailles Treaty imposed impossibly high reparations on Germany, and the U.S. Government imposed equally destructive demands on the Allies to pay their World War I arms debts, ending in the 1929–31 global financial breakdown. But until it finally became apparent that the volume of official inter-government debts could not be paid, the economies of Germany, Britain and France were impoverished and polarized. Since the 1960s many nations also have been subjected to austerity and economic shrinkage, leaving them less and less able to extricate themselves from debt.

---

[492] Budgen and Kouvelakis, *op. cit.*

Repeating that situation today has prompted Varoufakis to call the troika's demands on Greece a "new Versailles." There is no legal framework to write down debts owed to the IMF, the ECB or European and American creditor governments – and they in turn act on behalf of banks and bondholders, having been captured by anti-labor, anti-government financial warriors.

Relinquishing sovereign power to today's internationalism means austerity

In the wake of World War II many idealists advocated replacing national governments with regional or global groupings, on the logic that only nations make war. They were thinking of military warfare, of course. But today's global institutions are waging an economic war that is just as lethal. Instead of guiding the world toward greater prosperity, the IMF, World Bank, World Trade Organization, European Central Bank and NATO are backing creditor-oriented austerity.

As for the eurozone, instead of promoting further European integration, its deflationary policy has prompted an Irish columnist to comment: "The European Union as we have known it ended over the weekend. That EU project was all about the gradual convergence of equal nations into an 'ever closer union.' That's finished now."[493] The Greek crisis has shown that nations need to keep their currency under their own control, along with tax policy. A Bloomberg editorial opined bluntly:

> Enough is enough: Greece should leave the euro system. ... Such a compact is no longer possible. Trust has collapsed to such a point that Greece is being told it must become an EU colony, not a sovereign state. It is being forced into a deal it will resent for years, and to which it will feel no sense of obligation. Under these circumstances, leaving is the best available choice.[494]

In a similar vein, editorialist Wolfgang Münchau wrote for the Financial Times: "Greece's creditors ... have destroyed the eurozone as we know it and demolished the idea of a monetary union as a step towards a democratic political union."[495] Members of the eurozone have ceded their economic sovereignty to the European Union, but the EU is not a state. It has no

---

[493] Fintan O'Toole, "Tormenting Greece is about sending a message that we are now in a new EU," *The Irish Times*, July 14, 2015.

[494] "Greece Should Just Quit," Bloomberg editorial, July 13, 2015. http://www.bloomberg view.com/articles/2015-07-13/greece-should-just-quit.

[495] Wolfgang Münchau, "Brutal creditors have gutted the eurozone project," *Financial Times*, July 14, 2015.

Treasury or central bank to monetize public spending deficits. (At least, the ECB is not willing to do so, and EU rules even limit deficits to only 3 percent of GDP.) This means that members of the eurozone must give up their rights as a state.

This explains the rise in popularity of anti-euro parties from France and England to Denmark, Italy, Spain and Portugal. Post-Soviet countries joining the European Union also see the handwriting on the wall. Poland's former deputy foreign minister Witold Waszczykowski told a reporter: "We will try to stay away from the eurozone as long as possible." In Hungary, Prime Minister Viktor Orban's international spokesman, Zoltan Kovacs, said that the absence of a fixed deadline "opens Hungary to a lot of advantages not to adopt the euro, such as keeping control of our taxation and fiscal policy."[496]

Lacking a fully empowered Euro-Parliament in Brussels, policy-making power is financial, left to the ECB and European Council. Limiting these administrative organs to the monetary sphere – and running them on behalf of commercial banks and bondholders – smashes what used to be a mixed public/private economy into a portfolio of creditor claims on property and income. Debtor governments are stripped of the power to protect their interests, those of labor or their economy's future.

This *rentier* counter-revolution is not the product of reasoned economic logic. Even neoliberal economists claim to retain the classical opposition to rent seeking, and few would endorse chronic austerity and debt peonage. By the end of the 1920s it was recognized that debts should be annulled when they derange social balance by exceeding the reasonable ability to pay. And political theorists define the right of nations to control their own money and financial systems, resist debt leverage and tax *rentier* income – or keep or take basic infrastructure, land, natural resources and other chokepoints into the public domain. That is what makes them sovereign. But the arenas of power are in the worldly political sphere. Financial lobbyists control lawmaking by dominating election campaigns, the media and the courts, while financial centers use debt leverage backed by the threat of brute monetary sanctions by the IMF and ECB.

No nation should be made subject to chronic unemployment and depression to pay banks and bondholders. Defense against this rentier takeover therefore must start by reaffirming the right of nations to put their growth ahead of demands by creditors to appropriate their property and plunge them into

---

[496] Rick Lyman, "Greek Crisis Dulls Appetite for Euro in Countries Waiting to Adopt It," *The New York Times*, July 15, 2015.

austerity. Every nation has the sovereign right to issue its own money, levy taxes and write its laws, including those relations between creditors and debtors governing the terms of bankruptcy and debt forgiveness. Such sovereignty is needed to defend against the past half-century of financialized globalization.

Yet what used to be social democratic parties have come to support globalism even when it has turned neoliberal. By doing so, they have rejected their own former classical blueprint for how to free industrial capitalism and markets from the legacies of feudalism. The effect is to support neofeudalism

Where do we go from here?

The internationalist idealism that emerged as a pacifist reaction to World War II has been untracked, in large part because the political left has abandoned its focus on economic policy. The terms of globalism and European integration entail subordination to a neoliberal agenda. Finance always has been cosmopolitan, but not benign. It has replaced military warfare with a fight of *rentiers* against society, while the financial sector imposes austerity and debt dependency leading to privatization.

The eurozone is showing itself to be a false step toward unity, threatening to drive its members apart. The left's failure to address this dynamic came to a head in the case of Greece, as Kouvelakis has argued:

> The Left is filled with lots of people who are well-meaning, but who are totally impotent on the field of real politics. But it's also telling about the kind of mental devastation wrought by the almost religious belief in Europeanism. This meant that, until the very end, those people believed that they could get something from the troika, they thought that between "partners" they would find some sort of compromise, that they shared some core values like respect for the democratic mandate, or the possibility of a rational discussion based on economic arguments.[497]

Underlying the European problem is the continent's subservience to U.S. neoliberal strategists using debt leverage to create a neo-*rentier* society. As one recent observer has written:

> The European surrender to the United States occurred about seventy years ago. It was welcomed as a liberation, of course, but it has turned into lasting domination. It was simply reconfirmed by the July 12, 2015, Greek surrender. And that surrender has been enforced by an increasingly hegemonic ideology of anti-nationalism, particularly strong in the left, that considers "nationalism" to be the source of all evil, and the European Union the source of all good, since it destroys the sovereignty of nations. This ideology is so dominant on the left that very few leftists dare challenge it …

---

[497] Sebastian Budgen & Stathis Kouvelakis, *op. cit.*

As a result, only "right-wing" parties dare defend national sovereignty. Or rather, anyone who defends national sovereignty will be labeled "right-wing." It is too easily forgotten that without national sovereignty, there can be no democracy, no people's choice. … Much of the European left is finding itself increasingly caught in the contradiction between its anti-nationalist "European dream" and the destruction of democracy by the EU's financial bureaucracy. The Greek drama is the opening act of a long and confused European conflict.[498]

The neoliberal strategy is to cloak itself in universalism while blocking any alternative body of economic theory or ideology. The end of history is to be a new Dark Age of enclosures and privatization that will bury the Enlightenment's drive to free economies from *rentier* privilege, which is now re-christened "wealth creation."

There is an alternative, of course. The starting point must be to realize that an economic war is being waged, and has been for many centuries. In this war the financial powers and other *rentiers* fight all the more intensively and often covertly precisely because they realize that there is no moral justification for income and wealth that is obtained by extractive means instead of earned productively.

Those who obtain or inherit predatory wealth and privilege realize that the ultimate means of imposing austerity and demolishing the power of democracies is resort to the tactics of deception, junk economics and ideological camouflage, to use financial sanctions and act as monetary wreckers, with backup in the form of more overt violence in Pinochet/Chicago-style coups.

To prevent this pro-*rentier* "end of history" it is necessary for populations to revive the long classical fight to free economies. The alternative is neofeudalism.

---

[498] Diana Johnstone, "Greece Surrendered: But to Whom Exactly?" *Counterpunch*, July 17, 2015.

CPSIA information can be obtained
at www.ICGtesting.com
Printed in the USA
FSHW022250230320
68415FS

9 783981 484281